T0336738

E–Government Service Maturity and Development:

Cultural, Organizational and Technological Perspectives

Mahmud Akhter Shareef
McMaster University, Canada

Norm Archer
McMaster University, Canada

Shantanu Dutta
University of Ontario Institute of Technology, Canada

Information Science
REFERENCE

Senior Editorial Director: Kristin Klinger
Director of Book Publications: Julia Mosemann
Editorial Director: Lindsay Johnston
Acquisitions Editor: Erika Carter
Development Editor: Joel Gamon
Production Editor: Sean Woznicki
Typesetters: Natalie Pronio, Milan Vracarich Jr., Jennifer Romanchak
Print Coordinator: Jamie Snavely
Cover Design: Nick Newcomer

Published in the United States of America by
     Information Science Reference (an imprint of IGI Global)
     701 E. Chocolate Avenue
     Hershey PA 17033
     Tel: 717-533-8845
     Fax: 717-533-8661
     E-mail: cust@igi-global.com
     Web site: http://www.igi-global.com

                    Library of Congress Cataloging-in-Publication Data

E-government service maturity and development: cultural, organizational and technological perspectives / Mahmud Akhter Shareef, Norm Archer and Shantanu Dutta, editors.
     p. cm.
  Includes bibliographical references and index.
  Summary: "This book discusses important concepts for public administration reformation, taking into account the complex social, administrative, cultural, and legal problems of implementing modern digital systems"--Provided by publisher.
  ISBN 978-1-60960-848-4 (hardcover) -- ISBN 978-1-60960-849-1 (ebk.) -- ISBN 978-1-60960-850-7 (print & perpetual access) 1. Internet in public administration. 2. Public administration--Technological innovations. I. Shareef, Mahmud Akhter, 1966- II. Archer, Norm, 1937- III. Dutta, Shantanu, 1971-
  JF1525.A8E238 2011
  352.3'802854678--dc22
                         2011016806

British Cataloguing in Publication Data
A Cataloguing in Publication record for this book is available from the British Library.

All work contributed to this book is new, previously-unpublished material. The views expressed in this book are those of the authors, but not necessarily of the publisher.

To my father Md. Murshed Ali and mother Mrs. Lutfunnahar.

-- Mahmud Akhter Shareef

To Marybelle, my beloved wife and best friend.

-- Norm Archer

To my parents Subhas Dutta and Mamata Dutta.

-- Shantanu Dutta

Table of Contents

Section 2
Strategic Development of E-Government: Interoperability and Capability

Section 3
E-Governance Implementation in Competitive Reformation of Financial Markets

Section 4
E-Government Adoption Perspectives

Detailed Table of Contents

Section 1
Adoption of E-Government Globally: Vision, Mission, and Objectives

Mahmud Akhter Shareef, McMaster University, Canada
Norm Archer, McMaster University, Canada

This is a general introduction to e-government (EG), as an alternative channel to regular brick and mortar government offices. This information and communication technology (ICT) driven delivery system can offer government services to stakeholders in a more comprehensive, efficient, and effective way than through physical government offices. This chapter conceptualizes the fundamental development of EG. It explains the components, stakeholders, and development stages of EG as it progresses towards service maturity.

Mahmud Akhter Shareef, McMaster University, Canada
Uma Kumar, Carleton University, Canada
Vinod Kumar, Carleton University, Canada
Morteza Niktash, Public Works and Government Services, Canada

This chapter provides illustrations of initiatives from different countries that have launched EG. Different countries develop their initiatives from different perspectives and attempt to achieve different ends, although their means are very similar. This chapter addresses and analyzes the strategies and objectives for EG of different countries. It also delineates subtle differences in their targets to achieve the implementation and proliferation of EG.

Chapter 3

Mahmud Akhter Shareef, McMaster University, Canada
Norm Archer, McMaster University, Canada

This chapter extends the case studies presented in the second chapter on mission, vision, objectives, and strategies of EG initiatives adopted and implemented by different developed and developing countries, at local, regional, or national levels. It reviews literature on EG adoption and service. This chapter also illustrates the studies on EG initiatives of different countries, which will provide a consolidated research references for the future endeavours of prospective EG researchers.

Section 2
Strategic Development of E-Government: Interoperability and Capability

Chapter 4

Rakhi Tripathi, Indian Institute of Technology Delhi, India
V. Ranga Rao, Govt. of N.C.T. of Delhi, India
M. P. Gupta, Indian Institute of Technology Delhi, India

Chapter four contributes to the literature by documenting the interoperability aspects of EG. Data integration and interoperability among departments are critical research issues. These two issues are highlighted by the problems posed, concerns, challenges, and the ways of addressing them. It addresses the multiple benefits and challenges of personal information integration and provides relevant solutions in order to achieve personal information integration for one-stop government portals. The chapter also explains the need for integration among various departments of government.

Chapter 5

P. Senthil Priya, PSG College of Arts and Science, India
N. Mathiyalagan, PSG College of Arts and Science, India

This chapter highlights the central significance of different EG initiatives in the Indian context. Since India is a leading country in adopting and diffusing ICT, Indian EG service and digital preparedness provide significant learnings for other countries when developing interoperable EG service. An analysis of the impact and sustainability of two EG schemes is presented. The main conclusion is that, since there is no integration and interoperability between government departments, there is only sub-optimal utilization of the established infrastructure at present in this Indian EG service system.

Chapter 6

Mahmud Akhter Shareef, McMaster University, Canada
Norm Archer, McMaster University, Canada

The sixth chapter delineates the development procedure of mobile-government or m-government with extensive illustrations of the scope of services that are offered or could be offered through m-government. A major significance is the real time information that can be capitalized on by hand held mobile devices like wireless phones. This identifies the development of the fundamental capabilities needed to adopt and manage ICTs to successfully implement citizen-focused m-government systems.

Section 3
E-Governance Implementation in Competitive Reformation of Financial Markets

Chapter 7

Mary M. Oxner, St. Francis Xavier University, Canada
Ken MacAulay, St. Francis Xavier University, Canada
Gerald Trites, Zorba Research Inc., Canada

There are potential implications of e-governance in shaping the performance of future capital market functions. Primary stakeholders in capital market such as investors and creditors, and agencies like stock exchanges and securities commissions require information to support the assessment of stewardship and resource allocation. The dissemination of this information is now available electronically. This chapter encapsulates the stages of adoption and proliferation of XBRL (eXtensible Business Reporting Language), a part of the evolution of the electronic medium and of e-governance.

Chapter 8

Shantanu Dutta, University of Ontario Institute of Technology, Canada
Ken MacAulay, St. Francis Xavier University, Canada
Mary M. Oxner, St. Francis Xavier University, Canada

This chapter gives a fundamental conceptual paradigm for the adoption of EG by corporate financial institutions. The ICTs utilized by governments are often adopted from the corporate environment and subsequently used by governments to improve transparency and responsiveness. The use of ICTs as a medium to enhance governance is examined, focusing in particular on the Canadian capital market. Parallels are drawn between the e-governance issues faced by governments and capital markets.

Chapter 9

This chapter summarizes the evidence on trading behaviour in stock exchanges. Studies of corporate governance in the capital markets area have focused on the mechanisms and structures of governance and less on the medium through which it is accomplished. Fuelled by technological innovation, the New York Stock Exchange (NYSE) was able to move from fractional to decimal pricing. This is a revolutionary change that required conversion of traditional quoting methods to decimalization.

Chapter 10

Online banking and trading through virtual media are addressed and explored as a widely diffused and accepted issue of corporate online functionality. In the recent past, online or Internet based banking has become quite common. Banks have also realized the potential of Internet banking and have recognized that it is necessary to integrate new customer lifestyles and Web based activity preferences with their business models. This chapter analyzes different features of online banking and trading and their potential significance in shaping future financial market reformation and performance.

Section 4
E-Government Adoption Perspectives

Chapter 11

Chapter eleven provides insights into the application of open source software for the technological interfaces of EG. Opportunities for open source software in EG, the characteristics of open source software developers, and their motivation to volunteer by contributing to open source software projects are examined. This is followed by a discussion of the advantages and issues associated with open source software, and possibilities, scope, and significance of the adoption of open source software for successful EG operations.

Chapter 12

Teta Stamati, National and Kapodistrian University of Athens, Greece

Athanasios Karantjias, University of Pireaus, Greece

Drakoulis Martakos, National and Kapodistrian University of Athens, Greece

Chapter twelve gives a fundamental and conceptual framework for the adoption criteria of EG, grounded in the perceptions of the demand-side stakeholders (i.e., the end users or citizens). Citizen adoption criteria for EG are tailored to their perceptions of different aspects of EG, such as security, user friendliness, relative advantage, reliability, et cetera. Through an extensive empirical study and in-depth statistical analysis, this chapter reveals factors that can either drive or inhibit the adoption process.

Chapter 13

Ramaraj Palanisamy, St. Francis Xavier University, Canada

Bhasker Mukerji, St. Francis Xavier University, Canada

This chapter addresses one of the most researched issues of ICT-dominated projects such as EG, which are the security and privacy concerns that affect EG acceptance. It is unambiguously acknowledged that the transformation process of the public sector requires vast investments in new Internet technologies. The purpose of the chapter is to provide guidance for administrators and IT professionals in terms of investing in best practices for security and privacy technologies.

Foreword

Just over five years ago, a hundred key professionals in e-government came together at the University of Sussex, UK to discuss the emerging field of mobile e-government, at a conference I organized. Among the key participants was Professor Norm Archer, one of the editors of this book, who has made contributions to the field of e-government and who has helped to establish "mobile government" as an umbrella domain to create an identity for all professionals working with mobile technologies in e-government.

Since then, a number of exciting developments and approaches have helped to modernize public sector organizations and to serve the public better through the use of Information and Communication Technologies (ICT). These innovative approaches in the public sector are mainly driven by two major incentives. One is related to the modernization of activities and roles of public sector organizations, so that governments can act more efficiently and improve their reputations. The second is related to offering services to citizens that are convenient for them and that serve their needs better. Since e-government has become recognized as a field of research and practice, these incentives, perhaps, remain the same in general, but it continues to be challenging to achieve desired outcomes via various systems, applications, and services. Serious work in this area is always linked with overcoming these challenges by producing innovative ideas and practical solutions.

In recent years, these challenges have taken a quite unusual shape and form. There are a number of issues in successfully adopting and implementing e-government projects country-wide, by key public sector organizations that wish to improve key government activities. These issues range from cultural and social (e.g. having effective leadership backing, implementing effective change management, etc.) to technical and organizational (e.g. project management, interoperability, financial planning, etc.). New social networking methodologies, the evolution of Web 2.0, and the bottom up strengthening of the ability of citizens to participate and influence policies and decisions are also having a great impact, but they also create challenges for successful e-government system implementations.

These new developments and challenges have led to new considerations in e-government. Our understanding of, and approaches to, e-government are moving from the conventional to more complicated and broader views. In these views, e-government is more comprehensive and distributed to many activities that take place in any organizations having business or other relations with public sector organizations. It is no longer easy to view e-government simply as technology that is presented as a central portal and a gateway backed up with certain key back office capabilities. Such systems are designed mainly top-down and are more or less closed to (or have slower responses to) changes in requirements from highly IT sophisticated citizens and both governmental and non-governmental organizations. In this way, e-government becomes a distributed effort involving these activities, which were not in the past an aspect of ordinary e-government implementations. An important difference from past developments is that this approach requires a bottom up design to respond to citizens who may be participating more actively in government operations as reporters, publishers, and other participants in the networked civil society. E-government is therefore becoming a much broader concept than what it was originally conceived to be.

The collection in your hands is a significant effort by the editors to bring together articles containing knowledge on these new developments and to provide the e-government community with an opportunity for a deeper understanding of recent developments in e-government. The collection starts with a number of (country-based) cases where ideas on the very definition and content of what e-government actually involves are revisited and evaluated in the light of recent developments. It then continues to discuss interoperability - a core issue in e-government – from the point of view of an expanding and more comprehensive nature of e-government that involves recent challenges in (personal) data handling, revenue generation, and adoption of mobile technologies. The next group of articles examines how e-government is reflected itself in a relatively new area: financial and capital markets. Finally, the collection contains articles discussing an essential but mostly neglected implementation issue: adoption and application of e-government services by citizens, and related issues in this challenging domain.

Similarly to all domains of ICT work, e-government is a field which continues to evolve quickly in order to respond to needs emerging from organizational dynamism in the public sector and the changing needs and improved capabilities of citizens in the networked world. Drs. Shareef, Archer, and Dutta, and the contributing authors of this book present a range of valuable examples and cases showing recent approaches and responses to emerging needs in the ever changing domain of e-government. In this way, the book contributes significantly to the body of cumulative knowledge on e-government, even as this domain continues to change continuously both in terms of technological breakthroughs and innovative applications and services. This book will serve e-government professionals, both as a source of practical knowledge and an interesting reading experience for establishing a deeper understanding of the e-government domain.

Ibrahim Kushchu
Mobile Government Consortium International, UK

Ibrahim Kushchu *is an expert in mobile government with a background in management systems and artificial intelligence. Combining his management studies and his expertise in artificial intelligence, Prof. Kushchu has been working for business schools in the UK and in Japan, and teaching various information communication technology courses especially related to electronic business and mobile business. Prof. Kushchu is an internationally recognized pioneering practitioner and researcher in developing the mobile government field by bringing into the light the issues related to the use of mobile technologies in electronic government. His work also extends to impact of mobile technologies for economic and social development. He has edited and co-edited three books and has a number of publications in various international journals and in the proceedings of reputable conferences. He is also very active in international community of researchers through speaking, organizing, chairing, and co-chairing various international conferences and serving on the committees. He has been working with various multinational companies including Gates Foundation, Cisco, Nokia, Hitachi, and NTT DoCoMo on projects involving consultancy, research, and educational events. He also offers advisory services to local and central government organization and their agencies. Prof. Kushchu holds a first degree (BSc) in management. He also has an MBA and a Master's degree (MSc) in artificial intelligence from the University of Edinburgh, UK. He was awarded a PhD degree in evolutionary artificial intelligence from the University of Sussex, UK.*

Preface

E-government (EG) is the use of technology to enhance the access to and delivery of government services to benefit citizens, businesses, and employees. An EG system can also be seen as a powerful approach for government administrative reformation. The concept of EG originated in the early 1990s in the USA. Since that time, EG has been quickly adopted in many countries. The United Nations now recommends that member countries provide all ministry information on their own Web pages on the World Wide Web. Currently, the majority of countries are using or on the way to using the Internet to provide at least some access to government information, posted on government websites. E-government includes services ranging from static information to interactive and transaction oriented services that vary from country to country and among government levels (municipal, state, and national) within countries.

The EG concept can be viewed from technological, economic, organizational, socio-cultural, and political perspectives. Its aims are to provide information to citizens, to reduce government cost, to make government service delivery systems more efficient and participative, and to ensure transparency and accountability; ultimately, it should lead to citizen-centric government. Many developed countries, as well as developing countries, are determined to reform public service management and to reengineer government services by adopting EG. But the visions, strategies, initiatives, and final targets for EG in different countries are not necessarily the same. Subtle differences are noticeable in the implications of the visions and the final targets that governments set for its adoption. For some countries, the implementation of EG is only or primarily a technological manifestation. Some countries extend these views to include marketing and economic perspectives with their implementation strategies of EG. Other countries add management and organizational aspects to the strategic perspectives already mentioned. Finally, some countries target the achievement of a political agenda and good governance, in addition to other aspects, as the ultimate goal of EG. Because different countries adopt EG from many different perspectives, the overall structure, service patterns, technological association, interoperability, architecture, and service maturity of EG also follow different paths.

Throughout the world, governments are realizing the potential of placing traditional government services online. All the essential functions of a government – legislative, judicial, and executive – may use EG as a way to provide information, reduce the cost of rendering services, improve internal management, enhance efficiency of service delivery, and promote the processes of democratic governance. Corporate sectors can also benefit from the application of e-governance, which is profoundly evident in the reformation of the worldwide financial sector.

Because of the expansion and increasing reliance on government websites, researchers and practitioners are equally concerned with the issues of understanding and managing EG. However, although

EG offers promise to modern government systems, it also poses considerable challenges to government and public administrations, private sectors, and individuals in building trust, confidence, and security. Consideration of these EG issues is essential for management in planning to implement, adopt, sustain, expand, diffuse, and gain competitive advantage while making the capital investments required for effective EG systems.

Keeping in mind its global impact, cohesiveness in setting the missions and objectives of EG systems is an important managerial issue. There are a number of factors that have significant implications for progressive and successful development in setting the course of EG, and identifying and establishing the explicit missions and objectives that are needed for transforming the traditional government information structure into the electronic version. These factors include reaching unanimous consensus on EG development; determining the state of readiness through policy making; addressing key issues; strategizing leadership, boundaries, structures, and activities; deciding on technology infrastructure; and defining governance structures and policies. Identifying clear objectives for implementing EG is important in order to capitalize on the full opportunities that lie behind the EG system so that the many different stakeholders maintain an interest in adopting EG systems within the globalization context.

This book, "*Electronic Government Service Maturity and Development: Cultural, Organizational and Technological Perspectives,*" explores and conceptualizes paradigms of the strategic development of EG and its implementation and adoption process. This is addressed theoretically, but with many practical illustrations. In addition, the book provides insight into financial reformation through e-governance and describes corporate EG, with a focus on Internet banking and trading. As an extension of EG, this book also provides an outlook on m-government development. Other related technological, cultural, and organizational aspects of the successful development and proliferation of EG are also discussed.

The book is organized to provide academicians, researchers, practitioners, and policy makers with the necessary background information to assist in setting strategic vision, mission, and goals for EG in both developed and developing countries. It examines and identifies the major stakeholders of EG and reveals the stages of growth or service maturity levels. Many countries are striving to develop interoperable EG through horizontal and vertical information integration to ensure a seamless flow of service and information through a one stop Web interface or portal. This book elaborates on interoperable concepts with many practical implications. Although m-government is a closely related sub-set of EG, it still differs in terms of certain technological, cultural, social, and organizational perspectives that impact its implementation and proliferation. This book attempts to postulate m-government development concepts that reflect practical relevance. On another very fundamental topic, it sheds light on the paradigms and functional discourses of e-governance in financial markets. Basically, financial sector reformation can benefit significantly from successful implementation strategies of e-governance. An appealing corporate EG system is delineated by exploring Internet banking and online trading. Finally, the book discusses some potential issues like technological and software integration into EG development, user adoption criteria, and the substantial impact of security and privacy on this virtual interface.

The book contains four main sections. The first section has three chapters that discuss the background and general concepts related to EG development and its ancillary components, association of stakeholders, sequential service maturity, and stages of growth to facilitate further proliferation of this new wave of government service systems. In addition, the implementation of EG is demonstrated with the differentiated vision, mission, and objectives of case studies from several countries. The second section, also divided into three chapters, explains the related concepts and frameworks of EG development, focusing particularly on standardization and synchronization of tasks of different departments through interoperable service systems. As the latest extension of EG, this section also presents a directional view of m-government development. The third section includes four chapters that identify how implementation of e-governance systems can help redefine and streamline the financial sector. Internet banking and online trading facilities reflect an extended view of corporate EG in the banking sector. The fourth and final section has three chapters that shed light on certain implementation issues of EG. Implementation and successful adoption of EG from the developer and the users' side must address potential issues such as technology choice, users' cultural, social, and behavioral perspectives, and eternal privacy and security issues for the virtual environment. A brief description of each section, chapter, and section is provided below.

SECTION ONE

Many governments are enthusiastic about adopting E-government at one or more of the local, regional, and national levels. Before moving ahead with EG, it is vitally important to develop a strategy that sets explicit vision, mission, and objectives. The first section focuses on the components, stakeholders, and service maturity of EG development as a global phenomenon. Then it sequentially explores and analyzes through case studies strategic vision, mission, and objectives of EG of different countries. For authors, researchers, practitioners, and policy makers, this section synthesizes literature that helps EG to focus on country affairs. Conceptually this section presents a general view of implementing EG. This section has three chapters that address these issues.

The first chapter conceptualizes the fundamental development of EG. It explains the components, stakeholders, and development stages of EG through gradual service maturity. EG is an alternative and/ or parallel channel to regular brick and mortar government offices. The delivery system that is driven by information and communication technology (ICT) offers government services to its different stakeholders in a more comprehensive, efficient, and effective way than is possible through physical government offices. At different stages of EG development and growth, the functions, patterns, and capacities of offered services are distinctively different. As such, the association of technology is also different at these different stages.

The second chapter discusses the overarching strategic management of EG that has been initiated by several countries. Developed countries have initiated EG primarily for national, regional, and local governments during the last decade of the twentieth century. Developing countries tend to start their adoption of ICT with the reformation of public administration, although at the same time they align their mission to develop efficient government sectors that can satisfy citizens from multiple perspectives. Different countries develop their initiatives from different visions and attempt to achieve different ends, although their means are very similar. This chapter addresses and analyzes the strategies and objectives for EG of different countries. It also delineates subtle differences in their approaches to achieve the implementation and proliferation of EG.

The third chapter is an extension of the case studies presented in the second chapter on mission, vision, objectives, and strategies of EG initiatives that been adopted and implemented by different developed and developing countries at the local, regional, or national levels. This chapter first presents initiatives in developing EG. Then it describes well documented empirical instruments that reveal EG development capability in the country-context. From the practitioner's point of view, these instruments will provide the ability to measure government capability and to develop a capability index or parameters for different countries who are preparing to develop EG at any level of government. Finally, this chapter illustrates studies of EG initiatives in several countries, providing a consolidated research reference basis for the future endeavors of EG researchers.

SECTION TWO

The second section explains the most appealing target of EG, i.e., interoperable service systems, and illustrates the capability of EG by describing projects that have been implemented. Countries which adopted EG long ago such as Canada, USA, UK, Singapore, Malaysia, South Korea, Sweden, Denmark, and Australia are striving to develop standardized service systems that focus on providing citizen agency-based service from single Web portals. Interoperability, which can be achieved through synchronization and standardization of services among the work of different departments is the ultimate strategic goal of diffusing EG. This section also focuses on new directions and substantial extensions of EG through mobile EG or m-government, which can support real time information. These issues are covered in three chapters.

Chapter four examines different aspects of interoperability of EG. Data integration and interoperability among government departments are critical research issues in EG. The chapter focuses on these two issues by highlighting the problems posed, concerns, challenges, and the ways of addressing them. Examples are given to illustrate the benefits of achieving integration and interoperability. In the Introduction section, a list of projects to integrate government services at the national, state, and local levels is given, along with a number of examples of one-stop Web portals. Concerns and challenges for "personal information integration" are articulated in this chapter.

The potential to use the Internet to enhance government operations has been recognized throughout the world. A number of regional initiatives promoted by the government of India have brought e-services within the reach of millions of Indians. The fifth chapter makes a contribution to the literature by documenting the preparedness and digitization of services in Indian cities. Since India is a leading country in the world in adopting and diffusing ICT, Indian EG service and digital preparedness has significant implications for other countries in setting their interoperable EG service agendas. This chapter presents an analysis of the impact and sustainability of two EG schemes. It concludes that since there is no integration and interoperability between government departments, there is only sub-optimal utilization of the established infrastructure at present in the Indian EG service system.

The emergence of mobile technologies has not only revolutionized business procedures, but it has also resulted in transformation and reengineering of public service adoption mechanisms in more traditional EG systems. The sixth chapter delineates the development of mobile EG or m-government with illustrations of the scope of services that are offered or that could be offered through m-government. Its central significance is in real time information, which can be realized through hand held mobile devices like wireless phones. This chapter identifies the development of the fundamental capabilities needed to adapt and manage ICT to successfully implement citizen-focused m-government systems.

SECTION THREE

Section three is designed to impart specific knowledge about the reformation process of the financial capital market through the strategic implementation of e-governance. Through the application of specific knowledge of EG and with the inclusion of the impact of ICT, capital market reformation and stock exchange digitization can create enhanced opportunities. This section addresses different issues of capital markets with a particular emphasis on stock exchange decimalization, and it conceptualizes how e-governance systems can reshape and develop future optimization of financial market performance. Although ICT has been generally adopted in the banking sector to facilitate personal and corporate online banking, EG offers potential for the successful adoption of traditional EG in the banking sector. This section is organized into four chapters to conceptualize the adoption and implementation of an electronic governing framework to streamline future endeavors of financial capital markets.

Drawing inferences from the electronic governing adoption framework, or e-governance, in the capital markets, chapter seven describes the potential implications of e-governance in shaping the performance of future capital market functions. Prime stakeholders of the capital market, such as investors, creditors, and agencies like stock exchanges and securities commissions, require information that allow for the assessment of stewardship and resource allocation. The dissemination of that information is now available electronically. Financial capital markets increasingly require more effective governance, and much of that governance is disclosed and managed through an electronic medium. This chapter presents efficient, interactive, and transparent e-governance systems for the continuous evolution and service-centric reformation of the capital market. It also encapsulates the stages of adoption and proliferation of XBRL (eXtensible Business Reporting Language), a part of the evolution of e-governance.

Chapter eight gives a fundamental and conceptual paradigm for the adoption of EG by corporate financial institutions. The ICTs utilized by governments are often adapted from the corporate environment and subsequently used by governments to improve transparency and responsiveness. This chapter examines the use of ICTs as a medium to enhance governance in capital markets, focusing in particular on the Canadian capital market. Parallels are drawn between e-governance issues faced by governments and capital markets. Like national, regional, and local governments, the next frontier in e-governance is toward more stakeholder engagement, which may be possible through more sophisticated technological applications. The financial market is the prime corporate sector which has enhanced its services through the substantial adoption and widespread implementation of e-governance structures. Chapter eight broadly conceptualizes this phenomenon, particularly focusing on Canadian financial regulatory system optimization through digitization.

Fuelled by technological innovation, the New York Stock Exchange (NYSE) moved from fractional to decimal pricing. This was a revolutionary change which initiated a conversion of traditional quoting methods to decimalization. Chapter nine examines the impact of changing the smallest tick size from $1/16 to $0.01 in four areas, including market quality, trading behavior, the comparison between NYSE and NASDAQ, and evidence from other markets and securities. This chapter also summarizes evidence on trading behavior.

Chapter ten explores online banking and trading through virtual media, a widely diffused and accepted issue of corporate online function. During the last decade, Internet banking and online trading, supported by corporate EG, have been adopted in most countries and represent a popular format for banking service offerings to both individuals and corporations. Internationally, banks have also recognized the potential of Internet banking and have found that it is necessary to reconcile customer lifestyles and

Web based activity preferences with their business models. This chapter analyzes different features of online banking and trading, and their potential significance in shaping future financial market reformation and performance.

SECTION FOUR

Section four deals with the applied side of EG implementation, by identifying some application issues of EG initiatives. In particular, it investigates the anatomy of the technology interface and Open Source Software in the light of EG development. Technological, cultural, behavioral, organizational, and political aspects of EG adoption by its prime stakeholders are analyzed, and the growing importance of security and privacy issues for the implementation of EG are discussed in this section. This section has three chapters to deal with these topical issues.

Chapter eleven provides insights into the application of open source software for technological interfaces of EG. Across the world, almost all governments are implementing EG projects powered by ICT and trying to capture the benefits of dynamic, effective, and efficient public service systems. The most important advantage of adopting open source software for this purpose is that it helps to reduce a government's Information Technology (IT) expenditures, may encourage local software development, and it thereby promotes EG. This chapter investigates opportunities offered by open source software in EG. It also discusses the characteristics of open source software developers and their motivation to volunteer by contributing to open source software projects. The advantages and issues associated with open source software are described, along with the possibilities, scope, and significance of the adoption of open source software in EG.

Chapter twelve presents a fundamental and conceptual framework for the adoption criteria of EG, grounded in the perceptions of demand-side stakeholders, i.e. the end users or citizens. Citizens' adoption criteria of EG are tailored to their perceptions of different EG aspects, such as its security, user friendliness, relative advantage, reliability, et cetera. Basically, the adoption criteria of citizens have several interactive characteristics that include social, cultural, technological, organizational, and behavioral perspectives. Chapter twelve investigates the impact of security, trust, and legislative perceptions on citizen willingness to adopt virtual government services and information. Through an extensive empirical study and in-depth statistical analysis, this chapter reveals factors which can either drive or resist the adoption process.

Chapter thirteen addresses the most researched issues of ICT dominated projects in EG, which are security and privacy concerns for EG acceptance. It is unambiguously acknowledged that the transformation process of public sector requires vast investments in new technologies across the Web. In order to provide added value services to citizens, the governments around the world must build an infrastructure that ensures secure access to the Internet. Additionally, the adoption process of e-services is highly related to perceived security and perceived privacy. The chapter presents an overview of the security and privacy issues faced within EG initiatives. The purpose of the chapter is to provide guidance for administrators and IT professionals on this topic, and it reveals the necessity of investing in best practices for security and privacy technologies.

In summary, this book covers various and currently relevant issues of EG that concern the development, implementation, adoption, resistance, application, and performance of real EG projects. The editors hope that this will be a valuable contribution to the area of EG capability development in many different countries, with a specific focus on setting strategic achievement, offering interoperable government service systems, reforming the financial sector, and resolving ICT application issues in public service management.

However, in order to continue designing capable EG and m-government service systems in the public sector, and corporate e-governance in different private sectors to meet citizens' expectations from the 21st century public administration and private entities and facilitate development of effective and efficient services from both public and private sectors, we earnestly welcome constructive feedback and suggestions about this book. Feedback from academics, researchers, practitioners, and policy makers, based on their experience with actual EG initiatives in different countries in both the public and private sectors, is particularly welcome. Comments and constructive suggestions can be sent to us in care of IGI Publications Inc. at the address provided in this book's flyleaf.

Mahmud Akhter Shareef
McMaster University, Canada

Norm Archer
McMaster University, Canada

Shantanu Dutta
University of Ontario Institute of Technology, Canada

Acknowledgment

Scholars of virtual organizational behaviour, marketing, and information and communication technology — both academicians and practitioners were involved and contributed in the development of concepts and organization of the studies presented in this book. It is their enormous and relentless guidance at various stages of development of this work that pursues and confirms the highest quality of this book. This book would not have been possible without the contribution and guidance of the authors, advisors, reviewers, and our colleagues. We take this unique opportunity to convey our regards and gratitude to those scholars.

We must bestow our earnest regards to the staff at IGI Global who gave this opportunity to publish this book and supported the entire lengthy process of developing the book. The editors would like to thank the people at IGI Global, namely: Kristin M. Klinger for handling the book proposal, Jan Travers for managing the contract, and Joel A. Gamon for managing this project, especially for answering queries and keeping the project on schedule with highest responsiveness. In all aspects, we are highly obligated to reviewers for their useful and constructive comments to improvise the quality of all the book chapters. We are highly grateful to Dr. Professor Ibrahim Kushchu for providing the foreword.

We bestow our unbounded gratitude and deepest sense of respect to our families whose blessing, concerted efforts, constant encouragement, and wholehearted co-operation enabled us to reach this milestone.

Mahmud Akhter Shareef
McMaster University, Canada

Norm Archer
McMaster University, Canada

Shantanu Dutta
University of Ontario Institute of Technology, Canada

Section 1
Adoption of
E–Government Globally:
Vision, Mission, and Objectives

Chapter 1
E–Government Service Development

Mahmud Akhter Shareef
McMaster University, Canada

Norm Archer
McMaster University, Canada

ABSTRACT

E-government (EG) is an alternative channel to regular brick and mortar government office. This information and communication technology (ICT) driven delivery system offers government services to its different stakeholders in a more comprehensive, efficient, and effective way than it was through physical government office. At different stages of EG development and growth, functions, pattern, and capacities of offered services are distinctively different, and as such, association of technology is also different with these different stages. This chapter is designed to understand prime components, recognize stakeholders, and identify differentiable growth stage of EG. To fulfill this objective, this chapter is divided into four sections.

INTRODUCTION

Al Gore, former Vice President of the USA, has said: "In this fast-moving, fast-changing global economy — when the free flow of dollars and data are the source of economic and political strength, and whole new industries are born every day — governments must be lean, nimble, and creative, or they will surely be left behind" (Al

DOI: 10.4018/978-1-60960-848-4.ch001

Gore, 1993). This was the mission of EG when it was first introduced in the era of the fierce proliferation of information and communication technology (ICT). As a new and rapidly growing field, the concepts and theories of EG are still being developed. Researchers from different disciplines – such as political science, information systems, sociology, and organizational study – address the phenomenal paradigms of EG from the viewpoint of their fields. We have analyzed many different studies that discuss EG initiatives and missions, development strategies, proliferation and adoption, service maturity, and interoperability (Reddick, 2006; Al-Mashari, 2007; Gil-Garcia and Martinez-Moyano, 2007; Heeks and Bailur, 2007; Schedler and Summermatter, 2007; Wang and Liao, 2008; Van Dijk *et al.* 2008; Kim *et al.,* 2009; Robin *et al.,* 2009; Shareef et al. 2010a). It is clear that EG from its inception until now has aimed to accomplish not only the benefits of ICT in the public administration system, but also competence and competitive advantage in the present open market competition with the private sector. It can do this by introducing top quality, cost effective, and efficient citizen-centric service; offering a political gain through good governance; reforming organizations through power decentralization; and providing a citizen-centric administration system in the government organizational structure through cultural reformation. Other important aspects of EG are equal service availability for privileged and underprivileged groups across the country, and behavioral and attitudinal changes in individual and group performance. EG offers domestic economic gain from effective government service design and from the international attention received through proper image building of the country online and global interaction.

As a new and rapidly growing field, the concepts and theories of EG are still being conceptualized. Researchers from different disciplines – such as political science, information systems, sociology, and organizational study – address the phenomenal paradigms of EG from the viewpoint of their fields. After addressing and analyzing different studies representing EG initiatives and missions, development strategies, proliferation and adoption, service maturity, and interoperability (Reddick, 2006; Al-Mashari, 2007; Gil-Garcia and Martinez-Moyano, 2007; Heeks and Bailur, 2007; Schedler and Summermatter, 2007; Wang and Liao, 2008; Van Dijk *et al.* 2008; Kim *et al.,* 2009; Robin *et al.,* 2009; Shareef *et al.* 2010a) it is clear that EG from its inception until now has had several targets. Not only do governments

adopting EG hope to accomplish the benefits of ICT in the public administration system, but also competence and a competitive advantage in the present open market competition for some services with the private sector. To reach these goals, they have introduced top quality, cost effective, and efficient citizen-centric service and have worked to gain politically by offering good governance, organizational reformation through power decentralization, a citizen-centric administration system in the government organizational structure through cultural reformation, and equal service availability for privileged and underprivileged groups across the country. Governments have worked to establish behavioral and attitudinal changes in individual and group responses, and economic gain from domestically effective government service design, international attention through proper image building of the country online, and global interactions. The World Bank website (2005) viewed EG as: "information technologies…that have the ability to transform relations with citizens, businesses, and other arms of government... [and] can serve a variety of different ends: better delivery of government services to citizens, improved interactions with business and industry, citizen empowerment through access to information, or more efficient government management... benefits can be less corruption, increased transparency, greater convenience, revenue growth, and/or cost reductions." Shareef *et al*. (2010b) defined the comprehensive concept of EG as: "EG as an applied system can be defined as the modern evolution of government organizational structure for the presentation and delivery of all types of government information, services, and functions to all its users and stakeholders. It provides increased efficiency and efficacy in terms of service quality, time, and cost and in availability and accessibility. It also provides ease of use, transparency, participation in the public service function and decision making, democratization, and globalization through the use of modern ICT."

PRINCIPAL COMPONENTS

"We have a networked society and economy... and an industrial-aged government," Stephen Goldsmith, Harvard Professor and Presidential Advisor (Turner and Desloges, 2002).

For the last two decades, different governments have realized that without making government service more effective and efficient, ensuring maximum benefits to citizens for their tax money, providing more opportunities for them to participate in government decision making, it is difficult for them to be competitive with the private sector and fulfill the promise of the 21st century. Day by day, citizens are becoming frustrated with the performance of the government service system and believe that they are not receiving benefits from their tax money. Different developed and developing countries understood that public administration reformation and reengineering is inevitable. Considering some initial missions of public administration reformation, different governments have adopted an alternative channel to the traditional government service system: EG.

ICT is the primary tool which makes EG possible. Electricity, telecommunications, integrated circuits, networking, and the Internet have supported the revolutionary reformation in public administration service delivery system that is primarily adopted through political commitment and financial investment to bring efficiency and higher quality in government service. Continuing involvement of human capital – such as government, politicians, public administrators, policy makers, public and associated private employees, programmers, and technicians – is imperative for the successful implementation, operation, and maintenance of EG. Efficiency, effectiveness, cost-cutting, quality improvement, wider participation, easy accessibility, availability from anywhere round the clock, decentralization, and transparency are transformations that can be ensured with the application of ICT in the public

administration system. The supplementary support of political commitment, financial investment, human resources engagement, cultural change, and long-term vision are also essential (Shareef *et al.*, 2010a).

Reddick (2005) conducted an empirical study of EG implementation at the local level of the province of Ontario to determine how EG has changed the performance of municipalities. He revealed some results worth noting: 47% indicated that the business processes of the local government were re-engineered, 44% admitted that business processes and functions of government through EG were more efficient, 39% indicated that there is an obvious change in the role of staff, 30% agreed that the efficiency of employees was enhanced in respect to time management, and 20% said that administrative costs had been reduced. ICT has become one of the core elements of managerial reform, and EG may figure prominently in future governance. ICT has enlarged the scope of possibilities for improving managerial efficiency and the quality of public service delivery to citizens (Moon, 2002). During the last decade, technology has contributed to the revolutionary change in politics (Nye, 1999; Norris, 2001), government structure, institutional concepts, public administration, the process of governance (Fountain, 2001), performance management (Brown, 1999), bureaucracy and corruption reduction (Moon and Bretschneider, 2002), and reengineering (Anderson, 1999). Analyzing this discussion of EG development initiatives, we can categorize the major and fundamental components of the EG system as:

- Clear vision, mission, and objectives
- Governance structure and policy
- Continuing service transformation and improvement mechanism
- Huge and continuing financial investment
- Technology procurement and maintenance
- Web presence through ICT, Internet, and World Wide Web

- Country-wide telecommunication system
- Country-wide ICT network
- Country-wide Internet system with reasonable price and speed
- Related infrastructure including kiosks, cyber cafés, call centres, etc., particularly in rural areas
- Continuing up-grading of ICT
- Security and privacy
- Computer systems, and
- Human capital.

PRINCIPAL USERS/STAKEHOLDERS

The initiative, policy, development, reformation, functionality, interactivity, and interoperability of EG are substantially different from the traditional government service delivery mechanism (Schware and Deane, 2003; Van Dijk *et al.* 2008). The interaction between a customer/citizen and a business/government takes place with the Internet as the interface. Since the service delivery in EG has no human presence, the importance of trust, security, and privacy is substantial (Gefen et al., 2003). EG is more efficient, effective, democratic, accountable, participatory, and transparent (Shareef *et al.*, 2010a). It is an integration of government functions and, ultimately, aims at one-stop public service. The availability of and access to information is much more open. It saves in cost and time. It reflects the demand of the market/business/globalization mechanism in the 21ˢᵗ century and is citizen centered, because, at present, the long term strategy of EG reflects initiatives to remove the hierarchy and implement good governance. In EG, the initiative comes from the top level of government. Policy is associated with long-term political commitments to establish good governance. The development of EG is associated with huge financial and human capital investments and maintenance. It also requires adaptation of ICT in the core business of public administration. Reformation is done

in traditional public administration systems to ensure decentralization of power, breaking of the power of the bureaucracy, and revolutionary change in cultural adaptation, particularly in top level management. The functionality of EG accomplishes round-the-clock government service that is less expensive, efficient, and effective. Interactivity promotes the prime mission of EG adoption, which includes more accessibility for citizens and other stakeholders to government information and more participation in government decision making. Interoperability works for developing matured EG services through the virtual interface and standardizing functions and services of different organizations in a single domain (Carter and Bélanger, 2005).

In EG, stakeholders are treated as customers of the government/public system so that EG can be efficient and effective in meeting the requirements of a competitive market (Sakowicz, 2007). EG strategy includes the evolution of ICT, the reformation of public administration, and the integration of stakeholders. Since government service is a monopoly, unlike a private entity, the number of customers for EG is huge. Governments from the local, regional, or national levels develop EG to offer an alternative service delivery channel to stakeholders, which is a revolutionary change. Therefore, government is the supply side stakeholder. Government employees also use EG channels for internal efficiency, communication, and effectiveness (Internal Effectiveness and Efficiency, IEE). So, governments are representing both supply and demand side users.

Governments are designed to serve the citizens of the country. Citizens are the prime customers of any government; consequently, citizens are the prime users of EG (G2C). The most popular form of EG is G2C, i.e., government to citizen. This EG domain provides citizens government services and information through an online channel. Business organizations interact with governments for their business functions (G2B). This category supports the interaction between government and businesses so that through this alternative channel governments can provide efficient and effective services to private organizations, arrange information in an organized way, support business operations through interoperable functions, and reduce the cost of conducting business. These two types of users are the dominating stakeholders of EG from the demand side. Another demand side stakeholder is other governments – either at the local, regional, or national level – inside a country or governments of different countries (G2G). Different governments often share information and functions or collaborate for domestic service support or for international globalization.

The US government, while developing EG and categorizing service domains for public administration, has defined the stakeholders of EG into four groups. These are supporting service to: Government-to-citizen (G2C), Government-to-business (G2B), Government to-government (G2G), and Intra-government (IEE) (Evans and Yen, 2006; Lee *et al.*, 2005; Reddick, 2004; West, 2004). Among these four groups, IEE is for reformation inside an organization to expedite efficiency and effectiveness among employees while conducting business internally and externally. For the other three groups, the US EG initiative has figured out the following precise functions (USA.gov, 2002):

G2C – Government to Citizens:

1. Free online tax filing
2. Job search
3. Information about Social Security
4. Personal documents (birth and marriage certificates, passport applications, driver's license)
5. Immigration services
6. Health and related services
7. Government benefits information
8. Student loans
9. Disaster help
10. Other useful information (i.e., for sales, weather forecast, recreation).

G2B – Government to Business:

1. Comments on federal regulations
2. Corporation tax
3. Business opportunities
4. Registration of a new company
5. Business laws and regulations
6. Central contractor registration
7. Government auctions and sales
8. Employer ID number
9. Wage reporting
10. Subcontracting opportunities
11. File patents and trademarks
12. Export portal.

G2G - Government to Government:

1. Federal Pay Tables
2. Grants
3. Background Investigation Applications
4. e-Training Initiative for Federal Workers
5. Sale to Government Buyers
6. First Government Search for Federal Agencies
7. Per Diem Rates
8. Employee Directory
9. Federal Personnel-Payroll Changes.

The European Council has conceptualized and summarized EG service in a very comprehensive manner, listing 20 basic public services (12 for citizens and eight for businesses) (European Union, 2002). This list is as follows:

G2C – Government to Citizens:

1. Income taxes: notification of assessment
2. Job search services by labor offices
3. Social security contributions
    a. Unemployment benefits
    b. Family allowances
    c. Medical costs (reimbursement or direct settlement)
    d. Student grants

Table 1. Characteristics of types of e-government

Items	Information	Communication Online	Transaction
G2C and C2G	Information requests of a firm or the citizen regarding taxes, business licenses, registers, laws, political programs, administrative responsibilities, etc.	Information requests and discussion regarding administrative processes and products; communication with politicians, authorities, etc.	Online delivery of service and posting of results; electronic voting, providing solution online, and participation online, etc.
G2B and B2G	Information requests of a firm or the citizen regarding taxes, business licenses, registers, laws, business programs, business policy, administrative responsibilities, etc.	Information requests and discussion regarding administrative processes for business and products; communication with politicians, authorities, etc.	Online delivery of service and posting of results; electronic transactions of accounting, e-auditing, e-procurement, e-shopping, etc.
G2G	Exchange of information among different authorities and different hierarchical levels, regarding administrative acts and laws, policy making, data, projects or programs, background information to decisions, etc.	Information is exchanged among different authorities and different hierarchical levels; discussion fora; communication in negotiation and decision making; interaction regarding administrative acts and laws, projects or programs, etc.	Inter-organizational workflow and exchange of data, exchanging policy and solution online, information and knowledge management, etc.

Source: Fang (2002)

4. Personal documents (passport and driver's license)
5. Car registration (new, used, and imported cars)
6. Application for building permission
7. Declarations to the police
8. Public libraries (availability of catalogues, search tools)
9. Certificates (birth, marriage): request and delivery
10. Enrolment in higher education / university
11. Announcement of moving (change of address)
12. Health-related services (e.g., interactive advice on the availability of services in different hospitals; appointments for hospitals)

G2B – Government to Business:

1. Social contribution for employees
2. Corporation tax: declaration, notification
3. VAT: declaration, notification
4. Registration of a new company
5. Submission of data to statistical offices

6. Customs declarations
7. Environment-related permits (including reporting)
8. Public procurement

Fang (2002) has grouped EG services depending on stakeholders and stages of development. The following table, Table 1, has been borrowed from his work.

It is a significant and important issue to visualize users and stakeholders of a system prior to defining the functions of the system; otherwise its purpose, objectives, and missions might be jeopardized in the long run. Now, for EG, we can divide the prime stakeholders or users of EG into two major function-based groups: supply side and demand side. From the **supply side**, the prime stakeholders are:

1. Public administrators and employers (initiator organization)
2. Governments: national/regional/local (initiator)

From the **demand side**, the following prime stakeholders of EG can be identified and classified:

3. Citizens
4. Businesses
5. Government employees and also governments of other countries

SERVICE MATURITY LEVELS

Developed countries have implemented their own versions of an E-service system. Developing countries are also pursuing their own EG framework. Implementation and successive up-grades of an EG system follows certain paths, levels of maturity, stages, or phases. Traditional organizational growth models suggest that the growth of organizations goes through sequential maturation stages; these stages are hierarchical and the progressions of service maturity are irreversible (Nolan, 1979). These models reflect the conjecture that organizations transform their functionalities to the next higher stage, which is necessitated by the requirement to fulfill the challenges of different stakeholders; reformation to next stages can be classified as identifiable and discrete (Janssen and Van Veenstra, 2005). Different countries that implement EG in their ICT framework have different missions and objectives; however, the gradual development of an EG system in any country follows some unique levels of service maturity in their evolution. Researchers and practitioners have addressed, identified, and revealed those levels of service maturity of EG. However, methodologies followed to identify those levels of service maturity and categorization and, consequently, naming those levels of development do not follow the same track. Several researchers suggest that transformation of organizational functions to provide more flexible, efficient, and effective service to fulfill advance requirements of users that is more matured may not follow the same sequence (Klievink and Janssen, 2009). More specifically

it is not essential for organizations to follow the same order of service maturity; they can skip any service stage and still attain the upper maturation stages. This depends on the requirements, internal capabilities, and organizational strategy of the organization (Klievink and Janssen, 2009).

However, the evolution history of public administration has shown that the reformation and reengineering with the application of ICT has been tailored to successive up-grades of service maturity to fulfill the growing demand of the users (Gottschalk, 2009; Klievink and Janssen, 2009). Different researchers have identified different levels of service maturity and provided different names according to the methodologies, concepts, or theories applied in this identification. However, the generic meanings of those levels of development for EG identified by different researchers have very similar significance. Based on the conceptualization of service development stages of EG by different researchers (Layne and Lee, 2001; Fang, 2002; Accenture, 2003; Andersen and Henriksen, 2006; Evans and Yen, 2006; Irani *et al.,* 2006), Shareef *et al.,* (2010b) have defined the levels of service maturity of EG as: "*the pattern of service that a government develops, successively enhances interactivity, and delivers for stakeholders' acceptance and usage with up-grading of technological sophistication and functional characteristics.*"

In order to understand how the concepts of institution, organization, and isomorphism affect the evolution of EG, it is necessary to first comprehend the way in which researchers and practitioners have characterized and classified different levels of service maturity in the EG evolution (Hiller and Bélanger, 2001; Layne and Lee, 2001; UN/ASPA, 2002; Chen *et al.,* 2007; Gottschalk, 2009; Klievink and Janssen, 2009). The evolutionary approach suggests that EG gradually matures to provide interactive services (Schelin, 2003). Each of the stages represents different functions of services, different patterns of service characteristics, different levels of technological sophistication, and different orientations of stakeholders' association (Moon, 2002; Holden *et al.,* 2003).

Wong (2000) argued that EG deployment could be described in six levels of service maturity. These are: 1) information dissemination via websites; 2) two-way transaction via Internet connectivity; 3) multipurpose portals; 4) portal personalization; 5) clustering of common services; and 6) full integration and enterprise transformation.

Howard (2001) classified EG service maturity levels into three stages:

- **Stage 1: Publish:** This is the static stage where information of government is available online.
- **Stage 2: Interact:** Citizens can do certain two-way interactions with their governments, such as sending e-mail or joining chat rooms.
- **Stage 3: Transact:** In this stage, a complete two-way communication is established to provide different government service users with full benefits of transactions over the Internet.

A study addressing the development level of EG in 190 nations (UN/ASPA, 2002) identified five stages of EG: emergence or broadcasting, enhanced, interaction, transaction, and integration (seamless). Depending on the functions of EG, several authors (Trinkle, 2001; Wagner *et al.,* 2003; Bélanger and Carter, 2005) also divided web-based government services into five classified groups, as mentioned. This classification is based on the type of interaction or development path of maturity.

Chandler and Emanuels (2002) described EG service maturity levels in the following four stages:

- **Stage 1: Information:** This is a one-way communication which postulates the static presence of government information similar to the suggestion of Howard (2001.

- **Stage 2: Interaction:** This is a two-way communication denoting simple interaction between citizens and governments as advocated by Howard (2001).
- **Stage 3: Transaction:** This phase also resembles the transaction phase as proposed by Howard (2001): In this stage, a complete two-way communication is established to provide different government service users with full benefits of transactions over the Internet.
- **Stage 4: Integration:** This is the extension of Howard's model (2001). Here different functions are integrated among departments inside organizations and among different organizations to reduce duplication of service and ensure citizen-centric service in a flexible manner.

West (2004) suggested the same model of service delivery through EG suggested by Chandler and Emanuels (2002). The only difference is his conceptualization in defining stage 4, i.e., the integration stage. West advocates for the fourth stage to accomplish good governance and democracy with more government's accountability and citizens' participation.

Based on the stage model developed by the World Bank for EC (World Bank, 2003) where the model postulates that EC has evolved already through four stages: 1) publishing, 2) interactivity, 3) completing transactions, and 4) delivery (Figure 1), the United Nations has identified five stages of service delivery growth in attaining successive efficiency for higher interactivity and functionality that essentially capture the same issues. The emerging stage is the first presence of government service delivery to users through ICT. The enhanced stage is the extension of service offered through information gathered in EG websites. Stage three represents the interactive stage where users can directly interact with government to inquire or seek some information using web portals. At the fourth stage, i.e., transac-

Figure 1. The World Bank stage model of e-government (World Bank, 2003)

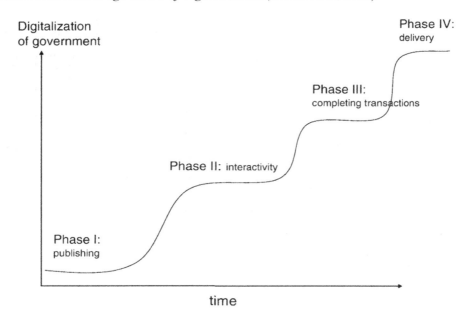

tional stage, a complete two-way communication provides more flexibility in seeking government service and performing individual and business functions through web interactions like paying taxes, utility bills, other charges, etc. Stage five, the seamless level, is actually integration of the functions inside organizations or among organizations across administrative boundaries, which ensures interoperability.

Chen *et al.* (2007) developed a four stage growth model that differs slightly in the concept of successive growth to offer flexible service. According to Chen *et al.* (2007), the growth stages are likely:

- **Stage 1:** Catalogue stage where government information can only be viewed and forms can be downloaded
- **Stage 2:** Transaction stage where a two-way communication is fully supported for service delivery
- **Stage 3:** Vertical integration is a higher stage where tasks within similar functionalities are integrated to provide more flexibility

- **Stage 4:** Horizontal integration is the final citizen-centric service system where different functions are integrated among organizations and it, finally, offers one-stop service delivery for users.

Layne and Lee (2001) postulate a comprehensive growth model that can be used to reflect EG development stages. Through this stage model, levels of service maturity of EG have been categorized into four groups, which mutually indicate a continuous process of development (Figure 2).

Klievink and Janssen (2009) classified EG development from the perspective of interoperability – more specifically shedding light on the capability to vertically integrate different functions inside an organization and horizontally integrate different tasks to standardize different organizations for harmony. They conducted an extensive study among different levels of people regarding service requirements, prolonged demands, and service design in the organizational and municipality levels and concluded that the successive up-gradation of service maturity offers more flexibility to fulfill further demands of users. Their

Figure 2. The Layne and Lee model

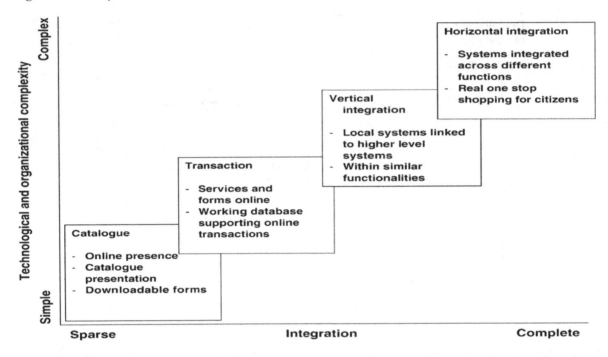

classification of EG service maturity, which is quite different from other researchers, is like this:

- **Stovepipes:** Delivery of different services is fragmented. No interconnection either intra- or inter-organizational.

- **Integrated organizations:** In intra-organization, there is standardization among different functions and tasks. This is vertical integration.

- **Nationwide portal:** Users can get access to the government service system through a nationwide portal.

- **Inter-organizational integration:** This is a horizontal integration and standardization of service among organizations.

- **Demand-driven, joined-up government:** This is customization or personalization of the service arrangement in the government EG initiative so that citizens can seek any service through a single interface. This is the optimization of a government service delivery mode which is customer driven.

The last stage as identified by Klievink and Janssen (2009) is also supported by several researchers ((Bertot and Jaeger, 2008).

What we find from exploring different models is that in the preliminary stages, EG offers different tasks organized around functions and not citizen demand. While service delivery systems matured, more flexible service is offered which can fulfill users' advance requirements. These matured service delivery options integrate functions inside organizations and, finally, among different bodies of government in a single portal. This requires higher levels of processing capability, technological up-gradation, service standardization, and security implementation (Shareef *et al.*, 2007, 2010). Synthesizing their classifications can be demonstrated in the following manner:

- **Initial presence:** This is primarily static website presenting government information for their users. No interaction is possible through this service delivery option.

- **Interactive presence:** At this service maturity level, government departments launch their individual websites to provide their information and invite users queries through email or chat rooms. It is fundamentally a two-way communication between government departments and users.

- **Transactional presence:** This is a more matured, higher level of service delivery of government departments where a complete two-way interaction is possible. EG allows secure transaction between governments and users.

- **Vertical integration:** Now the service delivery systems of EG has gained sufficient maturity. Gradually government departments move to synchronize their services, functions, and tasks vertically to integrate similar services provided by different levels of government. It is a continuous reengineering process, reformation of service delivery, and reconstruction of governmental structures.

- **Horizontal integration:** This is the advanced level integration among different government organizations that ensures better efficiency and convenience for citizens and other stakeholders in seeking similar services from different departments. At this stage, proper standardization of functions among organizations for interoperability is the essential strategy.

- **Customization or Personalization:** This level of service maturity refers to the ultimate citizen-centric delivery where users do not need to interact with any government organizations individually. All the services will be delivered through a single government portal and users will get services according to their needs from this portal.

So, what we can conclude? Several scholars have identified and classified service maturity levels of EG in different stages, although they argue that these maturity levels are not necessarily mutually exclusive or progressive (Hiller and Bélanger, 2001; Layne and Lee, 2001; UN/ASPA, 2002; Moon, 2002; Sandoval and Gil-García, 2005; Gil-Garcia and Martinez-Moyano, 2007, Gottschalk, 2009; Klievink and Janssen, 2009). Different authors have not only classified EG service maturity levels into different stages but also have provided different names for those maturity levels. From our studies we have determined that there is no strong theoretical background for differentiating EG development stages into such groups. There is also no clear evidence that the EG development process has to follow sequentially the different levels of service maturity. However, from those models we can learn the functional progress of EG development. It can also be inferred that these service maturity levels describe the development of maturity of service in a sequential manner.

REFERENCES

Andersen, K. V., & Henriksen, H. Z. (2006). E-government maturity models: Extension of the Layne and Lee model. *Government Information Quarterly, 23*, 236–248. doi:10.1016/j.giq.2005.11.008

Anderson, K. (1999). Reengineering public sector organizations using Information Technology. In Heeks, R. (Ed.), *Reinventing government in the information age* (pp. 312–330). New York, NY: Routledge.

Bélanger, F., & Carter, L. (2005). Trust and risk in e-government adoption. *Proceedings of the 11th Americans Conference on Information Systems*, Omaha, NE, USA.

Bertot, J. C., & Jaeger, P. T. (2008). The e-government paradox: Better customer service doesn't necessarily cost less. *Government Information Quarterly, 25*(2), 149–154. doi:10.1016/j.giq.2007.10.002

Brown, D. (1999). Information Systems for improved performance management: Development approaches in US public agencies. In Heeks, R. (Ed.), *Reinventing government in the information age* (pp. 113–134). New York, NY: Routledge.

Carter, L., & Bélanger, F. (2005). The utilization of e-government services: Citizen trust, innovation and acceptance factors. *Information Systems Journal*, *15*, 5–25. doi:10.1111/j.1365-2575.2005.00183.x

Chandler, S., & Emanuels, S. (2002). Transformation not automation. *Proceedings of 2nd European Conference on E-government*, (pp. 91-102). St Catherine's College Oxford, UK.

Chen, Z., Gangopadhyay, A., Holden, S. H., Karabatis, G., & McGuire, P. (2007). Semantic integration of government data for water quality management. *Government Information Quarterly*, *24*(4), 716–735. doi:10.1016/j.giq.2007.04.004

European Union. (2002). *Evolution of e-government in the European Union*. Report commissioned by the Spanish Presidency of the Council of the European Union. Retrieved from http://www.map.es/csi/pdf/ eGovEngl_definitivo.pdf

Evans, D., & Yen, D. C. (2006). E-government: Evolving relationship of citizens and government, domestic, and international development. *Government Information Quarterly*, *23*(2), 207–235. doi:10.1016/j.giq.2005.11.004

Fang, Z. (2002). E-government in digital era: Concept, practice and development. *International Journal of the Computer. The Internet and Information*, *20*, 193–213.

Fountain, J. (2001). *Building the virtual state: Information Technology and institutional change*. Washington, DC: Brookings Institution Press.

Gefen, D., Karahanna, E., & Straub, D. W. (2003). Trust and TAM in online shopping: An integrated model. *Management Information Systems Quarterly*, *27*, 51–90.

Gil-Garcia, J. R., & Martinez-Moyano, I. J. (2007). Understanding the evolution of e-government: The influence of systems of rules on public sector dynamics. *Government Information Quarterly*, *24*(2), 266–290. doi:10.1016/j.giq.2006.04.005

Gore, A., Jr. (1993). *From red tape to results: Creating a government that works better and costs less*. Washington DC: Government Printing Office. Retrieved from http://govinfo.library.unt.edu/ npr/library/nprrpt/annrpt/ redtpe 93/index.html

Gottschalk, P. (2009). Maturity levels for interoperability in digital government. *Government Information Quarterly*, *26*(1), 75–81. doi:10.1016/j.giq.2008.03.003

Hiller, J. S., & Bélanger, F. (2001). Privacy strategies for electronic government. In Abramson, M. A., & Means, G. E. (Eds.), *E-government 2001* (pp. 162–198). Lanham, MD: Rowman & Littlefield Publishers.

Holden, S. H., Norris, D. F., & Fletcher, P. D. (2003). Electronic government at the local level, progress to date and future issues. *Public Performance and Management Review*, *26*(4), 325–344. doi:10.1177/1530957603026004002

Howard, M. (2001). E-government across the globe: How will "E" change government? *Government Finance Review*, *17*(4), 6–9.

Irani, Z., Al-Sebie, M., & Elliman, T. (2006). Transaction stage of e-government systems: Identification of its location & importance. *Proceedings of the 39th Hawaii International Conference on System Sciences*.

Janssen, M., & Van Veenstra, A. F. (2005). Stages of growth in e-government: An architectural approach. *Electronic. Journal of E-Government, 3*(4), 193–200.

Klievink, B., & Janssen, M. (2009). Realizing joined-up government — Dynamic capabilities and stage models for transformation. *Government Information Quarterly, 26*(2), 275–284. doi:10.1016/j.giq.2008.12.007

Layne, K., & Lee, J. (2001). Developing fully functional e-government: A four stage model. *Government Information Quarterly, 18,* 122–136. doi:10.1016/S0740-624X(01)00066-1

Lee, J. K., Kim, D. J., & Rao, H. R. (2005). An examination of trust effects and preexisting relational risks in e-government services. *Proceedings of the 11th Americas Conference on Information Systems*, Omaha, NE, USA.

Moon, M. J. (2002). The evolution of e-government among municipalities: Rhetoric or reality? *Public Administration Review, 62*(4), 424–433. doi:10.1111/0033-3352.00196

Moon, M. J., & Bretschneider, S. (2002). Does perception of red tape constrain IT innovativeness in organizations: Unexpected results from simultaneous equation model and implications. *Journal of Public Administration: Research and Theory, 12*(2), 273–291.

Nolan, R. L. (1979). Managing the crises in data processing. *Harvard Business Review, 57*(March/April), 115–126.

Norris, P. (2001). *Digital divide: Civic engagement, information poverty, and Internet worldwide*. New York, NY: Cambridge University Press.

Nye, J. S. Jr. (1999). Information Technology and democratic governance. In Democracy.com? In Ciulla, E., Joseph, K., & Nye, S. Jr., (Eds.), *Governance in networked world* (pp. 1–18). Hollis, NH: Hollis Publishing Company.

Reddick, C. G. (2005). Citizen-initiated contacts with Ontario local e-government: Administrators' responses to contacts. *International Journal of Electronic Government Research, 1*(4), 45–62. doi:10.4018/jegr.2005100103

Report, A. (2003). *E-government leadership – Realizing the vision*. The Government Executive Series.

Sakowicz, M. (2007). *How to evaluate e-government? Different methodologies and methods*. Retrieved from http://unpan1.un.org/intradoc /groups/public/documents/ NISPAcee/ UNPAN009486.pdf

Sandoval, R., & Gil-García, J. R. (2005). *Assessing e-government evolution in Mexico: A preliminary analysis of the state portals*. Paper presented at the 2005 Information Resources Management Association International Conference, San Diego.

Schelin, S. H. (2003). E-government: An overview. In Garson, G. D. (Ed.), *Public Information Technology: Policy and management issues* (pp. 120–137). Hershey, PA: Idea Group Publishing.

Schware, R., & Deane, A. (2003). Deploying e-government program: The strategic importance of 'I' before 'E.'. *Info, 5*(4), 10–19. doi:10.1108/14636690310495193

Shareef, M. A., Kumar, U., & Kumar, V. (2007). Developing fundamental capabilities for successful e-government implementation. *Proceedings of ASAC Conference,* Ottawa.

Shareef, M. A., Kumar, U., Kumar, V., & Dwivedi, Y. K. (2010b). (in press). E-government adoption model (GAM): Differing service maturity levels. *Government Information Quarterly*.

Shareef, M. A., Kumar, V., Kumar, U., Chowdhury, A. H., & Misra, S. C. (2010a). E-government implementation perspective: Setting objective and strategy. *International Journal of Electronic Government Research, 6*(1). doi:10.4018/jegr.2010102005

Trinkle, S. (2001). *Moving citizens from in line to online: How the Internet is changing how government serves its citizens*. Retrieved from http://www.bcinow.com/demo /oel /Resources Articles.htm

Turner, M., & Desloges, C. (2002). *Strategies and framework for government online: A Canadian experience*. World Bank E-Government Learning Workshop, Washington D.C., June 18.

UN/ASPA. (2002). *Benchmarking of e-government: A global perspective*. New York, NY: United Nations Division of Public Economics and Public Administration and the American Society for Public Administration.

USA.gov. (2002). *Home page*. Retrieved from http://www.firstgov.gov/

Van Dijk, Jan A. G. M., Peters, O., & Ebbers, W. (2008). Explaining the acceptance and use of government Internet services: A multivariate analysis of 2006 survey data in the Netherlands. *Government Information Quarterly, 25*(3), 379–399. doi:10.1016/j.giq.2007.09.006

Wagner, C., Cheung, K., Lee, F., & Ip, R. (2003). Enhancing e-government in developing countries: Managing knowledge through virtual communities. *The Electronic Journal on Information Systems in Developing Countries, 14*(4), 1–20.

West, D. M. (2004). E-government and the transformation of service delivery and citizen attitudes. *Public Administration Review, 64*(1), 15–27. doi:10.1111/j.1540-6210.2004.00343.x

Wong, W. (2000). *At the dawn of e-government*. New York, NY: Deloitte Research, Deloitte and Touche.

World Bank. (2003). *A definition of e-government*. Washington, DC.

KEY TERMS AND DEFINITIONS

E-Government (EG): EG is government's service and information offered through the use of ICT for citizens, business organizations, and other stakeholders of government. It provides higher efficiency and effectiveness in terms of service quality, time, and cost.

Government Services: Government services are those services which are offered by governments for its stakeholders like citizens, business organizations, government employees etc.

Growth Model: Implementation and successive up-grading of the services offered through EG system follow certain paths, stages, or phases. This is called growth model.

Information and Communication Technology (ICT): ICT can be defined as the modern computer and Internet based technology used for managing and processing information in different public and private sectors.

Public Administration: It is the management of government service and information conducted through governments departments.

Service Maturity: In EG, service pattern, functionality, technological sophistication, interaction, and reengineering processes gradually upgrade. This is called service maturity.

Stakeholder: Different members in the society who develop and or seek government information and services.

Chapter 2
Electronic-Government Vision:
Case Studies for Objectives, Strategies, and Initiatives

Mahmud Akhter Shareef
McMaster University, Canada

Uma Kumar
Carleton University, Canada

Vinod Kumar
Carleton University, Canada

Morteza Niktash
Public Works and Government Services, Canada

ABSTRACT

Different countries adopt Electronic-government (EG) from different perspectives, although they align their mission to develop efficient government sectors that can satisfy citizens. However, countries develop their initiatives from different visions and attempt to achieve different ends, although their means are very similar. This chapter addresses and analyzes the strategies and objectives for EG of different countries. It also delineates subtle differences in their targets to achieve the implementation and proliferation of EG. It has three sections; the first gives the background of this case study, the second examines the EG initiatives of some selected countries, and the third discusses the summary of these initiatives.

BACKGROUND

It is now well recognized that the application of information and communication technology (ICT) in the bureaucratic public administration system can make it dynamic and ensure that service quality is modernized. However, it is also obvious from literature reviews that business process engineering in public service reformation must be supported by financial capability and political commitment (Kraemer and King, 2003; Stokes and Clegg, 2003; Dawes *et al.*, 2004; Titah and Barki, 2005; Reddick, 2006; Irkhin, 2007; Schedler and Summermatter, 2007). Different countries are pursuing EG as a national policy to reform public

DOI: 10.4018/978-1-60960-848-4.ch002

administration and developing an efficient, effective, and cost-cutting service delivery system to improve their national economy. Governments are learning from large corporations to treat customers as the first stakeholder to satisfy and, through this approach, creating loyal customer groups. Government organizations in both developed and developing countries now understand that without treating citizens as customers and satisfying their needs with the highest quality of service, they cannot compete with the private sector in areas where their services overlap. So public organizations are now working hard to reform their management system to be like private corporations and create close ties with their stakeholders. Therefore, the prime and fundamental objective of EG in any country is to satisfy customers with better quality and efficient services (Moon and Norris, 2005; Parent *et al.*, 2005; Evans and Yen, 2006; Irkhin, 2007; Shareef *et al.* 2009, 2010c).

However, different countries adopt this objective from different perspectives (Shareef *et al.*, 2010a). Some countries take this notion of citizen-centric service to make the service system more dynamic so that it can be cost effective. Other countries implement the objective of a citizen-driven system to make the public sector as dynamic as a private corporation and boost the national economy as well as establishing themselves on the global marketplace. Some countries do, however, approach the goal satisfying citizens so they can develop an interconnected government among all the stakeholders and pursue good governance through a transparent and participative government. We can observe these different approaches by different governments to pursue EG through ICT from the definition of EG given by Shareef *et al.* (2010b) that gives the accomplishment of ultimate objectives and goals of EG as: "EG as an applied system can be defined as the modern evolution of government organizational structure for the presentation and delivery of all types of government information, services, and functions to all its users and stakeholders. It pro-

vides increased efficiency and efficacy in terms of service quality, time, and cost and in availability and accessibility. It also provides ease of use, transparency, participation in the public service function and decision making, democratization, and globalization through the use of modern ICT."

We find that getting a comprehensive picture of the strategies and objectives of different countries in pursuing EG in the core public administration system through ICT, organizational reengineering, socio-cultural change, and political commitment has significant implications for any realistic managerial initiatives. The objective of this study is to analyze the vision, objectives, and strategies adopted by different countries in terms of their capability, technological beliefs, and political commitment.

CASE STUDY: EG INITIATIVES

To accomplish the aforementioned objective we have selected some countries as case studies for EG initiatives; these countries have a high profile in exploring ICT in the reformation capacity of public administration management, adopting a long-term vision in strategizing national policy, and developing mature service through EG. So, in one sense, we have selected the leading countries in the world in implementing transformational government through online means. But we also considered socio-cultural variations in choosing countries for our case study. To do this, we decided to analyze and interpret the EG development of at least one country from each continent so that we can compare and contrast the EG vision, mission, objectives, and long-term goal of different countries that have socio-cultural, political, economic, and technological variations. This will allow our conclusions to be generalized. For the case studies, we have addressed the EG policy and target of eight leading countries in the world.

Australia

Australian government began embracing EG with a clear vision that it would use ICT in the reformation of public administration systems to provide better services to its stakeholders (Accenture, 2004). Australia has a long history of implementing EG at the local, regional, and state and territorial government levels by using the full potential of ICT (Shareef *et al.*, 2010a). As Shareef *et al.* (2010a) illustrated from a through analysis of Australian EG initiatives and strategies, Australia is primarily motivated to develop EG as an alternative channel to traditional government service delivery systems. They want to provide better government service to their stakeholders in a more efficient and effective way through the extensive application of ICT as they reform public administration. Political commitment, good governance, citizen participation in government decision making, transparency, accountability, and more democracy are not yet directly reflected in their EG mission. We carefully examined different features, new extension and up-gradation, interactivity, maturity of service delivery, functionality, and degree of integration through interoperability of the Australian government's official EG website, http://australia.gov.au. The Australian government has created a new company, NBN Co Ltd, to extend the national broadband network so that Australian telecommunication systems can be efficient in speed, networking, and cost throughout the country.

In 2009, out of the 31 OECD countries the Australian fixed broadband was ranked 17th in terms of fixed broadband take-up (See Appendix B) and 5th in terms of service usage expense (The World Economic Forum reports, 2010). According to that report, Australia is 27th for accessibility of digital content, 21st for availability of new technology, and 16th on the Networked Readiness Index. The Australian central government portal has extended their service from static to interactive to transaction stages in several areas.

It is also attempting to achieve interoperability among different government departments through horizontal integration and standardization of services among departments. Citizens can now claim government service through a single account that allows them to sign on to multiple agencies and they can customize their requirements from their own needs.

We also reviewed several studies concerning Australian EG strategies (Accenture, 2005/2009; Evans and Yen, 2006; IMF, 2008; All About Market Research, 2008; Robin *et al.*, 2009; Shareef *et al.*, 2010a). These studies showed that the Australian EG initiative, primarily introduced at the end of the last century, is now pushing very hard to achieve seamless interoperable service through a single portal and aiming to fulfill the customized requirements of citizens and other stakeholders.

Accenture (2003) reported that Australian EG now has 105 services available out of the 115 services that the Australian government could deliver online. Australian EG is expanding quickly; among the regular Australian users of the Internet, 81 percent use EG (Accenture, 2004/2009). Australia now ranks 4th in providing mature services through EG among 22 leading global countries (See Appendix A). The Australian Taxation Office (ATO), Australia's principal revenue collection agency, has developed one of the most effective, efficient, and personalized tax return systems of countries worldwide; they developed this system based on community response.

In its inception Australian EG was more focused on developing ICT hubs in public administration systems that were capable in providing easier, cost effective, and efficient service to ensure higher quality in government performance. The Australian EG initiative is now gradually extending its functional periphery by embracing a more enlightened view of good governance. This is shown in the proclamation of the Australian Government 2.0 Taskforce Final Report. The report (Australian Government 2.0 Taskforce Final Report, 2009) claims that by embracing the government's 2.0 initiative, the Australian federal government has made it possible to:

- "make our democracy more participatory and informed
- improve the quality and responsiveness of services in areas like education, health and environmental management, and at the same time deliver these services with greater agility and efficiency
- cultivate and harness the enthusiasm of citizens, letting them more fully contribute to their wellbeing and that of their community
- unlock the immense economic and social value of information and other content held by governments to serve as a precompetitive platform for innovation
- revitalize our public sector and make government policies and services more responsive to people's needs and concerns by:
- providing government with the tools for a much greater level of community engagement
- allowing the users of government services much greater participation in their design and continual improvement
- involving communities of interest and practice outside the public sector - which offer unique access to expertise, local knowledge and perspectives - in policy making and delivery
- more successfully attracting and retaining bright, enthusiastic citizens to the public service by making their work less hierarchical, more collaborative and more intrinsically rewarding".

However, from their present efforts in EG, it can be noted that good governance through E-democracy, E-election, and E-participation in government decision making is still not their priority in EG mission. They are primarily engaged in delivering top quality service by capitalizing the enormous benefits of EG. The Australian govern-

ment has articulated their 2010 vision to achieve over the next five years (AGIMO, 2006) as:

- Citizens' requirements would be fulfilled with satisfaction.
- Through EG, digital inclusion and interconnected government would be established.
- Government service system would be efficient enough to realize value for money.
- Public sector capability, effectiveness, and efficiency would be enhanced and dynamic.

Finally, we can conclude that Australia is now a leading country in developing a clear vision to implement E-government. In the beginning they were very slow in achieving the benefits of EG by reformation of the public administration bureaucracy; however, they have now taken the final steps to accelerate interoperable, customized, and citizen-centric EG systems among all government departments. They are very eager to develop interconnected government systems and deliver the most efficient service to their stakeholders. Australian EG has achieved not only transactional capacity in several government services but also interoperable capacity by which they can provide customized and citizen-based service through a single portal. Nevertheless, they are still struggling to focus priority on E-democracy.

Brazil

Brazilian President Luiz Inácio Lula da Silva announced the expansion of EG and their political commitment towards its implementation in this statement – "The Brazil Portal marks a new stage in the communication from the State with society and the media," – during the launch of the new version of www.brasil.gov.br, Brazil's official EG website (Northxsouth, 2010). This commitment strongly indicates Brazil's long-term vision to capture the benefits of ICT by implementing it in public administration reformation and the development of EG.

Although Brazil is a developing country, it is very advanced in ICT and has remarkable competence in the application of ICT in the reformation of their traditional public administration system, which is bureaucratic, corrupt, and non-transparent. So the Brazilian federal government is enthusiastic enough to set a public policy and adopt a strategic initiative on knowledge management through the use of EG. At the beginning, starting in 2001, it was working at a very slow pace to deliver more sophisticated online government services. However, at present, Brazil has realized the potential of EG in boosting the national economy and positioning the country globally through online government (Accenture, 2009). From the beginning, Brazil's EG initiative was concentrated fundamentally on some specific services of education, health, public safety, justice, elections, legislation, and public administration. Brazil is a country where the digital divide is extremely high, which is seen in the differences in accessing government information from urban areas and rural zones. The country has now attempted to reduce this class difference by digital inclusion, i.e., bridging the gap digitally between privileged and unprivileged groups. Brazil's long-term commitment for reformation of federal public administration to implement EG and make the service accessible across the country has set the following strategic targets (Tavares, 2001; Knight, 2007):

1. Through the application of ICT in all levels of public administration improve the efficiency, effectiveness, and quality of public service for all Brazilians.
2. Ensure an efficient management system in public administration by reducing red tape and corruption.
3. Promote transparency and accountability in public management.

4. Reduce the digital divide by making government service equally available for all citizens countrywide.
5. Develop EG networks in such a way that all government services are available to citizens through the Internet, with better quality, lower costs, and easier access.
6. Boost the national economy through proper interconnectedness among different levels of governments.
7. Reduce government expenditure through capitalization of the benefits available with the application of ICT.
8. Confirm cultural change in public administration to ensure citizen-centric service.
9. Implement technology-intense infrastructure and communications to standardize service and security with higher quality in performance.
10. Make the public sector competitive with private counterparts.
11. Enhance the domestic image through online government and capitalize on the enormous opportunities of globalization.

The Brazilian government has been ensuring the presence, to some extent, of 103 government services online out of 135 types of public services. Though most of the services offered by Brazilian EG are still at the publish (static) level, the Brazilian government is steadily improving its service presence, maturity, and interactivity and is working to transform some services from the publish level to the interaction and transaction levels (Accenture, 2003). Brazil's position overall among 22 leading countries in implementing EG is 21 (Accenture, 2004) (See Appendix A).

As Knight (2007) remarked about mismanagement and lack of commitment in implementing a comprehensive EG structure and visionary plan in Brazil: "without strong leadership, these important initiatives are unlikely to result in radical improvements... Brazil needs a national e-Development strategy as an integral and high-priority element of a broader vision of where it wants to go and how to get there." This statement uncovers the present status of Brazilian EG initiatives and the reasons behind this. From the overview of the missions and objectives set forth by the Brazilian government in implementing EG, it is clear that the government is giving priority to the adoption of new ICT within its administrative processes and the services offered to the general public. However, Brazil has a long history of social class problems rooted in a highly unequal distribution of income. Its education, health, and land sectors are not equally available to all citizens. Although Brazil has a competitive economic force with wealth and capital, at the same time its rural areas suffer from extremely backwardness. The political system is still not transparent and the bureaucracy in public administration creates barriers to achieving economic competitiveness and social integrity. As a developing country, these are common socio-cultural, economic, and political phenomena. However, Brazil is addressing these problems, identifying the steps necessary to remove these barriers to development, and meeting objectives to advance the country through the successful implementation of EG by providing better government services to citizens and businesses, integrating the whole country with adoption of ICT, and minimizing the digital divide.

This new wave in drastically reforming Brazilian EG is evident in several recent initiatives to modernize domestic ICT-based infrastructure and long-term vision. "The world has entered a new era of open, interactive, real-time communication and with the launch of Brazil.gov.br, Brazil is ready to harness the opportunities presented by digital media to apply those qualities to official State communications," said the Secretariat for Social Communication Minister Franklin Martins (Banas and Hillard — SECOM, 2010). At the same time, Brazil is developing an extended version of the Brazilian government web portal that is very dynamic and efficient in meeting citizens require-

ments of the 21st century. The Secretariat further states: "Portal Brasil underlines our institutional beliefs in social equality and transparency. This website is one of the largest open-source undertakings ever attempted. We will use its flexible platform to quickly, efficiently and dynamically inform and communicate with local and foreign citizens of the world." This reflects the Brazilian involvement in developing a new digital era.

We can summarize with several points:

1. Brazilian EG is still not matured enough in comparison to other leading countries in the world, as can be expected from Brazil as a global growing power.

2. Its progress from the inception of ICT in public administration system and implementation of EG is very slow and not associated with great leadership.

3. However, recently Brazilian EG has gotten a much expected momentum and set certain long term visions with a strong political commitment to provide citizen-centric service.

4. Its strategic objective in adopting EG is to provide cost-effective and efficient service that will ensure higher quality service.

5. Brazilian EG is also active in achieving dynamic functionality in government service systems and reducing government expenditure by capitalizing on the enormous benefits of ICT.

6. Brazil has set the target in its EG initiative to attain global competence and higher economic performance.

7. Brazilian EG also includes some issues like transparency, bureaucracy, corruption, and accountability in their recent movement to maker visionary changes in EG, E-democracy, E-election, and E-participation of citizens in government decision making. These are all preconditions of EG, but Brazil still has a long way to go.

Denmark

Denmark's overall position among 22 leading countries in implementing EG is 5th (Accenture, 2004) (See Appendix A). This reflects the initiatives, strategies, and achievements of Denmark in developing a more efficient and effective public sector through EG. Danish EG, in their vision, took extensive use of the opportunities of ICT to reach people across the country in a more efficient and effective round-the-clock way. Their aim was to boost the national economy, provide the best and most efficient public service to citizens with the help of digital administration, and encourage citizen participation in democracy to finally establish an inclusive government (OECD e-Government Studies, 2010). According to the report of the OECD e-Government Studies (2010), in terms of the broadband penetration rate, Denmark is the top among the OECD member states; it has a fixed broadband penetration of 37.3% over a EU27 average of 23.9%, and an OECD average of 22.8%. Further, from an assessment of the impact of Danish EG on public administration reformation and reengineering in pursuing citizen-centric and efficient service, the report of OECD e-Government Studies (2010) revealed that "the Danish government has realized that e-government has a key instrumental value to push reforms forward at all levels of government and that where it is used it should be clearly integrated. The Government has made considerable efforts to ensure the alignment of the e-government programme with targeted public sector reform initiatives (e.g. the Quality Reform and De-bureaucratization Programme) and the co-ordination of the various governance bodies in charge of their implementation."

Denmark has been using ICT in public administration reformation and reengineering from the beginning of the computer and Internet era to capitalize on the benefits of modern technology (OECD, 2009). At the reformation stage, their primary vision was aimed at providing better quality service to citizens and fulfilling the needs of taxpayers (SAFAD, 2000; Löfgren, 2007). However, they soon extended their missions from only a seamless flow of competitive government service to citizens through adopting ICT to a digital inclusion of citizens with the government decision making process. They attempted to gain not only the known benefits of technology but also the social and political aspects of developing good governance. This is the ultimate mission of EG in achieving E-democracy (Okot-Uma and Caffrey, 2000; Shareef *et al.* 2008). This new approach demonstrated that Danish EG has taken a much broader view of establishing good governance through proper execution of government reformation. We can get some understanding from the following figure (Figure 1), which was developed from an extensive survey among different organizations in Denmark conducted by the OECD (2009) to understand Danish EG initiatives. The survey question was: "What are the main drivers of collaboration and co-operation with sub-national (regional and municipal) organisations?" In response, the Danish organizations focused primarily on efficient, effective, and innovative service delivery in their EG strategies. They also wished to gain competitiveness in the public sector through ICT. However, they are gradually becoming engaged in fulfilling the citizens' democratic demand of good governance (OECD e-Government Studies, 2010).

The vision of the preliminary EG strategy of Denmark was: "Digitalization must contribute to the creation of an efficient and coherent public sector with a high quality of service, with citizens and businesses at the centre" (OECD, 2005). However, from several recommendations of the OECD study on Danish EG and also from the political visionary commitment in providing better quality service, Denmark has a renewed vision in launching EG in its 2007-2010 policy program: "Towards Better Digital Service, Increased Ef-

Figure 1. Danish EG objectives for public organizations (Source: OECD survey of e-government in Denmark 2009)

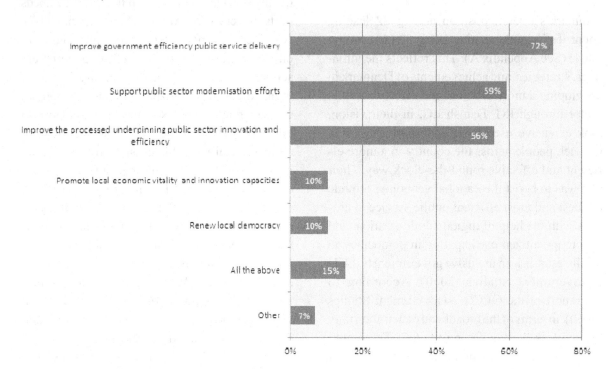

ficiency and Stronger Collaboration" (OECD e-Government Studies, 2010). The primary concentration of this overarching reformation is to ensure achieving a highly effective and customer-focused ICT-based EG structure that is capable in providing top quality services to citizens and businesses. They identified the following three priorities for their EG initiatives (OECD e-Government Studies, 2010):

1. To create easily accessible government services with better quality.
2. To support administrative reformation for achieving higher efficiency in public administration management.
3. To ensure effective collaboration between government and administration and within the administration.

Denmark has targeted to enhance its online service quality from interoperable "whole-

of-government" to its prime stakeholders by creating the www.borger.dk government portal for citizens and www.virk.dk for business organizations (OECD e-Government Studies, 2010). Denmark's achievement in an EG implementation scheme is its consistent development to provide mature service. Its initiatives are associated with strong citizen demand, political commitment, and long-term vision. Out of a possible 136 government services, 121 services are available in EG; several services are matured enough to provide the interaction and transaction phases of services (Accenture, 2003).

Now, if we carefully analyze the principles of Danish EG, we observe that, though the early vision of the Danish government was aimed at capitalizing the advantages of ICT and distributing it among citizens, the vision gradually shifted to establishing higher quality services to citizens and establishing good governance, democracy, and accountability of public administration. The fiscal and financial constraints, which are the consequences of the economic recession in 2008-2010, forced European governments, including Denmark, to reinforce public administration reformation to achieve a digital government that is more economic and efficient in government expenditure as well as effective in providing higher quality service and better welfare to citizens (OECD e-Government Studies, 2010). Denmark addresses the problem from the political perspective and tries to leverage citizen participation in the democratic movement and government decision making by involving citizens with the digital government. So, finally, by providing efficient and higher quality services to citizens by assisting citizen participation in government functions, Denmark is ultimately moving forward to achieve the widely proclaimed good governance that is essentially citizen-centric. This vision was adopted from the highest level of political commitment and is compatible with their socio-cultural, economical, and political structures as a Scandinavian country.

Japan

Japan's thrust of developing EG is directed to create a "knowledge-emergent society" by extensive application of innovative ICT in every sector of government to ensure that all stakeholders of government, such as citizens and business organizations, can actively utilize ICT and fully enjoy its benefits. Consequently, this country has showed strong commitment in building a countrywide infrastructure and regulatory and security policies of an ICT strategy in support of its EG initiatives (Koga, 2006). Japan's approach of launching EG fundamentally aims to diffuse where plausible all benefits of ICT in public administration reformation and reengineering.

From the beginning of this century, the Japanese government realized that to keep Japan a leader in the global economy, they had to utilize the full potential of ICT and reform the public administration system. In this connection, in July 2000, they established an "IT Strategy Headquarters" and the "IT Strategy Council" to streamline the overarching strategic priority for an ICT policy, to coordinate ICT-based government reformation, and to promote Japan's global image as a technology intensive nation. The Japanese EG initiative set out their primary goals in 2003 to launch an online government and achieve the following objectives (Muta, 2005):

1. Create a citizen-centric EG that can fulfill citizen demands in a secure fashion and be easily available round-the-clock through the Internet.
2. Online service should be very simple, efficient, and cost-effective. To set this goal, they attempted to perform business process reengineering (BPR) and enterprise resource planning (ERP) in all branches of government and to extensively reform public administration.

Taking exhaustive implementation efforts to present Japan as a leader in an ICT renovated government system, Japan achieved some basic milestones for developing citizen-focused EG. "As of March 2005, about 14,000 (i.e., 96 per cent) of the targeted national administrative procedures could be conducted and completed online, including in such areas as real estate registration, national taxation and social insurance. Several legal and technological initiatives have been put into effect for this purpose. With the introduction of the Government public key infrastructure through an encrypted key code, citizens can securely perform online transactions with any ministry. They are able to obtain a digital certification that confirms their respective identity, thus reducing identity theft and fraud" (United Nations, 2006).

Nevertheless, the Japanese EG initiative was not very successful in alleviating the digital divide and making government service available for all, which is an essential feature of a worldwide EG mission and an essential precondition for providing good governance through EG. As Koga (2006) discovered from a detailed analysis of Japan's strategic advancement in achieving targets initiated through an EG vision: "one of the challenges identified in this regard is to ensure 'accessibility' or to enable everyone, including the elderly and those with disabilities, to access the infrastructures and services of an electronic government."

According to Accenture (2004), Japan is ranked 13th for service maturity in EG out of 22 leading countries in the world in terms of taking EG initiatives (See Appendix A). In the field of telecommunication diffusion, Japan is placed 16th for fixed broadband penetration out of 31 OECD countries (OECD, 2009) (See Appendix B).

Something like 113 services are available through Japan's EG portal out of the 126 services that the Japanese government could deliver online (Accenture, 2003). Japan's EG initiative is severely affected by their economic goal. So they are more interested in extending their service through EG to renovate the market with the application of ICT in the business core. Japan is one of the leading countries in the world in developing multi-dimensional interaction and transaction services through the government website and interconnecting the private and public sectors. E-tax is one of the major Japanese public service reform efforts through EG. Citizens can return their taxes through a very easy and user-friendly interface of EG and this E-tax has a potential impact on Japan's effort in reforming the public administration system to adopt EG (Chatfield, 2009).

Japan's EG initiatives are fundamentally business-centric. Its initiatives and strategies are concentrated on achieving efficiencies in government service that are compatible with the private sector and can support E-commerce. This aim is compatible with Japan's socio-economic and political conditions. In terms of political openness, transparency, and democratic practice, Japan is not a leading country. However, Japan is one of the leaders in the global economy in achieving high performance in technology and quality. Therefore, Japan's primary goal in implementing EG is to use and maintain its authority in modern ICT, which confirms their competence in the global economy. They are also reforming their public administration systems to make them more citizen-focused. Japan is enthusiastic to provide effective and cost-cutting services to citizens and business organizations so that they perceive a higher quality government service. Achieving the previously mentioned goal necessarily means more access to government information, reformation of public administration focusing on the needs of citizens and businesses, more transparency, collaboration with the private sector, and effective and efficient service that ultimately promotes democratic movement of a government. However, it is still not their main target in the core of their EG vision to promote interconnected government, digital inclusion, citizen participation in government decision making, and, finally, to achieve good governance. Political commitment is far behind E-democracy where both privileged and unprivileged citizens will have access to government information and participate in government decisions with equal rights through the proliferation of EG.

Malaysia

While developing a strategy for public administration reformation, launching EG, and setting a long-term vision for digital government, the Malaysian government determined to continue its economic growth through capitalizing on the revolutionary benefits of ICT (Alhabshi, 2008). The government vision was to provide effective and efficient services to all its stakeholders so that the government could move forward in public administration management (Al-Mashari, 2007). The Malaysian official government web portal is www.malaysia.gov.my and through this single gateway the Malaysian government is providing citizens with agency-based services through integration among the different organizations' functions. According to their statement in www.malaysia.gov.my, "The project involves the development of an interface system called MyGovXchange which functions as a Public Service Gateway delivering Government services through an integrated and connected Klang Valley. Services are accessible via the myGovernment Portal, which is the front-end single window and one-stop center for my-Bayar (ePayment) and myForms (eSubmission)."

Starting in 2005, this new single gateway portal was undertaken by Malaysia Administrative Modernization and Management Planning Unit (MAMPU), a central agency working directly under the supervision of the Department of the Prime Minister. So we understand that this new initiative to reform public administration and to provide connectivity for citizens with the government comes from the highest political commitment and vision. The portal aims to ensure citizen connectivity with the government management system, 24 hours a day and 7 days a week, and provide the essential directories of government information and services (myServices, myForms, myBayar, myNews) through a single window. What we observe from their citizen-centric service offering from the online government is that the Malaysian government is committed to reengineer their management system, make it more effective and efficient, modernize the management system in public administration, and develop close ties with citizens. The important aspect of the Malaysian EG initiative of 2005 was that they are more interested in providing citizens with their needful services rather providing organizations' agency-based services. That means that through the interoperability of government organizations, they are attempting to standardize the protocols of functions of different organizations and, through synchronization, they are providing it through single window so that citizens can customize it (Alhabshi, 2008). In this way Malaysian EG is

trying to make the service delivery system more efficient and establish digital interconnectedness.

Of the 140 services that the Malaysian Government could deliver online, 103 are available to some degree (Accenture, 2003). Their overall rank in providing service through EG is jointly 17th among the leading 22 countries globally (See Appendix A). After critically reviewing the objectives set in the Malaysian EG implementation projects, the following characteristics were observed:

1. In its EG initiative, Malaysia puts more thrust on diffusing ICT in all the government branches.
2. It emphasizes achieving the enormous advantages of modern ICT through the reformation of public administration that is still bureaucratic, non-transparent, and non-participative.
3. It places great focus on promoting ICT among citizens and preparing them to be skilled in ICT usage.
4. As a developing country working to get very quick competence in the high-tech field, the Malaysian EG vision is focused on making E-business efficient and creating organized partnership with the private sector.
5. The prime objectives of launching EG are delivering better quality and efficient service to citizens and treating them as customers so that government services will be cost effective.
6. Basically, Malaysia is working to boost the public sector and make it as competitive as the private sector.
7. The prime reasons for launching EG are developing market mechanisms, improving the economy, and positioning Malaysia as the technology and economic hub of Asia.
8. Finally, Malaysia desires to gain enormous benefits in globalization through the online government functionality.

We can observe that accountability of government, good governance, transparency, better accessibility for citizens to government information, less corruption, participation of citizens in government decision making, and democracy are not well focused or prioritized in this vision of EG implementation. This observation is well supported and can be easily explained by reviewing their socio-cultural and political situation. Although Malaysia has been developing very quickly for the last two decades and now has a moderate industrial economy, its democratic and socio-cultural condition is very similar to other developing countries. It is still not an advanced country in promoting inclusion of citizens in government decision making and diffuse citizen reformation of government. Human rights, equality, judicial impartiality, and good governance are still not part of the Malaysian focus. It appears that the political vision and government culture of Malaysia is only aimed at making the country more prosperous, not focusing on good governance. Therefore, the mission of EG reflects the political agenda and socio-economic culture of Malaysia.

South Africa

South Africa, after getting rid of apartheid has tried to consolidate their resources to compete globally. In this connection, they realized that the reformation of their post-colonial government management system is unlikely to yield the competence in public administration which is desired for a citizen-focused government service system (SITA [Pty] Ltd, 2002). So South Africa moved to extensively adopt ICT in all sectors of public administration because they realized only ICT in public administration system can provide a modernized government with efficient management; this is quite clear from the statement of the member of the South Africa Presidential ICT Task Team for developing EG: "Information technology, and the ability to use it and adapt it, is the critical factor in generating and accessing

wealth, power, and knowledge in our time...." (Castells, 2000).

South Africa started their initiative to launch EG in 2001 spearheaded by the minister of public service and administration (DPSA) with the collaboration of the information and communication technology agency. Their ten-year plan to achieve certain milestones articulated the vision stated by DPSA, South Africa, "to leverage ICT to deliver public services and products structured around life episodes of citizens from cradle to grave" (Kyama, 2010). They set some specific targets to achieve gradually through the ten years of EG development.

The strategies are focused on the following four areas: developing interoperability through standardization of tasks of different departments, achieving economies of scale in the government sector, providing security in digital government, and improving service efficiency through eliminating duplicate services of different departments (Kyama, 2010). Through these objectives, the South African EG plan set forth the following objectives (Kyama, 2010):

- Make the government service efficient in delivery
- Lower government costs both for access and delivery
- Develop a very easy and convenient service system for citizens.

South Africa's official web portal is www.gov.za. As stated in their government portal, their primary mission, which comes from their political agenda, is to develop an easily accessible, high quality government service system that will ensure accountability and transparency in government administration. The government service system should satisfy citizens and other stakeholders. Their principles show in the proclaimed slogan – putting people first – and are as follows (Department of Public Service and Administration, 2007):

- regularly consult with customers
- set service standards
- increase access to services
- ensure higher levels of courtesy
- provide more and better information about services
- increase openness and transparency of services
- remedy failures and mistakes
- give the best possible value for money.

Accenture (2003) reported that out of the 130 services that the government could deliver online, 82 services are available through the South African EG. Their service maturity breadth is 63.1, which is far below the global average of 85.8. Out of 22 leading countries in providing mature EG services, South Africa scores the lowest (Accenture, 2004) (See Appendix A). However, the significant observation about their EG development process is that they are progressing with a clear steady pace and diffusing ICT-related infrastructure throughout the country (Trusler, 2003; Shareef *et al*., 2010a).

If we focus on analyzing the different initiatives and overall efforts with the overarching strategies of implementing EG by the South African government, we easily notice some important but definite characteristics of their endeavors. These are:

1. Their ICT infrastructure is still not well developed, which is an essential precondition for the proliferation of digital government.
2. Their public administration is not very dynamic and modern.
3. For more transparency and accountability and giving citizens confidence in the government, their government reformation scheme was inevitable.
4. Like other developing countries, their first movement for modernizing the public service system was to develop a country-wide telecommunication system and other ICT infrastructure with a clear long-term strategy.
5. Standing on this strong ICT network, this African government is now pushing their EG initiatives with a clear goal of providing citizen-centric service.
6. This post-apartheid, democratic government is zealous to construct organized, effective, and efficient government service delivery with lower cost through a government interoperable portal.
7. They are determined and have the political vision to make government service easily accessible for all citizens.
8. The South African EG development goal also has an explicit economic target. Through their online presence, this country expects to regain their strong position in Africa as well as in the global economy.

If we look at their socio-cultural, technological, economic, and political movements, we find that their ICT-grounded EG strategies and targets are compatible with those aspects. Their strategy and targets to achieve EG are based on ICT proliferation and economic improvement. They are trying to make the public system dynamic so that it will be efficient in terms of cost, availability, accessibility, and quality. Actually, these are essential and basic steps for an economic boost. They are at the preliminary stage of EG success and digital inclusion. "At present, they are focusing on the economic perspective rather than bringing transparency, accountability, democracy, and good governance—the focus of the western developed countries" (Shareef *et al*., 2010a).

United Kingdom (UK)

The UK initiative of launching an online government came from frustration with the service of public administration (Norris and Demeter, 1999). Different countries had adopted EG at the local, regional, and federal levels in the aim of bringing back confidence in public service. Political leaders had a mission of providing satisfaction to their stakeholders through higher quality and transparent service, and this was made possible through the application of ICT in public administration (Damodaran *et al.*, 2005; Robin *et al.*, 2009). ICT in reformation of public administration resolves some political issues, a resolution that has been sought by different stakeholders for a long time. These issues are power decentralization in government management, transparency and accountability, more efficiency and effective service at a lower cost, and more accessibility, and availability (Schware and Deane, 2003; Van Dijk *et al.* 2008). So it is obvious that, even though it is very complex, there is an explicit relation between the fundamental paradigms of democracy and the anticipated achievements of a successful EG mission operated through ICT.

The UK, with their political commitment towards digital inclusion of citizens with the government, conceived the vision of EG implementation as "exploiting the power of information and communications technology to help transform the accessibility, quality, and cost-effectiveness of public services and to help revitalize the relationship between customers and citizens and public bodies who work on their behalf" (Local Government Association, 2002). Former Prime Minister Tony Blair envisaged the mission of EG in their political agenda in the Prime Minister's speech to the National Policy Forum on July 9, 2005 as "This is a time to push forward, faster and on all fronts: open up the system, break down its monoliths, put the parent and pupil and patient and law-abiding citizen at the centre of it. We have made great progress. Let us learn the lessons of it not so as to rest on present achievements but to take them to a new and higher level in the future" (Cabinet Office, 2005). The strategy of "Transformational Government" was initiated in 2005 to meet the needs of citizens and business organizations from the highest level with the application of ICT. According to Britain's e-envoy, Alex Allan, "Government is going to have to behave more like the innovatory businesses on

the Internet in recognizing the role of individual initiative" (Grande, 1999).

The official UK web portal is www.direct.gov. uk. Most of the required interactions of citizens with the government can be conducted online. This UK one-stop web portal provides several matured services from static to transaction. Citizens and business organizations can transact for most of the payable government fees, including taxes and court fees. Accenture (2003) revealed that out of the 129 services that the government could deliver online 121 services are available through the UK EG. Their service maturity breadth is 93.8 percent, which is far above the global average of 85.8. Out of 22 leading countries in providing mature EG services, the UK EG maturity score stands 10th (Accenture, 2004).

The overarching UK government strategic objectives provide priority in three key areas (Cabinet Office, 2005):

1. The transformation of public services for the benefit of citizens, businesses, taxpayers, and front-line staff.
2. Improved efficiency of the corporate services and infrastructure of government organizations, thus freeing resources for the front-line.
3. The steps necessary to achieve the effective delivery of technology for government.

According to their overall EG maturity score from the Accenture (2004) report, the UK is positioned in the middle of the leading 22 countries. So, it is not exactly in the front line. However, based on different reports on the UK EG, their statements, mission, and vision set forth in their web portal and strategic documents on EG to achieve in the long run show a clear direction toward establishing good governance. They, through the application and use of ICT in the public service design and implementation of online government service delivery, treat citizens and other government stakeholders as their closest allies and develop an interconnected government among all partners. A government is developed through citizens; so the government's first priority is to satisfy them with the highest quality of service. Government service should be easily available, accessible, and open to all equally. Government's decision making in governing the country should be consistent with the views of citizens. As a top democratic country, the UK always views citizens as the first to be valued. In the last decade, the British labor party that conceived a social democratic doctrine in their long political vision, pursued public administration reformation through initiating online government to establish good governance in the UK where citizens will be the prime authority of governing the country (Shareef *et al.*, 2010a). We are able to conclude that the UK EG initiative is more focused on providing better quality service to citizens and satisfying them (Mosse and Whitley, 2009). Effective and efficient public service sector will also be an asset for a better economy. However, their mission is more focused on reducing the digital divide; confirming digital inclusion, accountability, and transparency in the government decision process; and streamlining the democratic process in the early 21st century. And this long view of EG is compatible with their political commitment. However, at the same time, we should raise the point that although digital inclusion is a popular slogan, making it real is very complex. Since, from the ICT based infrastructure perspective, there is an explicit difference between rural and urban areas, the UK is still struggling to alleviate this difference through EG and to create a level playing field between people in rural and urban areas (Choudrie *et al.*, 2005).

United States (US)

Al Gore, former Vice President of the US, has said: "In this fast-moving, fast-changing global economy – when the free flow of dollars and data are the source of economic and political strength, and whole new industries are born every day –

governments must be lean, nimble, and creative, or they will surely be left behind" (Al Gore, 1993).

Beginning from the 9th decade of the last century, the US government started to realize that citizens are daily frustrated by a public service system that is inefficient, non-transparent, and bureaucratic. They have no confidence in the public administration system. "The average American believes we waste 48 cents of every tax dollar. Five of every six want 'fundamental change' in Washington. Only 20 percent of Americans trust the federal government to do the right thing most of the time -- down from 76 percent 30 years ago" (NPR, 1993a). Since citizens are paying taxes to government, they deserve to receive the same top quality service which they get from American corporations. The government is elected by citizens. So, fulfilling citizens' needs is the first priority of a government. All government agencies must understand citizens' requirements, transform their service pattern according to those needs, and be careful to deliver services to satisfy them. This was the fundamental premise of the US government reformation vision. The National Performance Review (NPR, 1993a) focused completely on citizens' needs in the core public administration reformation program. They envisaged all of their efforts to transform government services to be competitive with the private sector. This is clear in their policy statements: "The National Performance Review seeks a government where services are customer-driven. If government services are to be customer-driven they must be judged based on the public's expectations. These expectations are being set, in large part, by the quality of services delivered each day by America's corporations. Federal Express says, 'When it absolutely, positively has to be there overnight.' Government can learn from the kind of commitments that America's best corporations make and how they view service" (NPR, 1993b). For improving customer service, The NPR (NPR, 1993b) recommended that government should reform all branches drastically and reengineer service patterns to satisfy citizens and treat them as customers. NPR (1993b) advocated that all government departments take the following actions to standardize their services: "The President should issue an Executive Order that would establish this overall standard for quality in services to the public: Customer services equal to the best in business. The Executive Order would state that the following principles govern the provision of customer services:

- Survey customers frequently to find out what kind and quality of services they want
- Post service standards and results measured against them
- Benchmark performance against the best in business
- Provide choices in both source of service and delivery means
- Make information, services, and complaint systems easily accessible
- Provide redress for poor services
- Handle inquiries and deliver services with courtesy
- Provide pleasant surroundings for customers"

Based on this action plan, the US government invented online government and applied ICT in the reformation strategy of public administration. Application of ICT in the core of government service functions can initiate some certain advantages (Steyaert, 2000; Hernon *et al*., 2002; Riley 2002; Gil-Garcia and Martinez-Moyano, 2007):

1. Streamlining of different functions, service delivery patterns, and internal administration of public sector can be reformed drastically.
2. ICT is a panacea to reduce the cost of service delivery, make service system effective and efficient, and ensure availability of service around the clock.
3. Through the use of ICT, departmental functions could be more effective, which

directs higher quality, effective, and efficient services.
4. The public sector can perform more competitively with the private sector.
5. Government service and information can be easily accessible from anywhere.
6. More transparency and accountability can be ensured.
7. ICT can assist to break down bureaucracy and promote decentralization, which is essential for economic management and better performance.
8. Government service can be available for all citizens.

Following those actions plans and realizing the potential of ICT in public administration systems, the US set some visionary strategies for their long-term reformation plan (Vice President Albert Gore's National Performance Review, 1994) which initiated the overarching principles of EG:

- Cutting red tape,
- Putting customers first,
- Empowering employees to get results, and
- Cutting back to basics: producing better government for less.

The US Administration is continuing this strategy in focusing public requirements on the development of citizen-centered electronic service. Different studies on the US EG implementations strategies (EOP, 2001; Accenture, 2003/2005; Evans and Yen, 2006; Al-Mashari, 2007; Guijarro, 2007; Reddick, 2009; Shareef *et al*., 2010a) revealed that the prime objective of this effort is to provide the most effective, efficient, high quality, and citizen-centric service for all its stakeholders. To ensure this phenomenal objective, some supplementary issues are achievable. These are:

1. Expenditures in providing and rendering government service will be minimized and the system will be cost effective.

2. Bureaucracy will be redundant through power decentralization and cultural reformation.
3. Service will be available all the time from anywhere.
4. Interconnectedness among different stakeholders will be ensured.
5. With proper partnership with the private sector, government will be able to improve the national economy.
6. The global leading position of the US will be confirmed.

The official US government's web portal, www.USA.gov, started with that stipulated mission. The US EG offers very outstanding and mature service with transactional facilities. Citizens can do most of their transactions with the government through the web portal. Around 115 government services are available through the web portal out of the 117 services for which the US government is responsible (Accenture, 2003). The US EG has one of the highest rates of online service delivery among the developed countries (Accenture, 2005/2009) and is ranked 3 out of 22 leading countries in the world in offering mature online government service (Accenture, 2004).

Now if we analyze the phenomenal objectives and surrounding strategies in achieving those objectives, we observe some exclusive characteristics of the US EG. Their EG is primarily reforming government service management system to gain cost effectiveness. They try to reduce government expenditure, make the service system more efficient, and connect citizens with government functions. By this means, they are eager and motivated from their strong political and social commitment, technological beliefs, and organizational reformation to achieve a strong national economy and position the US as the global leader. This long-term target is justifiable and compatible with their political and economic condition. As a top capitalist country having the highest grade market economy with leading world class corporate sectors, they try to achieve the full potential of public sector reformation. With an effective service mechanism, the US can boost the public sector, the largest sector in the US economy (Shareef *et al.*, 2010a). For a citizen-driven governing system, the US EG mission provides more accountability, transparency, and participation. Nevertheless, promoting good governance, reducing the digital divide, and encouraging citizen participation in government decision making are not profoundly visible in the US EG initiatives (Shareef *et al.*, 2010a). Therefore, although developing a citizen-centric service mechanism is their visible target; their ultimate purpose is economically driven. Through the application of ICT and reformation of the public administration system, the US is focused to reform their market mechanism and create an effective partnership with the private sector to sustain their expected economic growth and keep their position as the leader and catalyst of the global economy.

DISCUSSION

We have discussed here the vision and objectives of implementing EG and strategic goals to achieve through this EG implementation of eight leading countries in the world representing all the continents. We find certain similarities in their initiatives, strategies, and objectives. However, we also discovered certain subtle differences in their targeted achievements.

For instance, the Australian EG initiative is more focused on and directed towards achieving an efficient and cost-effective public sector. Finally, they want through public service reformation and reengineering to satisfy citizens and develop an interconnected government leading to good governance.

Brazil is more enthusiastic to reform the government sector to achieve a dynamic public management in order to maintain a cost-effective and modernized system. This country introduced ICT in the public sector to alleviate corruption, bureaucracy, and power politics in public organizations. So, through their EG vision and with the application of ICT, Brazil ultimately targets development of a dynamic government service system that resembles the private sector and boosts the national economy and country image globally.

Denmark is primarily taking the objective of public sector reformation through EG by using ICT in all branches of government to provide higher quality service and satisfy their citizens. They want to ensure transparency and accountability, and develop an interconnected and participative government. So, through the means of efficient, effective, and citizen-centric government, Denmark's EG vision directs them towards E-democracy and good governance as the end.

Japan is a global leader in ICT and the economic sector. Japan's EG initiative and strategy is aimed at achieving the enormous benefits of ICT from the public sector. So they target using ICT extensively in all public organizations, developing an interconnected government, and making the public sector as dynamic as a private corporation. To deliver cost-effective, efficient, and higher quality government service online, Japan's ultimate target is economic benefits and a leading global position.

Malaysia is a rising industrial country. This country is gradually positioning itself as an innovative leader in the application of ICT and reforming their public administration system towards that aim. This country is also enthusiastic to achieve higher competence in delivering government service to citizens through EG. Malaysia sets their objectives as reforming the government management system to create greater liaison among the different branches of government, gain the opportunities of modern ICT, streamline the partnership between the private and public sectors, and, finally, enhance the performance of government to realize a better economy.

South Africa is a developing country that, after apartheid, is struggling to reform its government service system. By using ICT in the traditional government service mechanism, this country has targeted to provide better quality service to citizens and, at the same time through its EG initiative, reform its market mechanism to capture economic benefits.

The UK is a leading democratic country in the world and is very enthusiastic to reform its public sector to satisfy its citizens with participative government. They have the vision of creating a citizen-driven government system where citizens will get round-the-clock service with higher quality. The UK EG is pushing transparency and accountability in their public management. So, through the means of dynamic and participative government, the UK EG is showing a concept of good government through ICT.

The US is the global leader in economy, free market development, and private sector management. This country realized that without reforming their public sector and developing a cost-effective, modern management system, it would be difficult to maintain its leading role globally in this competitive era. Also, if the country's public service system cannot satisfy citizens and business organizations, the prime stakeholders of government, the government could not develop a dynamic and citizen-focused public service. Therefore, the US adopted ICT in its reformation strategy of the public service system and developed a top quality public service sector to be competitive with private corporations. Its ultimate target, through a citizen-centric government service system, is to become more efficient and competence, which will ensure the US's overall position as the market leader.

Now we can contrast and compare different visions, strategies, and end objectives through a comprehensive table showing the perspectives of the different parameters of EG initiatives (Table 1).

Table 1. EG initiatives of different globally leading countries

Country	Issues						
	ICT adoption	Strategy for ICT	Intrinsic sense of EG development vision	EG strategy as the means	Political commitment	End goal	Service maturity
Australia	extensive	ICT strategy for government service reformation	To develop an interconnected government and ensure digital inclusion	Make the government service easily accessible and develop an interoperable system	Long term political vision is associated with democratic movement through EG implementation	Citizen-centric public service system	Top quality matured service with improved interactivity
Brazil	extensive	ICT strategy for government service reformation	To alleviate corruption and bureaucracy, reduce digital divide, and ensure transparency and more accountability	Improve performance of public sector through socio-cultural, political, and technological reformation	Political commitment is not very profound in achieving good governance. Political vision is engaged in modernizing management of public sector.	Efficient management in public service system	Service maturity is developing from the initial stage
Denmark	extensive	ICT strategy for government service reformation	Citizen-driven government service system for good governance and E-democracy	Satisfy citizens	Long term political vision is directed towards good governance through EG implementation	Citizen-driven public service system	Very matured service with top quality interactive facilities
Japan	very extensive	Long term ICT strategy to capitalize enormous benefits and position this country as the market leader in ICT innovation	Develop an effective and dynamic government sector to compete in the 21st century	Application of ICT to enhance efficiency of government sector	Political commitment is not very profound in presenting good government rather it is directed for innovative government equipped with modern technology	Economic benefits as the market leader	Top quality matured service with the highest application of ICT as much as possible
Malaysia	very extensive	Long term ICT strategy to ensure modernization of public and private sectors and position as the technology hub in the Asian zone	Adopt a connected government among different branches of public service sector to gain efficiency	Application of ICT to enhance efficiency of government sector	Political commitment is not very profound in presenting good government rather it is directed for innovative government equipped with modern technology	Economic benefits and global positioning	Service maturity is developing from the initial stage, however, application of ICT is extensive
South Africa	extensive	ICT strategy for government long term policy development	Reform public sector to make it dynamic, citizen-focused, modern and also to reduce digital divide	Improve performance of public sector through socio-cultural, political, and technological reformation	Political commitment is not very profound in achieving good governance. It is more focused on standardizing and modernizing post-colonial government system	Efficient management in public service system	Service maturity is developing from the initial stage

continued on the following page

Table 1. Continued

Country	Issues						
	ICT adoption	Strategy for ICT	Intrinsic sense of EG development vision	EG strategy as the means	Political commitment	End goal	Service maturity
UK	extensive	ICT strategy for government service reformation	Satisfy citizens and establish E-democracy and good governance	Satisfy citizens	Long term political vision is directed towards good governance through EG implementation	Citizen-driven public service system	Very matured service
US	extensive	ICT strategy for government service reformation, effectiveness, and global positioning	Develop a cost effective, efficient, and dynamic public sector which will be a global leader	Provide higher quality and efficient service so that stakeholders will adopt it	Political commitment for dynamic and competitive government.	Economic benefits as the market leader	Very matured service with top quality transactional and interactive facilities

REFERENCES

Accenture. (2003). *E-government leadership – Realizing the vision.* The Government Executive Series.

Accenture. (2004). *E-government leadership: High performance, maximum value.* The Government Executive Series.

Accenture. (2005). *Leadership in customer service: New expectations, new experiences.*

Accenture (2009). From e-government to e-governance: Using new technologies to strengthen relationships with citizens.

AGIMO (Australian Government Information Management Office). (2006). *Responsive government- A new service agenda.* Department of Finance and Administration, Australian Government.

Al-Mashari, M. (2007). A benchmarking study of experiences with electronic-government. *Benchmarking: An International Journal, 14*(2), 172–185. doi:10.1108/14635770710740378

Alhabshi, S. M. (2008). E-government in Malaysia: Barriers and progress. (International Federation for Information Processing (IFIP) Working Group 9.4). *Information Technology in Developing Countries, 18*(3), 6–15.

All About Market Research. (2008). *Internet world stats.* Retrieved from http://www.allaboutmarketresearch.com /internet.htm

Australian Government 2.0 Taskforce Final Report. (2009). *Engage getting on with government 2.0.*

Banas, M. J., & Hillard, F. (SECOM). (2010). *Brazil embraces digital age with new interactive e-gov portal - Brasil.Gov.Br.* The Secretariat for Social Communication (SECOM) of the Presidency of Brazil.

Cabinet Office. (2005). *Transformational government enabled by technology.* Retrieved from www.cabinetoffice.gov.uk

Castells, M. (2000). *End of millennium, the information age: Economy, society and culture (Vol. III).* Cambridge, MA/ Oxford, UK: Blackwell.

Chatfield, A. T. (2009). Public service reform through e-government: A case study of "e-tax" in Japan. *Electronic Journal of E-Government, 7*(2), 135–146.

Choudrie, J., Weerakkody, V., & Jones, S. (2005). Realising e-government in the UK: Rural and urban challenges. *Journal of Enterprise Information Management, 18*(5), 568–585. doi:10.1108/17410390510624016

Damodaran, L., Nicholls, J., & Henney, A. (2005). The contribution of sociotechnical systems thinking to the effective adoption of e-government and the enhancement of democracy. *The Electronic. Journal of E-Government, 3*(1), 1–12.

Dawes, S. S., Gregg, V., & Agouris, P. (2004). Digital government research: Investigations at the crossroads of social and Information Science. *Social Science Computer Review, 22*(1), 5–10. doi:10.1177/0894439303259863

Department of Public Service and Administration. (2007). *South African government information.* Retrieved from www.gov.za

Evans, D., & Yen, D. C. (2006). E-government: Evolving relationship of citizens and government, domestic, and international development. *Government Information Quarterly, 23*(2), 207–235. doi:10.1016/j.giq.2005.11.004

Gil-Garcia, J. R., & Martinez-Moyano, I. J. (2007). Understanding the evolution of e-government: The influence of systems of rules on public sector dynamics. *Government Information Quarterly, 24*(2), 266–290. doi:10.1016/j.giq.2006.04.005

Gore, A., Jr. (1993). From red tape to results: Creating a government that works better and costs less. Washington, DC: Government Printing Office. Retrieved from http://govinfo.library.unt.edu/npr/library/nprrpt/annrpt/ redtpe 93/index.html

Grande, C. (1999, 10 December). E-envoy vows to raise Internet use by ministries. *Financial Times.*

Guijarro, L. (2007). Interoperability frameworks and enterprise architectures in e-government initiatives in Europe and the United States. *Government Information Quarterly, 24*, 89–101. doi:10.1016/j.giq.2006.05.003

Hernon, P., Reylea, H. C., Dugan, R. E., & Cheverie, J. F. (2002). *United States government information: Policies and sources* (p. 388). Westport, CT: Libraries Unlimited.

IMF. (2008). *World economic outlook database-*October 2008, Washington, DC.

Irkhin, I. U. V. (2007). Electronic government and society: World realities and Russia (a comparative analysis). *Sociological Research, 46*(2), 77–92. doi:10.2753/SOR1061-0154460206

Knight, P. T. (2007, June). *Knowledge management and e-government in Brazil.* Paper Prepared For The Workshop On Managing Knowledge To Build Trust In Government, 7th Global Forum on Reinventing Government, 26-29 June 2007, Vienna, Austria. Retrieved from www.e-brasil.org.br

Koga, T. (2006). *Policy issues regarding electronic government and Web accessibility in Japan.* World Library and Information Congress: 72nd Ifla General Conference and Council 20-24 August 2006, Seoul, Korea.

Kraemer, K. L., & King, J. L. (2003). *Information Technology and administrative reform: Will the time after e-government be different?* CRITO, Center For Research On Information Technology And Organizations. Retrieved from http://www.crito.uci.edu

Kyama, G. W. (2005). E-government: A view from South Africa. Retrieved from http://www.uneca.org/aisi/ NICI/ Documents/eGovernment %20A%20view%20from% 20Southern%20Africa%20- %20Godfrey%20Kyama.ppt

Local Government Association. (2002). *egov@ local: Towards a national strategy for local e-government.* London, UK: Local Government Association.

Löfgren, K. (2007). The governance of e-government. *Public Policy and Administration, 22*(3), 335–352.

Moon, M. J., & Norris, D. F. (2005). Does managerial orientation matter? The adoption of reinventing government and e-government at the municipal level. *Information Systems Journal, 15,* 43–60. doi:10.1111/j.1365-2575.2005.00185.x

Mosse, B., & Whitley, E. A. (2009). Critically classifying: UK e-government website benchmarking and the recasting of the citizen as customer. *Information Systems Journal, 19*(2), 149–173. doi:10.1111/j.1365-2575.2008.00299.x

Muta, M. (2005). *Japanese e-government and e-commerce since Dec. 2001.* Retrieved from http://www.manaboo.com/ english/egov_japan.htm

Northxsouth. (2010). *Brazil launches new version of their electronic government portal.* Retrieved from http://news.northxsouth.com/ 2010/03/07/brazil-launches-new-version-of-their-electronic-government-portal/

OECD. (2009). *Rethinking e-government services: User-centered approaches.* Paris, France: OECD.

OECD E-Government Studies. (2010). *Denmark, efficient e-government for smarter public service delivery.*

Parent, M., Vandebeek, C. A., & Gemino, A. C. (2005). Building citizen trust through e-government. *Government Information Quarterly, 22,* 720–736. doi:10.1016/j.giq.2005.10.001

Reddick, C. G. (2006). Information resource managers and e-government effectiveness: A survey of Texas state agencies. *Government Information Quarterly, 23,* 249–266. doi:10.1016/j.giq.2005.11.006

Reddick, C. G. (2009). Factors that explain the perceived effectiveness of e-government: A survey of United States city government information technology directors. *International Journal of Electronic Government Research, 5*(2), 1–15. doi:10.4018/jegr.2009040101

OECD Report. (2005). *OECD peer review of e-government in Denmark.* Pre-Publication Draft: Version 2 – 29, September 2005.

NPR Reports. (1993a). *From red tape to results: Creating a government that works better and costs less.*

NPR Reports. (1993b). Improving customer service, ICS01: Create customer-driven programs in all departments and agencies that provide services directly to the public.

NPR Reports. (1994). *Vice President Albert Gore's national performance review.*

Riley, T. B. (2002). *Government and the invisible current of change.* Retrieved from http://www.electronicgov.net

Robin, G., Andrew, G., & Sasha, M. (2009). How responsive is e-government? Evidence from Australia and New Zealand. *Government Information Quarterly, 26*(1), 69–74. doi:10.1016/j.giq.2008.02.002

SAFAD. (2000). *The 24/7 agency criteria for 24/7 agencies in the networked public administration.* The Swedish Agency For Administrative Development Publication Service. Retrieved from http://www.statskontoret.se/ upload/ Publikationer/2000 /200041.pdf

Schedler, K., & Summermatter, L. (2007). Customer orientation in electronic government: Motives and effects. *Government Information Quarterly, 24,* 291–311. doi:10.1016/j.giq.2006.05.005

Schware, R., & Deane, A. (2003). Deploying e-government program- The strategic importance of 'I' before 'E.'. *Info, 5*(4), 10–19. doi:10.1108/14636690310495193

Shareef, M. A., Archer, N., Kumar, V., & Kumar, U. (2010b). (in press). Developing fundamental capabilities for successful e-government implementation. *International Journal of Public Policy.* doi:10.1504/IJPP.2010.035133

Shareef, M. A., Kumar, U., & Kumar, V. (2008). The e-government and e-governance: Conceptual alignment or subtle difference. *International Journal of Knowledge, Culture, and Change Management*, 8(1), 129–136.

Shareef, M. A., Kumar, U., Kumar, V., & Dwivedi, Y. K. (2010c). (in press). E-government adoption model (GAM): Differing service maturity levels. *Government Information Quarterly*.

Shareef, M. A., Kumar, V., Kumar, U., Chowdhury, A. H., & Misra, S. C. (2010a). E-government implementation perspective: Setting objective and strategy. *International Journal of Electronic Government Research*, 6(1). doi:10.4018/jegr.2010102005

SITA (Pty) Ltd. (2002). *Government experience in South Africa*. Retrieved from http://www.sita.co.zae

Steyaert, J. (2000). Local government online and the role of the resident. *Social Science Computer Review*, 18, 3–16. doi:10.1177/089443930001800101

Stokes, J., & Clegg, S. (2003). Once upon a time in the bureaucracy: Power and public sector management. *Organization*, 9(2), 225–247.

Tavares, M. (2001). *Brazilian policy for electronic government*. Federal Republic Of Brazil Ministry Of Planning, Budget And Management, Constituent Units and E-Government, organized by The Forum of Federations, Montreal.

Titah, R., & Barki, H. (2005). *E-government adoption and acceptance: A literature review*. HEC Montréal.

Trusler, J. (2003). South African e-government policy and practices: A framework to close the gap. In R. Traunmüller (Ed.), *EGOV 2003* (LNCS 2739, pp. 504-507).

United Nations. (2006). *Compendium of innovative e-government practices* (*Vol. II*). Department of Economic & Social Affairs.

Van Dijk, Jan A. G. M., Peters, O., & Ebbers, W. (2008). Explaining the acceptance and use of government Internet services: A multivariate analysis of 2006 survey data in the Netherlands. *Government Information Quarterly*, 25(3), 379–399. doi:10.1016/j.giq.2007.09.006

KEY TERMS AND DEFINITIONS

E-Government (EG): EG is government's service and information offered through the use of ICT for citizens, business organizations, and other stakeholders of government. It provides higher efficiency and effectiveness in terms of service quality, time, and cost.

Information and Communication Technology (ICT): ICT can be defined as the modern computer and Internet based technology used for managing and processing information in different public and private sectors.

Public Administration: It is the management of government service and information conducted through governments departments.

Government Services: Government services are those services which are offered by governments for its stakeholders like citizens, business organizations, government employees etc.

Service Maturity: In EG, service pattern, functionality, technological sophistication, interaction, and reengineering processes gradually upgrade. This is called service maturity.

Citizen: Residents of a country who use government service and information.

Implementation of EG: After setting initial missions of EG, different governments reform and reengineer public administration and develop an EG system through the use of ICT to achieve certain long term targets.

Objective of EG: It is the initial target which a government sets to achieve through the development of an EG system.

APPENDIX A

Figure 2. E-government maturity scores (Source: Accenture, 2004)

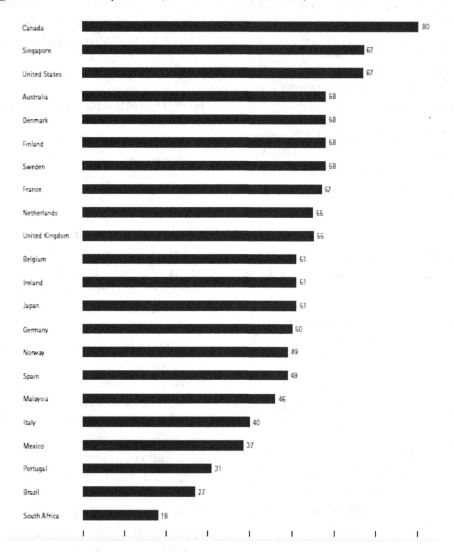

APPENDIX B

Figure 3. OECD fixed broadband subscribers per 100 inhabitants, by Technology, December 2009 (Source: OECD Broadband Portal, 2009) www.oecd.org/document/46/0,3343, en_2649_34225_39575598_1_1_1_1,00.html

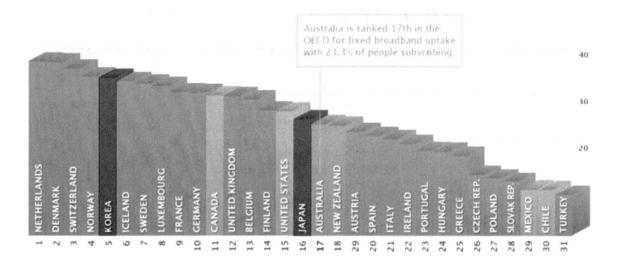

Chapter 3

E–Government Initiatives:
Review Studies on Different Countries

Mahmud Akhter Shareef
McMaster University, Canada

Norm Archer
McMaster University, Canada

ABSTRACT

This study is an extension of the case studies presented in the previous chapter (Chapter 2) on mission, vision, objectives, and strategies of E-government (EG) initiatives adopted and implemented by different developed and developing countries in the local, regional, or national levels. This chapter has three sections. In the first section, an introductory note regarding the initiatives to develop EG is presented. The second section describes two instruments to reveal EG development capability empirically in the country-context. The third section illustrates the studies on EG initiatives of different countries.

INTRODUCTION

A government can use information and communication technology (ICT) for several internal and external purposes. Internal purposes include but not limited to electronic data storage; electronic communication among employees like E-mail, chat rooms; different types of web postings like hiring, organizational rules and regulations, salary, pension schemes, organizational activities; electronic data sharing horizontally and verti-

cally among organizational members. External purposes include but not limited to web posting information, different kinds of forms, and policies for its all external stakeholders like citizens, business organizations, non-for-profit organizations, other government departments, other levels of governments inside country (local, provincial, and federal/national), and other governments globally to view those postings and download forms through online. External purposes may also include electronic communication of public organizations with its all stakeholders through e-mail, chat rooms to provide government services.

DOI: 10.4018/978-1-60960-848-4.ch003

External purposes are also aimed to facilitate its stakeholders, such as citizens and business organizations to perform different functions with governments like financial transactions with government; participating in bids, tenders, procurements etc.; sharing government information; participating in government decision making. As an extended external purpose, even citizens can vote electronically. For these purposes, different functions of government organizations might be integrated horizontally and vertically to provide services from one central web portal, organized based on stakeholders demand. Internal and external users of these services can get electronic access through Internet using PC and laptop or from mobile devices like mobile phone.

External users can view, search, and/or download forms from federal/provincial/local government websites to apply for jobs, file taxes, register to renew driving or other licenses, and register births and marriages registration. Government websites also yield information on educational, health care, human resource, justice, postal, and different types of government rules and regulations. In addition to the purposes mentioned here, other possible interactions with government websites include getting answers to further queries, e-mailing government departments for assistance, and registering for an appointment such as a driving license exam. Stakeholders might also use government websites for transactions such as paying taxes; renewing licenses; registering vehicles; and paying property taxes, hydro bills, and other federal/provincial/city fees. These interaction modes are backed by internal policy and systems of the departments.

Therefore, it is now possible to interact electronically via Internet using PC or laptop or via wireless device such as mobile phone, personal digital assistants (PDAs), smart phone, and other handheld devices with government departments/agencies such as Human Resources and Social Development, Justice, Revenue, National Defense, Public Works and Government Services, Education, Transport, Citizenship and Immigration (this is only a sample, not a complete listing) instead of going to physical government offices. We have called all these internal and external functions as Electronic-government or E-government (EG).

In this era of fierce competition, world-wide proliferation of private sectors, and globalization, it is important for all governments and public sectors to understand and conceptualize their own capability in terms of ICT management, resource availability and allocation, overall reengineering and transformation, and operation and maintenance knowledge necessary to implement EG using the proper ICT. Evidence suggests that particularly developed countries and developing countries with extensive ICT and financial capability are capable of adopting ICT, maintaining well-developed infrastructure, investing required capital in public service restructuring, and developing advance stage matured service through EG (Anderson and Narus, 1998). This raises the vulnerable question as to whether knowledge management and ICT advancement requires investment capability of enormous financial and ICT resources and, specifically, whether EG is largely a question of resources (Wagner et al., 2003). The answer to this issue, and thus the development of a framework regarding the plausible solutions of managing ICT and implementing EG, is important for researchers, practitioners, and policy-makers (Madu, 1989; Madon, 2004). This research study is designed to provide researchers and policy makers to investigate fundamental capabilities of a government to manage ICT and implement EG. In this regard, this study, from extensive exploration of different measurement techniques, presents empirical instruments to reveal the status of ICT diffusion and EG development in any country. This chapter also addresses several studies on different issues of EG in country-context in either local, regional, or national levels to provide with references for future researchers who are keen to understand EG implementation strategies, development capabilities, service maturity, interoperable systems, security and privacy issues, functional achievements, and driving forces, barriers and challenges in advancing EG projects from versatile experiences of different countries.

Instruments to Reveal EG Development Capability

In order to design appropriate EG systems, it is important to learn different issues related to different levels of government like, federal/national, provincial/state, and local/municipal. Different scholarly articles confirm that issues related to successful EG implementation, including institutional weakness, human resources, funding arrangements, local environment, technology absorption, and citizen acceptance and/or interest vary significantly based on differences in functions, objectives, and strategies of different countries and also of different levels like federal/national, provincial/state, and local/municipal governments (West, 2005; Evans and Yen, 2006; Reddick, 2006; Gil-Garcia and Martinez-Moyano, 2007). The previous chapter has explicitly demonstrated differences in EG initiatives, strategies, objectives, and end-goals for different countries. Now as an example of differences of characteristics of EG projects in different levels, in the United States of America, there is a clear disparity in the contexts of EG mission, objective, strategy, and functions among federal, state, and local governments (Moon, 2002; Edmiston, 2003; Holden et al., 2003; West, 2005). In fact, at the objective, strategic, and functioning levels there seem to be clear differences among federal/national, provincial/state, and local/municipal governments (Holden et al., 2003). Generally, federal governments have both the financial and human resources to be able to continuously move toward more extensive and sophisticated EG in the global context. Arguably, they also have the least direct democratic control from their stakeholders (Gil-Garcia and Martinez-Moyano, 2007). However, gradually provincial and local governments are also implementing EG with different capabili-

ties. Therefore, it is important to emphasize that developing fundamental capabilities to implement EG vary among national contexts and levels of government. Under the above paradigms, it is important to address the fundamental capabilities to implement EG in different countries at different government levels: federal, provincial, and local, separately.

In this aspect, we have reviewed literature, different empirical studies, and theories on computer-enabled technology and information systems, viz., ICT adoption, diffusion, and disruption; functions of governments, public administration and EG; and online behavior, organizational behavior, economics, sociology, behavioral characteristics, marketing, and political science to develop an extensive empirical instrument to explore the issues mentioned above of an EG system. In addition to literature, we reviewed the following empirical instruments, i) Networked Readiness Index (NRI) (Dutta and Mia, 2009), ii) E-Government Readiness Index (United Nations, 2008), iii) World Telecommunication/ICT Indicators (ITU, 2008), iv) E-readiness Indicators (Economist Intelligence Unit, 2009), v) Readiness for the Networked World (CID, 2006), and vi) Capability Model for EG Adoption (Shareef et al., 2010b), and synthesized the epistemological and ontological paradigms and concepts of those questionnaires to develop two separate questionnaires for government-context and organization-context inquiry. These are:

INTERVIEW QUESTIONNAIRE FOR GOVERNMENT POLICY MAKER

A. **Empirical tool to investigate government general policy decisions for all departments**: It should be administered among government policy makers at the central level, like the department of chief information officer, regarding the ICT adoption and EG development and implementation strategy and policy. The questionnaire is illustrated in Table 1.

E-Government Initiatives

Table 1. (Please check in the appropriate box that applies. In Question 1, you can check more than one answer, if you think those are applicable. You can skip answering any questions, if you think those are not applicable to you)

1. What are the precise targets of developing eGovernment/Mobile-government
    □ reduce government expenditure
    □ improve service quality for users
    □ reduce digital divide between urban and rural population
    □ boost national economy
    □ attract foreign investment and positioning globally
    □ reduce bureaucracy and corruption and enhance transparency
    □ promote good governance and democracy?

No.	Questions	Extensive (7)	Slightly below than Extensive (6)	Moderately below than extensive (5)	Not extensive nor limited (4)	Limited (3)	Very Limited (2)	Not at all (1)
2	Do you have resources to implement eGovernment?							
3	Do you have scarcities in implementing eGovernment?							
4	Do you think eGovernment initiative is achieving the results as targeted in your mission?							
5	Do you have the ability to offer all government services in eGovernment?							
6	Do you have the ability to offer all government services in eGovernment through a single web portal?							
7	Do you want to allow citizens and business organizations to get access in government information?							
8	Is there any coordination for eGovernment policies and related budgets and planning for the different federal agencies?							
9	Do you want to promote accountability in government by adopting eGovernment?							
10	Do you want to promote transparency in government by adopting eGovernment?							
11	Do you want to help reduce or prevent corruption by adopting eGovernment?							
12	Do you want to reduce bureaucracy in public administration by adopting eGovernment?							
13	Do you want to delegate authority among employees by adopting eGovernment?							

continued on the following page

Table 1. Continued

No.	Questions	Extensive (7)	Slightly below than Extensive (6)	Moderately below than extensive (5)	Not extensive nor limited (4)	Limited (3)	Very Limited (2)	Not at all (1)
14	Do you have policies for equal ICT infrastructure availability in urban and rural areas?							
15	Do you launch any specific program to develop citizens' awareness about eGovernment in both urban and rural areas?							
16	Do you launch any specific program to develop citizens' equal ability to use eGovernment in urban and rural areas?							
17	Do you think any promotional offer can serve as the relative advantage of using eGovernment over traditional government service?							
18	Do you have any specific plan to build users' trust on EG?							
19	Do you have any policy to create partnership with private entities?							
20	Have you launched any empirical studies to measure the need for eGovernment services by citizens in urban and rural areas?							
21	Have you launched any empirical studies to measure the need for eGovernment services by business organizations?							

INTERVIEW QUESTIONNAIRE FOR DEPARTMENT LEVEL POLICY MAKER

B. **Empirical tool to investigate organizational level decisions to implement ICT-based projects and develop EG in own organization**: It should be administered among managers who are engaged in policy making inside organizations regarding ICT adoption and EG development and implementation strategy and policy. The questionnaire is illustrated in Table 2.

Please answer the following questions with appropriate information. You can skip answering any questions, if you think those are not applicable to you)

21. What is the proportion of investment in ICT based projects (in terms of total budget) in your organizations (ICT procurement, ICT expertise hiring, ICT training)?

22. What is the proportion of investment in research and development (R/D) projects (in terms of total budget)?

23. What is the proportion of fund you get from external sources for ICT based projects (external sources/all sources)?

Table 2. (Please check in the appropriate box that applies. You can skip answering any questions, if you think those are not applicable to you)

No	Questions	Extensive (7)	Slightly below than Extensive (6)	Moderately below than extensive (5)	Not extensive nor limited (4)	Limited (3)	Very Limited (2)	Not at all (1)
1	Are you familiar with the term e-government?							
2	What is your opinion about the effect of implementing such a project in your agency?							
3	Do you have possible sources of funding for eGovernment?							
4	Do you have lack of technical staffs to develop ICT based projects?							
5	Do you have lack of ICT management staffs to develop ICT based projects?							
6	Do you have outside sources of vendors/contractors/consultants for any of your ICT projects?							
7	Do your authorities and employees have any specific education and training to implement eGovernment projects in your organization?							
8	What is the current status of ICT in the department in terms of use?							
9	Do you have major ICTs that your agency is using in relation to the public service?							
10	What is the level of expertise among the employees in your organization in terms of computer use?							
11	What is the level of expertise among the employees in your organization in terms of Internet use?							
12	What is your opinion about the effectiveness of your current information systems in your agency?							
13	We found from a recent empirical study that perceived security of eGovernment is one of the most significant criteria for citizens to transact with eGovernment websites. In this connection, we have some specific questions.							
	i	Do you have specific privacy policies for eGovernment projects?							
	ii	Do you implement specific measures to protect external users' privacy while accessing government information online?							

continued on the following page

Table 2. Continued

No		Questions	Extensive (7)	Slightly below than Extensive (6)	Moderately below than extensive (5)	Not extensive nor limited (4)	Limited (3)	Very Limited (2)	Not at all (1)
	iii	Do you implement specific measures to protect employees' privacy while accessing official information online?							
	iv	Do you have specific security policies for eGovernment projects?							
	v	Do you implement specific measures to protect external users' security while accessing government information online?							
	vi	Do you offer secure Internet access for external users while accessing government information online?							
	vii	Do you implement specific measures to protect employees' security while accessing official information online?							
	viii	Do employees in your organization have secure Internet access?							
	ix	While accessing official information from outside source, do employees have secure Internet access?							
14		Do you have capability to implement any eGovernment project by your own employees?							
15		Do you have capability to manage problems created by developing any eGovernment project in your own agency?							
16		If your organization has implemented a major new eGovernment project, you may have experienced changes triggered by this new ICT.							
	i	What do you think has been the impact of information technology in your organizational function?							
	ii	Has it ever influenced your organizational structure?							
	iii	Has it changed your employee tasks or procedures?							
17		Is there funding to handle maintenance required for ICT (hardware and software) regularly in your organization?							
18		Do you upgrade your ICT (hardware and software) regularly in your organization?							

continued on the following page

Table 2. Continued

No	Questions	Extensive (7)	Slightly below than Extensive (6)	Moderately below than extensive (5)	Not extensive nor limited (4)	Limited (3)	Very Limited (2)	Not at all (1)
19	Do you have required human resources to maintain and upgrade your ICT (hardware and software) regularly?							
20	Do you have a centralized ICT agency for maintenance?							

24. How many skilled technical personnel you have in your organization (no. of ICT experts/ total employees)?

25. How many skilled ICT management personnel in your organization (no. of ICT experts/ total employees)?

26. How many PCs/100 employees in your organization?

27. How many employees have knowledge/ professional training to use Computer/100 employees?

28. How many employees have knowledge/ professional training to use Internet/100 employees?

(Please check in the appropriate answer that applies. You can check more than one answer, if you think those are applicable)

29. How do you manage communication among employees internally?
    i.   Telephone
    ii. E-mail
    iii. Voice mail
    iv. Web post
    v.   Chat room
    vi. Paper based file system

30. How do you manage communication with other departments externally?
    i.   Telephone
    ii. E-mail
    iii. Voice mail
    iv. Web post
    v.   Chat room
    vi. Paper based file system

31. How do you archive your information?
    i.   Electronically
    ii. Paper based

32. Where do the new ideas related to modern ICT come from, i) locally or ii) abroad?

33. What are the most critical problems that you faced in initiating and managing eGovernment project, in terms of i) personnel, ii) funding, iii) other resources, iv) knowledge and training, and v) management?

Studies on EG Initiatives of Different Countries

Researchers who are interested in addressing, identifying, and revealing specific country experiences of vision, mission, and objectives for ICT and EG development initiatives, implementation strategies, service maturity growths, public service restructuring and reengineering, interoperability system, E-governance, performance in local, regional, and or national levels, adoption perspectives, adoption criteria, and over all adoption behavior find serious lacks in a comprehensive literature review on the related issues of EG. As Dwivedi (2009) postulated, ".... electronic government research may have opening in various journals and conferences from its reference disciplines (such as information systems, electronic commerce, public administration etc.). However, such wide distribution of the research publications on electronic government poses problems to potential researchers searching publications sparsely located across various disciplines. Such challenges become more severe if researchers unfortunately do not have access to academic search databases representing various reference disciplines. A thorough literature search and analysis is critical for establishing research gap and providing basis for new research and to identify relevant theoretical and methodological approaches". However, it is very important to explore issues like objectives, initiatives, and strategies, service maturity, stages of growth, development and implementation, interoperability, and barriers of EG of different countries to conceptualize knowledge-based epistemological and ontological paradigms of EG adoption behavior for future advancement. In this section, we reviewed the studies which were conducted on different countries' EG issues following the same procedure of Dwivedi (2009), "Bibliometrics approach". We also comprehensively analyzed all the EG papers mentioned in the study by Dwivedi (2009) to screen the studies related to any EG issues, however, focused on specific country-context. This research also explored the academic journal database provided by Thomson Scientific (previously known as the Institute for Scientific Information (ISI). We identified a total 375 research papers from different IS, EC, EG, public policy, political science journals and conference proceedings which deal country-specific experiences of multi-faceted issues of EG adoption, implementation, and development. These papers are published in the period of 2000 to 2010. They will be very helpful for future researchers, practitioners, and government policy makers who are engaged in developing policies and strategies for EG in local, regional, and or national level projects for any countries. We have provided the names of those papers as the additional readings in the reference section.

REFERENCES

Anderson, J. C., & Narus, J. A. (1998). Business marketing: Understand what customers value. *Harvard Business Review*, *76*(6), 53–65.

CID. (2006). *Readiness for the networked world: A guide for developing countries*. Center for International Development at Harvard University.

Dutta, S., & Mia, I. (Eds.). (2009). *The global Information Technology report 2008–2009*. Geneva, Switzerland: INSEAD and World Economic Forum.

Economist Intelligence Unit. (2009). *E-readiness rankings 2009: The usage imperative*.

Edmiston, K. D. (2003). State and local e-government: Prospects and challenges. *American Review of Public Administration*, *33*(1), 20–45. doi:10.1177/0275074002250255

Evans, D., & Yen, D. C. (2006). E-government: Evolving relationship of citizens and government, domestic, and international development. *Government Information Quarterly*, *23*(2), 207–235. doi:10.1016/j.giq.2005.11.004

Gil-Garcia, J. R., & Martinez-Moyano, I. J. (2007). Understanding the evolution of e-government: The influence of systems of rules on public sector dynamics. *Government Information Quarterly*, *24*(2), 266–290. doi:10.1016/j.giq.2006.04.005

Holden, S. H., Norris, D. F., & Fletcher, P. D. (2003). Electronic government at the local level, progress to date and future issues. *Public Performance and Management Review*, *26*(4), 325–344. doi:10.1177/1530957603026004002

ITU. (2008). *World telecommunication/ICT indicators 2008*. International Telecommunication Union.

Madon, S., Sahay, S., & Sudan, R. (2007). E-government policy and health information systems implementation in Andhra Pradesh, India: Need for articulation of linkages between the macro and the micro. *The Information Society, 23*(5), 327–344. doi:10.1080/01972240701572764

Madu, C. N. (1989). Transferring technology to developing countries – Critical factors for success. *Long Range Planning, 22*(4), 115–124. doi:10.1016/0024-6301(89)90089-7

Moon, M. J. (2002). The evolution of e-government among municipalities: Rhetoric or reality? *Public Administration Review, 62*(4), 424–433. doi:10.1111/0033-3352.00196

Reddick, C. G. (2006). Information resource managers and e-government effectiveness: A survey of Texas state agencies. *Government Information Quarterly, 23*(2), 249–266. doi:10.1016/j.giq.2005.11.006

Shareef, M. A., Archer, N., Kumar, V., & Kumar, U. (2010b). (in press). Developing fundamental capabilities for successful e-government implementation. *International Journal of Public Policy.* doi:10.1504/IJPP.2010.035133

United Nations. (2008). *From e-government to connected governance*. E-government survey 2008.

West, D. M. (2005). *Digital government: Technology and public sector performance*. Princeton, NJ: Princeton University Press.

ADDITIONAL READING

Abdelghaffar, H., & Kamel, S. (2008). The impact of eReadiness on eGovernment in developing nations - Case of universities and colleges admission services. Paper presented at the 9th International-Business-Information-Management-Association Conference (IBIMA), Marrakech, Morocco.

Abusin, M. (2007). Government of Sudan e-Government initiative: Challenges and opportunities. Paper presented at the 7th European Conference on e-Government (ECEG 2007), The Hague, Netherlands.

Accenture. (2003). E-government leadership – realizing the vision. The Government Executive Series. New York: Author.

Accenture (2004), eGovernment Leadership: High Performance, Maximum Value, The Government Executive Series.

Accenture. (2005). Leadership in customer service: New expectations, new experiences. New York: Author.

Accenture (2009), From e-Government to e-Governance Using new technologies to strengthen relationships with citizens.

Adeshara, P., Juric, R., Kuljis, J., Paul, R., & Ieee (2004). A survey of acceptance of e-government services in the UK. Paper presented at the 26th International Conference on Information Technology Interfaces, Cavtat, Croatia.

AGIMO (Australian Government Information Management Office). (2006). *Responsive Government A New Service Agenda*. Department of Finance and Administration, Australian Government.

Aichholzer, G. (2005). Service take-up and impacts of e-government in Austria. Paper presented at the 4th International Conference on Electronic Government (EGOV 2005), Copenhagen, Denmark.

Aichholzer, G., & Sperlich, R. (2001). Electronic government services for the business sector in Austria. Paper presented at the 12th International Conference on Database and Expert Systems Applications (DEXA), Munich, Germany.

Akramov, F., & Khudoyberganov, B. (2007). The e-Government in Uzbekistan: On a way to information society. Paper presented at the 3rd International Conference on e-Government, Montreal, Canada.

Akther, M. S., Onishi, T., & Kidokoro, T. (2005). E-government practice: What one country could learn from other. Paper presented at the 4th International Conference on Electronic Government (EGOV 2005), Copenhagen, Denmark.

Al Gore, J. (1993), From Red Tape to Results: Creating a Government that Works Better and Costs Less, Washington DC: Government Printing Office, http://govinfo.library.unt.edu/npr/ library/ nprrpt/annrpt/redtpe 93/index.html.

Al-Kindi, A., Al-Gharbi, K., & Al-Salti, Z. (2007). E-government initiative in the Sultanate of Oman. Paper presented at the 8th International-Business-Information-Management-Association Conference (IBIMA), Dublin, Ireland.

Al-Mashari, M. (2007). A Benchmarking Study of Experiences with Electronic-government, Benchmarking. *International Journal (Toronto, Ont.)*, *14*(2), 172–185.

Al-Shehry, A., Rogerson, S., Fairweather,N. B., & Prior, M., (2006), The Motivations for Change towards E-Government Adoption: Case Studies From Saudi Arabia, eGovernment Workshop '06 (eGOV06), September 11, Brunel University, West London, UB8 3PH.

Al-Turki, S., & Tang, K. (1998), Information Technology Environment in Saudi Arabia: A Review, Discussion Papers in Management and Organization Studies, University of Leicester. ISSN 1461-6017.

Alexander, C. J. (2001). Wiring the nation! Including First Nations? Aboriginal Canadians and Federal e-government initiatives (Canada). *Journal of Canadian Studies. Revue d'Etudes Canadiennes*, *35*(4), 277–296.

Alhabshi, S. M., (2008), E-government in Malaysia: Barriers and Progress, Information Technology in Developing Countries (International Federation for Information Processing (IFIP) Working Group 9.4), 18(3), 6-15.

Alkhatib, G., Bataineh, E., Fraihat, H., & Maamar, Z. (2007). An intelligent integrated e-Government framework: The case of Jordan. Paper presented at the 7th European Conference on e-Government (ECEG 2007), The Hague, Netherlands.

All About Market Research. (2008). Internet world stats. Retrieved from http://www.allaboutmarke-tresearch.com /internet.htm.

Australian Government 2.0 Taskforce Final Report (2009), Engage Getting on with Government 2.0.

Awan, M. A. (2003). E-government: Assessment of GCC (Gulf Co-Operating Council) countries and services provided. Paper presented at the 2nd International Conference on Electronic Government (EGOV 2003), Sep 01-05, Prague, Czech Republic.

Backhouse, J. (2007). e-Democracy in Australia: The challenge of evolving a successful model. Paper presented at the 7th European Conference on e-Government (ECEG 2007), Jun 21-22, The Hague, Netherlands.

Baines, S., Gannon-Leary, P., & Wilson, R. (2005, Oct 28-30). Practitioner buy-in and resistance to e-enabled information sharing across agencies - The case of an e-government project to join up local services in England. Paper presented at the 5th IFTP Conference on E-Commerce, E-Business, and E-Government, Poznan, Poland.

Baldoni, R., Fuligni, S., Mecella, M., & Tortorelli, F. (2008, May 19-21). The Italian e-Government Enterprise architecture: A comprehensive introduction with focus on the SLA issue. Paper presented at the 5th International Service Availability Symposium (ISAS 2008), Tokyo, Japan.

Balimann, C., & Zimmermann, F. (2005, Jul 14-17). Inter-governmental e-Government processes: Comparison of different solution approaches - Based on examples from Switzerland/Europe. Paper presented at the 3rd International Conference on Politics and Information Systems - Technologies and Applications/International Symposium on Social and Organizational Informatics and Cybernectics, Orlando, FL.

Ballardini, L., Germagnoli, F., Pagani, M., Picchi, M., Stoppini, A., & Cristiani, P. (2004, Sep 07-11). Putting e-government to work in healthcare environment: a Multiregional project funded by the Italian innovation & technology ministry. Paper presented at the 11th World Congress on Medical Informatics, San Francisco, CA.

Banas, M. J. and Hillard, F., (SECOM) (2010), Brazil Embraces Digitial Age with New Interactive E-Gov Portal - Brasil.Gov.Br, The Secretariat for Social Communication (SECOM) of the Presidency of Brazil.

Banas, P. A. (2010). International ideal and local practice – access to environmental information and local government in Poland. *Environmental Policy & Governance*, *20*(1), 44–56. doi:10.1002/eet.528

Barbosa, A., Junqueira, A., Diniz, E., & Prado, O. (2007, Sep 27). Electronic government in Brazil: A historical perspective of its development based on a structured model of analysis. Paper presented at the 3rd International Conference on e-Government, Montreal, Canada.

Bartels, U., & Steimke, F. (2004, Aug 30-Sep 03). How to modernize the people registration process. Experiences in the leading e-government project in Germany. Paper presented at the 3rd International Conference on Electronic Government (EGOV 2004), Zaragoza, Spain.

Baskoy, T. (2007, Sep 27). The European union and e-democracy: Interactive policy-making initiative (IPM). Paper presented at the 3rd International Conference on e-Government, Montreal, Canada.

Basu, S. (2004). E-government and developing countries: An overview. *International Review of Law Computers & Technology*, *18*(1), 109–132. doi:10.1080/13600860410001674779

Bavec, C., & Vintar, M. (2007, Sep 03-07). What matters in the development of the e-government in the EU? Paper presented at the 6th International Conference on Electronic Government, Regensburg, Germany.

Beddie, L., Macintosh, A., & Malina, A. (2001, Oct 03-05). E-democracy and the Scottish Parliament. Paper presented at the 1st IFIP International Conference on E-Commerce, E-Business, and E-Government (I3E 2001), Zurich, Switzerland.

Bednar, P., Furdik, K., Kleimann, M., Klischewski, R., Skokan, M., & Ukena, S. (2008, Aug 31-Sep 05). Semantic integration of eGovernment services in Schleswig-Holstein. Paper presented at the 7th International Conference on Electronic Government, Turin, Italy.

Bekkers, V. (2005, Aug 22-26). The governance of back office integration in e-government: Some Dutch experiences. Paper presented at the 4th International Conference on Electronic Government (EGOV 2005), Copenhagen, Denmark.

Berce, J., Bianchi, A., Centeno, C., Osimo, D., Millard, J., & Shahin, J. (2006, Sep 04-08). The organisation and coordination of European e-government research for the EU in 2010. Paper presented at the 5th International Conference on Electronic Government (EGOV 2006), Cracow, Poland.

Beynon-Davies, P. (2005, 2004). Constructing electronic government: The case of the UK inland revenue. Paper presented at the European Conference on Information Systems, Turku, Finland.

Beynon-Davis, P., & Williams, M. (2002), Electronic Local Government in the UK, Proceedings of the 2nd European Conference on E-Government, St Catherine's College, Oxford, UK, 79–89.

Bhatnagar, S., (2002), E-government: Lessons from Implementation in Developing Countries, Regional Development Dialogue, 24, UNCRD, (Autumn Issue), 1-9.

Biasiotti, M. A., & Nannucci, R. (2004, Aug 30-Sep 03). Teaching e-government in Italy. Paper presented at the 3rd International Conference on Electronic Government (EGOV 2004), Zaragoza, Spain.

Blakemore, M. (2006). *Think Paper 4: eGovernment Strategy Across Europe – a Bricolage Responding to Societal Challenges*. Birmingham: Ecotec Research and Consulting.

Bof, F., & Previtali, P. (2007, Sep 27). Is e-Government on the agenda of small municipalities? Empirical evidence from an Italian case study. Paper presented at the 3rd International Conference on e-Government, Montreal, Canada.

Bolivar, M. P. R., Perez, C. C., & Hernandez, A. M. L. (2007). E-government and public financial reporting - The case of Spanish regional governments. [Article]. *American Review of Public Administration, 37*(2), 142–177. doi:10.1177/0275074006293193

Brunschwig, C. (2002, Sep 02-06). Legal design and e-Government: Visualisations of cost & efficiency accounting in the wif! e-learning environment of the Canton of Zurich (Switzerland). Paper presented at the 1st International Conference on Electronic Government (EGOV 2002), Aix Provence, France.

Brunschwig, C. R. (2003, Jul 31-Aug 02). Good Practice in Swiss e-Government? How the Swiss authorities pay lip service to the multi-coding potential of the new information and communication technologies. Paper presented at the International Conference on Politics and Information Systems - Technologies and Applications (PISTA 03), Orlando, FL.

Bu, D. (2005, Aug 15-17). The application study on Chinese e-government construction. Paper presented at the 7th International Conference on Electronic Commerce (ICEC 2005), Xian, Peoples R. China.

Cabinet Office. (2005), Transformational Government Enabled by Technology, www.cabinetoffice. gov.uk.

Cardin, L., Holmes, B. J., Leganza, G., Hanson, J., & McEnroe, W. (2006). *Who are Canada's e-government consumers? Canadian demographics, tech attitudes, and purchasing power*. Boston: Forrester.

Castells, M. (2000). *End of Millennium, The Information Age: Economy, Society and Culture (Vol. III)*. Cambridge, MA; Oxford, UK: Blackwell.

Cegarra Navarro, J. G., Dewhurst, F. W., & Briones Penalver, A. J. (2007). Factors affecting the use of e-Government in the telecommunications industry of Spain. [Article]. *Technovation, 27*(10), 595–604. doi:10.1016/j.technovation.2007.03.003

Chadwick, A., & May, C. (2001, Aug 30-Sep 02). Interaction between states and citizens in the age of the internet: "e-government" in the United States, Britain, and the European Union. Paper presented at the 97th Annual Meeting of the American-Political-Science-Association, San Francisco, California.

Chan, C. M. L., Lau, Y. M., & Pan, S. L. (2008). E-government implementation: A macro analysis of Singapore's e-government initiatives. [Article]. *Government Information Quarterly, 25*(2), 239–255. doi:10.1016/j.giq.2006.04.011

Chan, C. M. L., & Pan, S. L. (2008). User engagement in e-government systems implementation: A comparative case study of two Singaporean e-government initiatives. [Article]. *The Journal of Strategic Information Systems, 17*(2), 124–139. doi:10.1016/j.jsis.2007.12.003

Chaney, P., & Fevre, R. (2002). Is there a demand for descriptive representative? Evidence from the UK's devolution program. *Political Studies, 50*(5), 897–915. doi:10.1111/1467-9248.00399

Chappelet, J. L. (2004, Aug 30-Sep 03). e-government as an enabler of public management reform: The case of Switzerland. Paper presented at the 3rd International Conference on Electronic Government (EGOV 2004), Zaragoza, SPAIN.

Chappelet, J. L., & Kilchenmann, P. (2005, Mar 02-04). Interactive tools for e-democracy: Examples from Switzerland. Paper presented at the International Conference on E-Government (TCGOV 2005), Bolzano, Italy.

Charalabldis, Y., Lampathaki, F., Sarantis, D., Sourouni, A. M., Mouzakitis, S., Gionis, G., et al. (2008, Aug 28-30). The Greek Electronic Government Interoperability Framework: Standards and Infrastructures for One-Stop Service Provision. Paper presented at the 12th Pan-Hellenic Conference on Informatics, Samos Isl, Greece.

Charif, H., & Ramadan, M. (2003, May 26-28). E-government attempts in ESCWA member countries. Paper presented at the 4th Annual International Working Conference on Knowledge Management in Electronic Government, Rhodes, Greece.

Chatfield, A. T. (2009). Public Service Reform through e-Government: a Case Study of 'e-Tax' in Japan, Electronic. *Journal of E-Government, 7*(2), 135–146.

Chatfield, A. T., & Al Hujran, O. (2007, Jun 21-22). The role of strategic leadership in driving transformative e-government: A comparative analysis of the Arab states in the Middle East. Paper presented at the 7th European Conference on e-Government (ECEG 2007), The Hague, Netherlands.

Chatzidimitriou, M., Koumpis, A., & Int Assoc, E. (2007, Jul 02-04). Matters of conceptualization and security in the building of one-stop-shop e-Government solutions in europe: Experiences from the European OneStopGov project. Paper presented at the World Congress on Engineering 2007, London, England.

Chen, X. X. (2002, Sep 02-06). The E-GOV action plan in Beijing. Paper presented at the 1st International Conference on Electronic Government (EGOV 2002), Aix Provence, France.

Chen, Y. N., Chen, H. M., Huang, W., & Ching, R. K. H. (2004, Dec). E-government strategies in developed and developing countries: An implementation framework and case study. Paper presented at the 1st International Symposium of IS/IT in Asia-Pacific (ISAP 2004), Washington, DC.

Chernov, S., Larichev, A., & Chernova, T. (2007, Sep 27). e-Government in Russia: Obstacles on the way to improve public management in a federal state. Paper presented at the 3rd International Conference on e-Government, Montreal, Canada.

Chiang, J. K., Huang, K., & Yen, E. (2007, Dec 02-05). e-Government reform and shared services in Taiwan. Paper presented at the IEEE International Conference on Industrial Engineering and Engineering Management, Singapore, Singapore.

Choudrie, J., Weerakkody, V., & Jones, S. (2005). Realising E-government in the UK: Rural and Urban Challenges. *Journal of Enterprise Information Management, 18*(5), 568–585. doi:10.1108/17410390510624016

Christy, O., (2002), Study: More Americans Become e-Citizens, CNN.com, Wednesday, April 3, 2002.

Ciborra, C., & Navarra, D. D. (2003, Jun 15-17). Good governance and development aid - Risks and challenges of e-government in Jordan. Paper presented at the Working Conference on Information Systems Perspectives and Challenges in the Context of Globalization, Athens, Greece.

Civilka, M. (2004, Jul 21-25). Situation of e-government in Lithuania and principles of regulation. Paper presented at the International Conference on Politics and Information Systems, Orlando, FL.

Connolly, R. (2007, Mar 03-06). Citizen trust in e-government in Ireland - The role of website service quality. Paper presented at the 3rd International Conference on Web Information Systems and Technologies, Barcelona, Spain.

Connolly, R., & Bannister, F. (2006b, Jun 19-21). The revenue Online service in Ireland: The relationship between website service quality & consumer trust in eGovernment. Paper presented at the 6th International-Business-Information-Management-Association Conference (IBIMA), Bonn, Germany.

Cook, I., & Horobin, G. (2006). Implementing eGovernment without promoting dependence: Open source software in developing countries in Southeast Asia. [Article]. *Public Administration and Development, 26*(4), 279–289. doi:10.1002/pad.403

Córdoba-Pachón, J.-R., & Orr, K. (2009). Three patterns to understand e-government: the case of Colombia. *International Journal of Public Sector Management, 22*(6), 532–554. doi:10.1108/09513550910982887

Costake, N. (2002, Sep 02-06). Some specific e-government management problems in a transforming country. Paper presented at the 1st International Conference on Electronic Government (EGOV 2002), Aix Provence, France.

Costake, N. (2003, Sep 01-05). Anti-corruption information systems and e-Government in transforming countries. A point of view. Paper presented at the 2nd International Conference on Electronic Government (EGOV 2003), Prague, Czech Republic.

Coursey, D., & Norris, D. F. (2008). Models of e-government: Are they correct? An empirical assessment. [Article]. *Public Administration Review, 68*(3), 523–536. doi:10.1111/j.1540-6210.2008.00888.x

D'Elia, I. (2004, Aug 30-Sep 03). e-Government and information society: The first regional law in Italy. Paper presented at the 3rd International Conference on Electronic Government (EGOV 2004), Zaragoza, Spain.

Damodaran, L., Nicholls, J., & Henney, A. (2005). The Contribution of Sociotechnical Systems Thinking to the Effective Adoption of e-Government and the Enhancement of Democracy, The Electronic. *Journal of E-Government, 3*(1), 1–12.

Danish Government. (2004), The Danish E-government Strategy 2004-06- Realizing the Potential, Strategy Paper, Denmark – Policy/Strategy, http://www.e.gov.dk/

Dawes, S. S., Gregg, V., & Agouris, P. (2004). Digital Government Research. Investigations at the Crossroads of Social and Information Science. *Social Science Computer Review, 22*(1), 5–10. doi:10.1177/0894439303259863

De, R. (2005, Aug 22-26). E-government systems in developing countries: Stakeholders and conflict. Paper presented at the 4th International Conference on Electronic Government (EGOV 2005), Copenhagen, Denmark.

De, R., & Sen, C. (2004, Aug 30-Sep 03). The complex nature of e-government projects: A case study of Bhoomi, an initiative in Karnataka, India. Paper presented at the 3rd International Conference on Electronic Government (EGOV 2004), Zaragoza, Spain.

De Petra, G., & De Pietro, L. (2003, May 30-31). The Italian approach to local e-government. Paper presented at the International Conference On Line Citizenship, Venice, Italy.

Department of Public Service and Administration. (2007), South African Government Information, www.gov.za.

Devadoss, P. R., Pan, S. L., & Huang, J. C. (2003). Structurational analysis of e-government initiatives: a case study of SCO. [Article]. *Decision Support Systems*, *34*(3), 253–269. doi:10.1016/S0167-9236(02)00120-3

Diez, C., & Prenafeta, J. (2002, Sep 02-06). e-Government applied to judicial notices and inter-registrar communications in the European Union: The AEQUITAS Project. Paper presented at the 1st International Conference on Electronic Government (EGOV 2002), Aix Provence, France.

Dimitrova, D. V., & Chen, Y. C. (2006). Profiling the adopters of e-government information and services - The influence of psychological characteristics, civic mindedness, and information channels. [Article]. *Social Science Computer Review*, *24*(2), 172–188. doi:10.1177/0894439305281517

Doty, P., & Erdelez, S. (2002). Information micropractices in Texas rural courts: methods and issues for E-government. [Article]. *Government Information Quarterly*, *19*(4), 369–387. doi:10.1016/S0740-624X(02)00121-1

Doucet, K. (2001). Canada Ranks First in E-Government Services. *CMA Management*, *75*(4), 8.

Du, J. P., & Ye, K. P. (2005, Aug 15-17). A study on the development and tactics of E-government construction of Jiangxi province. Paper presented at the 7th International Conference on Electronic Commerce (ICEC 2005), Xian, Peoples R. China.

Dunleavy, P., Margetts, H., Bastow, S., & Tinkler, J. (2008). Australian e-government in comparative perspective. [Article]. *Australian Journal of Political Science*, *43*(1), 13–26. doi:10.1080/10361140701842540

Durrant, F. (2002, Sep 02-06). e-government and the Internet in the Caribbean: An initial assessment. Paper presented at the 1st International Conference on Electronic Government (EGOV 2002), Aix Provence, France.

Dwivedi, Y. K. (2009), A Bibliometric Analysis of Electronic Government Research, In Ganesh P. Sahu; Yogesh K. Dwivedi; Vishanth Weerakkody (Ed.) E-Government Development and Diffusion: Inhibitors and Facilitators of Digital Democracy, 176-256.

Eka, M. I. (2008, May 04-07). E-government in Africa - Strengthening it through European cooperation. Paper presented at the 4th International Conference on Web Information Systems and Technologies, Funchal, Portugal.

Ekelin, A. (2003, Jul 31-Aug 02). It takes more than two to TANGO co-constructing situated accountability through a local e-government arena. Paper presented at the International Conference on Politics and Information Systems - Technologies and Applications (PISTA 03), Orlando, FL.

Elayoubi, M. (2008, Jan 04-06). E-government and marketing communication strategies of Moroccan public institutions: basis and implications. Paper presented at the 9th International-Business-Information-Management-Association Conference (IBIMA), Marrakech, Morocco.

Elsas, A. (2003a, Jul 31-Aug 02). E-government in Germany: Status quo and perspectives. Paper presented at the International Conference on Politics and Information Systems - Technologies and Applications (PISTA 03), Orlando, FL.

Eriksen, S., Dittrich, Y., Fiedler, M., & Aurell, M. (2003, Sep 01-05). It takes more than two... developing a TANGO arena for regional cooperation around e-government. Paper presented at the 2nd International Conference on Electronic Government (EGOV 2003), Prague, Czech Republic.

Eriksen, S., Ekelin, A., Elovaara, P., Dittrich, Y., Hansson, C., & Winter, J. (2004, Aug 30-Sep 03). What have we learned from the TANGO arena for regional cooperation around e-government in Southern Sweden? Paper presented at the 3rd International Conference on Electronic Government (EGOV 2004), Zaragoza, Spain.

Esteves, J. (2007, Jun 21-22). A semiotic analysis of Spanish local e-government websites. Paper presented at the 7th European Conference on e-Government (ECEG 2007), The Hague, Netherlands.

European Union. (2005). An application if this strategy by a member state is the e-envoy office set up by the UK government. Retrieved from http://www.e-envoy.gov.uk/

Evangelidis, A., Akomode, J., Taleb-Bendiab, A., & Taylor, M. (2002, Sep 02-06). Risk assessment & success factors for e-Government in a UK establishment. Paper presented at the 1st International Conference on Electronic Government (EGOV 2002), Aix Provence, France.

Evangelidis, A., Macintosh, A., & Davenport, E. (2004, Aug 30-Sep 03). FRAMES towards risk modelling in e-government services: A UK perspective. Paper presented at the 3rd International Conference on Electronic Government (EGOV 2004), Zaragoza, Spain.

Ezz, I., Papazafeiropoulou, A., & Serrano, A. (2009). Challenges of interorganizational collaboration for information technology adoption: Insights from a governmental financial decision-making process in Egypt. *Information Technology for Development, 15*(3), 209–223. doi:10.1002/itdj.20123

Facis, R., Torres, C. A. N., & de Vasconcelos, J. B. (2007, Sep). Sao Paulo state e-gov: LabIHC and e-poupatempo's experience. Paper presented at the 11th IFIP International Conference on Human-Computer Interaction, Rio de Janeiro, Brazil.

Feng, Y. Q., & Li, Y. (2002, Oct 22-24). Research on E-government and its development in China. Paper presented at the International Conference on Management Science and Engineering, Moscow, Russia.

Fernandez, E., Fernandez, I., Jimenez, S., & Salvador, J. (2006). E-government for water management in Spain. The case of Hispagua. [Article]. *Profesional De La Informacion, 15*(2), 99–113.

Ferrer, E. (2009). ICT Policy and perspectives of Human Development in Latin America: the Peruvian Experience. *Journal of Technology Management & Innovation, 4*(4), 161–170. doi:10.4067/S0718-27242009000400014

Fischmann, L., Jakisch, G., & Riedel, R. (2001, Sep 03-07). E-Vienna living situation based eGovernment and eDemocracy. Paper presented at the 12th International Conference on Database and Expert Systems Applications (DEXA), Munich, Germany.

Freya, K. N., & Holden, S. H. (2005). Distribution channel management in e-government: Addressing federal information policy issues. [Article]. *Government Information Quarterly, 22*(4), 685–701. doi:10.1016/j.giq.2006.01.001

Gadda, L., & Savoldelli, A. (2002, Sep 02-06). The local e-government best practice in Italian country: The case of the centralised desk of "area berica". Paper presented at the 1st International Conference on Electronic Government (EGOV 2002), Aix Provence, France.

Gallemore, C. (2005). Of lords and (cyber)serfs: eGovernment and poststructuralism in a neome-dieval Europe. [Article]. *Millennium-Journal of International Studies, 34*(1), 27–55. doi:10.1177 /03058298050340011001

Garcia, T. H. B., Theiss, I., Zimath, P., Hoeschl, H. C., Donatti, F., Loureiro, G. M., et al. (2003, Sep 01-05). Consumer-SC: An E-gov portal for consumers rights protection in Brazil. Paper presented at the 2nd International Conference on Electronic Government (EGOV 2003), Prague, Czech Republic.

Garcia-Martinez, G., Romero Civera, A., Segui Mas, E., & Villalonga Granana, I. (2006, Dec 14-16). Corporative e-government in the digital era: empirical study of rural Spanish cashiers. Paper presented at the 7th International-Business-Information-Management-Association Conference (IBIMA), Brescia, Italy.

Garimella, S., & Vanka, S. (2004, Jul 21-25). E-government in the developing context - The Indian experience. Paper presented at the International Conference on Politics and Information Systems, Orlando, FL.

Garofalakis, J., Koskeris, A., & Vopi, A. (2007, Jun 21-22). An e-government application for in-tegrated, multi-level management of large scale resources of the Greek primary and secondary education. Paper presented at the 7th European Conference on e-Government (ECEG 2007), The Hague, Netherlands.

Gauld, R. (2007). Public Sector Information System Project Failures: Lessons from a New Zealand Hospital Organization. *Government In-formation Quarterly, 24*, 102–114. doi:10.1016/j. giq.2006.02.010

Germanakos, P., Christodoulou, E., & Samaras, G. (2007, Sep 03-07). European perspective of e-Government presence - Where do we stand? The EU-10 case. Paper presented at the 6th Inter-national Conference on Electronic Government, Regensburg, Germany.

Ghaziri, H. (2003), Prerequisites for Building E-Government: The Case of the Arab Countries, Proceedings of the 2003 International Business Information Management Conference, December 16-18th, Cairo, Egypt.

Gisler, M., & Spahni, D. (2000, Sep 04-08). eGovernment experiences of the Swiss Federal Institute of Intellectual Property. Paper presented at the 11th International Workshop on Database and Expert Systems Applications, London, England.

Glassey, O., & Chappelet, J. L. (2003, Sep 01-05). From e-Government to e-Governance: A survey of the federal and cantonal e-Policies in Switzerland. Paper presented at the 2nd International Confer-ence on Electronic Government (EGOV 2003), Prague, Czech Republic.

Goh, B. H. (2007, Oct 14-16). E-government for construction: The case of Singapore's CORENET project. Paper presented at the 2nd International Conference on Research and Practical Issues of Enterprise Information Systems, Beijing, Peoples R. China.

Gomez-Perez, A., Ortiz-Rodriguez, F., & Villazon-Terrazas, B. (2006). *Legal ontologies for the Spanish e-Government Current Topics in Artificial Intelligence (Vol. 4177*, pp. 301–310). Berlin: Springer-Verlag Berlin.

Gonzalez, R., Gasco, J., & Llopis, J. (2007). E-government success: some principles from a Spanish case study. [Article]. *Industrial Man-agement & Data Systems, 107*(5-6), 845–861. doi:10.1108/02635570710758752

Grande, C. (1999, December). E-Envoy Vows to Raise Internet Use By Ministries. *Financial Times (North American Edition)*, 10.

Groznik, A., & Vicic, D. (2005, Jun 01-04). Towards E-government: Business renovation of public sector in Slovenia. Paper presented at the 19th European Conference on Modelling and Simulation (ECMS 2005), Riga, LATVIA.

Guijarro, L. (2007). Interoperability frameworks and enterprise architectures in e-government initiatives in Europe and the United States. [Article]. *Government Information Quarterly, 24*(1), 89–101. doi:10.1016/j.giq.2006.05.003

Gupta, M. P., & Jana, D. (2003). E-government evaluation: A framework and case study. [Article]. *Government Information Quarterly, 20*(4), 365–387. doi:10.1016/j.giq.2003.08.002

Hackney, R., Jones, S., & Losch, A. (2007). Towards an e-Government efficiency agenda: the impact of information and communication behaviour on e-Reverse auctions in public sector procurement. [Article]. *European Journal of Information Systems, 16*(2), 178–191. doi:10.1057/palgrave.ejis.3000677

Heeks, R., & Stanforth, C. (2007). Understanding e-Government project trajectories from an actor-network perspective. [Article]. *European Journal of Information Systems, 16*(2), 165–177. doi:10.1057/palgrave.ejis.3000676

Heinderyckx, F. (2002, Sep 02-06). Assessing e-government implementation processes: A pan-European survey of administrations officials. Paper presented at the 1st International Conference on Electronic Government (EGOV 2002), Aix Provence, France.

Henriksen, H. Z., & Damsgaard, J. (2007). Dawn of e-government - an institutional analysis of seven initiatives and their impact. [Article]. *Journal of Information Technology, 22*(1), 13–23. doi:10.1057/palgrave.jit.2000090

Hernon, P., Reylea, H. C., Dugan, R. E., & Cheverie, J. F. (2002). *United States Government Information: Policies and Sources* (p. 388). Westport, CT: Libraries Unlimited.

Hilton, S. (2006). Developing local e-democracy in Bristol - From information to consultation to participation and beyond. [Article]. *Aslib Proceedings, 58*(5), 416–428. doi:10.1108/00012530610692366

Ho, A. T. K., & Ni, A. Y. (2004). Explaining the adoption of e-government features - A case study of Iowa County treasurers' offices. [Article]. *American Review of Public Administration, 34*(2), 164–180. doi:10.1177/0275074004264355

Holden, S. H. (2002, May 19-22). Electronic authentication initiatives in the IRS e-file program: Enabling e-government through electronic signatures. Paper presented at the International Conference of the Information-Resources-Management-Association, Seattle, Wa.

Holden, S. H., & Millett, L. I. (2005). Authentication, privacy, and the federal E-Government. [Article]. *The Information Society, 21*(5), 367–377. doi:10.1080/01972240500253582

Holliday, I. (2002). Building E-government in East and Southeast Asia: Regional rhetoric and national (in)action. [Article]. *Public Administration and Development, 22*(4), 323–335. doi:10.1002/pad.239

Holliday, I., & Kwok, R. C. W. (2004). Governance in the information age: building e-government in Hong Kong. [Article]. *New Media & Society, 6*(4), 549–570. doi:10.1177/146144804044334

Holliday, I., & Yep, R. (2005). E-government in China. [Article]. *Public Administration and Development, 25*(3), 239–249. doi:10.1002/pad.361

Hollosi, A., Leitold, H., & Posch, R. (2002, Sep 26-27). An open interface enabling secure e-Government - The approach followed with the Austrian citizen card. Paper presented at the 6th IFIP Working Conference on Communications and Multimedia Security, Portoroz, Slovenia.

Hollosi, A., Naber, L., & Liehmann, M. (2004, Oct 27-29). Personal identity and proxy identities in Austria's eGovernment. Paper presented at the eChallenges e-2004 Conference, Vienna, AUSTRIA.

Hoogwout, M. (2003, Sep 01-05). Super pilots, subsidizing or self-organization: Stimulating E-government initiatives in Dutch local governments. Paper presented at the 2nd International Conference on Electronic Government (EGOV 2003), Prague, Czech Republic.

Hornung, H., Baranauskas, M. C. C., & Tambascia, C. A. (2008, Jun 12-16). Assistive Technologies and Techniques for Web Based Egov in Developing Countries. Paper presented at the 10th International Conference on Enterprise Information Systems, Barcelona, SPAIN.

Horst, M., Kuttschreuter, M., & Gutteling, J. M. (2007). Perceived usefulness, personal experiences, risk perception and trust as determinants of adoption of e-government services in The Netherlands. [Article]. *Computers in Human Behavior*, *23*(4), 1838–1852. doi:10.1016/j.chb.2005.11.003

Huang, C. (2006, Oct 23-26). Analysis on the construction of management modes of e-government information exchange in China. Paper presented at the 7th International Conference on Web Information Systems Engineering, Wuhan, Peoples R. China.

Huang, W., D'Ambra, J., & Bhalla, V. (2002). An empirical investigation of the adoption of eGovernment in Australian citizens: Some unexpected research findings. [Article]. *Journal of Computer Information Systems*, *43*(1), 15–22.

Huang, Z. Y. (2007). A comprehensive analysis of US counties' e-Government portals: development status and functionalities. [Article]. *European Journal of Information Systems*, *16*(2), 149–164. doi:10.1057/palgrave.ejis.3000675

Hwang, S. D., Choi, Y., & Myeong, S. H. (1999). Electronic government in South Korea: Conceptual problems. [Article]. *Government Information Quarterly*, *16*(3), 277–285. doi:10.1016/S0740-624X(99)80028-8

Hyden, G., Court, J., & Mease, K. (2003), Government and Governance in 16 Developing Countries, World Governance Survey Discussion Paper, 6 July 2003.

Imai, H., & Yamagishi, A. (2000, Dec 03-07). CRYPTREC project - Cryptographic evaluation project for the Japanese electronic government. Paper presented at the 6th International Conference on the Theory and Application of Cryptology and Informnation Security (ASIACRYPT 2000), Kyoto, Japan.

Ioannidis, A., Spanoudakis, M., Priggouris, G., Eliopoulou, C., Hadjiefthymiades, S., & Merakos, L. (2002, Sep 02-06). EURO-CITI security manager: Supporting transaction services in the E-Government domain. Paper presented at the 1st International Conference on Electronic Government (EGOV 2002), Aix Provence, France.

Iovan, A. A., & Iovan, S. (2005, Jul 14-17). e-Government in Romania; Methodological and legal aspects. Paper presented at the 3rd International Conference on Politics and Information Systems - Technologies and Applications/International Symposium on Social and Organizational Informatics and Cybernectics, Orlando, FL.

Iovan, S., Feher, A. A., & Iovan, A. A. (2005, Jul 14-17). e-Government in Romania; Theoretical and practical aspects. Paper presented at the 3rd International Conference on Politics and Information Systems - Technologies and Applications/ International Symposium on Social and Organizational Informatics and Cybernectics, Orlando, FL.

Irani, Z., Love, P. E. D., Elliman, T., Jones, S., & Themistocleous, M. (2005). Evaluating e-government: learning from the experiences of two UK local authorities. [Article]. *Information Systems Journal, 15*(1), 61–82. doi:10.1111/j.1365-2575.2005.00186.x

Irani, Z., Love, P. E. D., & Jones, S. (2008). Learning lessons from evaluating eGovernment: Reflective case experiences that support transformational government. [Article]. *The Journal of Strategic Information Systems, 17*(2), 155–164. doi:10.1016/j.jsis.2007.12.005

Irkhin, I. U. V. (2007). Electronic Government and Society: World Realities and Russia (A Comparative Analysis). *Sociological Research, 46*(2), 77–92. doi:10.2753/SOR1061-0154460206

Jackson, P., & Curthoys, N. (2001, Sep 03-07). E-Government: Developments in the US and UK. Paper presented at the 12th International Conference on Database and Expert Systems Applications (DEXA), Munich, Germany.

Jaeger, P. T. (2004). Beyond Section 508: The spectrum of legal requirements for accessible e-government Web sites in the United States. [Article]. *Journal of Government Information, 30*(4), 518–533. doi:10.1016/S1352-0237(04)00057-7

Jaeger, P. T. (2006). Assessing Section 508 compliance on federal e-government Web sites: A multi-method, user-centered, evaluation of accessibility for persons with disabilities. [Article]. *Government Information Quarterly, 23*(2), 169–190. doi:10.1016/j.giq.2006.03.002

Jaeger, P. T., & Thompson, K. M. (2004). Social information behavior and the democratic process: Information poverty, non-native behavior, and electronic government in the United States. [Article]. *Library & Information Science Research, 26*(1), 94–107. doi:10.1016/j.lisr.2003.11.006

Jansen, A. (2006, Sep 04-08). What role has Scandinavian IS tradition in eGovernment implementations. Paper presented at the 5th International Conference on Electronic Government (EGOV 2006), Cracow, Poland.

Janssen, M., Kuk, G., & Wagenaar, R. W. (2005, Aug 15-17). A survey of e-government business models in the Netherlands. Paper presented at the 7th International Conference on Electronic Commerce (ICEC 2005), Xian, Peoples R. China.

Janssen, M., Kuk, G., & Wagenaar, R. W. (2008). A survey of Web-based business models for e-government in the Netherlands. [Article]. *Government Information Quarterly, 25*(2), 202–220. doi:10.1016/j.giq.2007.06.005

Jho, W. (2005). Challenges for e-governance: protests from civil society on the protection of privacy in e-government in Korea. [Article]. *International Review of Administrative Sciences, 71*(1), 151–166. doi:10.1177/0020852305051690

Jiang, Y., & Dong, H. (2008, Sep 14-19). Towards Ontology-Based Chinese E-Government Digital Archives Knowledge Management. Paper presented at the 12th European Conference on Research and Advanced Technology for Digital Libraries, Aarhus, Denmark.

Jung, H., & Kim, S. (2003, Jul 31-Aug 02). The value of a city-owned broadband network for e-Government: The case of e-Seoul Net. Paper presented at the International Conference on Politics and Information Systems - Technologies and Applications (PISTA 03), Orlando, FL.

Kaaya, J. (2009). Determining types of services and targeted users of emerging e-government strategies: The case of Tanzania. *International Journal of Electronic Government Research, 5*(2), 16–36. doi:10.4018/jegr.2009040102

Kahraman, C., Demirel, N. C., & Demirel, T. (2007). Prioritization of e-Government strategies using a SWOT-AHP analysis: the case of Turkey. [Article]. *European Journal of Information Systems, 16*(3), 284–298. doi:10.1057/palgrave. ejis.3000679

Kalja, A., Reitsakas, A., & Saard, M. (2005, Jul 31-Aug 04). eGovernment in Estonia: Best practices. Paper presented at the Portland International Conference on Management of Engineering and Technology, Portland, OR.

Kalu, K. N. (2007). Capacity building and IT diffusion - A comparative assessment of E-government environment in Africa. [Article]. *Social Science Computer Review, 25*(3), 358–371. doi:10.1177/0894439307296917

Kampen, J. K., Snijkers, K., & Bouckaert, G. (2005). Public priorities concerning the development of e-government in Flanders. [Article]. *Social Science Computer Review, 23*(1), 136–139. doi:10.1177/0894439304271557

Kaylor, C., Deshazo, R., & Van Eck, D. (2001, Mar). Gauging e-government: A report on implementing services among American cities. Paper presented at the Workshop on Foundations of Electronic Government in Americas Cities, Chicago, Illinois.

Ke, W. L., & Wei, K. K. (2004). Successful e-government in Singapore - How did Singapore manage to get most of its public services deliverable online? [Article]. *Communications of the ACM, 47*(6), 95–99. doi:10.1145/990680.990687

Kettani, D., & Ghailani, M. (2004, Jul 21-25). E-Government for better governance: Morocco's first pilot experience. Paper presented at the International Conference on Politics and Information Systems, Orlando, FL.

Kettani, D., & Maghraoui, D. (2003, Jul 31-Aug 02). Practicing E-government in Morocco. Paper presented at the International Conference on Education and Information Systems - Technologies and Applications (EISTA 03), Orlando, FL.

Kim, H. J., Pan, G., & Pan, S. L. (2007). Managing IT-enabled transfonnation in the public sector: A case study on e-government in South Korea. [Article]. *Government Information Quarterly, 24*(2), 338–352. doi:10.1016/j.giq.2006.09.007

Kim, Y. S., & Icact (2006, Feb 20-22). Challenges and barriers in implementing e-government: Investigation on NEIS of Korea. Paper presented at the 8th International Conference on Advanced Communication Technology, Phoenix Pk, South Korea.

Kita, T., & Murakami, T. (2006, Jul 16-19). A colaborative approach for the next generation of "e-government" in Japan. Paper presented at the 10th World Multi-Conference on Systemics, Cybernetics and Informatics/12th International Conference on Information Systems Analysis and Synthesis, Orlando, FL.

Klischewski, R. (2003, Sep 01-05). Semantic Web for e-government. Paper presented at the 2nd International Conference on Electronic Government (EGOV 2003), Prague, Czech Republic.

Klumpp, D. (2002, Sep 02-06). From websites to e-government in Germany. Paper presented at the 1st International Conference on Electronic Government (EGOV 2002), Aix Provence, France.

Knight, P. T. (2007), Knowledge Management And E-Government In Brazil, Paper Prepared For The Workshop On Managing Knowledge To Build Trust In Government, 7th Global Forum on Reinventing Government, 26-29 June 2007, Vienna, Austria, www.e-brasil.org.br.

Koga, T. (2003). Access to government information in Japan: a long way toward electronic Koga, T. (2006), Policy Issues Regarding Electronic Government and Web Accessibility in Japan, World Library and Information Congress: 72nd Ifla General Conference and Council 20-24 August 2006, Seoul, Korea.

Kong, W. C., & Chen, S. F. (2005, Aug 15-17). The characteristics, problems and solutions of e-government in China. Paper presented at the 7th International Conference on Electronic Commerce (ICEC 2005), Xian, Peoples R. China.

Korteland, E., & Bekkers, V. (2007, Sep 03-07). Diffusion of e-government innovations in the dutch public sector: The case of digital community policing. Paper presented at the 6th International Conference on Electronic Government, Regensburg, Germany.

Kraemer, K. L., & King, J. L. (2003), Information Technology and Administrative Reform: Will The Time After E-Government Be Different? CRITO, Center For Research On Information Technology And Organizations, http://www.crito.uci.edu.

Krishna, S., & Walsham, G. (2005). Implementing public information systems in developing countries: Learning from a success story. *Information Technology for Development*, *11*(2), 123–140. doi:10.1002/itdj.20007

Kristin, D. (2001). Canada Ranks First in E-government Services. *CMA Management*, *75*(4), 8–11.

Kudo, H. (2008). Does E-Government Guarantee Accountability In Public Sector? Experiences in Italy and Japan. *Public Administration Quarterly*, *32*(1), 93–120.

Kuk, G. (2003). The Digital Divide And The Quality Of Electronic Service Delivery In Local Government In The United Kingdom. *Government Information Quarterly*, *20*(4), 353–363. doi:10.1016/j.giq.2003.08.004

Kumar, R., & Best, M. L. (2006). Impact and sustainability of e-government services in developing countries: Lessons learned from Tamil Nadu, India. [Article]. *The Information Society*, *22*(1), 1–12. doi:10.1080/01972240500388149

Kunstelj, M., Jukic, T., & Vintar, M. (2007, Sep 03-07). Analysing the demand side of e-government: What can we learn from slovenian users? Paper presented at the 6th International Conference on Electronic Government, Regensburg, Germany.

Kyama, G. W. e-Government: A View from South Africa, http://www.uneca.org/aisi/ NICI/ Documents/eGovernment%20A %20view%20 from%20Southern%20 Africa%20- %20God-frey%20Kyama.ppt., [Accessed, 2010].

Lam, T. M. (2008, Jul 26-29). The private and public partnership strategy in e-government ESDlife in Hong Kong. Paper presented at the International Conference on e-Business (ICE-B 2008), Oporto, Portugal.

Lan, L. (2004, May 17-19). E-government: A catalyst to good governance in China. Paper presented at the 5th IFIP Interenational Working Conference on Knowledge Management in Electronic Government, Krems, Austria.

Lan, L. (2005, Mar 02-04). Enhancing e-democracy via fiscal transparency: a discussion based on china's experience. Paper presented at the International Conference on E-Government (TCGOV 2005), Bolzano, Italy.

Lassnig, M., & Markus, M. (2003, Sep 01-05). Usage of e-government services in European regions. Paper presented at the 2nd International Conference on Electronic Government (EGOV 2003), Prague, Czech Republic.

Latre, J. L. B. (2003, Sep 01-05). Implementing E-Government in Spain. Paper presented at the 2nd International Conference on Electronic Government (EGOV 2003), Prague, Czech Republic.

Lau, T. Y., Aboulhoson, M., Lin, C., & Atkin, D. J. (2008). Adoption of e-government in three Latin American countries: Argentina, Brazil and Mexico. [Article]. *Telecommunications Policy, 32*(2), 88–100. doi:10.1016/j.telpol.2007.07.007

Lay, K., Alam, M. S., & Phu, H. E. L. (2007, Dec 05-06). Different stages of developing e-government between Cambodia and japan. Paper presented at the 4th International Conference on Innovation and Management, Ube, Japan.

Lee, S., & Cho, J. E. (2007, Jul 22-27). Usability evaluation of Korean e-Government portal. Paper presented at the 4th International Conference on Universal Access in Human-Computer Interaction held at the HCI International 2007, Beijing, Peoples R. China.

Lee, S., Kim, B. G., & Kim, J. G. (2007, Jul 22-27). Accessibility evaluation of Korean e-Government. Paper presented at the 4th International Conference on Universal Access in Human-Computer Interaction held at the HCI International 2007, Beijing, Peoples R. China.

Lee, S. M., Tan, X., & Trimi, S. (2005). Current practices of leading e-government countries. [Article]. *Communications of the ACM, 48*(10), 99–104. doi:10.1145/1089107.1089112

Lemon, W. F., Holden, S. H., & Preece, J. J. (2003, May 18-21). A descriptive framework for federal electronic government: A necessary step prior to field research. Paper presented at the International Conference of the Information-Resources-Management-Association, Philadelphia, PA.

Leutgeb, A., Utz, W., Woitsch, R., & Fill, H. G. (2007, Jun 12-16). Adaptive processes in E-government - A field report about semantic-based approaches from the EU-project "FIT". Paper presented at the 9th International Conference on Enterprise Information Systems (ICEIS 2007), Funchal, Portugal.

Levillain, P., Jourdan, A., & Hill, N. (2005). E-government: The new collaborative environment for user-centric public administrations. [Article]. Alcatel Telecommunications Review(1), 84-87.

Leyland, P. (2003). Devolution, the British Constitution and the distribution of power. *The Northern Ireland Legal Quarterly, 53*(4), 408–434.

Li, B. L. (2005, Aug 15-17). On the Barriers to the development of e-government in China. Paper presented at the 7th International Conference on Electronic Commerce (ICEC 2005), Xian, Peoples R. China.

Li, H. G., Fan, B., Zheng, X. X., & Alfred, U. (2007, May 26-27). The top layer design theory and its revelations on the application of e-government in China. Paper presented at the 6th Wuhan International Conference on E-Business, Wuhan, Peoples R. China.

Li, Y., & Ieee (2006, Jun 21-23). Evaluation of public service maturity of e-government: A case in Chinese cities. Paper presented at the IEEE International Conference on Service Operations and Logistics and Informatics, Shanghai, Peoples R. China.

Liao, S. H., & Jeng, H. P. (2005). E-government implementation: Business contract legal support for Taiwanese businessmen in Mainland China. [Article]. *Government Information Quarterly, 22*(3), 505–524. doi:10.1016/j.giq.2005.08.002

Lim, J. H., & Tang, S. Y. (2008). Urban e-government initiatives and environmental decision performance in Korea. [Review]. *Journal of Public Administration: Research and Theory, 18*(1), 109–138. doi:10.1093/jopart/mum005

Liu, W. Y., & Wang, J. L. (2007, Aug 18-20). The enlightenment to China of e-government application in rural areas from Japan, South Korea and India. Paper presented at the 1st International Conference on Computer and Computing Technologies in Agriculture (CCTA 2007), Wuyishan, Peoples R. China.

Liu, Y. B., & Liu, J. (2004, Jun 04-07). How e-government helps combat corruption in developing countries. Paper presented at the 3rd Wuhan International Conference on E-Business - Global Business Interface, Wuhan, Peoples R. China.

Local Government Association. (2002), egov@ local: Towards a National Strategy for Local E-government, Local Government Association, London.

Löfgren, K. (2007). The Governance of E-government. *Public Policy and Administration, 22*(3), 335–352.

Lowe, C. (2003, Sep 01-05). Experiences of take-up of e-Government in Europe. Paper presented at the 2nd International Conference on Electronic Government (EGOV 2003), Prague, Czech Republic.

Lu, X. (2007, Jul 30-Aug 01). Distributed secure information sharing model for e-government in China. Paper presented at the 8th ACIS International Conference on Software Engineering, Artificial Intelligence, Networking and Parallel/Distributed Computing/3rd ACIS International Workshop on Self-Assembling Wireless Networks, Qungdao, Peoples R. China.

Ma, L. J., Chung, J. P., & Thorson, S. (2005). E-government in China: Bringing economic development through administrative reform. [Article]. *Government Information Quarterly, 22*(1), 20–37. doi:10.1016/j.giq.2004.10.001

Maciel, C., Nogueira, J. L. T., & Garcia, A. C. B. (2005, Sep 12-16). An X-ray of the Brazilian e-Gov Web sites. Paper presented at the International Conference on Human-Computer Interaction, Rome, Italy.

Madon, S. (2004). Evaluating the Developmental Impact of E-Governance Initiatives: An Exploratory Framework. *The Electronic Journal on Information Systems in Developing Countries, 20*(5), 1–13.

Mahrer, H., & Krimmer, R. (2005). Towards the enhancement of e-democracy: identifying the notion of the 'middleman paradox'. [Article]. *Information Systems Journal, 15*(1), 27–42. doi:10.1111/j.1365-2575.2005.00184.x

Makhera, N., Moloisane, A., & Busler, M. (2004, Aug 14-17). Lesotho's migration path to e-government. Paper presented at the International Conference on Computing, Communications and Control Technologies (CCCT 2004), Austin, TX.

Makolm, J. (2005, Jul 14-17). Holistic approach and stakeholder integration: The Austrian way to successful e-Government applications. Paper presented at the 3rd International Conference on Politics and Information Systems - Technologies and Applications/International Symposium on Social and Organizational Informatics and Cybernectics, Orlando, FL.

Manuela, W. S., & Tiglao, N. M. C. (2006, Dec 14-16). E-government applications in the Philippines. Paper presented at the 7th International-Business-Information-Management-Association Conference (IBIMA), Brescia, Italy.

Margetts, H. (2006). E-government in Britain - A decade on. [Article]. *Parliamentary Affairs*, *59*(2), 250–265. doi:10.1093/pa/gsl003

Marques, I. C., Lima, D. L. M., & Martins, M. L. C. (2004, Jul 21-25). E.gov, the government and citizens: a study of the government's official web portal in Brazil. Paper presented at the International Conference on Politics and Information Systems, Orlando, FL.

Maumbe, B. M., Owei, V., & Alexander, H. (2008). Questioning the pace and pathway of e-government development in Africa: A case study of South Africa's Cape Gateway project. [Article]. *Government Information Quarterly*, *25*(4), 757–777. doi:10.1016/j.giq.2007.08.007

McCall, C., & Williamson, A. (2002). Governance and Democracy in Northern Ireland: The role of the voluntary and community sector after the agreement. *Governance*, *14*(3), 363–384. doi:10.1111/0952-1895.00165

McGregor, M. A., & Holman, J. (2004). Communication technology at the federal communications commission: E-government in the public interest? [Article]. *Government Information Quarterly*, *21*(3), 268–283. doi:10.1016/j.giq.2004.04.005

McNeal, R., Schmeida, M., & Hale, K. (2007). E-disclosure laws and electronic campaign finance reform: Lessons from the diffusion of e-government policies in the States. [Article]. *Government Information Quarterly*, *24*(2), 312–325. doi:10.1016/j.giq.2006.06.006

McPherson, M., & Ramli, R. (2004, May 23-26). Lessons learned from the implementation of a Malaysian eGovernment project. Paper presented at the International Conference of the Information-Resources-Management-Association, New Orleans, LA.

Mecella, M., & Batini, C. (2001a, Oct 03-05). A review of the first cooperative projects in the Italian e-government initiative. Paper presented at the 1st IFIP International Conference on E-Commerce, E-Business, and E-Government (I3E 2001), Zurich, Switzerland.

Mecella, M., & Batini, C. (2001b). Enabling Italian e-government through a cooperative architecture. [Article]. *Computer*, *34*(2), 40. doi:10.1109/2.901166

Mele, V. (2007, Apr 03). Explaining programmes for change: Electronic government policy in Italy (1993-2003). Paper presented at the 11th International Research Symposium on Public Management, Potsdam, Germany.

Miesenberger, K., & Puhretmair, F. (2005, 2005). Help.gv.at - Accessible e-Government in Austria. Paper presented at the 8th European Conference for the Advancement of Assistive Technology, Lille, France.

Millard, J. (2002, Sep 02-06). e-Government strategies: Best practice reports from the European front line. Paper presented at the 1st International Conference on Electronic Government (EGOV 2002), Aix Provence, France.

Mirchandani, D. A., Johnson, J. H., & Joshi, K. (2008). Perspectives of citizens towards e-government in Thailand and Indonesia: A multigroup analysis. [Article]. *Information Systems Frontiers*, *10*(4), 483–497. doi:10.1007/s10796-008-9102-7

Mitra, R. K., & Gupta, M. P. (2008). A contextual perspective of performance assessment in eGovernment: A study of Indian Police Administration. [Article]. *Government Information Quarterly*, *25*(2), 278–302. doi:10.1016/j.giq.2006.03.008

Moody, R. (2007, Sep 03-07). Assessing the role of GIS in e-government: A tale of e-participation in two cities. Paper presented at the 6th International Conference on Electronic Government, Regensburg, Germany.

Moon, M. J., & Norris, D. F. (2005). Does Managerial Orientation Matter? The Adoption of Reinventing Government and E-Government at the Municipal Level. *Information Systems Journal, 15*, 43–60. doi:10.1111/j.1365-2575.2005.00185.x

Mosse, B., & Whitley, E. A. (2009). Critically Classifying: UK E-government Website Benchmarking and the Recasting of the Citizen as Customer. *Information Systems Journal, 19*(2), 149–173. doi:10.1111/j.1365-2575.2008.00299.x

Moukdad, H. (2004, Jul 21-25). Canadian E-government sites: An exploratory study of the political dimensions of disseminating information. Paper presented at the International Conference on Politics and Information Systems, Orlando, FL.

Mousavi, S. A., Pimenidis, E., & Jahankahni, H. (2007, Jun 21-22). e-business models for use in e-Government for developing countries. Paper presented at the 7th European Conference on e-Government (ECEG 2007), The Hague, Netherlands.

Mrugalla, C. (2005, Sep 27-29). The Virtual MailOpening: Usable cryptography in German e-government. Paper presented at the Information Security Solutions Europe Conference, Budapest, Hungary.

Muta, M. (2005), Japanese eGovernment and eCommerce since Dec. 2001, http://www.mana-boo.com/english /egov_japan.htm

Naidoo, G. (2007, Sep 27). e-Government in South Africa: A perspective on issues and challenges. Paper presented at the 3rd International Conference on e-Government, Montreal, Canada.

Ndou, V. D. (2004). E-government for developing countries: Opportunities and challenges. *Electronic Journal of Information Systems in Developing Countries, 18*(1), 1–24.

Neeta, V., & Alka, M. (2010). India's Approach in Constructing One-Stop Solution Towards e-Government. *Journal of E-Governance, 33*(3), 144–156.

Neumann, L., & Sekanina, P. (2007, Jun 21-22). Strengths and weaknesses of the European interoperability framework related to the real application of ICT in e-government. Paper presented at the 7th European Conference on e-Government (ECEG 2007), The Hague, Netherlands.

Ni, A. Y., & Bretschneider, S. (2007). The decision to contract out: A study of contracting for e-government services in state governments. [Article]. *Public Administration Review, 67*(3), 531–544. doi:10.1111/j.1540-6210.2007.00735.x

Ni, A. Y., & Ho, A. T. K. (2005). Challenges in e-government development: Lessons from two information kiosk projects. [Article]. *Government Information Quarterly, 22*(1), 58–74. doi:10.1016/j.giq.2004.10.005

Ni, J., Zhao, X. L., & Zhu, L. J. (2007, Dec 05-06). A Semantic Web Service Oriented Architecture for Chinese e-government. Paper presented at the 4th International Conference on Innovation and Management, Ube, Japan.

Nikolaidou, M., Laskaridis, G., Panayiotaki, A., & Anagnostopoulos, D. (2006, Jul 20-23). What is the affect of providing e-government services based on existing legacy systems and applications? The case of the Hellenic ministry of economy and finance. Paper presented at the 4th Int Conf on Education and Information Syst/2nd Int Conf on Social and Organizational Informatics and Cybernetics/4th Int Conf on Politics and Information Syst, Orlando, FL.

Norris, D. F. (2004, Aug 30-Sep 03). e-government impacts at the American grassroots: An initial assessment. Paper presented at the 3rd International Conference on Electronic Government (EGOV 2004), Zaragoza, Spain.

Northxsouth (2010), Brazil Launches New Version of Their Electronic Government Portal, http://news.northxsouth.com/2010 /03/07/ brazil-launches-new-version-of-their-electronic-government-portal/

OECD. (2009). *Rethinking E-government Services: User-centered Approaches, Paris, France. OECD e-Government Studies, (2010)*. Denmark: Efficient E-Government for Smarter Public Service Delivery.

Ogurlu, Y. (2007, Jun 21-22). e-Government applications and its effects on public service in Turkey. Paper presented at the 7th European Conference on e-Government (ECEG 2007), The Hague, Netherlands.

Oleskow-Szlapka, J., & Przybylska, J. (2008, Sep 08-10). E-government in Poland against the background of other EU countries. Paper presented at the 9th Working Conference on Virtual Enterprises, Poznan, Poland.

Ouyang, Z. H. (2005, Aug 15-17). The epitome of middle city's e-government in China: Quanzhou. Paper presented at the 7th International Conference on Electronic Commerce (ICEC 2005), Xian, Peoples R. China.

Panayiotou, P. (2007, Sep 27). e-Government in Cyprus: The reality and the perspective. Paper presented at the 3rd International Conference on e-Government, Montreal, Canada.

Parent, M., Vandebeek, C. A., & Gemino, A. C. (2005). Building Citizen Trust Through E-Government. *Government Information Quarterly, 22,* 720–736. doi:10.1016/j.giq.2005.10.001

Paris, M. (2005). Local E-government and devolution: Electronic service delivery in Northern Ireland. [Article]. *Local Government Studies, 31*(3), 307–319. doi:10.1080/03003930500095137

Paris, M. (2006). Local e-government and devolution: Electronic service delivery in Northern Ireland. [Article]. *Local Government Studies, 32*(1), 41–53. doi:10.1080/03003930500453450

Parisopoulos, K., Tambouris, E., & Tarabanis, K. (2007, Sep 27). Analyzing and comparing European e-Government strategies. Paper presented at the 3rd International Conference on e-Government, Montreal, Canada.

Peled, A. (2001). Centralization or diffusion? Two tales of online government. [Article]. *Administration & Society, 32*(6), 686–709. doi:10.1177/00953990122019622

Peristeras, V., & Tarabanis, K. (2005, Aug 22-26). Providing Pan-European e-Government services with the use of semantic Web services technologies: A generic process model. Paper presented at the 4th International Conference on Electronic Government (EGOV 2005), Copenhagen, Denmark.

Petrakaki, D. (2008, Aug 10-13). E-government and changes in the public sector: The case of Greece. Paper presented at the International Working Conference on Information Technology in the Service Economy - Challenges and Possibilities for the 21st Century, Toronto, Canada.

Petralkaki, D., Hayes, N., & Introna, L. (2007, Jun 21-22). e-government and the joing-up of the Greek Public Sector. Paper presented at the 7th European Conference on e-Government (ECEG 2007), The Hague, Netherlands.

Pollard, P. (2003, Sep 01-05). Spatial Data Infrastructure and e-government: A case study of the UK. Paper presented at the 2nd International Conference on Electronic Government (EGOV 2003), Prague, Czech Republic.

Povalej, R., Horvatek, R., & Tomicic, M. (2007, Jun 20-22). Trainings courses in eGovernment for civil servants in Croatia: The EU project eGovCRO - An actual overview. Paper presented at the 8th International-Business-Information-Management-Association Conference (IBIMA), Dublin, Ireland.

Pries-Heje, J. (2005, Aug 22-26). eGovernment and structural reform on Bornholm: A case study. Paper presented at the 4th International Conference on Electronic Government (EGOV 2005), Copenhagen, Denmark.

Prosser, A., Guo, Y., Lenhart, J., & Insticc (2006, May 23-27). The attitude towards e-democracy - Empirical evidence from the Viennese population. Paper presented at the 8th International Conference on Enterprise Information Systems (ICEIS 2006), Paphos, Cyprus.

Reddick, C. G. (2004). A two-stage model of e-government growth: Theories and empirical evidence for US cities. [Article]. *Government Information Quarterly, 21*(1), 51–64. doi:10.1016/j.giq.2003.11.004

Reddick, C. G. (2009). Factors that explain the perceived effectiveness of e-government: A survey of United States city government information technology directors. *International Journal of Electronic Government Research, 5*(2), 1–15. doi:10.4018/jegr.2009040101

Reddick, C. G., & Frank, H. A. (2007). The perceived impacts of e-government on US cities: A survey of Florida and Texas City managers. [Article]. *Government Information Quarterly, 24*(3), 576–594. doi:10.1016/j.giq.2006.09.004

Reichstaedter, P. (2004, Oct 27-29). E-delivery - Based on the Austrian eGovernment law. Paper presented at the eChallenges e-2004 Conference, Vienna, Austria.

OECD Report, (2005), OECD Peer Review of E-Government in Denmark, Pre-Publication Draft: Version 2 – 29, September 2005.

NPR Reports, (1993a), From Red Tape to Results: Creating a Government that Works Better and Costs Less.

NPR Reports, (1993b), Improving Customer Service, ICS01: Create Customer-Driven Programs in all Departments and Agencies That Provide Services Directly to the Public.

Resca, A. (2004, May 17-19). How to develop e-Government: The Italian case. Paper presented at the 5th IFIP Interenational Working Conference on Knowledge Management in Electronic Government, Krems, Austria.

Riad, A. M., Fahmy, M. M., & El-Sharkawy, M. A. (2005, Dec). An architecture for Mining the Egyptian E-Government Network Traffic for Intrusion Detection. Paper presented at the ITI 3rd International Conference on Information and Communications Technology (ICICT 2005), Cairo, Egypt.

Riedl, R. (2004, Aug 22). Rethinking trust and confidence in European E-government - Linking the public sector with post-modern society. Paper presented at the 4th International Conference on E-Commerce, E-Business and E-Government held at the 18th World Computer Congress, Toulouse, France.

Riley, T. B. (2002), Government and the Invisible Current of Change, http://www.electronicgov.net.

Riquelme, H., & Buranasantikul, P. (2004, Aug 30-Sep 03). e-government in Australia: A citizen's perspective. Paper presented at the 3rd International Conference on Electronic Government (EGOV 2004), Zaragoza, Spain.

Robin, G., Andrew, G., & Sasha, M. (2009). How Responsive is E-government? Evidence from Australia and New Zealand. *Government Information Quarterly, 26*(1), 69–74. doi:10.1016/j.giq.2008.02.002

Robins, G., & Burn, J. (2001, Oct 03-05). Building value into e-government: An Australian case study. Paper presented at the 1st IFIP International Conference on E-Commerce, E-Business, and E-Government (I3E 2001), Zurich, Switzerland.

Rosiyadi, D. Nuryani, & Waskita, D. (2007, Sep 27). The development of e-Government framework based on open source in Indonesia. Paper presented at the 3rd International Conference on e-Government, Montreal, Canada.

Ross, P., Hutton, N., Peng, L. M., & Lei, J. (2004). Revolutionary e-Government strategies across Asia-Pacific. [Article]. Alcatel Telecommunications Review(3), 332-337.

Rotthier, S. (2004, Aug 30-Sep 03). e-Government policies, strategies and implementation: e-Government in the federal country Belgium. Paper presented at the 3rd International Conference on Electronic Government (EGOV 2004), Zaragoza, Spain.

Rupp, C. (2004, Oct 27-29). The Austrian eGovernment initiative - Good practice in European eAdministration. Paper presented at the eChallenges e-2004 Conference, Vienna, Austria.

Ryan, S. M. (1994). Uncle-Sam Online - Government Information on the Internet. [Article]. *Communication Education, 43*(2), 151–158. doi:10.1080/03634529409378972

Sabucedo, L. A., & Anido, L. (2004, Aug 30-Sep 03). A review of current e-government initiatives in Spain. Paper presented at the 3rd International Conference on Electronic Government (EGOV 2004), Zaragoza, Spain.

Saebo, O. (2006, Aug 31-Sep 02). How to identify objectives and genres in E-Democracy projects: Learning from an action case study. Paper presented at the 15th International Conference on Information Systems Development, Budapest, Hungary.

SAFAD. (2000), The 24/7 Agency Criteria for 24/7 Agencies in the Networked Public Administration, The Swedish Agency For Administrative Development Publication Service, Box 2280, SE-103 17 Stockholm, Sweden, http://www.statskontoret.se/upload/ Publikationer/2000/200041.pdf.

Sandoval, R., & Gil-García, J. R. (2005). Assessing e-government evolution in Mexico: A preliminary analysis of the state portals. Paper presented at the 2005 Information Resources Management Association International Conference, San Diego, CA.

Santos, J. M. V., & Alonso, A. I. (2006, Jun 12-14). E-democracy and citizen's empowerment: a case study of the city of Madrid. Paper presented at the 2nd International Conference on the Internet Society, New Forest, England.

Sardy, S., Asvial, M., & Jamal, A. (2007, Jul 12-15). E-government and FOSS policies in Indonesia. Paper presented at the International Multi-Conference on Society, Cybernetics and Informatics, Orlando, FL.

Schedler, K., & Summermatter, L. (2007). Customer Orientation in Electronic Government: Motives and Effects. *Government Information Quarterly, 24*, 291–311. doi:10.1016/j.giq.2006.05.005

Schuppan, T. (2009). E-Government in developing countries: Experiences from sub-Saharan Africa. *Government Information Quarterly, 26*(1), 118–127. doi:10.1016/j.giq.2008.01.006

Schware, R., & Deane, A. (2003). Deploying E-government Program the Strategic Importance of 'I' Before 'E'. *Info, 5*(4), 10–19. doi:10.1108/14636690310495193

Schweighofer, E. (2003, Sep 01-05). E-government in the European Commission. Paper presented at the 2nd International Conference on Electronic Government (EGOV 2003), Prague, Czech Republic.

Seaton, J. (2005). The Scottish Parliament and e-democracy. [Article]. *Aslib Proceedings, 57*(4), 333–337. doi:10.1108/00012530510612068

Shan, Z. G., Li, X. Y., Wang, Z. M., & Ning, J. J. (2004, Sep 13-15). Policies and practice of E-government construction in China. Paper presented at the IEEE International Conference on E-Commerce Technology for Dynamic E-Business, Beijing, Peoples R. China.

Shareef, M. A., Kumar, U., & Kumar, V. (2008). The E-government and E-governance: Conceptual Alignment or Subtle Difference. *International Journal of Knowledge, Culture, and Change Management, 8*(1), 129–136.

Shareef, M. A., Kumar, U., Kumar, V., & Dwivedi, Y. K. (2010c). (in press). E-government Adoption Model (GAM): Differing Service Maturity Levels. *Government Information Quarterly*.

Shareef, M. A., Kumar, V., Kumar, U., Chowdhury, A. H., & Misra, S. C. (2010a). (in press). E-Government Implementation Perspective: Setting Objective and Strategy. *International Journal of Electronic Government Research, 6*(1). doi:10.4018/jegr.2010102005

Sharifi, H., & Zarei, B. (2004). An adaptive approach for implementing e-government in IR Iran. [Article]. *Journal of Government Information, 30*(5-6), 600–619. doi:10.1016/j.jgi.2004.10.005

Shi, Y., & Ieee (2007, Aug 27-29). Improving e-government services should start with domain names: A longitudinal study of chinese e-government domain names. Paper presented at the IEEE International Conference on Service Operations and Logistics and Informatics, Philadelphia, PA.

Shi, Y. Q. (2006). E-government web site accessibility in Australia and China - A longitudinal study. [Article]. *Social Science Computer Review, 24*(3), 378–385. doi:10.1177/0894439305283707

Siegfried, T. (2002, Sep 02-06). The experience of German local communities with e-government - Results of the MEDIA@ Komm project. Paper presented at the 1st International Conference on Electronic Government (EGOV 2002), Aix Provence, France.

Simurina, J., Hruska, D., & Markovic, M. (2007, Dec 14-16). E-government in Croatia. Paper presented at the 6th WSEAS International Conference on E-ACTIVITIES, Puerto de la Cruz, Spain.

Singh, S., Lubbe, S., Naidoo, G., & Klopper, R. (2007, Jun 21-22). Towards a hypothetical e-government solution: A South African perspective. Paper presented at the 7th European Conference on e-Government (ECEG 2007), The Hague, Netherlands.

SITA (Pty) Ltd. (2002). Government experience in South Africa. Retrieved from http://www.sita.co.zae.

Snavely, E. C. (2002). e-Government evolution: The Richardson, Texas, experience. Government Finance Review, 34-36.

Sorrentino, M., & Ferro, E. (2008, Aug 31-Sep 05). Does the Answer to eGovernment Lie in Intermunicipal Collaboration? An Exploratory Italian Case Study. Paper presented at the 7th International Conference on Electronic Government, Turin, Italy.

Sou, G., & Cstp (2004, Nov 02-06). e-Government vis-a-vis logistics industry in the Hong Kong special administrative region. Paper presented at the World Engineers Convention 2004, Shanghai, Peoples R. China.

Soufi, B., & Maguire, M. (2007, Jul 22-27). Achieving usability within E-government web sites illustrated by a case study evaluation. Paper presented at the Symposium on Human Interface and the Management of Information held at HCI International 2007, Beijing, Peoples R. China.

Spahni, D. (2003, Sep 01-05). URN: Technology - A building block of the Swiss e-government platform. Paper presented at the 2nd International Conference on Electronic Government (EGOV 2003), Prague, Czech Republic.

Spremic, M., & Brzica, H. (2008, Apr 06-08). E-Government and its application in the Republic of Croatia. Paper presented at the WSEAS Conference on Recent Advances in Systems, Communications and Computers, Hangzhou, Peoples R. China.

Sriramesh, K., & Rivera-Sanchez, M. (2006). E-government in a corporatist, communitarian society: the case of Singapore. [Article]. *New Media & Society, 8*(5), 707–730. doi:10.1177/1461444806065661

Srivastava, S. C., & Teo, T. S. H. (2006, Jul 06-09). E-government payoffs: Evidence from cross-country data. Paper presented at the 10th Pacific Asia Conference on Information Systems, Kuala Lumpur, Malaysia.

Stefan, V., & Stefan, A. (2008, May 04-07). Live services for citizens with live technologies - e-payment in Romania as first step to an effective e-Government. Paper presented at the 4th International Conference on Web Information Systems and Technologies, Funchal, Portugal.

Steyaert, J. (2000). Local Government Online and the Role of the Resident. *Social Science Computer Review, 18*, 3–16. doi:10.1177/089443930001800101

Stokes, J., & Clegg, S. (2003). Once Upon a Time in the Bureaucracy: Power and Public Sector Management. *Organization, 9*(2), 225–247.

Streib, G., & Navarro, I. (2006). Citizen demand for interactive e-government - The case of Georgia consumer services. [Article]. *American Review of Public Administration, 36*(3), 288–300. doi:10.1177/0275074005283371

Strejcek, G., & Theil, M. (2003). Technology push, legislation pull? E-government in the European Union. [Article]. *Decision Support Systems, 34*(3), 305–313. doi:10.1016/S0167-9236(02)00123-9

Sukhbaatar, B., Odgerel, U., & Ieee (2005, Nov 09-10). A study on e-government policy in Mongolia. Paper presented at the 6th Asia-Pacific Symposium on Information and Telecommunication Technologies, Yangon, Myanmar.

Sullivan, S. J. (2004, Apr 20-23). Electronic records management (ERM) electronic government (E-Gov) initiative transferring permanent electronic records to the national archives of the United States. Paper presented at the 1st IS&T Archiving Conference, San Antonio, TX.

Susanto, T. D., & Goodwin, R. (2006, Jun 12-14). Opportunity and overview of SMS-based e-government in developing countries. Paper presented at the 2nd International Conference on the Internet Society, New Forest, England.

Sweisi, N. A., & Adams, C. (2007, Jun 20-22). Proposed framework to manage the change to e-Government (lessons from Libya). Paper presented at the 8th International-Business-Information-Management-Association Conference (IBIMA), Dublin, Ireland.

Sweisi, N. A., Eldresi, F. Y., & Adams, C. (2007, Sep 27). e-government services to support vaccination programmes: Libya, a successful implementation. Paper presented at the 3rd International Conference on e-Government, Montreal, Canada.

Tambouris, E., & Gorilas, S. (2003, Sep 01-05). Evaluation of an e-democracy platform for European cities. Paper presented at the 2nd International Conference on Electronic Government (EGOV 2003), Prague, Czech Republic.

Tan, C. W. (2005). Managing stakeholder interests in e-government implementation: Lessons learned from a Singapore e-government project. [Article]. *Journal of Global Information Management, 13*(1), 31–53. doi:10.4018/jgim.2005010102

Tan, C. W., & Pan, S. L. (2003). Managing e-transformation in the public sector: an e-government study of the Inland Revenue Authority of Singapore (IRAS). [Article]. *European Journal of Information Systems, 12*(4), 269–281. doi:10.1057/palgrave.ejis.3000479

Tang, Z. W., Jia, X. M., & Alfred, U. (2007, May 26-27). Citizen oriented e-government planning and case study at county level. Paper presented at the 6th Wuhan International Conference on E-Business, Wuhan, PEOPLES R. CHINA.

Tang, Z. W., Zhao, S. H., & Chen, L. L. (2006, May 27-28). The analysis of the structure of e-government theory system in China. Paper presented at the 5th Wuhan International Conference on E-Business, Wuhan, PEOPLES R. CHINA.

Tavares, M. (2001), Brazilian Policy for Electronic Government, Federal Republic Of Brazil Ministry Of Planning, Budget And Management, Constituent Units and E-Government, organized by The Forum of Federations, Montreal.

Teodosio, A. S. S. (2002, 2002). Participatory budgeting and e-democracy in Brazil: new strategies, new challenges in the city management. Paper presented at the 2nd International Conference on the Sustainable City, Segovia, Spain.

Thomas, C. A., LeBlanc, P. D., Mbarika, V. W., & Meso, P. (2004, May 23-26). E-government in Africa: A new era for better governance in sub-Saharan Africa. Paper presented at the International Conference of the Information-Resources-Management-Association, New Orleans, LA.

Thompson, C. S. (2002). Enlisting on-line residents: Expanding the boundaries of e-government in a Japanese rural township. [Article]. *Government Information Quarterly, 19*(2), 173–188. doi:10.1016/S0740-624X(02)00093-X

Tiglao, N. M. C., Manuela, W. S., & Verdillo, R. C. (2008, Jan 04-06). Barriers to e-government maturity: the Philippine experience. Paper presented at the 9th International-Business-Information-Management-Association Conference (IBIMA), Marrakech, Morocco.

Titah, R., & Barki, H. (2005). *E-government Adoption and Acceptance: A Literature Review*. HEC Montréal.

Tolbert, C. J., Mossberger, K., & McNeal, R. (2008). Institutions, policy innovation, and e-government in the American states. [Article]. *Public Administration Review, 68*(3), 549–563. doi:10.1111/j.1540-6210.2008.00890.x

Torres, L., Pina, V., & Acerete, B. (2004, Jul 21-25). Gauging e-government evolution in EU municipalities. Paper presented at the International Conference on Politics and Information Systems, Orlando, FL.

Torres, L., Pina, V., & Acerete, B. (2005). E-government developments on delivering public services among EU cities. [Article]. *Government Information Quarterly, 22*(2), 217–238. doi:10.1016/j.giq.2005.02.004

Torres, L., Pina, V., & Royo, S. (2005). E-government and the transformation of public administrations in EU countries - Beyond NPM or just a second wave of reforms? [Article]. *Online Information Review, 29*(5), 531–553. doi:10.1108/14684520510628918

Trusler, J. (2003, Sep 01-05). South African e-government policy and practices: A framework to close the gap. Paper presented at the 2nd International Conference on Electronic Government (EGOV 2003), Prague, Czech Republic.

Trusler, J. (2003). South African e-government policy and practices: A framework to close the gap. In R. Traunmüller (Ed.), EGOV 2003 (LNCS 2739, pp. 504-507).

Tseng, P. T. Y., Yen, D. C., Hung, Y. C., & Wang, N. C. F. (2008). To explore managerial issues and their implications on e-Government deployment in the public sector: Lessons from Taiwan's Bureau of Foreign Trade. [Article]. *Government Information Quarterly, 25*(4), 734–756. doi:10.1016/j.giq.2007.06.003

Tung, L. L., & Rieck, O. (2005). Adoption of electronic government services among business organizations in Singapore. [Article]. *The Journal of Strategic Information Systems, 14*(4), 417–440. doi:10.1016/j.jsis.2005.06.001

Turner, M., & Desloges, C. (2002). Strategies and framework for government on-line: A Canadian experience. Paper presented at the World Bank E-Government Learning Workshop, Washington, DC.

United Nations. (2006). *Compendium of Innovative E-government Practices (Vol. II)*. Department of Economic & Social Affairs.

Vahtera, A. (2008, Sep 24-26). e-government in the Finnish early childhood education: An analysis of current status and challenges. Paper presented at the 8th IFIP International Conference on e-Business, e-Service, and e-Society, Tokyo, Japan.

van der Vyver, B. (2007, Jun 20-22). A South African case study into the use of public Internet facilities for participation in e-democracy and e-governance. Paper presented at the 8th International-Business-Information-Management-Association Conference (IBIMA), Dublin, Ireland.

van Deursen, A., van Dijk, J., & Ebbers, W. (2006, Sep 04-08). Why e-government usage lags behind: Explaining the gap between potential and actual usage of electronic public services in the Netherlands. Paper presented at the 5th International Conference on Electronic Government (EGOV 2006), Cracow, Poland.

Van Dijk, Jan A.G.M., Peters, O., & Ebbers, W. (2008). Explaining the Acceptance and Use of Government Internet Services: A Multivariate Analysis of 2006 Survey Data in the Netherlands. *Government Information Quarterly, 25*(3), 379–399. doi:10.1016/j.giq.2007.09.006

van Overeem, A., Witters, J., & Peristeras, V. (2006, Jul 20-23). Semantic Interoperability in pan-European eGovernment services. Paper presented at the 4th Int Conf on Education and Information Syst/2nd Int Conf on Social and Organizational Informatics and Cybernetics/4th Int Conf on Politics and Information Syst, Orlando, FL.

van Velsen, L., van der Geest, T., ter Hedde, M., & Derks, W. (2008, Aug 31-Sep 05). Engineering User Requirements for e-Government Services: A Dutch Case Study. Paper presented at the 7th International Conference on Electronic Government, Turin, Italy.

Varavithya, W., & Esichaikul, V. (2003, Sep 01-05). The development of electronic government: A case study of Thailand. Paper presented at the 2nd International Conference on Electronic Government (EGOV 2003), Prague, Czech Republic.

Vergnolle, S., Amin, N., & Pritchard, H. (2007, Jun 21-22). Review and contrast of the French and German approaches to e-democracy. Paper presented at the 7th European Conference on e-Government (ECEG 2007), The Hague, Netherlands.

Vice President Albert Gore's National Performance Review, (1994), NPR Reports.

Virili, F. (2001, Sep 03-07). The Italian e-government action plan: from gaining efficiency to rethinking goverment. Paper presented at the 12th International Conference on Database and Expert Systems Applications (DEXA), Munich, Germany.

Viscusi, G., Thevenet, L. H., & Salinesi, C. (2008, Jun 16-20). Strategic alignment in the context of e-services - An empirical investigation of the INSTAL approach using the Italian eGovernment initiative case study. Paper presented at the 20th International Conference on Advanced Information Systems Engineering, Montpellier, France.

Wagner, C., Cheung, K., Lee, F., & Ip, R. (2003). Enhancing e-government in developing countries: managing knowledge through virtual communities. *The Electronic Journal on Information Systems in Developing Countries, 14*(4), 1–20.

Wang, S., Kim, A., & Shin, H. K. (2007, Aug 26-27). A research on multilateral cooperation system of public crisis management based on the e-government in China. Paper presented at the 2nd International Workshop on Information Systems for Crisis Response and Management, Harbin, Peoples R. China.

Wauters, P. (2006). Benchmarking e-government policy within the e-Europe programme. [Article]. *Aslib Proceedings, 58*(5), 389–403. doi:10.1108/00012530610692348

Weerakkody, V., & Dhillon, G. (2008). Moving from e-government to t-government: A study of process reengineering challenges in a UK local authority context. *International Journal of Electronic Government Research, 4*(4), 1–16. doi:10.4018/jegr.2008100101

Weerakkody, V., Jones, S., & Olsen, E. (2007). E-government: a comparison of strategies in local authorities in the UK and Norway. *International Journal of Electronic Business, 5*(2), 141–159. doi:10.1504/IJEB.2007.012970

Wei, X. J., & Zhao, J. (2005, Aug 15-17). Citizens' requirement analysis in chinese e-government. Paper presented at the 7th International Conference on Electronic Commerce (ICEC 2005), Xian, Peoples R. China.

Welp, Y. (2007, Mar 14-15). Latin America in the e-government era. Analysis of the introduction of new technologies to the improvement of democracy and government. Paper presented at the International Conference on Direct Democracy in Latin America, Buenos Aires, Argentina.

Wen, J., & Cheng, L. H. (2007, Aug 05-09). Innovation in e-government initiatives: New website service interfaces and market creation - The Taiwan experience. Paper presented at the Conference of the Portland-International-Center-for-Management-of-Engineering-and-Technology (PICMET 2007), Portland, OR.

Wescott, C. G. (2004, Jul 21-25). e-government in the Asia-Pacific region: Progress and challenges. Paper presented at the International Conference on Politics and Information Systems, Orlando, FL.

Westbrook, L. (2008). E-government support for people in crisis: An evaluation of police department website support for domestic violence survivors using "person-in-situation" information need analysis. [Review]. *Library & Information Science Research, 30*(1), 22–38. doi:10.1016/j.lisr.2007.07.004

Wiesmaier, A., Lippert, M., Karatsiolis, V., Raptis, G., & Buchmann, J. (2005, Jun 20-23). An evaluated certification services system for the German national root CA - Legally binding and trustworthy transactions in e-business and e-Government. Paper presented at the International Conference on E-Business, Enterprise Information Systems, E-Government and Outsourcing, Las Vegas, NV.

Williams, C. (2007, Sep 27). 24-7 government, the permanent campaign, and e-democracy: An analysis of Massachusetts governor Deval Patrick's interactive website. Paper presented at the 3rd International Conference on e-Government, Montreal, Canada.

Williamson, A., Dawson, A., & Barton, J. (2004, Jul 21-25). ASPECT: Digital election ephemera to support e-democracy in Scotland. Paper presented at the International Conference on Politics and Information Systems, Orlando, FL.

Xiong, J. A. (2006). Current status and needs of Chinese e-government users. [Article]. *The Electronic Library, 24*(6), 747–762. doi:10.1108/02640470610714198

Xu, W. H. (2006, May 27-28). Local e-government in China: A study in the context of administration reformation. Paper presented at the 5th Wuhan International Conference on E-Business, Wuhan, Peoples R. China.

Yammine, A. (2002, Sep 02-06). A new approach to the phenomenon of e-Government: Analysis of the public discourse on e-Government in Switzerland. Paper presented at the 1st International Conference on Electronic Government (EGOV 2002), Aix Provence, France.

Yang, B., & Shen, F. (2002, May 23-26). E-government: The case study of Nanhai's e-government practice. Paper presented at the International Conference on E-Business (ICEB2002), Beijing, Peoples R China.

Yang, F., & Wu, M. H. (2006, May 27-28). RE-SVM: Improving the safety in e-government of China by information retrieval based on SVM. Paper presented at the 5th Wuhan International Conference on E-Business, Wuhan, Peoples R. China.

Yang, W. (2003, Nov 28-30). Study on the Chinese reform and e-government adaptability. Paper presented at the International Conference on Management of e-Commerce and e-Government, Nanchang, Peoples R. China.

Yildiz, M. (2007). Impact of the international organizatons 39 on the e-government policies of Turkiye. [Article]. *Amme Idaresi Dergisi, 40*(2), 39.

Yun, H., Guo, S. J., & Liu, Q. Y. (2005, Jun 04-05). Empirical analysis of the e-government development level of Chinese foreign trade and economic cooperation. Paper presented at the 4th Wuhan International Conference on E-Business - Global Business Interface, Wuhan, Peoples R. China.

Zahan, E., & Costake, N. (2007, Sep 27). Priorities for e-Government in European transforming countries. Example of Romania. Paper presented at the 3rd International Conference on e-Government, Montreal, CANADA.

Zhang, J. H. (2002). Will the government 'serve the people'? The development of Chinese e-government. [Article]. *New Media & Society, 4*(2), 163–184. doi:10.1177/14614440222226325

Zhang, P. Z., Xu, F. F., Jiang, L. Q., & Ge, R. Y. (2005, Aug 15-17). G2C e-government: Shanghai social security and citizen services. Paper presented at the 7th International Conference on Electronic Commerce (ICEC 2005), Xian, Peoples R. China.

Zhao, X. Q., & Ye, J. (2008, Aug 04-05). Analysis of the E-government Operation Services of China in the Present Situation. Paper presented at the International Colloquium on Computing, Communication, Control, and Management, Guangzhou, Peoples R. China.

Zheng, Y. X., Lei, L., & Hai, W. (2007, Jul 23-27). State-based process description model in Chinese E-government affair system. Paper presented at the 31st Annual International Computer Software and Applications Conference, Beijing, Peoples R. China.

Ziedi, M. J., & Azizi, M. Z. (2008, Jan 04-06). E-government and business: G to B (Government to Business) - Contribution of e-government to the performance of Tunisian businesses. Paper presented at the 9th International-Business-Information-Management-Association Conference (IBIMA), Marrakech, Morocco.

Zobel, R. (2003, May 30-31). E-government: European commission policies and activities. Paper presented at the International Conference On Line Citizenship, Venice, ITALY.

KEY TERMS AND DEFINITIONS

Adoption of EG: It is the acceptance and use of EG by its stakeholders with satisfaction.

Citizen: Residents of a country who use government service and information.

Development Capability: It is the resource based ability of a country to meet targeted goals and deliver justified values to stakeholders through the development of e-government.

E-government (EG): EG is government's service and information offered through the use of ICT for citizens, business organizations, and other stakeholders of government. It provides higher efficiency and effectiveness in terms of service quality, time, and cost.

Implementation of EG: After setting initial missions of EG, different governments reform and reengineer public administration and develop an EG system through the use of ICT to achieve certain long term targets.

Information and Communication Technology (ICT): ICT can be defined as the modern computer and Internet based technology used for managing and processing information in different public and private sectors.

Objective of EG: It is the initial target which a government sets to achieve through the development of an EG system.

Public Administration: It is the management of government service and information conducted through governments departments.

Section 2
Strategic Development of E-Government:
Interoperability and Capability

Chapter 4

Interoperability in E-Government:
Select Aspects of Personal Information Integration

Rakhi Tripathi
Indian Institute of Technology Delhi, India

V. Ranga Rao
Govt. of N.C.T of Delhi, India

M. P. Gupta
Indian Institute of Technology Delhi, India

ABSTRACT

Integration and interoperability are critical issues for successful development of one-stop portal for the government. This issue involves integration of information among departments of government both vertically and horizontally. The following paper focuses on Personal Information Integration of citizens which is one of the aspects for achieving interoperability within the departments of government in India. Various challenges, benefits, and key issues of sharing personal information for one-stop portal are discussed. Potential solutions to overcome the challenges are detailed in the paper. In-depth research conducted through a set of interviews with high-ranking government officials forms the basis for the chapter.

INTRODUCTION

One of the key objectives under the e-government agenda is to achieve a one-stop government portal (Gupta et. al, 2005) and (Dias and Rafael, 2007) so that the citizens, businesses and other authorities have 24 hours access to public services from their home, their offices or even on the move. India has announced development of an India portal under National E-governance Plan approved in 2006. The objective is to integrate and provide access to government services to the citizens (NeGP, 2007). The portal will not only be a mirror for the

DOI: 10.4018/978-1-60960-848-4.ch004

Government and its departments but will also be very helpful and easily accessible for the citizens.

At present most of the Government departments; subordinate offices and government funded autonomous departments have their own websites but none of them have achieved a one-stop portal. The reason behind this is the lack of integration and interoperability of information among different departments. The term Interoperability has been defined by different organizations and authors: The European Commission (2003) has defined interoperability as "the means by which the inter-linking of systems, information and ways of working, whether within or between administrations, nationally or across Europe, or with the enterprise sector, occurs". Interoperability is the ability of government organizations to share information and integrate information and business processes by use of common standards and work practices (State Services Commission, 2007). According to the Government Interoperability Framework (e-GIF, 2004) and Government CIO (2007), if the coherent exchange of information and services between systems is achieved then the systems can be regarded as truly interoperable. When information and services are provided to and accepted between systems and organizations, they are said to inter-operate. Further, Scholl and Klischewski (2007) define integration as "the forming of a (temporary or permanent) larger unit of government entities for the purpose of merging processes [and systems] and sharing information".

Economic benefits of interoperability result in lower transaction costs typically utilizing standardized processes. Yet, most integration and interoperation efforts face serious challenges and limitations. Exchanges of information and services are fragmented and complex, plagued by technical and organizational problems (Gouscos et al., 2007).

A distinction should be made between interoperability and integration. Integration is the forming of a larger unit of government entities, temporary or permanent, for the purpose of merging pro-

cesses and/or sharing information. Interoperation in e-Government occurs whenever independent or heterogeneous information systems or their components controlled by different jurisdictions, administrations, or external partners work together (efficiently and effectively) in a predefined and agreed-upon fashion. E-Government interoperability is the technical capability for e-Government interoperation (Scholl & Klischewski, 2007).

For interoperability both horizontal and vertical integration forms the basis. Integration can be defined as "the forming of a (temporary or permanent) larger unit of government entities for the purpose of merging processes [and systems] and sharing information" (Klischewski & Scholl, 2006). Integration can be approached in various manners and at various levels (Vernadat, 1996) for example: (i) physical integration (computer networks), ii) application integration (integration of software applications and database systems) and (iii) business integration (co-ordination of functions that manage, control and monitor business processes).

As shown in Figure 1, there are projects going on in India on integrating the e-government services at national level, state level as well as local level (Bhatnagar et. al, 2007).

- **At national level:** MCA 21, Income Tax online and Customs on-line are working on providing a one-stop portal for their respective departments. The current objective of these projects is to integrate their departments vertically. This will help the citizens to use the services at one go.

- **At state level (IIM-A, 2007):** Property registration (CARD, KAVERI, SARITA); Bill payment (eSeva: One stop shop for many services in Andhra Pradesh have been operational for three years); Land records (BHOOMI: Karnataka); eProcurement (Online tendering in Andhra Pradesh); SmartGov (AP); Khajane (Computerization of treasuries in Karnataka). Achieving one-

Figure 1. Deployment of e-government projects in India (Source: http://www.hindustantimes.com/News-Feed/india/E-governance-programme-for-323-cities/Article1-246358.aspx and http://www.timesofindia. indiatimes.com/)

E-governance programme for 323 cities

HT Correspondent
New Delhi, September 4

THE GOVERNMENT has approved an ambitious programme for 323 cities in the country enabling citizens to register and then receive death and birth certificates, pay property tax, water and power-bills and submit building plans online, anywhere anytime.

ARC recommends e-governance of passport processing system
http://timesofindia.indiatimes.com/
25 Jan 2009, 0047 hrs IST, Bhaskar Roy, TNN
NEW DELHI: The dream of a hassle-free, online passport processing system has got a major boost with the Administrative Reforms Commission making a strong pitch for e-governance of the procedure. What is more, the latest ARC report has made a strong recommendation for integrating the method of issuing passports with the online police database and computerized records of citizens. The 11th report of the Commission released on Saturday, in fact, visualized the transformation of the crawling file culture into total e-governance by 2020.

stop portal at state level will help the citizens to use the online services offered by Government more efficiently.

- **At local level:** Municipality (Ahemdabad, Vijyawada) - 'One Stop Civic Shop' for availing various civic services in the Municipal Corporation premises; Lokvani (Sitapur) - Service Oriented e-Governance system which attempts to provide efficient and responsive online services to the common people and seeks to increase transparency and accountability in Government procedures (Ministry of IT) ; Rural Telecenters: e-Chaupal, Akshaya (district wide e-literacy project of Kerala Government), n-Logue, Drishtee. At local level, where the citizens are dependent on Government services most, availability of interoperability in one-stop portal will connect the local level to national level.

Further, substantial growth has also been seen globally in achieving a one-stop portal. The following countries are working towards one-stop web portal for their respective Governments:

- **The Government of Singapore:** (http://www.gov.sg/) a portal where citizens can access government departments, get information and carry out transactions.
- **The Government of USA:** (FirstGov.gov) is intended to serve as a portal to all of the federal government's publicly available, on-line information and services and links the government's more than 20,000 web sites and 500 millions of web pages.
- **United Kingdom:** (http://www.e-envoy.gov.uk) has launched e-Envoy that covers all public services available online by 2005 with the objective of setting "standards of service" and also involve the citizen in the decision making process.
- **The Government of Austria:** initiative towards an e-Government portal (www.help.gv.at) considers life-events in design where the services offered in a one-stop government should be easily understandable for any citizen or business partner.
- **The Dutch Portal:** (www.government.nl) allows citizens to customize the site by

postal code; this enables local and regional information to be displayed upon request.

There are several aspects of interoperability out of which one is personal information. At present Government of India has an inventory of more than a million different types of forms in different languages used for various transactions to improve efficiency and citizen services. Citizen's Personal information (Name, address, data of birth, place of birth etc.) is captured and stored by the departments separately. The personal information of a citizen is organized by various applications (e.g., email, spreadsheets). Also, most of the Government operations employ paperbound processes. Hence, finding a piece of information is mostly done manually. This creates multiple inconveniences for citizens e.g. they need to seek assistance at multiple Government offices and also stand in long queues.

The solution i.e. providing services and information to citizens through multiple channels under single window requires integration of Citizens' Personal Information among the public and private sector departments. Integration drives efficiency and effectiveness gains through better use of data, information or technology (especially across Government departments). It also improves security and reduces fraud.

Implementation of the Personal Information integration is a solution for integrated service delivery and for other services like G2E, G2G and G2B among the departments. Not an easy task to implement in the Government sector. But it is certainly a goal —A. Singh, IT Director, Indian Railways.

The paper is organized as follows: "Personal Information Integration" discusses the need for personal information integration and talks about the maturity level of department for data integration. Challenges and selected solutions for personal information integration are stated in "Challenges

with Personal Information Integration" and "Overcoming the Challenges" respectively. "Examples" gives the examples of few Government departments where integration is required and how beneficial it will be to have the information in departments interoperable. Expected benefits from personal information integration are listed in "Expected Benefits." Finally, concluding remarks are stated in "Concluding Remarks."

PERSONAL INFORMATION INTEGRATION

The increasing complexity of handling personal information by various Government departments has raised the issue of data sharing and integration. Earlier the key problem was the lack of sufficient standards and protocols, resulting in the development of proprietary data formats for transmitting personal information between Government departments. Also, transferring files in incompatible data formats create difficulty in sharing and exchanging data.

Personal Information Integration will help the Government departments to communicate smoothly with each other. This will not only share key information within departments but will be efficient for the citizens as they need not have to go to various departments or wait in long queues. Personal information integration requires data integration. Before adopting any framework for data integration, an estimation of maturity is required for the departments.

Concerns of Data Integration

- **The data domain:** What data does the department collect? How is it stored? What formal databases does it have?
- **The information system domain:** What is the information system environment of the department? What platforms, languages

and protocols are being used? What are the security measures taken?

- **The Decision support domain:** Is there an executive information system for the department? Do the end-users understand basic decision support system concepts? What decision support tools are in place?
- **The People domain:** Who are the end-users? Are they computer literate? What is their level of training? Where are they located?
- **The Privacy domain:** Privacy is more than confidentiality and security. It can't be an afterthought. It has to be built into the system from the outset. Indeed, privacy concerns may well determine how you build these systems and maybe even whether you build them at all.
- **Business Process Re-Engineering domain:** Manual processes of Citizen's Personal Information needs to be re-engineered among the Government in order to leverage maximum benefit.
- **Accessibility domain:** How are the citizens accessing the benefits of data sharing?
- **Local Languages:** Is the Citizen's Personal Information available in all Local languages (example: Indian Languages like Hindi, Telugu, Tamil, Bengali and Urdu etc.)?
- **Future Accessibility:** Is their compatibility with the existing technology?

The reason behind estimating maturity for the departments for data integration is to assess the current position of a department in terms of level of integration. Higher the level of data integration maturity, lesser resources will be required to achieve personal information integration and vice versa. Moreover, this will further help the government officials to focus on the relevant factors involved with data integration.

CHALLENGES WITH PERSONAL INFORMATION INTEGRATION

Personal information Integration is critical to the center and state government departments than any other sector. Political pressures, budget cuts and security issues bring many new and difficult challenges discussed below.

- **Incompatible Systems:** In Integrated Service Delivery (ISD) particularly in case of sharing personal information of a citizen among various Government departments, the citizen's information is created, managed and maintained by the individual departments separately. Also in a government environment, many different departments maintain citizen information on a variety of incompatible systems, making data sharing almost impossible. For example, a residential address might be stored in 10 unconnected computer systems.
- **Different forms or biometric data:** Generally many departments of Government would collect personal information of citizen through different forms (online/offline) or biometric data like thumb/finger impressions or signatures captured through various biometric devices on different occasions according to their needs. Since it is managed and maintained by the individual departments it may vary from one department to another. For instance, one department is capturing name and age and another department is capturing name as first name, middle name, last name and age as the date of birth. It means same citizen information is available with multiple departments and they are maintaining it separately.

Since separate databases are created for the same citizen at different point of time by different departments it has now become difficult for the

Government to modify the citizen information with a single click.

- **Different languages:** Another major challenge is how to integrate Personal Information, if different departments are using different languages (English, Hindi, Urdu, Teluguand Tamil etc.) for different application forms (online/Offline).

- **Diverse data sources:** Many Government departments capture Personal Information from wide variety of sources and formats like Databases, flat files, spread sheets and word formats. It can be difficult to locate, identify and select the data that needs to be extracted, cleaned and transformed.

- **Undefined polices:** Critical Personal Information often gets scattered across multiple departments making it difficult to access. Inconsistent standards for data, completeness, formats and security exist. Undefined polices for data access remain.

- **Unable to deliver reliable data:** The integrated personal information should be clean, consistent, accurate and reliable. It can be used to have a single consistent view of a citizen. But challenges to the Government are identifying, validating, collecting and consolidating the correct data among multiple departments.

- **Lack of appropriate methodology:** The main challenge to the Government is what methodology should be adopted to create and manage the citizen's personal information (similar to the employee's personal information of a department) so that it will be updated at one place. As far as citizen point of view, it becomes extremely difficult for them to update their details as and when a change occurs. If departments are maintaining the same citizen information separately (for an instance change of address) then he/she has to provide the same information to all departments repeatedly.

As long as the departments are not sharing their data it is very difficult for the government to create reports, analyze and forecast.

Government-led IT projects often suffer from institutional constraints (weak planning management and commitment etc.), human resources constraints and problems of technical adaptation. The success on a large scale often proves elusive for a number of reasons: First, some projects succeed largely because of the enthusiasm and competence of the initiators, a factor that cannot always be guaranteed. Second, the motivation to improve administration is often lacking. Third, the financial resources to scale up pilot projects are often inadequate. Finally, there is often unwilling on the part of Government bodies to identify and develop suitable ICT applications and/or re-engineer bureaucratic work accordingly.

Apart from the above, there are other challenges like disparate systems and data models, security concerns, large volume of data across individual government departments, departmental behaviours and cost prohibitive approaches to integration.

The following example makes the issue of integration and interoperability clearer (Figure 2):

- Land department will allot a piece of land to the citizen along proper plan to construct
- Banks will provide loan as per rules.
- Land will be registered with Revenue department based on the information given by the Land Department.
- Then the basic amenities like water and power will get from the respective departments.
- The necessary property tax has to be paid to property tax department.
- Citizen will get a Passport, since he has all the necessary documents, which are required by the concern department.

Figure 2. Example (Lack of personal information integration)

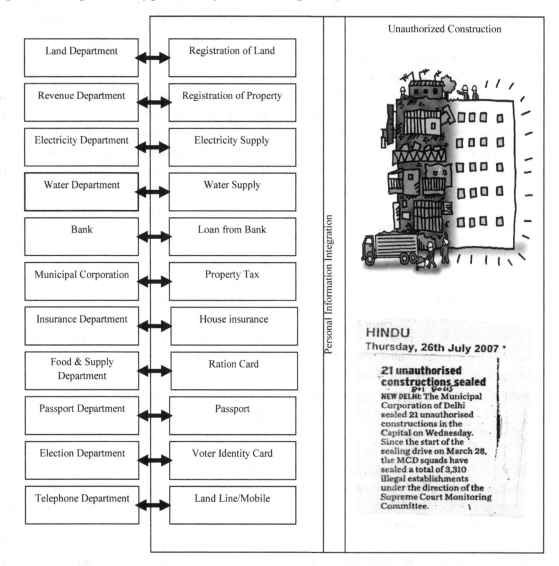

HINDU
Thursday, 26th July 2007

21 unauthorised constructions sealed
NEW DELHI: The Municipal Corporation of Delhi sealed 21 unauthorised constructions in the Capital on Wednesday. Since the start of the sealing drive on March 28, the MCD squads have sealed a total of 3,310 illegal establishments under the direction of the Supreme Court Monitoring Committee.

- Even citizen will get voter identity card form the election department based on the house identity.

  Similarly he will get all the benefits from other departments as mentioned in Figure 2. But lack of standard norms, policy guidelines and feasible strategies with the Government departments to deal with the problem of unauthorized or illegal construction, the Government and citizens are facing lots of problems.

From the above example the following problems may arise:

- Sometimes unauthorized construction may happen on the approved land (only three floors to be built, but more flats are built illegally). Lack of proper checks on the construction of buildings as per the plan approved by the concern department, illegal constructions may happen. Using false

Table 1. Relevant solutions to the challenges in achieving personal information integration

S. No.	Challenges	Relevant Solution
1.	Incompatible Systems	Back office integration and unique citizen identification number
2.	Different forms or biometric data	Uniformity
3.	Different languages	Local Language Computing
4.	Diverse data sources	Centralized data base; Maintenance of integrated data
5.	Undefined polices	Adoption of open standards; Policies regarding security; Uniformity
6.	Unable to deliver reliable data	Framework which distinguishes reliable and unreliable data e.g. Use of semantics
7.	Lack of appropriate methodology	Adoption of centralized methodology

documents, the illegal construction will be registered.

- Since the Land department is not sharing the information on the approved plot/flat/land for construction of building with the Registration department, illegal buildings may be registered with the Registration department.
- Banks will provide loan to illegal constructions as the information provided by the citizen for loan with the Land department and Registration department either through online/offline, which is not available with the many banks.
- Approval for basic amenities like electricity and water based on the registration documents.
- The citizen will pay property tax to the Tax department and it will accept the same, since Tax department do not have the right information about the property. Also the Tax department does not share their data either with the Land department or with the property registration department.
- Based on the property proof, he will get the voter identity card from the election department.

Also some internal and sub-branches of these departments are not connected with their Head departments. While many departments are maintaining this data, the government could not make use of it until the departments to benefit from interdepartmental data exchanges.

OVERCOMING THE CHALLENGES

Some of the solutions to the above challenges are discussed in this section. Table 1 summarizes the relevant solutions to the challenges in achieving personal information integration.

- **Uniformity:** A uniformity of all the application forms so that similar information is available with all the departments. Also a mechanism for updating the old data so that the citizen does not have to inform all the departments when changes occur.
- **Identification number:** The Government may adopt a methodology where citizen information can be updated and modified at a single location through their State Data Center using State Wide Area Network. This can be achieved by issuing a unique citizen identification number, which can be used for various Government services. If the citizen's information is available at one place the departments can use it for sharing, analyzing and forecasting. It is also useful to the citizens as they do not need to go to multiple departments for any change.

- **E-government Interoperability Framework (eGIF):** An eGIF is required that enables different departments to share data interchangeably at back office. The framework can use open standards, different methodologies like ontology search engines etc. according to the requirement of the individual department and hence the Government.

- **Common set of data processes and formats:** Implementation of Personal Information integration is a solution to leverage long-term investments in complex legacy data in the government and standardize on a single platform for department-wide data access, management and analysis. For this a *common set of data processes and formats* so that information can be shared between State Governments, Central Governments and its local bodies.

- **Establishment of ownership and responsibility for an integrated system that functions as data.** There are certain legal and security issues while sharing Personal Information sharing. For example, the personal information needs to pickup individual tax records at the department of taxation and drop them at the department of employment, the integration competency center will determine how to lock that information so only authorized individuals can access it. As said by Srivastava (2009), the IT Director of Madhya Pradesh portal, India 'The technology alone does not create change'. It takes commitment by individuals and requires a long implementation period. Some information sharing is already taking place in most governments (For example in India the portals www. MPonline.gov and www.APonline.gov). A team is required to identify such departments and that can be moved into the integration platform.

- **Government departments should drill down no deeper than necessary when** authenticating identity. Different departments need to know different things about a citizen, although there is some obvious overlap, such as name, address and date of birth. The architecture of the systems operated by different government departments must reflect that. Where anonymity is not possible, *authentication information* should be limited and segmented; the only personal information that's revealed should be the information that's needed for that specific transaction.

- **To create an integrated and interoperable activity across departments, an effective *means of communication* between departments both within and outside is needed.** The State and Central Government is the obvious body to drive this approach. Cross-agency cooperation is a huge challenge for data integration since every department has its own system. This has to be solved.

- **There is a need for *understanding factors* that affect participation from Government departments and stakeholders.** Strategies need to be devised to address these issues, both internally and externally, in particular, social entrepreneurship.

- **'The Change has to be come from the *grass root level*':** N. Mittal (Head of www. aponline.gov). The Government is about people – citizens and employees. These people must engage with e-Government.

- **There is need to understand how to create flexible systems that can adapt and change with demand.** Constant change is a natural occurrence in the government and it impacts people, processes and technology in equal measure.

- **The information sharing among departments should be complete, accurate and timely manner from disparate sources without redoing the whole sys-**

tem. Unfortunately for most departments, however, this information is often either unavailable or is incomplete and outdated. As a result, critical information is not always shared at key decision points in the government process.

- **A one-stop is required for the users where they can access various government services through single point.** In this case the basic IT infrastructure has to be *maintained centrally*. Further, standards need to be set to guarantee interoperability.
- **Local Language Computing:** As specified by Michel Gambier, General Manager - Information Worker Business Group, Microsoft APAC. (*Source: E-Gov magazine for the Asia & the Middle East, July 2007*) "The Local language computing is absolutely essential in enabling governments to communicate with citizens. Of the 6,000 languages spoken in the world today, 32 percent of them are from Asia. Yet, many of the word processing amenities (e.g. grammar and style checkers), do not exist for native Asian languages". Local Language Program provides great opportunities to people of all cultures, regions, locations and languages by facilitating access and promoting communication and interaction.
- All the sub-offices should be well connected with their Head and Main office and personal information data should be available in the electronic format then only share with other department is possible.

EXAMPLES

The following are examples where Personal Information Integration is required in different departments of the Government. Also how interoperability can provide flexibility, agility and responsiveness.

Personal Information Integration between Transport Department, Traffic Police Department and Judiciary Department

Government is focusing on improving methodologies for integrating Transport department, Traffic police department and Judiciary department (Figure 3). Unconnected transportation planning networks cannot use the information effectively to inform and coordinate their work. So there is a need to consolidate and standardize existing transportation data, offering a single source of consistent information for multi state transportation planning. Several problems occur every day due to lack of interoperability. For example, in the absence of centralized database of all the Road Transport offices in the country the traffic violators may cancel their license in one state and manage a new one from another state. Also, without regular update of data the Traffic Police may issue fine to citizen for a vehicle that has been already stolen/ sold/ destroyed.

If all the three departments are integrated and the information is being updated regularly then it can reduce fraud and duplication, citizens can update their information at one-stop and the information can be used for making further decisions (Figure 4). By integrating these departments the problem of biometric data and maintenance of diverse data will be solved.

Personal Information Integration between Universities, Employment Exchange and Offices and Recruitment Agencies

The students of different universities get registered at the employment exchange offices. They submit their personal information including their qualification and receive a card. The recruitment agencies contact the employment offices and find the suitable candidate. At present all this is done manually at Government departments. There is no

Figure 3. Centralized Database (Source: e-Paper Hindustan Times, Delhi Published on July 21, 2007, Page2)

A centralised database for driving licences coming up

Harish V. Nair
New Delhi, July 20

VERY SOON, it going to be difficult for a traffic violator whose licence was revoked in Delhi, to get another one discreetly from another state. The Delhi High Court on Friday asked the Transport Ministry to link Road Transport Offices (RTO) across the country within a year to stop this practice.

"Traffic violators whose licences are cancelled in one state manage a new one from other states. Some even get fake ones for a fee," a Bench led by Chief Justice M.K. Sharma and Justice R.S. Sodhi observed during the hearing of a PIL on the lack of road safety and infrastructure in the Capital.

The Ministry has also been asked to maintain a computerised 'register' of all driving licences issued, which can be accessed via a centralised database.

The Delhi government said driving licences were cancelled in 955 of 992 fatal accident cases recorded since 2004 but the Bench countered, "there is a possibility of these offenders procuring licences from other states." harishvnair@hindustantimes.com

mechanism for checking such documents online. This lack of interoperability leads to incorrect information (student gets a job but does not updates the profile, student goes for higher education) and duplication of cards (one student may have more than one card). Duplication will further lead to wrong assessment of unemployed people in India and hence a statistical flaw.

Personal information sharing is required among these departments to not only save time but it is also transparent and efficient (Figure 5). A central database will help in updating the personal information and all the three departments can view the profile at the same time. The problem of security and handling of incompatible systems will be solved by integrating different agencies. Moreover, for a centralized data base there will be use of open standards.

Personal Information Integration between Passport Offices, Post Offices and Police Stations

Validity of a passport is five to ten years. During this period there might be change of address, change of name (after marriage the name might change) etc. This information needs to be updated.

Figure 4. Integration of Transport department, Police department and Traffic department

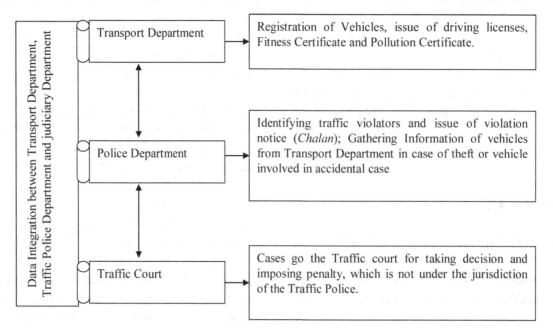

Figure 5. Integration of universities, employment exchange offices and recruitment agencies

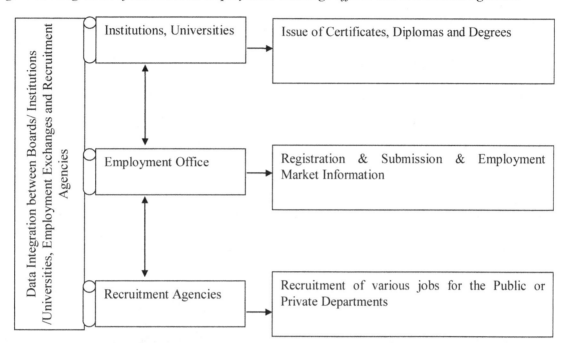

Also, a citizen with criminal background can have a passport by giving false information as the departments are not integrated. Personal Information Integration between passport offices, post offices and police stations is essential to identify fraud and misuse. For example www.bangaloreOne. com (portal of Bangalore) in association with the Ministry of External Affairs, Government of India has launched a new service "Acceptance of applications for a new Passport" through its Integrated Citizen Service Centers. Citizens can now apply for fresh passports at these centers (Figure 6). Citizen-friendly executives at elegant centers assist in filing an application for issue of a fresh passport. Applications received at this portal are forwarded to the passport office within two working days after submission. The centre generates the file reference number and enters the personal details of the applicant into the system. The data is transferred to the passport office electronically and the papers relating to police verification are sent directly from these centers to the concerned police authorities. The applications are physically sent

to regional passport office (RPO) Bangalore for further processing. (Source: www.bangaloreone. gov.in). After the verification, passport is issued to the citizen and sent through mail. Same as above, with integration among departments the challenge of biometric data, undefined policies will be solved.

EXPECTED BENEFITS

Integration and interoperability between the government departments for achieving one-stop portal is very beneficial for both citizens as well as for the Government. Dayanidhi Maran, Minister of Communications & Information Technology, India has mentioned in his presentation (NeGP, 2006) the benefits of interoperability to the citizens: Integrated and enhanced access to government services, clearly defined service levels, Services at the doorstep with substantial rural outreach, Increased Efficiency, Improved Reliability and Bridging the digital divide. Further more benefits

Figure 6. Integration of passport offices, post offices and police stations

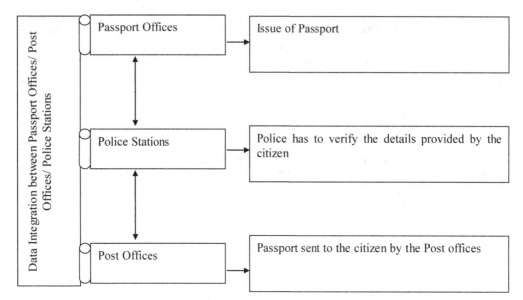

to the citizens have been discussed by Bhatnagar et. al (2007): Affordable Cost, Reduced transaction time and elapsed time, Less number of trips to Government offices, Expanded time window and convenient access, Reduced corruption – need for bribes, use of influence, Transparency – clarity on documents and procedures, Fair deal and courteous treatment, Less error prone, reduced cost of recovery, Empowered to challenge action - greater accountability. Interoperability is very useful for the Government in many ways Traunmüller (2004) and Bhatnagar et. al (2007):

• Introduces transparency in data, decision and actions, rules, procedures and performance of Government departments.
• Makes decisions traceable – tracks actions
• Builds accountability – great access to information through web publishing – role of civil society
• Provides documentation to citizens for follow-up
• Centralizes and integrates data for better audit and analysis.

• Enables unbiased sampling for audit purposes.
• Personal information can be used to locate and identify an individual including name, sex, address
• Duplication can be avoided

CONCLUDING REMARKS

Achievement of one-stop portal for the Government requires interoperability of information among different departments of the Government. The problem of interoperability is large and complex which not only includes technical but also managerial issues. This paper is an attempt to cover one of the aspects of interoperability, Personal Information. Personal Information integration is essential for integrated service delivery and for other services like G2E, G2G, and G2B among the departments in Government. Using personal information integration among departments of the Government and its agencies, not only to share key information across multiple departments but also to make better management and deeper insights possible with a more efficient use of resources across the state or center Government. Also it provides accurate, current, and timely information for Govt. initiatives. Personal Information sharing among government departments and its agencies does not exist and there is an urgent need to not only accelerate information distribution, but also to broaden the scope of organization that can share data. Sharing personal information among all agencies and departments and leveraging information to reduce costs while enabling decision makers to make more effective decisions faster and minimizes the amount of hardware that must be installed and upgraded.

The contribution of the paper is three fold. First, it has addressed the multiple benefits and challenges of personal information integration. Second, it provides relevant solutions to the challenges in order to achieve personal information integration for one-stop Government portal. Third, examples of personal information integration are given that explain the need for integration among various departments of Government.

As future work, other aspects of interoperability may be targeted apart from data integration such as process integration, communication integration. Also, the organizational and socio-economic factors should be considered for achieving a one stop Government portal.

REFERENCES

ADPIP. (2007). *Government interoperability frameworks for Asia-Pacific countries.* Retrieved March 20th, 2007, from http://www.apdip.net/ projects/ gif/ project

Bhatnagar, S., Rao, T. P., Singh, N., Vaidya, R., & Mandal, M. (2007). *Impact assessment study of e-government projects in India.* Retrieved Aug 14th, 2007, from www.mit.gov.in/ download/ impact-assessment-study- dit-31jan%20(2).pdf

Caldow, J. (1999). *The quest for electronic government: A defining vision.* Institute for Electronic Government, IBM Corporation De', R. (2005). *Assessment of e-government projects - A case study of Bhoomi, India.*

Dias, G. P., & Rafael, J. A. (2007). A simple model and a distributed architecture for realizing one-stop e-government. *Electronic Commerce Research and Applications, 6,* 81–90. doi:10.1016/j. elerap.2006.02.001

EC: Commission of the European communities. (2003). *Linking-up Europe: The importance of interoperability for e-government services.* Staff Working Document.

Edina. (2004). *E-government interoperability framework,* version 6.0. Retrieved April, 2004, from http://edina.ac.uk/ projects/ interoperability/ e-gif-v6-0_.pdf

Electronic Privacy Information Center. (2007). *National identification cards: Legal issues.* Retrieved March, 2007, from http://www.epic.org/ events/ id/ resources/ RS21137.pdf

Finger, M., & Pécoud, G. (2003). From e-government to e-governance? Towards a model of e-governance. *Electronic. Journal of E-Government, 1*(1), 1–10.

Gouscos, D., Kalikakis, M., Legal, M., & Papadopoulou, S. (2007). A general model of performance and quality for one-stop e-government service offerings. *Government Information Quarterly, 24,* 860–885. doi:10.1016/j.giq.2006.07.016

Government, C. I. O. (2007). *The HKSARG interoperability framework.* Office of the Government Chief Information Officer, The Government of the Hong Kong Special Administrative Region. Retrieved November 2007 from www. ogcio.gov.hk

Government of India. (2007). *National e-gover-nance action plan*. Retrieved March, 2007, from http://india.gov.in/ govt/ csd06 _initiatives.php

Government of Karnataka. (2007). Retrieved March 20th, 2007, from http://www.bangaloreone. gov.in/ public/ GovtoCitizenLinks.aspx

Government of New Zealand. (2000). *E-govern-ment - A vision for New Zealanders*. E-government Unit of the State Services Commission, New Zealand

Gupta, M. P., Kumar, P., & Bhattacharya, J. (2005). *Government online: Opportunities and challenges*. Tata Mc Graw-Hill Publishing Com-pany Limited.

Heeks, R. B. (2001). *Understanding e-governance for development. I-Government paper no. 11*. UK: IDPM, University of Manchester.

Hilbert, M. (2005). *Development trends and challenges for local e-governments: Evidence from municipalities in Chile and Peru*. Santiago, Chile: United Nations.

Institute of Electrical and Electronics Engineers. (1990). *IEEE standard computer dictionary: A compilation of IEEE standard computer glossa-ries*. New York. Retrieved from http://www.sei. cmu.edu/ str/ indexes/ glossary/ interoperability. html

Klischewski, R., & Scholl, H. J. (2006). *Informa-tion quality as a common ground for key players in e-government integration and interoperability*. In Hawaii International Conference on System Sciences (HICSS).

Marshall, S., Taylor, W., & Yu, X. H. (2005). *Encyclopedia of developing regional commu-nities with Information and Communication Technology*. Hershey, PA: Idea Group Reference. doi:10.4018/978-1-59140-575-7

Riley, T. B., & Riley, C. G. (2003). *E-governance to e-democracy: Examining the evolution*. Ottawa, Canada: Commonwealth Centre for e-governance and Riley Information Services.

Scholl, H. J., & Klischewski, R. (2007). E-government integration and interoperability: Framing the research agenda. *International Jour-nal of Public Administration, 30*(8), 889–920. doi:10.1080/01900690701402668

Srivastava, A. (April 13, 2009). *Personal interview with IT director of Madhya Pradesh, India*.

State Services Commission. (2007). *New Zea-land e-government interoperability framework*. Retrieved October, 2007 from www.e.govt.nz

Traunmüller, R. (2004). *Electronic government*. Springer.

Vernadat, F. B. (1996). *Enterprise modelling and integration: Principles and applications*. London, UK: Chapman & Hall.

Wimmer, M., Liehmann, M., & Martin, B. (2006). Offene standards und abgestimmte spezifikationen - dasosterreichische interoperabilittskonzept. *Proceedings MKWI* (2006).

World Bank. (2007). *Case studies - Better service delivery for citizens*. Retrieved Aug 16th, 2007, from http://www1.worldbank.org/ publicsector/ egov/

KEY TERMS AND DEFINITIONS

E-Government: E-government is using infor-mation technology to deliver government services at all times directly to citizen, business or even another government entity.

Integration: The forming of a (temporary or permanent) larger unit of government entities for the purpose of merging processes [and systems] and sharing information.

Interoperability: Interoperability is the ability of government organizations to share information and integrate information and business processes by use of common standards and work practices.

One-Stop Portal: One-stop Government refers to a single point of access to electronic services and information offered by different public authorities where all public authorities are interconnected and that the citizen has 24 hours access to public services by a single point even if these services are provided by different public authorities or private service providers.

Maturity: The extent to which an organization has explicitly and consistently deployed processes that are documented, managed, measured, controlled, and continually improved.

Data Integration: Data integration is combining data residing at different sources and providing the user with a unified view of this data.

Chapter 5

A Qualitative Study of E–Governance in Coimbatore Revenue Administration with Special Reference to "Tamil Nilam" and "Star" Projects in Tamilnadu, India

P. Senthil Priya
PSG College of Arts and Science, India

N. Mathiyalagan
PSG College of Arts and Science, India

ABSTRACT

Land revenue constitutes a major part of revenue for any state government in India. Land administration is one of the most crucial functions of any government, and land records make the foundation of land administration. For decades, maintenance of land records has been one of the most notorious areas of governance in the country in terms of efficacy and transparency. In recent years, with the advent of Internet and newer Information Technology applications, many e-governance initiatives have been implemented at the national and state level to facilitate one on one communication link between the government bureaucracy and the citizenry. Two such projects, Land Record Computerization Project and Computerization of Property Registration, that have totally revamped the land administration system in India, have been taken for analysis in the present study. The author has taken both the projects for analysis as for completion of any land transaction in India both these projects need to function in synchronization. These projects could be called as the first e-governance initiatives in the country that

DOI: 10.4018/978-1-60960-848-4.ch005

involved grass-root citizenry. The present study traces the implementation and inter-operability status of the land administration projects in Tamilnadu, India.

The study reveals that though the revenue earned by the projects grow every year, the awareness level of the projects remain relatively low. Findings also suggest that the land record data available in the website are obsolete, and to bring in more efficiency, the portal has to be constantly updated. Also, since there is no integration and interoperability between the revenue and registration department of the state, there is only sub-optimal utilization of the established infrastructure at present. The study recommends immediate integration of the projects to make it more effective.

INTRODUCTION

India, located in South Asia, is one of the oldest civilizations in the world with a kaleidoscopic variety and rich cultural heritage. It has achieved all-round socio-economic progress during the last 62 years of its Independence. It has become self-sufficient in agricultural production and is now one of the top industrialized countries and the second most populous nation in the world. English is the major language of trade and politics, but there are fourteen official languages in the nation. The country is divided into 29 states and 7 Union territories for administrative convenience. The central government is the federal institution of governance but the states elect their own provincial government with a chief minister at its helm to run the state administration (Indian Government portal, 2010).

Fragmentation of land is widespread in India and this fragmented nature of land holdings play a major role in decreased levels of agricultural productivity (Jha, 2005). Despite recent, rapid economic growth in India, the country still has the planet's largest concentration of poor people (defined as those living on less than $2 per day). Approximately 70% of Indians exist on less than $2 a day, a higher proportion than in Africa (Hanstad and Nielsen 2009). The two statistics are closely related as landlessness is the best indicator of rural poverty (World Bank, 2007). Civil courts are clogged by land disputes and 8 million of the 20 million pending civil cases in India as of the year 2000 pertained to land litigations in India. Most of the civil cases drag on for several years (RTI India, 2007). A study on land reforms in India remarked that land disputes affected 28% of all plots in peri-urban environments in the state of Andhra Pradesh (Deininger, 2007). Statistics have also revealed that 90% of land holdings in India are subjected to ownership disputes and the money spent in contesting law suits at judicial institutions constituted around 1.3% loss of Gross Domestic Product growth every year (Indian Brand Equity foundation, 2004).

"Land" is listed as a state subject under the constitution of India and hence land and related issues are governed by state (provincial) laws and regulations. Land revenues constitute the major part of income for any state government. For decades, maintenance of land records has been one of the most notorious areas of governance in terms of efficacy and transparency (Second Administrative reforms Commission, 2008). A study has identified that Indians paid substantial bribes to access 11 public service facilities and land administration department was one of the most corrupt public administration departments in India (India Corruption Study, 2005). It was often very difficult to get a certified copy of the land title deed (Record of Rights copy) from the village accountant (government employed distributor of land documents within a rural locality), which was very necessary for the farmer to avail bank loan to buy seeds and fertilizers.

This study is divided into seven sections. "Background of the Study" provides the introduction, background of land administration in Tamilnadu and the context of land transaction in Tamilnadu. "Need for the Study" presents need for the study, objectives of the study and the scope of the study. "Literature Review" presents the literature review of several land administration projects, the research questions formulated for analysis, methodology and theoretical framework used in the study and a brief description of the two projects. "Data Analysis" includes an analysis of the level of citizen participation and interviews with beneficiaries, "Findings and Discussion" encloses the research findings and discussion, the implications of the study and the conclusion and recommendations.

Background of the Study

Tamil Nadu is the seventh most populous state in India with a population of 66,396,000, as of July 1, 2008 (approximately 5.79% of India's population). The state has 32 districts, 206 taluks and 17,292 villages (www.tn.gov.in). It is the fifth largest contributor to India's GDP and the most urbanized state in India. For administrative convenience, the state is categorized into districts comprising villages and taluks comprising rural panchayats (www.tn.gov.in). It is one of the foremost states in the country in terms of overall development. Majority of the population are settled in rural areas and agriculture is the main source of livelihood for greater part of the population (www.tn.gov.in). This dependency status on agriculture has created a predominant need for land records and related details for the community at large.

Coimbatore municipality is the third largest and one of the top most industrialized cities of Tamilnadu. It is known as the 'Manchester of South India.' The municipality covers 9 rural taluks and 481 revenue villages (www.coimbatore.gov.in).

The manual system of maintaining land records in the state was very diverse. The procedure to record transfer and ownership of lands, shares and inheritance was generally based on particular identity numbers allotted for each individual plot of land. Revenue assessment, property tax and agricultural yield related details were also recorded against that specific identification number to keep track of the changes in the land records. But, the traditional methods have been changing over the years in each state according to local practices and traditions. But, in general, all states maintained and issued uniform copies of land title documents.

Traditionally, numerous formats of land records were maintained at the village, taluk and district levels. In every village (rural hamlet), Village Administrative Officers (VAO) were entrusted with the maintenance of land records and in case of change in ownership, transfer or inheritance of land, the records have to be manually updated to enforce the new changes (mutations) at once. But, in practice, the land records were not updated in time due to work load pendency of staffs within the revenue department as the staffs of the department were periodically utilized for developmental works undertaken by the government machinery such as elections to the local, civic bodies and corporations, welfare aid distribution and financial assistance to minorities. This situation led to incompetency in management of land records.

In the old system of land administration, the state revenue department maintained around 20 registers to store land related details of each individual plot within the villages or towns (Rita Ahluwat, 2008). In case of any litigation, the hand written record book with manual crypts used to be the only document with legal standing in the court and this document book with all recorded details of the land has to be produced for verification in courts. Hence, any civil litigation took many years to solve.

These circumstances emphasized the need for development of a novel land records management system that reduced the work pendency status of documents, work load of the staffs and created a transparent system of revenue accounts. The project planners wanted to facilitate an efficient, easier and accountable system of land administration. Though, it was a daunting task to transfer the legacy data to computers and motivate the rigid revenue staffs to adapt to the new computerized system of administration, the state government took adequate care to provide an effective and smoother transition.

Land Transaction Process in India

As land does not belong permanently to any single entity and it changes hands often, land records have to be constantly updated for effective land administration. Presently, land rules in India require that as soon as any transfer, partition and inheritance takes place, the name of new owners should be entered and updated in the relevant land registers without delay to avoid administrative hindrances. But, it was never done on time and users faced lot of inconveniences in the process.

In practice, any land transaction in India is done in two phases; the first stage is that the citizen, who acquires the land, has to attest his right of ownership in a deed of registration that is maintained at the land registration offices (District Registration office or Sub-Registration office) of the concerned locality. The second stage is that the person, who sells the land, has to fill in a form of mutation (change of ownership form) and transfer the land rights to the new owner. This process is done at the taluk office within the same locality. Hence, for any land transaction to be complete, the process has to be initiated at the office of land registration and followed up at the regional taluk office. Only, when the document entry is complete at both the places, the ownership right is accorded on the new owner. If the work of mutation (change of ownership) is not done on time, the records would remain out-of-date and the RoR copy would imply the old owner as the legal owner.

Hence, there is a critical need for both the offices to function in synchronization to complete any land transaction. Manual entry is carried out at both the departments to keep the records up-to-date. This process is time-consuming as land registers have to be passed on between the departments and changes have to be entered. It is also prone to human error.

The state government decided to streamline the process and initiate computerization at both the departments. The policy makers envisioned wide area network connectivity between the departments and facilitate automatic data flow between the departments. Information and Communication Technology tools were used to synchronize the data entry at both ends and bring down the workload of department staffs. This process of computerization has brought in lot of changes to the old system of land administration.

Land revenue department implemented "Tamil Nilam" project and the registration department of the state introduced "Star" project to harmonize the land transaction process. In this context, the present study provides an evaluation of these two projects implemented by the land administration department within Coimbatore district and municipality.

NEED FOR THE STUDY

Computerization has the potential to support most land administration reform initiatives in any developing country. In the present context, e-governance projects were introduced primarily to improve efficiency, effectiveness and transparency of revenue administration. Hence, there is a need to periodically assess the impact of Land Records Computerization (LRC) project and Computerization of Property Registration (CPR) facility in Coimbatore district and to find out the effectiveness and sustainability of both the projects. The study is relevant at present as a crucial first stage of evaluation is necessary to ascertain the extent to which these intended outcomes have been achieved. The intended benefits of the projects and the attained benefits of the projects are debated upon and a better framework suggestion is provided at the end. Citizen response to the projects and channelization of revenue generated from the projects are also analyzed.

The study also analyzes the impact, sustainability, new media penetration, adoption and diffusion of the projects within Coimbatore district and municipality. Thus, the proposed research will assess to what extent both the e-governance projects have benefitted the users and enforced transparency.

Objective of the Study

1. To find out the stages of maturity of both the projects at the Coimbatore municipality and taluks.
2. To find out the current stage of re-engineering and pace of implementation of both the projects at Coimbatore municipality and taluks.
3. An analysis of cross-departmental co-ordination and integration of services available within the departments.
4. To trace the interoperability factors between the departments in Coimbatore city and rural areas.
5. To find out the level of citizen participation in both the projects.

Scope of the Present Study

In recent years, with the advent of internet and newer information technology applications, many E-Governance initiatives have been implemented at the national and state level to facilitate one on one communication link between the government bureaucracy and the citizenry. Many governments in developing countries have chosen to go on-line in administrative departments that have a huge citizen interface and involve collection of money on a day to day basis.

The study analyzes the challenges and opportunities of growth to further evolve better

systems of land record administration in a wider perspective. It can be used as a benchmark study that analyses the current scenario of land administration in Tamilnadu state and it could be used as a ground level assessment of the two projects. The study is relevant at present as there is a need to constantly analyze the scope for betterment of the projects from time to time and locate the bureaucratic hurdles within the system to further extend the benefits of the projects and progress to the next phase of implementation.

LITERATURE REVIEW

Many studies have been done to analyze the suitability and sustainability of e-governance initiatives in some countries. Olsen et al (2005) employed the MeGAP-3 (Municipal E-Government Assessment Project) assessment tool to assess the status of municipal e-governance project in Agder region of southern Norway, an area with high internet penetration and mature information and communication technology use. It concluded that the dominant stakeholder in sustainability of the project was the bureaucratic administration rather than citizens or politicians and identified that a more citizen-centric approach would ensure long term success of the project. Zwahar et al (2005) employed Lausanne framework of analysis to evaluate the "e"- initiatives implemented in administrative functions like policy making, regulation and service delivery among the Flemish Community in Belgium. The study identified that e-initiatives had huge transformative potential within the state. Dale (1999) analyzed the use of technology in the acquisition, storage, and processing of cadastral data and concluded that to support sustainable land development, it was imperative to address the core issues of the information society such as the protection of intellectual property rights and the privacy of the individual.

There are some studies done to find out the efficiency of land administration system in the present context. Vilasini Ramachandran (2005) analyzed the impact of land administration projects in the state of Gujarat, India and concluded that these projects would be successful in India only when automatic data transfer and inter-operability facilities exist between the revenue and registration departments. Jayaradha (2003) addressed the impact of computerization of property registration project and has recommended the usage of regional language for successful participation of citizens in any regional projects within state. Bhatia (2004) carried out an assessment of five wide scope e-governance projects in India and asserted that users favored the land record computerization projects to a greater extent as there was visible reduction in corruption, shorter waiting times, fewer visits, error free transaction and greater transparency.

Some studies have stressed the need for more government co-ordination and involvement in land administration projects. Ossako (2006) has suggested for creation of a unified data registry in all developing countries under a government organization and this multipurpose unified land registry (cadastre) organization, as the owner and provider of legal data can fulfill all of the multi-purpose demands raised by the economy, decision makers and the society.

Few studies have analyzed the grass root impact of such projects. Raul Zambrano and Pierre Dandjinou (2003) analyzed the link between e-governance and the poor through two case studies, one from India and another from South Africa and noted that usage of ICT can be an effective tool not only to simplify government to citizen (G2C) interactions, but can also facilitate participatory communication within the country. Vinay Thakur et al (2004) studied the social impact of land record computerization project and listed out the lacunae in manual record keeping system of India. The study included a status report of land record computerization projects in all Indian states and found that greater impact of the project was felt by the people living in rural areas with low income capacity. Islam (2003) broadly analyzed the land

administration system and land record projects in three Indian states of Karnataka, Himachal Pradesh and Haryana. The author pointed out that mere computerization of government offices did not make projects successful. The new technologies have to be taken to the grass root citizenry to achieve overall economic development in any nation. Valentina Ndou (2004) has asserted that all well implemented e-governance projects in developing countries have the potential of reshaping the public sector activities and processes, building relationships between citizens and the government, enhancing transparency, increasing government capacity and providing a "voice" for those at the grass roots.

Research Questions and Methodology

The research study focuses on three principal research questions:

1. What is the status of implementation of the land administration projects in Coimbatore municipality and taluks? To what extent has the district administration implemented the projects?
2. What is the current stage of the maturity of the projects and its interoperability status?
3. What could be the role of stake holders in the projects?

The study was exploratory in nature. Primary data collection was done by conducting in-depth interviews with the policy makers, project implementers, department heads and technical and operational staffs of both the departments at the district level. 2 district level policy implementer of both the projects, 5 management personal working at the computerization department involved in software development of the projects, 2 administrative heads of the projects and 10 staffs from each department involved in day to day operations of the project were interviewed.

Around 25 beneficiaries of each project were also interviewed to find out about their awareness, usage and level of satisfaction.

Analysis of secondary data was done by scrutinizing all relevant materials published in websites, journals, magazines, web publications, newspaper articles, government reports, white papers, seminar papers and the previous research projects. Land administration project reports, white paper of Indian government administrative departments, e-assessment frameworks used in studies and land reform reports, that primarily pertained to developing countries were studied. Department web portals were analyzed in detail and some studies done in developed nations about the land information systems and cadastral data management were also analyzed to assess the suitability and sustainability of e-governance initiatives of developed nations. Land administration reports and articles published on the subject were also examined. Best practices literature of England, Hungary and Belgium that was available online were assessed.

Theoretical Framework of the Study

Four stages maturity model of Gartner (2000) and Layne and Lee (2001) maturity models are used in the analysis to position the state in the growth model of E-Governance.

According to Gartner, growth of E-Governance takes place in four-phases based on E-Governance maturity model. These phases have been defined based on experiences with E-Commerce and E-Governance plans in Europe and other developed western regions.

E-Governance Maturity Model (Gartner)

Early 90's Information → Presence

Mid 90's Interaction → Intake Process

Present Transaction → Complete transaction

Future Transformation → Integration and organizational changes

Another widely known maturity model suggested by Layne and Lee (2001) sees E-Governance as an evolutionary phenomenon, from which initiatives could be derived and implemented. They have included two more phases in the growth model for E-Governance. They are:

- **Vertical integration:** It refers to inter-departmental integration – a particular department fully integrated at the district, state and national level. At this level, all similar departments are integrated internally between themselves and any information regarding a district can be easily assessed at the state and vice versa. All details of the department are accessible from all other offices across the state or union. It is called as vertical integration and it is done to facilitate transactions between departments easier and up-to-date. Ideally, vertical integration precedes horizontal integration.
- **Horizontal integration:** It refers to integration of different departments of administration. An integration of similar departments within the same state, along with an integration of different departments as well as across various stake holder agencies lead to this kind of integration. The master database of a particular department is accessible to all other departments of administration within the union. This kind of departmental integration is done to facilitate easier trading of information between different departments and various stake holders involved in a transaction.

Description of "Tamil Nilam" and "Star" Projects

"Tamil Nilam" (Tamil is the regional language of the state, Nilam refers to land in Tamil) is an important E-Governance initiative of the Government of Tamilnadu, India that pertained to computerization of land records and related data of 206 taluks and 32 districts of the state. The project was fully funded by the central government and commenced by the state government in the year 1993. Data entry process was initiated in the same year and land records were brought online in the year 2003. Likewise, all states of the Indian union commenced the computerization operations at the same time. This project was a significant step to strengthen land record management at the national level.

The main component of the project was the computerization of alpha-numeric details of permanent land record details. For administrative convenience, Coimbatore city was divided into urban and rural sub-divisions. Urban sub-division constituted Coimbatore city and its peripherals and urban land records pertained to the maintenance of land records within the city.

Rural land records referred to the maintenance of land records within the district or rural taluks of the state and rural sub-division constituted the surrounding villages, taluks and small towns. Nine rural sub-divisions pertained to the rural classification. The data entry of all land record details of these sub-divisions have been completed and over 1.2 million land documents of land holders at the rural hamlets have been brought online for usage. Once, the process of manual data entry was completed, 3 verification check lists were prepared and cross-checked to make the land documents error free. And, the project was brought online for public access in the year 2002.

Land title document is also called as the Record of Right (RoR) copy. This legal document accords clear ownership title on any land holder within the country and it is of high importance for rural farmers as it is used to access bank loans and crop mortgages. Through this e-governance project, the copy of RoR is issued as a computerized print-out for all users at all taluk offices within the state.

"STAR", (Simplified and Transparent Administration of Registration) project was launched to facilitate easier and faster registration process. It is an e-governance project that pertains to easier registration, archival, index and storage of new registered documents. In India, registration of any new property is mandatory as only this facility confers clear ownership title on a new buyer. The registration department also creates and maintains up-to-date land information system for usage and verification of land title deeds. This system greatly reduces risk of fraud and helps to solve land disputes easily. The process of registration ideally takes place in the registration office or Sub Registrar Office (SRO) within a particular locality. This project was implemented in the early nineties and the details of all registered documents were brought online in the year 2002.

Coimbatore zone covers 13 SRO offices within its limit. In all SRO offices, a facility for scan and store module exists in the software system and around 5 million property records have been computerized in the zone so far. All old documents from the year 1987 onwards were scanned page wise with the photographs and finger prints of the buyer – seller along with the register office endorsement seal and the entire set of documents were indexed and archived in the computer system. Details were saved based on the survey and subdivision number of individual properties. In the computerized system of storage, all the land record details remain error-free as no manual entry was involved and data processing and storage was done entirely through the scan module.

The Star project web portal also issues application forms for marriage, Encumbrance Certificate (EC – document with year wise details of previous land transaction involving the same land), chit fund registration, welfare scheme beneficiaries, pension certificates and other related forms online. Filled

Table 1. Tamil Nilam project: Citizen participation and revenue for year 2008 (Source: District revenue division, 2008)

District	Taluk Name	Total Number of users	Total view Revenue in million	Number of Print Requests	Total Print Revenue in millions	Total Revenue in millions
Coimbatore	Palladam	100	.002	55963	1.119	1.119
	Pollachi	0	0	55007	1.100	1.100
	Avinashi	0	0	49602	.992	.992
	Tirupur	205	.004	38388	.767	.768
	Udumalpet	0	0	36037	. 720	.720
	Coimbatore(South)	0	0	30669	.613	.613
	Coimbatore(North)	0	0	24449	.488	.488
	Mettupalayam	0	0	21123	.422	.422
	Valparai	0	0	23	.004	.004
	Total	305	.006	311261	6.225	6.225

in forms can be submitted at any registration or sub-registration offices for processing.

The policy makers had two-fold objectives in the implementation of land administration projects. Primarily, the projects were executed to establish vertical integration of both the departments through State Wide Area Network Connectivity program as a first step. Secondly, the projects were meant to be integrated at a horizontal level as well as interoperability features would facilitate automatic data transfer between the departments without human intervention. This integration provision would have facilitated proper verification of clear land title ownership at the time of registration to avoid any land discrepancies.

DATA ANALYSIS

The project has brought in revenue of 6.22 million (Revenue Department, 2008) in the year 2008 in Coimbatore district taluks alone (see Table 1). Likewise, the project had also brought in revenue to the tune of 4.6 million (Revenue Department, 2008) for the year 2007, 3.8 million (Revenue Department, 2008) for the year 2006

and 3 million (Revenue Department, 2008) for the year 2005 from the taluks within Coimbatore district. Compared with the year 2005, the revenue generated and print requisitions for RoR copies have almost doubled within a span of 4 years. The statistics prove that awareness level of the project is on the rise as the revenue keeps growing every year. Information kiosks were not available for the public at some taluks, and hence the number of users and the viewing revenue is shown as nil in all these taluks.

The District Registration office controls 13 Sub-Registrars offices within the limit. During the year 2008, a total number of 1, 38,203 new registrations were carried out within Coimbatore Zone and the annual revenue generated was 2,966 million (see Table 2) (Revenue Department, 2008). During the year 2006, a total number of 2, 56,343 registrations of new properties were carried out in the zone. Due to economic recession, the real estate scenario has changed in Coimbatore zone and the number of registrations has come down by almost 46% in the subsequent year. STAR project also issues encumbrance certificates for all applicants. Users can apply for EC copy through online web service as well as across the counter.

Table 2. Star project: Citizen participation and revenue for year 2008 (Source: District revenue division, 2008)

Sub - Registration Offices	Number of Documents Registered	Revenue in million
Coimbatore Joint 1	8081	380
Coimbatore Joint 2	6627	192
Gandhipuram	9781	413
Singanallur	12759	259
Madhukarai	7320	146
Thondamuthur	8585	161
Perianaicken Palayam	17321	282
Mettupalayam	16107	156
Annur	10403	101
Avinashi	20517	174
Ganapathy	8226	202
Peelamedu	4738	235
Vadavalli	7738	265

In the year 2008, 2750 online applications for EC were received through the web portal. Applications received at the counter accounted to 9999 and the total revenue of counter (department counter) EC generated in the year 2008 amounted to 1.8 million (Revenue Department, 2008) whereas web EC revenue accounted to half a million only (Revenue Department, 2008). It shows that counter EC is the most prevalent mode of transaction and web EC is preferred by only 30% of the users (see Figure 1).

1. Stage of Maturity

Tamil Nilam Project: At present, land title copies of all rural taluks can be viewed online. Through the government web portal, a facility exists for the user to manually type in the identity number of the land and RoR copy can be viewed online. Land title information can be verified and a provision for print-out exists in the website. However, this print-out cannot be utilized for official documentation purposes. A legal authenticated version of the land title document is issued only at the district taluk office on payment of Rs.20

(Source: Revenue department, 2008) (Rs.44 equals 1 USD, Source: Indian Forex department, 2008). These authenticated copies, issued at the taluk office counter are only accorded legal sanctity. A facility for transaction is not available in the website and the user has to manually go to the counter at taluk office to get an authenticated copy of land title. There is no provision to apply for land title document online. A charge of Rs.20 per copy is collected as revenue by the government. This process is time-consuming as it involves travel, wait and requisition for land title document. Town survey details of Coimbatore municipality is not yet complete and land titles of town properties are not available through the website.

Using Gartner's (2000) four stages maturity model, the level of maturity of the project is only at the first stage of information provision for nine rural taluks in the district. Coimbatore municipality is still in the nascent stage of data entry.

Star Project: In the government portal, users can view all information like market values of land, percentage of stamp duty, preparation of model deed and details about the registration fees online. Registration forms for marriages,

Figure 1. The service levels of both the projects

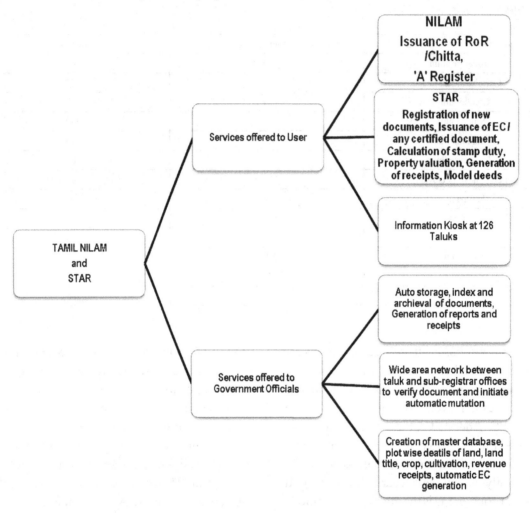

chit funds, welfare aid and pension forms can be downloaded through the web portal but the facility for transaction is not available. Only information access is possible for all these services.

Facility for issuance of Encumbrance Certificate (EC) has moved on to the next phase of maturity. EC forms can be filled in and applied online. The copy of EC would be dispatched to any address provided by the user. A facility for online delivery exists based on user needs only for EC copies. Hence, EC forms are in the transaction phase of maturity.

Using Gartner's (2000) four stages maturity model, on an implementation scale, the level of maturity of Star project in the department of registration is in the first stage. For the provision of EC forms, the project has moved on to the third phase of maturity and transaction facility is available for the users.

2. Level of Integration

The state government planned for interconnection of all SRO and taluk offices to carry out automatic mutation of land records once the registration process was completed. This process of automatic mutation would considerably reduce the time delay in carrying out the manual mutation changes. To achieve this status of Integration between the projects, it is essential to have Tamilnadu State Wide Area Network (TNSWAN) established at both the offices. At present, taluk office and SRO offices function in isolation and there is no interconnection or integration of services between both the departments. At present, there is absolutely no integration of the projects.

The Integration channel is available only at two taluks (Pollachi and Tirupur) as in the first phase of implementation, SRO and taluk offices that functioned within the same premises were provided with interconnection facility. But, the departmental integration process remains static even at these two taluks as there are some technical hitches in establishing integration and access. Infra-structure for integration and internal network is currently being established at two more taluks (Palladam and Udumalpet taluks) of the district. Within Coimbatore city, integration of the projects is not achieved as same platform of application software was not used for both the projects and this situation has created incompetency of operating systems and inter-departmental integration is proving to be very difficult. Suitable arrangements for integration are being done by the district administration.

Hence, at present, all taluk offices still function in isolation. Vertical integration is not available between taluk offices and this status of non-integration has resulted in sub-optimal utilization or non-utilization of these expensive assets.

With regard to Star project, it is fully integrated and operable at the Coimbatore municipality as well as at the district taluks. Registration offices and SRO within the state are inter-connected through a wide area network connection. Encumbrance Certificate (transfer of ownership) details of land documents are accessible at all registration offices within the state. But land ownership verification facility or clear land title verification facility for registered land documents is not available on line even at the department level. Vertical integration is thoroughly achieved in this project

and it is ready for horizontal integration with taluk offices.

3. Status of Interoperability

Nilam project is utilized by the taluk offices to facilitate data entry of land records and mutation of land records. STAR project is used by all registration offices for indexing of land documents. As integration facility is not achieved between both the projects there is no inter-operability of projects. The mutation entry of new land details is still manual. Anytime a new document is registered, the record details are manually entered and sent to the taluk office for effecting mutation certificates to the users. At present, both the departments function in isolation and no intra-net facility is available to track changes and status, manual entries are done by the staff at both offices.

This process is time consuming as three to four registers have to be simultaneously updated to complete a single transaction and hence this process is always time-consuming. Hence, at present, there is no cross-departmental coordination and interoperability of these projects at taluks and municipality.

4. Pace of Implementation

The pace of implementation of Nilam project is very slow, as even after a decade of implementation, the records of the entire district and municipality are not brought online. The project is currently functional at all nine rural taluks of Coimbatore and land title records can be verified online. Urban land records still remain in the nascent stage of data entry within Coimbatore municipality. Town survey of Coimbatore city is not yet complete, as it is a very time consuming and tedious process that involves recording details of each block, area and street wise data for all the available land records. Also, the Village Administrative Officers at panchayats (rural village) are not fully aware of the usage of computer systems

Figure 2. Stake holders

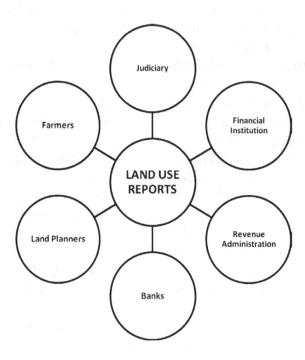

at present. All panchayat level transactions are still totally manual. All queries are referred to taluk offices in the city for processing.

STAR project was completed in time and it is fully functional at the municipality and district taluks. All registration offices within the taluk are inter-connected and EC details of any document can be seen at any other registration office within the state. But, provision for land title facility is not available for the department staffs. Only when this facility is made available for the staffs, clear land title records can be verified before registration. Efforts have to mooted to establish this facility within the registration department.

5. Role of Various Stakeholders

There are many stakeholders (Rahul De, 2006) involved in the process of computerization of land record details and master land database could prove useful for many organizations and institutions within the country. Farmers use land information and record of registration details for property transfers, financial loans and mortgage of property. Financial institutions use record of registration as credible evidence to provide land mortgage loans to farmers. Land planners use the land information for land classification surveys and for sustainable development of land. Judiciary uses record of registration details to decide on ownership issues and solve litigations. Revenue administrators use information of land to calculate revenue, tax and land under encroachment for better development programs. Hence, master land database is critical for many departments. Access could be given to the concerned departments and the projects could become even more beneficial for the public as well as the stakeholders (see Figure 2).

Interviews with Beneficiaries

Interviews of beneficiaries were done at both the project offices to evaluate the tangible benefits accorded by the project (see Table 3).

Table 3. Report of interviews at Taluk office (Tamil Nilam project)

Name, Age, Occupation of Interviewees	Place of residence	Feed back
Illango, 40, Retired Government Employee	Alandurai	He felt that the new project was definitely better than the old system. But, the objective of paperless governance has not been achieved in the department as the transaction was partly manual.
Ponnusamy, 52, Agriculturist	Narasipuram	He opined that the service efficiency of the project have to be improved as most often the department counter was closed without notice and the users had to come again the next day for transaction. Situations like this were very unfavorable for users who commute long distances to the taluk office for certificates.
Ramasamy, 49, Agriculturist	Pichanur	This agriculturist felt that the infra-structure available at the counters have to be improved and a separate room with chairs and drinking water facility needs to be provided for the users.
Kumaresan, 33, Agriculturist	Alandurai	This agriculturist asserted that he did not know about land title documents being accessible online and more publicity needs to be provided for the project.
Ramalingam, 45, Agriculturist	Alandurai	He added that the entire process was still time-consuming as the form has to be filled in and submitted for processing a day in advance and only then the document was made ready and issued at a later date.

Everyday around 50-100 users approached the taluk office counter for requisition of land title copies. The applications were received and processed. In case, the requisition was urgent, Rs.20 was collected immediately and a slip was issued to the user with the current date and identification number. The user has 2 options, either he can wait till 5 pm in the evening and collect the document or he can come back at his convenience within a week and collect the copy in person by producing the identification number (see Table 4).

The counter staff received around 10-30 applications per day. A special counter with computer is set up within the premises to handle queries and distribute copies.

FINDINGS AND DISCUSSION

As citizens' expectations of governance have changed, the pressure is on the government to improve public services. With Information access and reach at its peak, people are more knowledgeable, more vocal about their needs and more sophisticated in their expectations of how government should meet these citizen needs. Also,

Governments worldwide have begun developing strategies to not only enhance efficiency and effectiveness, but also to strengthen the relationship between government and citizens. During the last decade, e-government has largely been an one-way street—"government delivered and citizen received", but now, the users understand and emphasize the need for the government and citizen to partner with each other and other stakeholders in ensuring effective service delivery. Hence, for the future, conventional service delivery systems have to be modified in innovative ways to create public value.

The study revealed that both the projects have clearly benefitted the users, but the extent of benefits offered to the users at this stage is rather very limited. E-services offered through the websites act only as information provider and it is accessed by only a fraction of the population. The level of service delivery should be enhanced for an elaborate analysis as at present the e-governance projects are still in the initial stage of implementation. Genuine e-services can be provided to the users only at the transaction stage wherein the citizen can conduct a significant number of services through the web

Table 4. Report of interviews at district registration office (Star project)

Name, Age, Occupation of Interviewees	Place of residence	Feed back
Velusami, 55, Retired telecom employee	Vellimalaipattinam	He opined that the process of EC was very convenient as a facility for transaction was available online.
Sadasivam, 35, Agriculturist	Alandurai	He asserted that there was a critical need to make the master database accessible to the users as it would avoid multiple registration. He included that some cases of multiple registration were still prevalent in his hometown.
Kumarsan, 33, Factory worker	Alandurai	This employee felt the need for buyer and seller to be mandatorily present at the taluk office for authenticating mutation certificates.
Ramalingam, 45, Agriculturist	Alandurai	This agriculturist wanted the land database to be made available through the web portal for all users as it would show authenticated owners of all land titles and avoid land discrepancies.
Muthuraman, 58, Agriculturist	Chettipalayam	This farmer noted that the access facilities were good at the registrar's office. But the project would be much beneficial if the users were able to access the EC facility through citizen service centers or post-offices in their vicinity.

portal without having to be manually present in the administrative department.

Though, the projects have facilitated quicker processing of land records and brought in transparency to the once opaque system, the pace of implementation of the project within Coimbatore district is very slow when compared to other states of Indian Union. The land administration projects function more efficiently in other states like Karnataka, Maharashtra, Madhya Pradesh, Haryana, Andhra Pradesh and Goa where property registration process has been integrated with computerized land records at taluk offices. In these states, there exists a monitoring mechanism to facilitate genuine land transactions and identify fraudulent transactions. The horizontal and vertical integration process established between the land administration projects is proving to be very beneficial for the states in many ways. Compared to these states, Tamilnadu and in particular within Coimbatore district administration, the process of implementation of land administration projects is very slow and only limited arrays of services are offered to the users.

Even after a decade after implementation, Nilam project is functional only at nine rural taluks within the district and Coimbatore city land record details are still in the process of data entry. However, in terms of revenue generation, the project is very successful. All taluk offices still function in isolation with no data network facility between them.

Nilam project has still a long way to go in establishment of network connection between all taluk offices within the district as well as all taluk offices in the state. Vertical integration of all taluk offices has to be achieved at a priority basis and only when this level of connectivity is achieved, the pace of implementation could move on to the next level of integration with offices of registration. Also, Nilam project is inert at panchayat (village) level and issuance of land documents is still time consuming process.

Star project offers a provision for the users to view the stamp duty, guideline value and model deed online and to download applications for some certificates. Payment of stamp duty, registration fees and registration process is still entirely manual and at the time of registration, the payments can be manually done at the department counter. A facility exists for the user to submit the application of Encumbrance Certificate online and there is a provision to receive the document at any given address through postal services. Only issuance of EC has moved on to the next stage of maturity and transaction facility exists for the users.

Star project has been implemented successfully across all districts of the state and integration facility exists between District Registrar and SRO offices in the state. Exchange of data, EC detail, Land title search facility and certificate verification is possible between all offices. Vertical integration of the department of registration is completed and the project is ready for horizontal integration.

Individually, both the projects have proved to be useful at its current stage of implementation, but integration of the projects would be more beneficial for the users and for the staffs within the departments. This inter-connection through State Wide Area Network, if established, would create unhindered data flow between the taluk and registration offices. Soon after a registration process, the data module would automatically update the new ownership details and produce a mutation copy. As the entire process would be automatic, manual entries at both offices can be avoided. Clear land titles can be issued to the land owners and work load at the administrative departments would be considerably reduced. It would facilitate automatic exchange of land record details and land title documents would be up-to-date online.

Both the projects are still in the first phase of maturity and only at the third and fourth phase of maturity a more detailed analysis could be carried out. As of now, information access is only provided to the public and the users of Tamil Nilam project can conduct only part of the transaction online, as an attestation seal at the taluk office counter is mandatory on the land title document to make it legal and usable for official purposes. This seal is provided only at the taluk office counters after payment of Rs.20 (50 cents). This amount is accounted as revenue of the project and it is channelized back to the revenue department of the state.

As user demand for better quality service increases, E-Governance needs to improve along the line, not only across different levels of government but also different functions of government.

Only if service integration within the department as well as cross-departmental integration happens at the same time, it would serve helpful for the users. After this process is completed to the fullest capacity, it is possible for the user to visit a single portal contact one point of government and complete any level of government transaction – at a "one-stop" concept (Bhatnagar, 2000).

Also, Indian government has announced development of an India portal under National E-governance Plan in 2006 with an objective to integrate and provide access to all government services to the citizens (NeGP, 2007). The portal would provide a single door (web interface) of entry and access for multiple-services through a self-service portal. This one-stop government portal would require complete interoperability, both vertically and horizontally, between all the administrative departments to suit higher demands at a national level.

There are many on-going e-governance projects in India that envisages complete integration of government services at national, state level as well as local level. At national level, Income Tax online and Customs on-line are working on providing a one-stop portal for their respective departments. The current objective of these projects is to integrate the two departments vertically as well as horizontally. However, in practice, these projects were not specifically planned to get suit the objectives. To create a national portal of this magnificence, it is essential to establish integration at all levels. For a national portal with single point of entry, all administrative departments within the union should operate with open access software platforms that are compatible and operable with all type of web technologies. Hence, taking the long term goal of the government into consideration there is a need for land administration departments to adopt technologies that would suit such deviations. A research study by Ajay Ahuja (2008) revealed that interoperability challenges and issues can be best addressed by adopting and following solutions based on open standards, open source and open format. Such solutions provide leverage to the users and do not constrict the user to a particular technology or a vendor and most importantly inter-operate with each other. The author has recommended the usage of such solutions and technologies for Governments of developing nations like India.

Nevertheless, the land administration projects have helped to create immensely rich, technology-interactive land data base in the state. In terms of revenue, both the projects have proved to be successful. Each district within Tamilnadu has generated annual revenue of 1 million and Coimbatore district in particular has generated revenue to the tune of 6 million in the year 2008. Star project has incubated revenue to the tune of 29 million in the year 2008. Issuance of EC has generated revenue to the tune of 2 million in the year 2008. For the government, the land administration projects have clearly generated revenue of more than 35 million and the registration department and revenue departments have clearly seen the beneficial effect of computerization.

IMPLICATIONS

Some of the major lessons learned and challenges faced by the project at the implementation stage were:

1. Issuance of land title copy is still not instant and the process is time-consuming at taluk offices. The users have for 8 hours to receive the document or they have to come again to collect the document at another time.

2. The responsibility of document issuance still rests in the hands of the revenue officials; hence, the monitoring mechanism and efficiency of operation needs to be strengthened, as this serves as a crucial component for the success of the projects.

3. Issuance of land title document facility is not fully-automatic through the web portal.

4. Loan facility and other hindrances encountered by the farmers still remain unchanged.

5. Farmers still travel long distances to taluk head quarters to apply for land title document.

6. No significant change is felt by the farmers or other users as they still travel long distances, wait in line for access as well as wait for almost 8 hours to receive the certificate. Present stage of computersation of departments has not made any difference to them.

7. There has only been a shift of powerbase from the VAO to the taluk office staffs.

8. Land administration offices still function in isolation as no integration facility exists between the two departments.

9. Land title details online are not updated for weeks and the data often remains obsolete.

10. Different platform of soft wares used in the project has created interoperability challenges and open standard solutions should be utilized to avoid incompatibility and ensure inter-operability of future projects.

11. Stake holder access and land title verification facility is not offered for the public at present. This access facility would simplify the loan and financial difficulties encountered by the farmers. Hence the project offers only a limited scope for the users.

12. Networking of the projects at different levels to ensure data movement from district to provincial governments and at the level of union government through central web-hosting facility would be very beneficial for the departments.

13. Citizen Service centers needs to be created for convenient usage as, at present, the users need to travel to taluk offices for all land document copies.

14. Awareness level of the projects among the users seems to be low and publicity efforts have to be initiated.

15. Digitization of Cadastral Survey Maps should be done without which the land information system is incomplete.

CONCLUSION AND RECOMMENDATION

E-governance includes measures that allow a more participatory, interactive and meaningful interaction between the government and the citizen. This study tried to understand the nature (dimensions) and degree of impact of computerization of 2 projects in which the manual system was replaced through the usage of computers. The aim of the study was to produce a credible assessment of impact of these two projects in the state of Tamilnadu.

In order to ensure success and efficiency of any E-Governance initiatives in the country, it is important to assess the performance of E-Government projects periodically and take necessary actions based on these assessments. This research study has presented the growth stage model of E-Governance maturity of land administration projects at Coimbatore districts and municipality to assess the pace of implementation of the projects within the municipality and district taluks. At present, land administration projects are not fully functional in the district because of various operational and infrastructure problems. Findings reveal that the district administration needs to focus its attention on enhancing the service level of both the projects.

Taking the long term goal of a single portal for multiple service access into consideration, the state government should create a synchronized land administration portal that provides multiple service entries through a common access point to enhance service efficiency. This portal can be linked to the all India portal without any difficulty at any point of time. The usual website at its current phase of implementation that serves as an information provider is not sufficient for citizen usage as the services offered to the citizen is rather very limited at this stage.

E-government is not merely equipping the government offices with computers or automation of government departments, but it should be used as an effective tool of governance that increases the functional efficacy of administration. It is a process that requires planning, sustained dedication of resources and political will. Transactional and fully automatic services can only ensure greater customer satisfaction.

Analyzing the implementation scale of Tamil Nilam and Star projects, the pace of implementation of Tamil Nilam is very slow. Even after a decade since implementation the objectives of computerization of land records have not been achieved and town survey records are still in the process of data entry. Also, since there is no integration between both the projects, the land title record available through the web portal is obsolete. The land database that is online should be constantly refreshed as online mutation is crucial for uploading of fresh data.

Star project has come a long way since implementation and the registration department has successfully established a wide area network connection where in all registration offices within the state are interconnected and connection facility also exists with the IG of Registration, Chennai. Hence, all activities of the registration department are fully automated.

Only if integration and interoperability is achieved between the SRO and registration offices at district and municipality, the end user would avoid time delays, avail easier, up-to-date land titles and reap the true benefits as intended by the projects. A research study by Vilasini Ramanchandran (2005) has concluded that automatic data flow between the concerned offices would only result in online mutation and result in successful implementation of any E-Governance projects in the longer run.

According to a study on critical factors of E-Governance (2007), lack of Integration of various applications within or across various Government departments lead to silos, with each department having their own set of data, administrators, management procedures and related issues. These applications and projects, which are not based on standards, create use of varied technologies which may not interoperate. This leads to duplication of work, increasing cost of ownership and complexity in integration of any two projects.

At this juncture, integration and on-line access of land administration projects are necessary as only then clear ownership title of any land property is accessible for all. A number of cases of multiple registration of same plot of land have been observed in states like Bihar. As, the registration departments do not have any access to the land title for verification before registration of a new property, it is possible that deeds for the same property can be registered in multiple names. Until, integration is achieved between these projects and clear ownership titles are verified before any new registration, purchase of land in the state might have risks. Later on, for a single unified portal of all states, the system of integration could be used at a national level through webhosting facility. Land record data all through the 26 states of India could be integrated and brought online for citizen usage.

Furthermore, within Coimbatore municipality, the same platform of application software is not used for land administration projects and this situation has resulted in incompetency of operating systems. Inter-departmental integration is proving to be very difficult because of this reason. Suitable arrangements for integration process are currently being done by the district administration. This status of non-integration of the two projects has resulted in sub-optimal utilization or non-utilization of such expensive assets. Semantic factors should also be taken into consideration in the planning process of any e-governance projects as such differences normally make it more difficult for different platforms to co-exist through a single portal. A study by Rakhi Tripathi (2006)

has noted that semantic incompatibility can be minimized to a certain level when the operational systems are designed by using previously agreed data formats.

A research study by Ajay Ahuja (2008) revealed that interoperability challenges and issues can be best addressed by adopting and following solutions based on Open Standards, Open Source and Open Format. Such solutions provide leverage to the users and do not constrict the user to a particular technology or a vendor and most importantly inter-operate with each other. The author has recommended that Governments of developing nations like India should go in for such solutions and technologies. The City of Munich, Brazilian Government, French Government and People's Republic of China are amongst many of the government agencies who are evaluating and implementing Open Source based desktop solutions in recent times, to save on licensing costs and to move away from the proprietary and closed solutions.

If separate intra-net backbone proves costly, two departments of similar functions could be corroborated and the cost could be shared. As, taluk offices and SRO share similar functions and is mutually dependant on one another for total information access for the public. Hence, the funds obtained from the most successful, revenue obtainable projects like star could be channelized for the betterment of Tamil Nilam project as both are dependent on each other for information sufficiency.

One reason for delay could be the fact that there is no strong departmental head to take care of implementation schedules and meet up the deadlines of the project due to transfer or change of staffs in charge. The study on critical issues in E-Governance (2007) has clearly outlined lack of leadership at senior management level as the major cause for failure of any E-Governance initiative in India. Hence, efforts have to be mooted to bring a strong head of implementation of all E-Governance schemes at the district level.

Tamilnadu government has gone up the ladder of implementation by installing 127 information kiosks at many taluks to provide access to the users and to bridge the digital divide in the state. According to Critical issues in E-Governance study (2007), this facility is looked at as one of the most advanced stage of implementation across the country as it breaks down the barriers of technology access and reaches the mass easily. Now, this effort has to be appreciated and other hindrances have to be removed for more tangible benefits for the users.

Awareness level of the project seems to be low among the users. Mainly agriculturists, who use land title documents often to avail loan facilities, are aware of the fact that only computerized land title document can be used for official documentation purposes. But, the farmers are not aware of the fact that the land title document can be verified online, through the web portal. Lack of rigorous publicity of the projects has in fact led to this situation.

Even if users know about the projects, if it is only an information access website and part of the transaction could only be achieved online and to complete the transaction, a visit to the department of administration is necessary, then it is of little or no use to them. As, anyway to carry out part of the transaction they need to make a visit to the government office, they might not be interested in conducting part of the transaction online. There is a dire need to make the entire process fully automatic at the earliest.

Although access to land title document is easier now, the process of rural credit still remains unchanged for the farmers. The true impact of the projects can be seen only when the farmers are able to avail easier loan facilities. The departmental integrations should be done at the stake-holder level so that when a farmer arrives at a commercial bank for a loan, the officer at the bank should be able to type in the land title number and find all relevant details about the property right from his table. Mortgage details, crop details, cultivation details, title of the deed and size of his land holding should all be accessible for the loan officer. Based on the accessible details, loan can either be sanctioned or rejected at once.

In the earlier system of manual land records, the village accountant was an easily accessible government functionary within the village with whom the farmers could maintain a long-term relationship. With the new system, the power base had shifted to the taluks and the farmers need to make half a day's journey to the taluk headquarters and new functionaries are in charge. While, the projects have facilitated easier access to land title certificates, the rural farmers still travel long distance to reach the nearest taluk office for obtaining the copy. The number of trips that the farmer makes to the taluk office has reduced, but still he needs to travel to the neighboring taluk office to obtain a certificate. Also, the issuance of land title document still takes 1-3 days of processing time based on the number of applications received. Obtaining a land title copy is still not an instant service delivery facility. Provision for instant land titles have to be introduced for easier accessibility.

Even now, the common problems that a user encounters at the taluk office are unexpected delay in delivery due to frequent power cuts, technical snags, significant travel distances and delay in carrying out mutation process. These factors cause great inconveniences to the users. Hence, the infrastructure requires to be upgraded and delivery mechanism should also be improved.

Provision to issue the land title documents and certificates at convenient location would make the project more convenient for the farmers. In the state of Uttaranchal and Chhattisgarh, land title documents are issued at all rural schools for convenience of the users and Tamilnadu state can also replicate the same system and issue the land title document at post-offices or rural schools. In Chhattisgarh, 171 Citizen Service Centers has been set up in rural schools to facilitate easier citizen participation at all rural villages and taluks. Community Service Centers should be set up at strategic locations to facilitate more citizen access and participation. Land administration project in Karnataka has set up 800 citizen centers in towns and villages and this project generates more revenue for the government than all other E-Governance projects put together.

The land data should be allowed to access by various institutions i.e. financial institutions, judiciary, developmental departments etc for their respective domains. Stake holder access is very necessary now as only when all the identified stake holders like cooperative banks, commercial banks, judicial courts, land administrative wings of all government departments and land planners are able to access relevant details of the master database created by the web host facility, the projects would be truly beneficial for the grass root citizen. Direct central database access facility to all the stake holders would eliminate numerous trips to administrative departments of government machinery and commercial loan vendors.

In an UN E-Governance survey (2008), the United States scored the highest on e-participation index. The study revealed that it was primarily due to the nation's strength in e-information and e-consultation that enabled its citizens to be more interactive with their government. South Korea, though it is termed as a 'digital state' emerged second only as awareness level of citizen was low. Publicity measures should be enhanced within the district level to create a better impact.

Land administration projects have successfully brought in transparency into the system and eliminated corruption at lower levels of administration. Overall, Tamil Nilam and Star projects have transformed the lives of millions of farmers through efficient administration. The projects have resulted in the creation of voluminous data at the state level with 100 million landholders living in 17,292 villages within the state. Transaction mode of services would go a long way in empowering the citizens with knowledge of communication. Citizen needs and requirements should be integrated into the e-governance strategy to achieve maximum benefits from the projects. The land administration projects are still evolving through advanced technology. Automation, integration with cadastral mapping and registration process would improve the entire revenue administration system within the state.

RECOMMENDATIONS

1. A strong departmental head and commitment to deadlines is the most crucial factor in achieving the target. Deadlines are necessary for any project as that would hasten up the activities of the project.

2. Integration of Tamil Nilam and Star projects is vital to offer effective service delivery.

3. Stake holder access of land title documents is necessary to prevent multiple registration of same property. If clear title verification is possible online, any seller and buyer could verify the documents and access the true ownership details of a particular property.

4. If separate intra-net backbone proves costly, two departments of similar functions could be corroborated and integration cost could be shared.

5. Efficiency of service is the key to reform and provision to access and complete the entire transaction over the internet should be incorporated.

6. A provision to apply and receive land title documents online should be introduced. EC copies are currently provided efficiently through postal services.

7. Website has to be constantly updated for efficient service delivery as obsolete data makes the project unreliable.

8. Infrastructure available at the taluk office counters where the documents are issued need to be improved and a single room with waiting chairs, drinking water provision and token system should be introduced for the user convenience.

9. Instant issuance of land title, EC and other certified copies should be provided. The counter staff should be provided with a computer system, printer and they should be trained to issue a print out as soon as an application is received. This would reduce delay in service delivery.

10. A single counter at rural post office or schools could be used as distribution points to deliver land title and other certified documents.

11. Alternate provision can be introduced to accept land title extracts from the public without attestation. As, it would result in revenue loss for the government, a stamp of Rs.20 denomination can be mandatorily asked to be pasted on the document for legal sanctity. This would be very convenient for the internet users, as they could just download a print-out and they need not go to the counter for attestation. Here again, the revenue of Rs.20 is channeled back to the government but there is no need for the user to visit the counter for certified copies.

12. Central web-hosting facility can be initiated at the district or state level and all the details of master data base can be stored in a central server with link up of SRO and taluk offices of all districts within the state. All land data of SRO and taluk offices can be cumulatively deposited at a common information pool of the central server. Likewise, database of 206 taluks in the state can be pooled in at the central server.

13. Using web hosting technology, this database can be given access for all government administrative departments. Users can also be given access to the data pool.

14. Stake holder access remains as one critical factor of E-Governance. Access to the information pool can be given to all stake holders and a fee can be collected from them for utility of land record database. This kind of an access would truly benefit all the stake holders involved and the end users in many ways.

15. Convenience is the key word of any latest technology. Common service centers need to be created at strategic locations in cities and rural villages and these centers could be made to function on all days of the week. These centers could issue all land record copies and provide related details for all.

REFERENCES

Ahuja, A. (2008). Open and secure solutions for empowering governments. Retrieved September 21, 2009, from www.egovonline.net/.../ 4194-indian-society- is-it-ready-for- online-government-services.html

Bhatnagar, S. (2003). Access to information report: E-government. In Hodess, R., Inowlocki, T., & Wolfe, T. (Eds.), *Global corruption report 2003* (pp. 24–32). London, UK: Profile Books Lt.

Bhatnagar, S. (2006). *E-governance – An assessment framework. Department of Information Technology*. New Delhi: Government of India.

Bhatnagar, S. (2007). *E-government in Asia Pacific regions – An assessment of issues and challenges*. Ahmadabad: Indian Institute of Management.

Bodkar, S., et al. (2008). Framework for expanding e-government: The e-governance project. Paper presented at 5th Scandinavian Workshop on E-Government, Copenhagen.

Bonham, M., & Seifert, J. (2003). *The transformative potential of e-government in transitional democracies*. Congressional Research Service.

Chandra, S., & Lyons, K. (2001). *Undertaking land administration projects: Sustainability, affordability, operational efficiency and good practice guidelines*. Australian Government Overseas Aid Program, Quality Assurance Series, AusAid.

Chawla, R. (2004). Online delivery of land titles to rural farmers in Karnataka, India. A paper presented at Scaling up Poverty Reduction: A Global Learning Process: E-Governance Conference, Shanghai.

Chawla, R. (2007). Freedom in the fields: Bhoomi online delivery of land records. Retrieved on September 29, 2009, from www.bhoomi.kar.nic.in

Critical Issues in E-Governance. (2007). Summary of discussion using issue process methodology panel discussion. Paper presented at the 5th International Conference on e-Governance (ICEG 2007). Available at http://www.csi-sigegov.org/critical_issues_on_e_governance.pdf accessed on 21.9.2009

Dale, P. (1999, October). Is technology a blessing or a curse in land administration? Presented at the UN-FIG Conference on Land Tenure and Cadastral Infrastructure for Sustainable Development, Melbourne, Australia.

Dale, P. (2000). The importance of land administration in the development of land markets - A global perspective. Land Markets and Land Consolidation in Central Europe, TU Delft – Report of UDMS 2000.

De, R. (2005). E-government systems in developing countries: Stakeholders and conflict. In Wimmer, M. A. (Eds.), *E-Gov - 2005, LNCS 3591* (pp. 26–37).

De, R. (2006). The impact of e-government initiatives: Issues of poverty and vulnerability reduction. *Regional Development Dialogue, 27*(2), 88–100.

Deepak, B. (2004). *Measuring the impact of e-government. E-Government Applications Practice Lead, Global ICT Department*. World Bank.

Deininger, K. (2007). *Land policies for growth and poverty reduction. Organization for Economic Cooperation and Development*. India: World Bank.

Department of Information Technology. (2007). *National e-governance report*. New Delhi.

District, C. (2008). *Revenue department report*. India.

Dwivedi, P., & Sahu, G. P. (2008). *Challenges of e-government implementation in India. Emerging technologies in e-government* (pp. 210–215). E-Governance Publication.

EGAT/NRM/LRM/USAID. (2009). *Land tenure, poverty and economic growth in India*. Briefing Paper.

Gilmore, A., & D'Souza, C. (2006). Service excellence in e-governance issues – An Indian case study. *Journal of Administration and Governance, 1*(1).

Government of India. (2007). *Right to information India*. New Delhi.

Hanstad, T., & Nielsen, R. (2009). Land tenure reform in India. In Prosterman, R. L., Mitchell, R., & Hanstad, T. (Eds.), *One billion rising: Law, land and alleviation of global poverty*. Leiden University Press.

India, U. N. D. P. (2009). Project E-Setu: Reaching the unreached. New Delhi, India: United Nations Development Program. Retrieved from http://www.undp.org.in/events/ict-goa/e-setu15-16dec03goa.PPT

India Corruption Study. (2005). To improve governance. Centre for Media Studies, New Delhi.

Indian Brand Equity Foundation. (2004). *Ministry of Commerce*. Government of India.

Jayaradha, N. (2003). *E-governance: Tackling the hurdles. Tamil Inaiyam 2003*. India: Tamilnadu.

Jha, R. (2005). Land fragmentation and its implications for productivity: Evidence from Southern India. (ASARC Working Paper 2005/01).

Kochhar, S., & Dhanjal, G. (2004). *From governance to e-governance: An initial assessment of some of India's best projects*. Skoch E-Governance Report Card.

Kumar, R. (2006). Impact and sustainability of e-government services in developing countries: Lessons learned from Tamilnadu, India. *The Information Society*, *22*, 1–12. doi:10.1080/01972240500388149

Land Information and Management Report. (2005).

Maenpaa, O. (2004). E-governance: Effects on civil society, transparency and democracy. Paper presented at Challenges and Opportunities for Democracy, Administration and Law IIAS-ISA, Workshop, Helsinki.

Ministry of Information and Communication. (2005). E-readiness report of New Delhi.

Ministry of Rural Development. (2004). Land reforms. Retrieved on September 29, 2009, from http://rural.nic.in/ book01-02/ ch-24.pdf

National Informatics Centre. (2009). *Computerization of land records*. New Delhi: Land Records Division, Ministry of Information Technology.

Ndou, V. (2004). E – government for developing countries: Opportunities and challenges. *Electronic Journal on Information Systems in Developing Countries*, *18*(1), 1–24.

Olsen, D. (2005). Local e-government in Norway - Current status and emerging issues. *Scandinavian Journal of Information Systems*, *17*(2), 41–84.

Pacific Council on International Policy. (2002). *Roadmap for e-government in the developing world*. Report of the Working Group on E-Government in the Developing World.

PRISM. (2005). *Department of IT*. Government of Punjab.

Rai, K., & Bhalla, D. K. (2005). Computerization of land records in India. Retrieved on September 9, 2009, from http://www.gisdevelopment.net/ application/ lis/ overview/ lisrp0015.htm

Ramachandran, V. (2005). *E-Dhara: Land records management system*. India: Revenue Department, Government of Gujarat.

Oracle Report. (2004). Urban local bodies in Tamilnadu deliver improved citizen services. Oracle – E-Governance News, 6, pp 1- 14.

Reserve Bank of India. (2008). Foreign exchange department report.

Ritu, A. (2008). E-learning in land record Information System sharing good practices: E-learning in surveying, geo-Information Sciences and land administration. FIG International Workshop, Enschede, The Netherlands.

Sathyamurthy, D. (2002, October). KAVERI - Karnataka valuation and e-registration. Paper presented at the sixth national conference on E-Governance, Chandigarh.

Saxena, K. B. S. (2005). Towards excellence in e-governance. International Journal of Public Sector Management, 18, 498–513. Retrieved on September 29, 2009, from http://www.emeraldinsight.com/ 10.1108/ 09513550510616733

Second Administrative Reforms Commission. (2008). Government of India report.

Seifert, J. W. (2003). *A primer on e-government: Sectors, stages, opportunities and challenges of online governance*. Congressional Research Service, Library of Congress.

Sharma, L. P. (2006). Technology fusion for e-land record. Paper presented at 4th International Conference on E-governance held at IIT, Delhi.

Shastri, P. (2001, May 1). Digitizing land records key to reform. Hindustan Times. Retrieved on September 29, 2009, from http://www.hindustantimes.com/News/business/Digitising-land-records-key-to-reform/Article1-219609.aspx

Shirin, M. (2004). Evaluating the developmental impact of e-governance initiatives: An exploratory framework. *Electronic Journal of Information Systems in Developing Countries, 20*(5), 1–13.

Sipiar, J., et al. (2005). Bridging the digital divide for e-government inclusion: A United States case study. The Electronic Journal of E-Government, 3(3), 137-146. Retrieved on September 9, 2009, at www.ejeg.com

Thakur, V. (2005). *Social impact of computerization of land records. Adopting e-governance.* New Delhi, India: Computer Society of India Publications.

Tripathi, R. (2006). *Selected aspects of interoperability in one-stop government portal of India. Towards next generation e-governance.* New Delhi, India: Computer Society of India Publications.

Umashankar, C. (2002). Transforming district administration using e-governance - Tiruvarur experience. Retrieved on September 29, 2009, from http://www.groups/yahoo.com/group/India-egov

Umashankar, C., & Bhaskara, R. (2000, January). Implementation of an integrated land records system - A case study at Kudavasal Taluk, Tiruvarur District, Tamilnadu. Paper presented at Technical proceedings, Geomatics 2000.

UN E-Government Service. (2008). *From e-government to connected governance.* Department of Economic and Social Affairs Division for Public Administration and Development Management.

World Bank. (2007). *India: Land policies for growth and poverty reduction* (pp. 74–79). New Delhi, India: Oxford University Press.

Zambrano, R., & Dandjinou, P. (2003). *E-governance service delivery.* India and South Africa: United Nations Development Project.

WEBOGRAPHY

http://agmarknet.nic.in/agmarknet.htm

http://egov.mit.gov.in/elecgov.htm

http://Europe.eu.int/information_society/eeurope/index_en.htm

http://goidirectory.nic.in/ministry.htm

http://himachal.nic.in/lokmitra.htm

http://intra.tn.nic.in/kiosk/

http://www1.worldbank.org/publicsector/egov/apmandalscs.htm

http://www1.worldbank.org/publicsector/egov/gujaratcs.htm

http://www.digitalgovernance.org

http://www.dpindia.org/pub_case_drishtee.htm

http://www.mit.gov.in/actionplan/about.asp

http://www.unpan.org/e-government/global leaders index.htm

http://www.worldmarketsanalysis.com/e_gov_report.html

www.bhoomi.kar.nic.in

www.egov4dev.org

www.egov.gov.sg/

www.elcot.in

www.rti-india.com

www.taluk.tn.nic.in

www.tn.gov.in

www.tnreginet.net

KEYWORDS AND DEFINITIONS

E-Government: Electronic Governance or digital governance that enables citizen to conduct administrative transactions through internet or any other Information Communication Technology.

Land Record Computerization Project: Computerization or digitization of all land records within the state.

Computerization of Property Registration: Computerization or digitization of all property transactions facility.

Common Service Centers: Community service center that facilitates e-governance transactions of the users.

Stake-Holder Access: Integration or Accessibility provided to related players involved in the transaction at all levels of governance.

Master Database: Cumulative land record database of the entire population of state.

Citizen Access: Connectivity provided to the citizen or users.

Data-Warehousing: Data store house at a common server.

Inter-Operability: Inter-departmental access facility.

Chapter 6
Extension of E-Government:
M-Government Development Capabilities

Mahmud Akhter Shareef
McMaster University, Canada

Norm Archer
McMaster University, Canada

ABSTRACT

The emergence of mobile technologies has not only revolutionalized business procedures, but it has also resulted in transformation and reengineering of public service adoption mechanisms in more traditional e-government (EG) systems. Mobile-government or m-government (MG) is a subset of EG where interactions with government services can be conducted through mobile devices. In this chapter, we identify the development of the fundamental capabilities needed to adopt and manage information and communications technologies and to successfully implement citizen-focused MG systems. To accomplish this, we address the feasibility of adopting MG and the fundamental capabilities needed by a government to establish MG.

INTRODUCTION

The massive proliferation and diffusion of information and communication technology (ICT) has changed the concepts, techniques, economies, and cultures of society. Consumers and business organizations have developed an understanding of these changes and have been quick to adopt the full potential of ICT-based systems. Modern govern-

ments are typically engaged in planning, creating, organizing, regulating, and administering different sectors of governing systems – such as residence, education, health, commerce and trade, foreign policy, and all other affairs related to citizens and business. Governments also develop and adopt different rules and regulations to maintain established order and to amend existing systems according to the needs of a society – such as security, law and order, agreements with other states, and policies within the state. At the present time, most

DOI: 10.4018/978-1-60960-848-4.ch006

democratic governments realize that, for the sake of sustainability and popularity, citizen-focused service is the main vehicle for good governance, and it is also the main task of the government. Developed countries, among others, are seeking to enhance performance of government services and increase the participation of citizens in public systems through the application of ICT in public administration (Damodaran et al., 2005; Robin et al., 2009). This has resulted in the use of ICT as an essential component of many government organizations (Steyaert, 2000). This revolutionary movement by government organizations towards extensive ICT-based enablers is simply known as electronic government, or E-government (EG). The United Nations Public Administration Network (UNPAN, 2002) has defined EG as: "… utilizing the Internet and the World Wide Web for delivering government information and services to citizens."

Many developed and developing countries are striving to achieve the maximum potential of EG, basically providing access to government web sites through wired technology (Heeks & Bailur, 2007). Many countries are investing financial and human resources in achieving either static, interactive, and/or transactional phases of EG to facilitate the national economy, provide better quality and cost effective services to citizens, ensure global positioning of country images, and enhance citizen participation to establish accountable, transparent, and good governance (Accenture, 2005; Shareef et al., 2010b). However, some countries have completely or partially failed to achieve the precise mission of EG. The most significant reasons for these failures have been:

1. The proliferation of EG has created a digital divide which inevitably prevents the democratic participation of all citizens in the EG system.
2. A majority of citizens do not have enough computer and Internet competence to work with the system and interact with government web portals.
3. In rural areas, due to insufficiency of technological infrastructure, the unavailability of the Internet and computers, underprivileged groups cannot access the EG system.
4. Underprivileged people do not possess social and cultural compatibility with computers that can access the wired Internet system.
5. The wired Internet network and associated computers are costly systems which are not financially manageable for a majority of the people.
6. EG without the capabilities of mobile devices cannot provide time and location sensitive services which are imperative for disaster management, emergencies, terrorism alerts, severe weather forecasts, and certain other real time information.
7. Spontaneous two-way communication is difficult for the wired Internet and PC network.
8. EG has little mobility and it is difficult to access from remote village areas, particularly in developing countries.

All the above barriers to EG do not prohibit the emergence of a system for accessing government services, but rather expedite alternative and supplementary systems that could overcome the barriers to EG. One supplementary system exists in the form of mobile-government (MG) which is accessed through hand held devices such as cellular telephones, personal digital assistants (PDAs), smart phones, laptop computers, and/ or other handheld devices. MG is a subset of EG where interactions with government services can be conducted through mobile devices (Archer, 2007; Kumar & Sinha, 2007; Shareef & Archer, 2010a). In fact, MG is viewed by researchers and practitioners as providing the future direction in which governments must move to facilitate the proliferation of widespread access to online government systems. MG can provide many advantages: time and cost saving, instant information transfer, transparency, and democratization, as well as global communication without time and space constraints.

MG has been adopted by several European, Asian, and African countries to leverage government services where real time information is important, such as terrorism alerts, traffic information and road conditions, severe weather forecasts, police investigations, disaster management, land inspection, etc. (Blackman, 2006; Trimi & Sheng, 2008). MG has the potential for improved efficiency, effectiveness, urgent two-way communications, and user-friendly features. Citizens can be comfortable in adopting and participating in MG irrespective of class, education, and skill. As an extension or a supplement of EG, the diffusion and articulated implementation of MG has confronted many challenges which need explicit attention by any government intending to implement MG projects (Archer; 2007; Trimi & Sheng, 2008). However, compared to regular EG channels that require wired computer connections, wireless connections through mobile devices are much more vulnerable to security and privacy problems, are difficult for data management and data storage, cannot support large information displays, and are difficult for typing and reading (Trimi & Sheng, 2008). In addition, wireless Internet access may be costly, not easily available or easy to use, and often may not be able to access many websites that require different application protocols.

Therefore, before funding and implementing MG in any country, it is essential to identify the generic and distinctive characteristics of that country in terms of super-structural and infrastructural conditions, and the overall technology absorption capabilities of their government and citizens. In this era of globalization, the answer to this issue is of the utmost importance. The development of a framework that would provide plausible solutions for the implementation of MG and the supporting ICT infrastructure is of interest to researchers, practitioners, and United Nations organizations. This research addresses this issue in a comprehen-

sive manner and attempts to develop a framework from a government's perspective for designing, implementing, and managing ICT and MG.

In this study, we identify the development of the fundamental capabilities needed to adopt and manage ICT and to successfully implement citizen-focused MG systems. To meet this target, we will address the fundamental capability of a government to implement MG by analyzing the following issues:

1. Infrastructure
2. Knowledge management
3. Availability of resources
4. Digital divide
5. Operations
6. Maintenance

The next section describes the concepts and applications of MG. Then we encapsulate a theoretical typology framework for MG development capability. Finally, we discuss conclusions based on our framework.

M-GOVERNMENT: CONCEPT AND APPLICATION

M-government (MG) is a new trend in reforming public service that can supplement existing of EG services with more competitive and versatile application hand-held devices. MG can be defined as the evolution and extension of existing E-government organizational structures to facilitate uses of government service with more efficiency, mobility, scope of availability, participation, ease of use, and to some extent real time information where interactions between users and service providers are possible through mobile devices (Archer; 2007; Blackman, 2006; Global Dialogue, 2007; I-Ways, 2009; Misuraca, 2009; Naqvi & Al-Shihi, 2009; Trimi & Sheng, 2008).

EG can be defined from public administration, political, social, organizational, and technological perspectives. The key focus of EG has been on government information and service delivery through a networked environment to different stakeholders of government services. According to Riley (2002), the application of ICT and the reformation of public administration and government services have two main aspects: 1) Service delivery patterns and internal public sector administration have been reformed drastically, and 2) Interactions of government stakeholders with government agencies/departments have changed, prompting expectations of higher quality, effective, and efficient services.

The general concepts, paradigms, and definitions of EG do not provide any restrictions on the use the type of device used to gain access to the Internet and to government portals. These devices might be wireline connected through personal computers as end user devices, or wireless Internet connected through laptops, WiFi (wireless Fidelity), or mobile phones and any other hand held devices. In MG, devices include mobile phones or any other handheld mobile device or wireless Internet connection through laptops and other mobile device (Archer; 2007; Blackman, 2006; Global Dialogue, 2007; I-Ways, 2009; Misuraca, 2009; Naqvi & Al-Shihi, 2009; Trimi & Sheng, 2008). Therefore, MG is a dynamic sub-classification of EG. It is a new trend in EG which is now widely used by consumers in European, Asian, and African countries (Archer; 2007; Misuraca, 2009; Trimi & Sheng, 2008).

The adoption of mobile services is highly versatile. According to the ITU (International Telecommunication Union), the growth of mobile cellular subscribers worldwide has been very impressive. In 2000, global mobile penetration was only 12 per cent, but it surpassed 60 per cent by early 2009, and 95 percent of mobile phones currently sold include web browsers. Global mobile services were expected to reach 4 billion subscribers worldwide by the end of 2009, while PC usage has been left far behind at 1 billion users (Internet World Stats, 2009). The

functionality of mobile phones, including user proximity, accessibility, instantaneous messaging and real time information exchange, voice mail, anytime and anywhere connection, emergency notification, and web browsing with mobility, have made mobile phones the communications choice of a growing percentage of users worldwide. Coupled with extensive wireless infrastructure even in developing countries (sometimes the only communications technology available in these countries), makes mobile phones the latest revolution in the world ICT market (Lallana, 2008; Misuraca, 2009; Trimi & Sheng, 2008). This grass roots adoption of mobile phones, irrespective of a country's economic position or the social and economic status or technological knowledge of individuals, implies that mobile phones might become the panacea that fulfills the intriguing dream of implementing EG while at the same time minimizing the digital divide.

The growth of mobile use throughout the world makes it the most popular and viable wireless channel for voice mail, SMS, and wireless Internet services which can facilitate existing EG services and open the scope of new services among all classes of citizens, either privileged or unprivileged (I-Ways, 2009; Shareef et al, 2009b; Vincent and Harris, 2008). In that sense, MG is not only an extension of EG for certain stationary services, but it can also provide supplementary facilities like availability anytime and anywhere. At the same time, MG can be used for implementing new public projects where mobile devices are the only feasible means of interaction with certain government service applications (Archer; 2007; Scholl, 2005). Basically, the integration of existing EG services with some unique features of MG, which has been done in certain countries, particularly for providing real time information and disaster management, supports the comprehensive concept of ubiquitous-government or U-government, thus transforming public administration with the help of ICT (Anttiroiko, 2005; Archer, 2007).

Applications of MG have appeared in all four primary sectors of public service systems: M-communications, M-services, M-democracy, and M-administration (Lallana, 2008). Mobile devices have also been used for interaction in all EG categories, including government-to-citizen (G2C), government-to-business (G2B), government-to-employee (G2E), government-to-government (G2G), and internal effectiveness and efficiency (IEE) (Archer, 2007; Kumar & Sinha, 2007). However, for citizen use and internal effectiveness and efficiency, mobile applications are more common than other standard EG applications (Archer; 2007). Citizens frequently use mobile phones to interact with government and to seek the latest government information, including forecasts, news, emergency messages, and acknowledgements or notifications (Kumar & Sinha, 2007). These G2C or C2G interactions are leveraged by common facilities which mobile phones offer in comparison to connection through the wired Internet. Accessibility, user proximity, and wide area networking encourage governments to provide and receive real time information by interacting with their citizens. We now address versatile applications of MG in different countries.

Since mobile phones allow parties to communicate instantaneously anytime and from anywhere, even from remote areas, this is a convenient way to receive government services (Lallana, 2008). Several countries use mobile phone channels to inform citizens of real time information, emergency news, and important notifications. For example, Singapore uses SMS (Short Messaging Service) to circulate government information like road tax renewals, medical examination appointments for domestic workers, passport renewal notifications, parking reminders, parliamentary notices, and emergency national alerts (Lallana, 2008). M-technology enables government to maintain truly instantaneous two-way communication, a location-based personalized service, even when users are located in remote village areas (Trimi & Sheng, 2008). "My Mobile Virginia" is a popular wireless portal in the State of Virginia, USA through which the government can transmit instantaneous information for purposes such as emergency weather conditions, legislative information, tax related information, election notices, etc (Moon, 2004). "My California on the Go" is an example of M-communication implemented in the State of California, USA to provide citizens with information and government notices for traffic jams, state lotteries, press releases of government services, energy warnings, etc. (Trimi & Sheng, 2008). The New York City, USA fire department uses SMS services to communicate with citizens (wireless messaging services), and the Federal Aviation Administration (FAA), USA sends real-time airport status information to commuters and passengers via email (Trimi & Sheng, 2008). SMS services are used by the London, UK police department to inform citizens about security threats and emergency alerts. Also in London, the 'Bus Operator Metroline' uses a mobile tracking system to monitor locations of buses and their scheduling and to send text messages to alert drivers to maintain proper scheduling (Trimi & Sheng, 2008). SMS services are very common in India to provide citizens with government updates like agricultural information "Agri-watch" (Kapugama, 2009). In China 150 million mobile phone users can send SMS messages to deputies of the National People's Congress. The Hong Kong government communicates with citizens to alert them of emergencies, such as the SARS epidemic of 2002-2003 (i4d, 2007). Japan's Vehicle Information and Communication System (VICS), uses mobile technologies to inform citizens about traffic congestion, road work, car accidents, availability of parking lots, and weather information (Trimi & Sheng, 2008).

M-service is basically a broad category which can be conceptualized as citizen interactions with government portals through mobile devices to seek government services. For example, the "Government of Canada Wireless Portal" is an evolving project which encourages citizens to access certain government services using mobile devices, such as contact information for parliament members, Canada-USA border wait times, the latest economic indicators, passport services, and government emergency news releases concerning citizen affairs (Trimi & Sheng, 2008). The Indian income tax department has introduced an M-service for citizens to inquire online about tax challans (official payment receipts) and to upload the details of tax deposits through mobile devices (Kapugama, 2009). The Singapore National Library allows citizens to receive instantaneous service through mobile inquiry. The Helsinki Public Transport System in Finland sells transport tickets to commuters through mobile text messaging (i4d, 2007). M-services are very common in Sweden and Finland. Tax services, job related information, parking ticket payments, etc. are widely available in these countries through mobile devices (Trimi & Sheng, 2008). Muscat Municipality in Oman has developed a mobile parking ticket payment system, and the Muscat school board has launched an SMS system for receiving semester grades through mobile text messaging (Naqvi & Al-Shihi, 2009). In Bangladesh, citizens can pay utility fees like electricity, gas, and water bills through mobile devices. Students can get their school board results through mobile phones. Another interesting service offered by private mobile companies (not related to government services) in Bangladesh is medical advice. Subscribers of a mobile company can call to a specific number at any time to seek the advice of registered physicians who are employed by the mobile company, for any emergency health related problems. This service is provided at the regular outgoing call rate which is very low. Several African countries like Kenya, Mali, and Rwanda use money transfer services (M-banking) and health services to citizens through mobile phones (i4d, 2007). The M-PESA project in Kenya is a popular M-banking project through which citizens can transfer and receive money from any country in Africa (i4d, 2007).

M-democracy has become a very popular method through which certain governments have attempted to implement good governance. Although this has been a top priority mission for implementing EG, it is virtually impossible to achieve such a goal through a PC-based wired Internet, since this form of access is available mostly for urban, knowledgeable, economically solvent, and socially privileged groups (Shareef et al., 2009b; Shareef & Archer, 2010a). In several countries, citizens from all levels, classes, can anywhere and anytime now participate in government decision making and can interact with legislative bodies through mobile devices. This is formally designated as M-democracy (i4d, 2007). Local and regional governments of different European countries and some Asian countries use mobile phones as a means by which citizens can interact with election commissions and other legislative bodies to promote good governance by providing their opinions online (Lallana, 2008).

As stated by Archer (2007) M-administration is a fertile area where mobile devices are frequently used to upgrade administrative systems and enhance public management efficiency and productivity through connected employees (M-IEE or Mobile Internal Efficiency and Effectiveness). In many countries including the USA, Canada, UK, Malaysia, Singapore, Norway, Finland, Sweden, Japan, Germany, South Korea etc., the police, healthcare, fire, traffic, and land departments use mobile devices internally among employees to enhance service quality, efficiency, and productivity by instantaneous accessibility to records and by supporting versatile functionality with on-time or real time data exchange (Jeong & Kim, 2003).

The services mentioned here are some brief examples of the proliferation of mobile technologies as a supplement to EG and also some unique services of MG which can only be designed and implemented through mobile technology. If we analyze and compare the characteristics of EG and MG, we notice that MG applications differ from stationary EG applications through their mobility, and also that certain applications of MG require location-sensitivity, time-criticality, and personal identity (Archer, 2007). In addition EG, since it is accessed through the wired Internet, is less security vulnerable, its applications provide higher volume downloads, and display capacity is larger. MG is therefore not convenient for the secure transmission of private, voluminous and complex information. Since MG involves hand held devices in an open environment, it is more vulnerable to security and privacy related issues (Kumar & Sinha, 2007). The wireless Internet tends to be more costly, less available, and it has less capacity to perform versatile tasks (Sundar & Garg, 2009). Considering these aspects, the proliferation of MG and its acceptance by end users is a matter of real question and concern. It is a challenging job for governments to ensure that citizens have the capability and capacity as well as beliefs and behavioral intentions to adopt successfully this supplementary addition to EG.

THEORETICAL FRAMEWORK: TYPOLOGY OF MG DEVELOPMENT CAPABILITY

In this section, we conceptualize the critical issues which strengthen the development of MG for any country. The Capability Model for EG Adoption was developed by Shareef et al. (2010c) to investigate the factors which affect the development of a fundamental capability to implement EG. According to this model, the development of a fundamental EG capability by a country should lead to successful ICT adoption and EG implementation. Shareef et al. (2010c) defined the fundamental capability for EG "as the resource-based ability to adopt, implement, and maintain the system with accumulated knowledge." This model postulated that the following factors affect the development of a fundamental capability for EG.

- Central Government Support and Long-Term Political Commitment (CGS & LTPC)
- Government and Political Stability (GPS)
- Educated and Skilled Personnel (ESP)
- Reengineering of Processes (RP)
- Size of the Implementing Organization (SIO)
- Traditional Public Organizational Culture (TPOC)
- Partnership with the Private Sector (PPS)
- Strategic Alignment and Overall Readiness (SA & OR)

Based on this model, a case study was conducted in India to define a capability model for government MG development. We chose India as a case study for several reasons. In terms of Internet usage, availability of personal computers, telecommunications and other infrastructure, proliferation of mobile usage, the adoption of MG in different sectors, and ICT related human resources, India is currently a leading country (i4d, 2007). For example, about 50%-60% of EG operations can now be conducted in India through handheld mobile devices (i4d, 2007; Kumar & Sinha, 2007). These include land registrations, tax payments, utility bill payments, seeking information on agriculture, public health, and education through SMS, and several other government services which are now disbursed through MG (Jadhav, 2003; Nagarapalike Update, 2004).

Using a semi-structured questionnaire, we collected information through detailed interviews of Indian government policy makers. These interviews were conducted at different levels of administrative and engineering management authorities of both regional and central governments that are involved in MG implementation projects in India. Indian MG development projects have several phases. Some projects were developed where the only medium of interaction is mobile phones. For example, SMS for pension deposits, utility bill payments etc. (Kumar & Sinha, 2007). These services were developed so they are uniquely compatible with MG features. Some other online services are provided through both the wired Internet accessed by computers, and the wireless Internet accessed by mobile phones, including tax payments, fund transfer, education and health related information etc. (Trimi & Sheng, 2008). Central and regional governments have different projects for EG and MG. The Indian EG and MG projects have static, interactive, and transaction phases for the services they offer. However, for MG most of the services are designed for two-way communication where governments can easily transfer services to citizens who live in remote rural areas. At the same time citizens can seek certain real time government information from anywhere at anytime. We interviewed both central and regional policy makers. Respondents all requested anonymity as they are government employees.

In the semi-structured questionnaire and in the interviews, respondents were informed that the purpose of this research was to examine the fundamental capabilities necessary for a government to successfully adopt MG. The concepts of fundamental capability and ancillary issues of MG implementation were grounded in a detailed literature review (Archer; 2007; I-Ways, 2009; Kapugama, 2009; Kumar & Sinha, 2007; Naqvi & Al-Shihi, 2009; Shareef & Archer, 2010a; Trimi & Sheng, 2008). From their working experience concerning development of MG projects, the respondents contributed to an understanding of the required fundamental capability of a country to develop, implement, and successfully launch MG projects. They were asked to describe the essential features, strategies, supporting activities, functions, barriers, challenging issues, and resources that are imperative to develop the capabilities necessary for successful adoption of MG. In total, 12 interviews were conducted. Probing questions were used to capture their epistemological and ontological speculations. The primary questionnaire was comprised of eight fundamental semi-structured questions, developed

from different MG issues found in the literature (Archer; 2007; I-Ways, 2009; Kapugama, 2009; Kumar & Sinha, 2007; Naqvi & Al-Shihi, 2009; Shareef & Archer, 2010a; Trimi & Sheng, 2008). These are described in the following.

The respondents were requested to deliver their own opinion on these issues as well as to extend and elaborate their concepts on aspects of MG implementation.

1. Why did you decide to adopt Mobile-government (MG)?
2. What are the precise targets of developing MG— i) reduce government expenditure, ii) improve service quality for users, ii) reduce digital divide between urban and rural population, iv) boost up national economy, v) attract foreign investment and positioning globally, vi) reduce bureaucracy and corruption and enhance transparency, vii) promote good governance and democracy?
3. Who are the stakeholders (e.g. citizens, business organizations, international clients)?
4. What are the strategies you followed?
5. What are the resources you utilized?
6. What are the scarcities?
7. What are the inhibitors in developing MG?
   A. Technological barriers
   B. Social barriers
   C. Financial barriers
   D. Political barriers
   E. Cultural barriers
   F. Organizational barriers
8. What are the outcomes you expect?

From these 12 interviews, we gathered mostly descriptive information. To present that data in a consistent and meaningful way, the information gathered was rearranged according to the principles of matrix thinking for organizing, categorizing, conceptualizing, and analyzing qualitative data (Patton, 981). We reduced lengthy verbal and written information, categorized it, and then grouped it into well-defined attributes which are

Figure 1. Theoretical framework for the fundamental capability of MG development

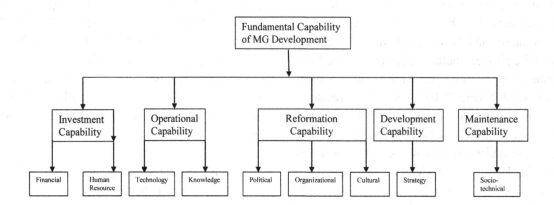

consistent with contemporary issues from the EG and MG literature. From the anatomy of the information gathered through the 12 interviews, we grounded a typology of the fundamental capability essential for MG development, as presented in Figure 1.

We encapsulate the basic concepts of the different capabilities and their leveraging components in the following discussion.

Investment Capability

This concept is similar to the same attribute of the Capability Model for EG Adoption (Shareef et al., 2010c). According to that model, investment capability can be conceptualized as "the ability of a country to take advantage of existing technological resources and identify its technological demand (that is, to determine the need); the availability of capital and labor resources; and the allocation, mission, objective, and outcome (or the cost-benefits)." Investment capability is comprised of financial investment capability and the availability of competent human resources to leverage the system resources. Government agencies must have the capability to maintain technical staff to support the technology hubs and link applications to multiple types of wireless

devices (Kumar & Sinha, 2007). Since one of the primary missions of MG development is to deploy a system that will be available for all the citizens, even from remote rural areas, technological networks should be extended throughout the whole country. Interviewees unanimously agreed that to interconnect customer interfaces with existing EG services through mobile devices and the Internet, significant financial investments and the availability of human resources are pre-requisite conditions. Although India trains more software engineers than any other country, in order to develop both unique MG projects and joint EG/MG projects, all the projects require significant investment streams.

Operational Capability

Most interviewees said that a major challenge they confront in deploying MG projects is to provide operational capability. Back-office support should be errorless in delivering the needed service in the shortest possible time that is promised in the strategic objectives of the project (Kumar & Sinha, 2007). According to the capability model for EG adoption (Shareef et al., 2010c), operational capability can be defined as "the skills and information needed to adopt, implement, operate, maintain, and repair EG systems to achieve the functional objectives." It is grounded in technological and knowledge management capability. Proper content management, page display, usability, and accessibility design are important technological capabilities which should be provided to operate the systems. Wireless devices use different browsers for presenting information. Wireless devices like mobile phones have limited display capabilities in size, support for color and graphics, and insufficient or complex keyboards or buttons. Different mobile device companies design their devices using a variety of supporting languages like WAP (Wireless Application Protocol) and WML (Wireless Markup Language), etc. "While government organizations may adopt a specific standard for mobile employees, citizen access to government information and services may require agencies to support multiple standards/technologies" (Kumar & Sinha, 2007). For MG, citizens seek time and location sensitive government services on travel, automated tools to leverage urgent services and accurate web searches; therefore intelligent software agents and knowledge management are essential to MG development (Sundar & Garg, 2009).

Reformation Capability

While developing online government systems for traditional EG or using the features of EG supported by mobile devices (MG), a government will specify some specific mission to be achieved by the system. This system is assumed to provide advantages such as: increased efficiency, lower service rendering cost, better and more available services, increased participation, and less corruption with more transparency (Shareef et al., 2010b). Although governments are realizing the potential of MG, varying degrees of complexity and success in this process have been observed in different countries. Different MG implementation results show that the development of MG systems needs to include multi-dimensional capabilities, with reformation capability assuming major

serious importance at the outset of the initiative. Previous experience also demonstrates that the proper implementation of MG is very complex and depends on many potential factors, ultimately linked with reengineering and transformation of the total system to a form that is compatible with MG features. Moreover, since its purpose is to support citizens, its implementation, development, and performance should be such that it can meet the criteria and facilitate factors that enable citizens to adopt MG. Several researchers have suggested that, without proper political, cultural, and organizational reformation, policy makers cannot ensure successful MG development. For example, the application of ICT in MG should be designed to reform the internal management of public administration and develop dynamic relations with external agencies (Sundar & Garg, 2009; Trimi & Sheng, 2008). The successful adoption of MG systems requires analyzing changes in social values over time. A society and culture produces values, ideas, intentions, and speculations about human traits, attitudes, and behavior. According to the theory of planned behavior (TPB) (Ajzen, 1991) and the theory of reasoned action (TRA) (Ajzen and Fishbein, 1980), social and cultural values affect beliefs and attitudes of certain behavior—in this case the citizen adoption behavior towards MG. Beliefs and attitudes about MG lead to formation of behavioral intentions to learn, accept, and use MG systems. By shedding light on the proposed system through socio-technical theory, we can encapsulate the complex interaction effects between public reformation and implementation of ICT and the various complementary variables of the organization. The political mission of a government is a potential factor in this aspect since an important mission of MG is to minimize the digital divide and promote good governance (Sundar & Garg, 2009; Trimi & Sheng, 2008). This points to the significance of management's role and leadership during the MG implementation process. MG implementation, development, and successful adoption have organizational, cultural, and political stimuli. In order to reform and re-engineer the public administration in a way that reflects a vision of successfully implementing MG, a number of important issues need to be resolved. First of all the top authorities must have a strong commitment to ensure transparency and account-ability. We can postulate reformation capability from the views of the respondents *as the ability to transform organizational structure, relation, and functions and overall administrative style and visualize and modify political mission consistent with the vision of MG development efforts.* This includes setting a political mission and reforming organizational structure and culture adherent with the dynamic nature of MG oversight. Second, government agencies need to overturn decades of embedded business culture in order to tackle the processes of the new government. They need to focus on being market-driven, citizen-centric, and results-oriented. Third, in order to reorganize public administration in accordance with the MG structure, a number of important conditions and prerequisites have to be in place. The authorities must have the necessary political will, commit-ment, and readiness to reduce bureaucracy and increase transparency; and society must have reached an adequate level in the globalization process. Fourth, a rational, feasible, and justified conception of new administrative structures must be formulated.

Development Capability

The ultimate success of MG depends on the adop-tion intentions of different stakeholders. However, a lack of consensus in setting similar explicit objectives diversifies the adoption criteria of MG. Therefore, a number of factors have significant implications for progressive successful develop-ment of an MG structure. First, identifying clear objectives for implementing MG is important, in order to capitalize on the full opportunities that lie behind the MG system, so that different stakehold-ers will be interested in adopting the MG system

under the globalization context. Second, users will not use the system and thus its mission will not be successful if the system cannot provide privacy, security, user-friendly accessibility, and availabil-ity from anywhere and anytime (Kumar & Sinha, 2007). Third, the digital divide is another problem: if a country cannot provide equal opportunities so all of the population can access MG systems, MG will increase the digital divide. Moreover, using public services that increases discrimination among citizens will seriously hamper the prime motivation for implementing MG (Bertot, 2003). Urban communities of any country are ahead of rural populations in the availability of technology infrastructure and using ICT in everyday life. In terms of availability, awareness, and opportunity, the gap between the urban and rural populations is already substantial, and the new wave of ICT in the public sector might potentially cause an increase in this gap. Fourth, the lack of availability of resources in rural communities is an eternal and acute problem (Parker, 2000). However, as a government structure, MG should create a level playground for both urban and rural popula-tions. Otherwise, the proliferation of MG in the modern world would increase the digital divide. Fifth, certain other managerial issues related to the education of rural people, inadequate electri-cal power in rural areas, the cost of computing, network expansion, prompt customer service, openness of information and citizen decision making participation etc. (Archer; 2007; Naqvi & Al-Shihi, 20009; Sundar & Garg, 2009; Trimi & Sheng, 2008) are all related to developing a suc-cessful strategy prior to launching MG projects. Interviewees asserted that the ultimate success of MG projects depends largely on the strength of the initial strategy upon which the system is built. According to the Canadian government (2002), at the outset of the implementation of EG (and the same for MG), the success of the system is largely grounded on setting the appropriate course and establishing objectives and strategizing – leader-ship, boundaries, structures, and activities. We can define development capability in the light of MG technical, cultural, organizational, political, and economic perspectives as *the capability to initiate, develop, and manage the system with appropriate, multi-dimensional, and strong fore-sighted strategies.*

Maintenance Capability

Interviewees confirmed the necessity of a maintenance capability for the proper development, diffusion, and successful performance of MG. Since MG represents a new technological advance in government systems, it is still in the experimental phase. To explicitly capitalize on the potentials and benefits of MG, a challenging and very important issue is to first identify and ensure the development of system maintenance capability. Without very advanced technical, financial, political, social, and individual ability, it is really difficult to progress and achieve the fundamental mission of MG implementation. Numerous studies of ICT projects (Basu, 2004; Ndou, 2004; Dada, 2006) have shown that ICT failed to achieve its desired goals in so many projects due to an inability to maintain the projects after they were implemented successfully. The maintenance capability of MG can be idealized as *the capability of a country with stable government and political mission to support the system continuously with financial, technical, and human resources, ensure dynamic technical learning and organizational relational and structural changes to manage the reformation introduced by MG, and achieve the technological know-how to support the system with regular updates.* This concept basically illustrates socio-technical capability. It also explains adaptability of the system by first finding stakeholder needs separately in urban and rural areas. Accordingly the system should be managed technically and socially. Technical adaptability means continuous upgrades of the system with user-friendly software, and maintaining easy accessibility, flexibility of the system, smooth flows of information, and other

stakeholder technical requirements (Shareef et al, 2010d). Governments must pay close attention to this issue and focus on the ancillary factors that enhance stakeholder technological and psychological capabilities to use the MG service. At the same time social adaptability means citizens should always be focused and concerned while any technological changes are introduced so that they will maintain social and behavioral adaptability with reformed system. To assist in this, citizens should get technological support and education regarding handling the technological interfaces associated with MG, and the associated mental motivation to use the system.

CONCLUSION

Growth in the use of mobile devices continues worldwide at a rapid pace. In 2000, mobile penetration was only 12 per cent, but it surpassed 61 per cent at the end of 2008, representing 4 billion subscribers worldwide. This revolutionary diffusion of mobile technologies presents both interesting possibilities and difficult challenges in implementing MG widely. All over the world, countries are striving to achieve the desired targets of EG by linking wired communications to mobile technologies. As MG is a recent concept, there has as yet not been a real theoretical dissection of how to bring an organized and structured MG to every layer of people in society.

The conceptual framework we propose here resulted from a rigorous discussion with MG policy makers in different sectors in India, grounded in the typology of capability development for setting a mission, proper planning and strategizing, implementation and development reflecting the mission at the root of the project, and finally performing successfully in order to achieve good governance. The grounded theory is based on ICT in government, and on the social, cultural, political, organizational, and behavioral aspects of the related stakeholders and resources required to implement MG. The epistemological and ontological paradigms used in the analysis of MG are based on the economic and human resource capability, ranging from the resource planning stage and on through the investment, operation, and maintenance stages. The framework also indicates the interactions of different stakeholders while introducing mobile features in traditional EG systems in order to provide unique features as well as to support existing features with supplementary additions. These interactions can affect and be affected by organizational structure and relations, culture, and society at large. At the same time, we also consider how political phenomena and neo-institutionalism are potential factors in the reformation of public administration, particularly in setting good governance and democracy that is characterized by transparency, accountability, and lessened corruption and bureaucracy through ICT and mobile technologies. Governments that are striving to acquire the capability to develop and implement MG in a manner that minimizes the digital divide can accelerate this through a complementary wired communication system applied to interactions with the public administration. In turn, this will make government services available for all classes of people from both urban and remote rural areas still unaware of this relatively new phenomenon whose potential is largely unknown and unexplored. The proposed framework for the proper development of MG can be used for planning, designing and implementing successful MG systems.

REFERENCES

i4d. (2007). From e-government to m-government. *ICTD Project Newsletter*, 33-36.

Al-adawi, Z., Yousafzai, S., & Pallister, J. (2005). *Conceptual model of citizen adoption of e-government*. The Second International Conference on Innovations in Information Technology (IIT'05), (2005).

Allison, P. D. (1999). *Logistic regression using the SAS system*. Cary, NC: SAS Institute.

Andersen, K. V., & Henriksen, H. Z. (2006). E-government maturity models: Extension of the Layne and Lee model. *Government Information Quarterly*, 23, 236–248. doi:10.1016/j.giq.2005.11.008

Anthopoulos, L. G., Siozos, P., & Tsoukalas, L. A. (2007). Applying participatory design and collaboration in digital public services for discovering and re-designing e-government services. *Government Information Quarterly*, 24, 353–376. doi:10.1016/j.giq.2006.07.018

Anttiroiko, A.-V. (2005). Towards ubiquitous government: The case of Finland. *E-Service Journal*, 4(1), 65–99. doi:10.2979/ESJ.2005.4.1.65

Archer, N. (2007). Mobile e-health: Making the case. In Kushchu, I. (Ed.), *Mobile government: An emerging direction in e-government* (pp. 155–170). Hershey, PA: IGI Global. doi:10.4018/978-1-59140-884-0.ch008

Bhatnagar, S. (2002). E-government: Lessons from implementation in developing countries. *Regional Development Dialogue*, 24, 1–9.

Blackman, M. (2006). Municipalities move to mobile government. *Government Procurement*, 54-55. Retrieved from www.govpro.com

Browne, M. W., & Cudeck, R. (1993). Alternative ways of assessing model fit. In Bollen, K. A., & Long, J. S. (Eds.), *Testing structural equation models*. Newbury Park, CA: Sage.

Carroll, J. (2005). Risky business: Will citizens accept m-government in the long term? In I. Kushchu & M. Halid Kuscu (Eds.), *The Proceedings of the 1st European Mobile Government Conference* (Euro mGov 2005), Brighton, UK, (2005), 10-12 July, Mobile Government Consortium International Pub, UK.

Chau, P. Y. K. (1997). Reexamining a model for evaluating information center success: Using a structural equation modeling approach. *Decision Sciences, 28*(2), 309–334. doi:10.1111/j.1540-5915.1997.tb01313.x

Chen, Y.-C., & Thurmaier, K. (2005). *Government-to-citizen electronic services: Understanding and driving adoption of online transactions*. The Association for Public Policy & Management (APPAM) Conference, Washington, D.C., November 3-6, (2005).

Churchill, G. A. (1979). A paradigm for developing better measures of marketing constructs. *JMR, Journal of Marketing Research, 16*, 64–73. doi:10.2307/3150876

Cronin, J. J., & Taylor, S. A. (1992). Measuring service quality: A reexamination and extension. *Journal of Marketing, 56*, 55–68. doi:10.2307/1252296

Davis, F. D. (1989). Perceived usefulness, perceived ease of use and user acceptance of Information Technology. *Management Information Systems Quarterly, 13*(3), 319–340. doi:10.2307/249008

Davis, F. D., Bagozzi, R. P., & Warshaw, P. R. (1989). User acceptance of computer technology: A comparison of two theoretical models. *Management Science, 35*(8), 982–1003. doi:10.1287/mnsc.35.8.982

eGovWorld. (2007). *Global dialogue, mobile innovations for social and economic transformation*.

Espinoza, M. M. (1999). Assessing the cross-cultural applicability of a service quality measure: A comparative study between Quebec and Peru. *International Journal of Service Industry Management, 10*(5), 449–468. doi:10.1108/09564239910288987

Evans, D., & Yen, D. C. (2006). E-government: Evolving relationship of citizens and government, domestic, and international development. *Government Information Quarterly, 23*(2), 207–235. doi:10.1016/j.giq.2005.11.004

Fishbein, M., & Ajzen, I. (1975). *Beliefs, attitude, intention, and behavior: An introduction to theory and research*. Reading, MA: Addison-Wesley.

Fornell, C., & Larcker, D. F. (1981). Evaluating structural equation models with unobservable variables and measurement error. *JMR, Journal of Marketing Research, 18*(1), 39–50. doi:10.2307/3151312

Gil-Garcia, J. R., & Martinez-Moyano, I. J. (2007). Understanding the evolution of e-government: The influence of systems of rules on public sector dynamics. *Government Information Quarterly, 24*(2), 266–290. doi:10.1016/j.giq.2006.04.005

Grande, C. (1999, 10 December). E-envoy vows to raise Internet use by ministries. *Financial Times*.

Grandi, F., Mandreoli, F., Scalas, M. R., & Tiberio, P. (2004). Management of the citizen's digital identity and access to multi-version norm texts on the Semantic Web. In *Proceedings of the International Symposium on Challenges in the Internet and Interdisciplinary Research*.

Heeks, R. B., & Bailur, S. (2007). Analyzing e-government research: Perspectives, philosophies, theories, methods, and practice. *Government Information Quarterly, 24*(2), 243–265. doi:10.1016/j.giq.2006.06.005

Hernon, P., Reylea, H. C., Dugan, R. E., & Cheverie, J. F. (2002). *United States government information: Policies and sources* (p. 388). Westport, CT: Libraries Unlimited.

Hu, L.-T., & Bentler, P. M. (1999). Cutoff criteria for fit indexes in covariance structure analysis: Conventional criteria versus new alternatives. *Structural Equation Modeling, 6*(1), 1–55. doi:10.1080/10705519909540118

I-Ways. (2009). E-government for development information exchange. *Journal of E-Government Policy and Regulation, 32*, 20–22.

Internet World Stats. (2009). Retrieved from http://www.allaboutmarketresearch.com/internet.htm

Jadhav, S. (2003). *Evaluation study on e-governance applications in ULBs*. Pune, India: YASHADA.

Jeong, K., & Kim, H. (2003). After the introduction of the government portal services: Evolution into the m-government initiatives. *Proceedings of the ICA 37th Conference*, (2003).

Kapugama, N. (2009). *Colloquium: Identifying conditions for the delivery of m-government services to the BOP: India*. Retrieved from www.lirneasia.net

Kline, R. B. (2005). *Principles and practice of structural equation modeling*. New York, NY: The Guilford Press.

Krishna, S., & Walsham, G. (2005). Implementing public Information Systems in developing countries: Learning from a success story. *Information Technology for Development, 11*(2), 123–140. doi:10.1002/itdj.20007

Kumar, M., & Sinha, O. P. (2007). *M-government – Mobile technology for e-government* (pp. 294–301). Computer Society of India.

Kumar, V., Kumar, U., & Shareef, M. A. (2006). Implementation of quality management practice in EC. *Proceedings of the Administrative Sciences Association of Canada Conference*, Banff, Calgary, Canada, 27, 146-163.

Kushchu, I., & Kuscu, H. (2003). *From e-government to m-government: Facing the inevitable*. 3rd European Conference on E-Government (ECEG03), July 1–2 at Trinity College, Dublin, (2003).

Lallana, E. (2008). *E-government for development information exchange*. University of Manchester's Institute for Development Policy and Management. Retrieved from http://www.egov4dev.org/mgovernment/ applications/

Loiacono, E. T., Watson, R. T., & Goodhue, D. L. (2002). WEBQUAL: A measure of website quality. In Evans, K., & Scheer, L. (Eds.), *Marketing educators' conference: Marketing theory and applications, 13* (pp. 432–437).

Misuraca, G. C. (2009). E-government 2015: Exploring m-government scenarios, between ICT-driven experiments and citizen-centric implications. *Technology Analysis and Strategic Management, 21*(3), 407–424. doi:10.1080/09537320902750871

Moon, J. (2004). *From e-government to m-government? Emerging practices in the use of m-technology by state governments*. IBM Center for the Business of Government.

Naqvi, S. J., & Al-Shihi, H. (2009). M-government services initiatives in Oman. *Informing Science and Information Technology, 6*, 817–824.

Ndou, V. D. (2004). E-government for developing countries: Opportunities and challenges. *Electronic Journal of Information Systems in Developing Countries, 18*(1), 1–24.

Netter, J., Kutner, M. H., Nachtsheim, C. J., & Wasserman, W. (1996). *Applied linear regression models* (3rd ed.). Chicago, IL: Irwin.

Nunnally, J. C., & Bernstein, I. H. (1994). *Psychometric theory*. New York, NY: McGraw-Hill.

Parasuraman, A., Zeithaml, V. A., & Berry, L. L. (1988). SERVQUAL: A multiple-item scale for measuring customer perceptions of service quality. *Journal of Retailing, 64*(1), 12–40.

Quick, S. (2003). *International e-government, special report: Government*. EBSCO Publishing.

Accenture Report. (2005). *Leadership in customer service: New expectations, new experiences*. E-Government Report.

IMF Report. (2007). *Global financial stability report, market developments and issues*.

Riley, T. B. (2002). *Government and the invisible current of change*. Retrieved from http://www.electronicgov.net

Rogers, E. M. (1995). *Diffusion of innovations*. New York, NY: The Free Press.

Scholl, H. J. (2005). The mobility paradigm in government theory and practice: A strategic framework. In Ibrahim Kushchu & M. Halid Kuscu (Eds.), *Proceedings of the 1ˢᵗ European Mobile Government Conference* (Euro mGov 2005), Brighton, UK, (2005), 10-12 July, Mobile Government Consortium International Pub, UK.

Segars, A., & Grover, V. (1993). Re-examining perceived ease of use and usefulness: A confirmatory factor analysis. *Management Information Systems Quarterly, 17*(4), 517–527. doi:10.2307/249590

Shareef, M. A., & Archer, N. (2010a). M-government adoption: A consumer study in India. *Proceedings of the Administrative Sciences Association of Canada Conference*, Regina, Saskatchewan, Canada, May.

Shareef, M. A., Archer, N., Kumar, V., & Kumar, U. (2010c). (in press). Developing fundamental capabilities for successful e-government implementation. *International Journal of Public Policy*. doi:10.1504/IJPP.2010.035133

Shareef, M. A., Dwivedi, Y. K., Williams, M. D., & Singh, N. (2009b). *Proliferation of the Internet economy: E-commerce for the global adoption, resistance and cultural evolution*, (pp. 186-213). Hershey, PA: Information Science Reference, IGI Global Publications.

Shareef, M. A., Kumar, U., & Kumar, V. (2010d). E-government adoption model (GAM): Differing service maturity levels. PhD Thesis, Sprott School of Business, Carleton University, Canada.

Shareef, M. A., Kumar, U., Kumar, V., & Dwivedi, Y. K. (2009a). Identifying critical factors for adoption of e-government. *Electronic Government: An International Journal, 6*(1), 70–96. doi:10.1504/EG.2009.022594

Shareef, M. A., Kumar, V., Kumar, U., Chowdhury, A. H., & Misra, S. C. (2010b). E-government implementation perspective: Setting objective and strategy. *International Journal of Electronic Government Research, 6*(1). doi:10.4018/jegr.2010102005

Sundar, D. K., & Garg, S. (2009). *M-governance: A framework for Indian urban local bodies*. Retrieved from http://www.mgovernment.org/resources/euromgov2005/PDF/41_R359SK.pdf

Trimi, S., & Sheng, H. (2008). Emerging trends in m-government. *Communications of the ACM, 51*(5), 53–58. doi:10.1145/1342327.1342338

Tung, L. L., & Rieck, O. (2005). Adoption of electronic government services among business organizations in Singapore. *The Journal of Strategic Information Systems, 14*, 417–440. doi:10.1016/j.jsis.2005.06.001

Turner, M., & Desloges, C. (2002). *Strategies and framework for government online: A Canadian experience*. World Bank E-Government Learning Workshop, Washington D.C., June 18, (2002).

Update, N. (2004). *Municipal Initiatives in E-Governance, 2(1)*. New Delhi: Institute of Social Sciences.

Vincent, J., & Harris, L. (2008). Effective use of mobile communication in e-government: How do we reach the tipping point? *Information Communication and Society, 11*(3), 395–413. doi:10.1080/13691180802025632

Wang, Y.-S. (2002). The adoption of electronic tax filing systems: An empirical study. *Government Information Quarterly, 20*, 333–352. doi:10.1016/j.giq.2003.08.005

Wangpipatwong, S., Chutimaskul, W., & Papasratorn, B. (2005). Factors influencing the adoption of Thai e-government websites: Information quality and system quality approach. *Proceedings of the 4th International Conference on eBusiness*, November 19-20, (2005), Bangkok, Thailand.

Wolfinbarger, M., & Gilly, M. C. (2003). eTailQ: Dimensionalizing, measuring, and predicting retail quality. *Journal of Retailing, 79*(3), 183–198. doi:10.1016/S0022-4359(03)00034-4

Yoo, B., & Donthu, N. (2001). Developing a scale to measure the perceived quality of an Internet shopping site (Sitequal). *Quarterly Journal of Electronic Commerce, 2*(1), 31–46.

Zhang, J. J., Yuan, Y., & Archer, N. (2002). Driving forces for m-commerce success. *Journal of Internet Commerce, 1*(3), 81–105. doi:10.1300/J179v01n03_08

KEY TERMS AND DEFINITIONS

M-Government (MG): MG is a subset of EG where interactions with government services can be conducted through mobile devices.

E-Government (EG): EG is government's service and information offered through the use of ICT for citizens, business organizations, and other stakeholders of government. It provides higher efficiency and effectiveness in terms of service quality, time, and cost.

Information and Communication Technology (ICT): ICT can be defined as the modern computer and Internet based technology used for managing and processing information in different public and private sectors.

Adoption of EG: It is the acceptance and use of EG by its stakeholders with satisfaction.

Public Administration: It is the management of government service and information conducted through governments departments.

Fundamental Capability: Fundamental capability for EG can be defined as the resource-based ability to adopt, implement, and maintain the system with accumulated knowledge.

Citizen: Residents of a country who use government service and information.

Section 3
E–Governance Implementation in Competitive Reformation of Financial Markets

Chapter 7
XBRL:
The Direction of E-Governance in the Capital Markets

Mary M. Oxner
St. Francis Xavier University, Canada

Ken MacAulay
St. Francis Xavier University, Canada

Gerald Trites
Zorba Research Inc., Canada

ABSTRACT

XBRL is a language that allows for the electronic communication of business information. In XBRL, tags are attached to items of information allowing that information to be exchanged and processed electronically. The architecture of XBRL facilitates more efficient electronic dissemination of information than does the traditional Web-based or PDF formats. The result is the potential for improved availability and accessibility of financial information and increased transparency. In effect, XBRL has the potential to improve electronic governance. For that potential to be realized, several challenges must be addressed. Concerns exist regarding data integrity, the costs of implementation, the training of employees, and the updating of XBRL taxonomies. Given both its potential and the limited number of studies on XBRL, more research is needed on XBRL implementation and use.

INTRODUCTION

Governance requirements and expectations in the global capital markets have changed dramatically over the last ten years. These changes are the result of the concurrence of corporate failures such as

DOI: 10.4018/978-1-60960-848-4.ch007

Enron, which resulted in extensive changes in corporate governance regulations, and the availability of technologies like the internet, which allowed for the electronic reporting of corporate results. New corporate governance regulations have emphasized increased dissemination of information to market participants, increased transparency of corporate policies and strategies, and increased accountability to stakeholders. To address the increased corporate governance requirements, companies have used the internet and other available technologies to deliver information to investors and regulators. Much of this governance information is now disclosed and managed through an electronic medium. The electronic medium is in continuous evolution which is allowing for more efficient, more interactive, and more transparent electronic governance (or e-governance[1]). XBRL is a part of the evolution of the electronic medium and of e-governance.

XBRL or eXtensible Business Reporting Language is a language for the electronic communication of business information which works by attaching tags to items of information so that the information can be read, exchanged and processed electronically. XBRL improves corporate governance by improving the accessibility and transparency of company information and provides significant benefits in the preparation, analysis and communication of business information (XBRL Canada, 2010). Because of its benefits, XBRL is being mandated by financial regulators around the world. As companies begin to embrace the benefits that XRBL offers, XBRL adoptions and XBRL applications to deliver e-governance will undoubtedly increase.

This chapter reviews the potential of XBRL as an instrument of e-governance in the capital markets. The structure of the chapter is as follows: first, XBRL is described; second, e-governance in the capital markets is briefly reviewed and the capabilities of XBRL as a language for electronic communication and e-governance are discussed; third, an overview of the limited empirical research on XBRL implementation and use is provided; fourth, the application of XBRL in the global capital markets (e.g., United States, Australia, China and Canada) is reviewed; and finally, a discussion of the future of XBRL as a tool in the evolution of e-governance in the capital markets is presented.

What is XBRL?

XBRL is a language for the electronic communication of business and financial data and is one of the family of XML languages. XML or Extensible Markup Language is a recognized text format that allows the electronic exchange of a wide variety of data on the internet. Under XML, identifying tags are applied to items of information so that they can be processed efficiently by computer software (XBRL International, 2010a). XML, however, was not developed for the electronic exchange of financial information. It was Charles Hoffman, a CPA in the United States, who adapted XML for financial information and this led to the development of XBRL (Efendi et al., 2009; Cohen et al., 2005). Subsequently an international non-profit consortium, XBRL International, was established (XBRL International, 2010a). A more extensive discussion of XBRL`s development can be found in Cohen (2009), Boritz and No (2004) and Cohen et al. (2005).

How XBRL Works

XBRL is designed to attach computer readable tags to financial and non-financial data. The tags identify the information along a number of dimensions such as the nature of the item (e.g., whether it is a monetary item) and the format of the data (e.g., whether it is a percentage or a fraction) (Boritz and No, 2004; XBRL International, 2010a). XBRL tags enable the automated processing (i.e., select, analyze, store and exchange) of financial information by computer software and the presentation of financial information to meet the reporting requirements that must be followed by most industries and companies (XBRL International, 2010a; Brashear, 2009; Cohen et al., 2005; Cohen, 2004). An XBRL report (i.e., instance document) is created by mapping company specific financial information to XBRL elements which are included in a taxonomy (Boritz and No, 2004). Taxonomies are hierarchical dictionaries which contain lists of elements (such as cash, accounts receivable, sales, and advertising expense) that are mapped to the individual matching items in the financial statements to create XBRL (instance) documents. It is the taxonomies that contain metadata, such as the descriptions of the elements, the accounting standards that guide their preparation, and the calculations that form part of the financial statements. Because the elements are mapped to the financial statements' items, these metadata, often referred to as tags, are essentially linked to the financial statement items. When the XBRL instance documents are received by a computer system, that system, with the appropriate software, can then read the metadata and understand a great deal about the related items, which is what enables automated analysis. Companies can develop multiple taxonomies for various reporting requirements (e.g., financial reporting, tax reporting, and internal reporting purposes) or use taxonomies developed by regulators such as securities commission, stock exchanges, national accounting boards and others (Boritz and No, 2004). Further, corporate information can be tagged using more than one taxonomy (Efendi et al., 2009). Taxonomies which have been officially recognized by XBRL International (XII) are listed at http://www.xbrl.org/FRTApproved/ and http://www.xbrl.org/FRTAcknowledged/. Most taxonomies used for public reporting are either "approved" or "acknowledged" by XII.

Although taxonomies include the most frequently used elements, one taxonomy cannot necessarily represent all the unique information that a company might want to present in its financial statements. Consequently, companies can customize their XBRL reports (Cohen, 2004). The 'X' part of XBRL is 'Extensible' and the extensible feature of XBRL allows for the customization of company data by extending a standard taxonomy. The extension is accomplished by adding elements and related metadata and/or by making modifications to the existing elements, definitions and interrelationships.

Benefits of XBRL

A multitude of benefits have been espoused by developers who support the adoption of XBRL, by regulators who have mandated XBRL, and by users who have extracted and utilized XBRL reports. From the user perspective, increased corporate transparency is realized as investors are better able to access and interpret information within financial statements. The users also benefit from the expanded dissemination of information (both from regulated disclosures and the functionality of XBRL). Users can receive, select, compare and analyze data much more efficiently if it is in XBRL format (Efendi et al., 2009). Users such as financial analysts can analyze data without having to manually enter that data into their own spreadsheets and models. Regulatory organizations like securities commissions and stock exchanges also realize the benefits of reduced processing time as XBRL data allows organizations to more efficiently review and process submitted filings. Auditors may also realize the benefits of XBRL through the application of statistical software developed for audit procedures (Boritz and No, 2004). Several of these applications are dependent, however, on software developers developing the necessary software, which to date has been somewhat limited.

From a company or preparer perspective, XBRL can increase the efficiency and reduce the costs of consolidating information for business and regulatory reporting. Reduced costs are realized by the increased speed of data processing and reduced occurrences of data redundancy and mistakes caused by human error (Graziano, 2002). Companies also benefit from the flexibility of XBRL to tag financial data as a way to communicate a company's uniqueness. XBRL's ability to disseminate business information is not limited to quantitative data and financial reporting. XBRL has the potential to communicate appropriately tagged quantitative and qualitative information in a much broader range of business reporting than financial reports (Cohen, 2009). Finally, companies can use financial information tagged in one or more taxonomies to generate reports for the differing requirements of investors, securities commissions, tax agencies and other regulatory organizations without reentering and reformatting data into traditional formats and prescribed forms.

CAPABILITIES OF XBRL AS A LANGUAGE FOR E-GOVERNANCE

The capital markets have an explicit need for information from companies to assist in the evaluation of firm performance, the assessment of management stewardship and investment allocation decisions. Information is required on strategic plans, risk management, business policies and corporate governance (Jiang et al., 2009). Regulations concerning the dissemination of information in the capital markets changed dramatically with respect to the level, timing and nature of that information in response to high profile corporate scandals. The changes in regulation centered on more extensive and comprehensive disclosure, continuous disclosure, broader dissemination and accessibility of information, greater personal accountability of management (i.e. CEOs and CFOs) and the required use of technology (e.g. the internet) to disseminate information (Jiang et al., 2009; Cohen et al., 2005).

The emergence of the internet as the predominant vehicle for disseminating information (CICA, 2010) has had implications for corporate governance. Capital market regulators globally have increasingly mandated the use of the internet for filing corporate information such as annual reports and financial statements (Trites, 2008). The internet has the potential to electronically and efficiently disseminate information, resulting in better quality disclosure and improved transparency leading to better corporate governance (Boritz & No, 2004, Jiang et al., 2009). In effect, the internet enables electronic governance. In

this context, XBRL is emerging as a language to facilitate the electronic dissemination of information and thus improving electronic governance.

XBRL has been described as the catalyst for change in terms of the format, the timing and the content of corporate disclosure (Cohen et al., 2005). In many countries, corporate disclosures are submitted electronically and stored in electronic repositories (e.g., EDGAR, the Electronic Data Gathering, Analysis, and Retrieval system in the United States and SEDAR, the System for Electronic Document Analysis and Retrieval in Canada). Most of this electronic reporting is in Web-based or Adobe Acrobat (PDF) formats which are electronic versions of the traditional paper reporting.

The Web-based and Adobe Acrobat (PDF) formats for current reporting have created inefficiencies. PDF files and Web-based files were developed to preserve the traditional hard copy reporting format of filings and are rigid in form, are difficult to manipulate and format, are labor-intensive to generate and are not designed to be read by computers (i.e., not downloadable or easily downloadable into an Excel spreadsheet). PDF files in particular have been criticized because of their size and limited ability to search within the file or report. From the preparer's perspective, the various regulators each have unique prescribed forms and reporting requirements which cannot be used for other purposes or shared with other applications (Trites, 2006). Consequently, companies need to maintain and support various applications and formats (i.e., one for each regulatory body to which the company is reporting). From the user's perspective, using the information contained in these electronic documents usually involves their manual re-entry into databases and spreadsheets which is costly and increases the possibility of human error (Cohen et al., 2005; Trites, 2006; Graziano, 2002). From the regulators' perspective, as they continue to require more frequent filings with more information, they have an increased need for resources to review and process those filings (Trites, 2006). Consequently, preparers and users such as investors, analysts and regulators are plagued with inefficiencies created by electronic reporting using PDF and Web based technology. A potential solution to the inefficiencies in electronic corporate reporting is XBRL.

XBRL allows for electronic filings that reduce the identified inefficiencies experienced by preparers and users of financial information using traditional vehicles. With XBRL, companies are able to generate a single piece of information that can be easily reused and delivered in multiple formats to Web pages, regulatory filings and internal management reports as needed (Graziano, 2002). "XBRL has, in a relatively short time, become the pre-eminent standard for the exchange of business-oriented reporting data in electronic form." (Piechocki et al., 2009, p. 238)

OVERVIEW OF THE EMPIRICAL RESEARCH ON XBRL

There are few empirical studies available on XBRL implementation and use. The empirical research that is available addresses: a) the lack of diffusion of XBRL, b) the profile of voluntary adopters of XBRL, and c) the XBRL implementation problems that may affect data quality.

Diffusion of XBRL

Despite its benefits, XBRL has not been embraced by companies even when it is encouraged by regulators. Cohen et al. (2005) suggest that companies which are not mandated by regulators to adopt XBRL are reluctant to do so because of concerns about the potential costs and an inability to see the benefits of XBRL adoption. In the United States, the Securities Exchange Commission (SEC) introduced voluntary XBRL reporting in 2005[2]. Only 1.37% of the more than 10,000 registrants participated in the program to use XBRL. In addition, of the more than 8,000 banks required

to file reports in XBRL to the Federal Financial Institutions Examination Council (FFEIC), less than 1 percent participated in the SEC's voluntary XBRL filing program (Gray and Miller, 2009). Two reasons have been suggested for the slow rate of adoption: 1) the poor communication of the benefits of XBRL and 2) the perception of XBRL as a compliance issue only (Cohen, 2009). These observations about XBRL diffusion have led some to conclude that the widespread use of XBRL is not possible without it being mandated by regulatory bodies (Cohen et al., 2005; Gray and Miller, 2009).

Gray and Miller (2009) investigated the potential adoption of XBRL by public companies in the United States. Using a focus group of internal auditors, each auditor was asked to provide an issue or concern that was challenging or problematic for their organization. Upon identification of those issues by the auditors, the authors identified how and where XBRL could address those identified issues. The main concern of the internal auditors in the study was the maintenance of data integrity. The issues and concerns identified by the internal auditors revolved around Sarbanes Oxley compliance, fear of spreadsheets which often become overwhelming because of their size and complexity, retrieving and consolidating accounting information, and the use of audit tools. The authors demonstrated that to achieve widespread adoption of XBRL companies need to be informed about the advantages XRBL offers and how XBRL addresses the issues the auditors in the study identified (Gray and Miller, 2009).

Profiles of Early Adopters of XBRL Reporting in Voluntary Regimes

Research on the characteristics of early adopters of XBRL focused on characteristics such as the level of corporate governance (Premuroso and Bhattacharya, 2008), operating performance (Premuroso and Bhattacharya, 2008), size (Callaghan and Nehmer, 2009; Efendi et al., 2009;

Premuroso and Bhattacharya, 2008), innovation or R&D spending (Efendi et al., 2009), financial leverage (Callaghan and Nehmer, 2009; Premuroso and Bhattacharya, 2008), liquidity (Callaghan and Nehmer, 2009), profitability (Premuroso and Bhattacharya, 2008) and risk (Callaghan and Nehmer, 2009). These studies however had small sample sizes and used different selection criteria for their matched sample procedures. Premuroso and Bhattacharya (2008) had a sample size of 20, Efendi et al. (2009) had a sample size of 82 and Callaghan and Nehmer (2009) had a sample size of 77. Further, with respect to the criteria to match firms, Premuroso and Bhattacharya (2008) used industry codes and revenue to match companies, Efendi et al. (2009) matched company attributes to industry averages, and Callaghan and Nehmer (2009) used industry, size and governance score availability to match companies.

The collective results of the empirical studies investigating the characteristics of early filers suggest that XBRL early adopters have superior performance (Premuroso and Bhattacharya, 2008), are more innovative (Efendi et al., 2009), are larger (Callaghan and Nehmer, 2009; Efendi et al., 2009; Premuroso and Bhattacharya, 2008) and are less financially leveraged (Callaghan and Nehmer, 2009). The results on corporate governance demonstrated that corporate governance was a factor that distinguished between early XBRL adopters and non-adopters however the relationship of corporate governance was mixed. Callaghan and Nehmer (2009) demonstrated that companies with lower corporate governance ratings were early adopters. In contrast, Premuroso and Bhattacharya's (2008) results suggest that companies with superior corporate governance ratings were early adopters. XBRL early adopters were not different from their counterparts in terms of liquidity (Callaghan and Nehmer, 2009), profitability (Callaghan and Nehmer, 2009; Premuroso and Bhattacharya, 2008), leverage (Callaghan and Nehmer, 2009; Premuroso and Bhattacharya, 2008), risk (Callaghan and Nehmer, 2009), audi-

tor type (Premuroso and Bhattacharya, 2008) or total assets (Premuroso and Bhattacharya, 2008). Due to the small sample sizes, methodological considerations over the matching processes and the limited number of empirical studies, these results may not be generalizable.

Implementation Problems Affecting Data Quality

Studies on XBRL implementation have reported the occurrence of errors in XBRL reports. Common errors include incorrect data entry, excluded subtotals in aggregated totals, the transposition of the sign of debits and credits, aggressive rounding, and incorrect mapping of the elements to the taxonomy (Bartley et al., 2010; Debreceny et al., 2010). Those errors create concern over the quality and integrity of data contained in XBRL reports. In the United States, the SEC introduced a multiyear transition to XBRL for submissions to its corporate filing reporting system (i.e., EDGAR). Debreceny et al (2010) studied the quality of the 2009 XBRL disclosures for 400 American companies that were required to file using XBRL. They identified six different classes of errors and found that 26% of companies that filed had errors. The primary cause of the errors was the incorrect entering of balances as debits or credits. These results generate concerns over the quality of information that results from an XBRL implementation.

APPLICATIONS OF XBRL: THE GLOBAL CONTEXT

The use of XBRL is continuing to grow worldwide. The Australian Prudential Regulatory Authority (APRA) was the first banking regulator in the world to both develop a taxonomy for its own needs and to use XBRL to monitor the financial information of financial institutions such as banks, credit unions, insurance companies, and superannuation funds (Efendi et al., 2009; Graziano, 2002). China was the first country to mandate XBRL reporting in the capital markets. China started its voluntary XBRL filing program in 2003 and then mandated XBRL reporting in 2004 for companies listed on both the Shanghai and Shenzhen Stock Exchanges (Efendi et al., 2009).

XBRL has become, on a mandatory or voluntary basis, part of many capital markets' compliance regimes. In addition to China, the mandated use of XBRL has been announced in the United States, Japan, the United Kingdom and numerous other countries around the world (Cohen, 2009). Many countries that have mandated the use of XBRL are using a phased in approach to ease the transition to XBRL. For example, in 2005, the SEC introduced XBRL for reporting entities and encouraged the voluntary use of XBRL. In 2009, the SEC introduced a mandatory transition plan to allow for required XBRL reporting for all public companies by 2011. The mandatory XBRL reporting requirement is being phased in over a three year period with companies with the largest market capitalizations subject to the new requirements in 2009. All other companies with large market capitalizations using US Generally Accepted Accounting Principles (GAAP) were subject to the XBRL requirements in 2010. All remaining filers using U.S. GAAP and all foreign private issuers using International Financial Reporting Standards (IFRS) will be subject to the XBRL requirements in 2011 (Brashear, 2009).

The use of XBRL for reporting in other countries such as the Netherlands and Canada is optional (Cohen, 2009). For example, in Canada, a voluntary program has been introduced to help the Canadian marketplace gain practical knowledge in preparing, filing, and using XBRL information and to help the regulators assess the usefulness of XBRL. Companies choosing to participate can file their financial statements in XBRL format. XBRL financial statements are not a substitute but a compliment to financial statements which are required to be filed under Canadian securities

legislation. Interestingly, the use of XBRL reporting will likely require changes to the SEDAR website because SEDAR was developed more than a decade ago and is not easily compatible with XBRL.

Finally, several countries such as Australia and the Netherlands are developing standard business reporting (SBR) in which XBRL is used to streamline private company to government reporting (Alles, 2009). Australia made its SBR program mandatory in 2010 (Australian Government, 2010). New Zealand is also developing a similar program.

FUTURE OF XBRL AS AN EVOLUTION OF E-GOVERNANCE IN THE CAPITAL MARKETS

The success of XBRL as an instrument for e-governance will depend on the possibility of extended regulatory requirements, the use of XBRL Global Ledger, and the development of software that explicitly incorporates XBRL. The future of XBRL adoption however is hindered by concerns over data integrity, the limited knowledge of employees about XBRL, the perceived cost of XBRL adoption relative to its benefits and the challenges of flexible taxonomies.

Future Applications of XBRL

XBRL as a tool for e-governance has the potential to significantly change the format, amount and timeliness of the dissemination of information to capital market participants. That potential will be realized in an environment with advancing technology which makes use of social networking (e.g., Facebook) and hardware innovations (e.g., handheld devices). The dialogue on the future of XBRL includes expanded regulatory requirements, the use of XBRL Global Ledger, and software incorporating XBRL capabilities.

1. **Extended Regulatory Requirements:** The most common applications of XBRL are for financial statement reporting, corporate filings such as insider reports, registration with regulators, and submission of corporate tax returns. XBRL has however a broader use than is currently mandated by regulators (Cohen et al., 2005). XBRL also allows for filings beyond the most common applications to include corporate actions such as mergers, dividends, stock splits, etc. Using XBRL for corporate actions will provide stakeholders with the same transparency, filing speed and accuracy as afforded to the financial statements (Anonymous, 2010). XBRL also allows for the tagging of non-financial data. As companies become capable of producing increasing amounts of both financial and non-financial data, regulators may consider mandating additional disclosures. For example, the SEC has indicated that it is not currently requiring XBRL tagging of the Management's Discussion and Analysis (MD&A) which usually includes both financial and non-financial information but it will consider additional regulated disclosure in the future (Brashear, 2009). Further, XBRL allows for more efficient internal reporting processes. Where XBRL is used for both external reporting by preparers and the consumption of external reports by their users, the integration of the internal and external reporting systems can be made easier with the use of XBRL and XBRL Global Ledger (Cohen, 2009).

2. **XBRL Global Ledger:** XBRL Global Ledger (GL) is a taxonomy which can be used to tag and access data right down to the transaction level. The tagged data can then be used for a variety of reporting purposes and also can provide a linkage of detail (e.g., transactional data) to aggregated financial statement elements (e.g., accounts receivable). XBRL GL is a particular taxonomy(s)

that is used primarily for internal reporting (Cohen, 2009). The use of XBRL GL is growing for internal reporting systems because it provides a means of making a vast array of data readily available and also facilitates the integration of internal functions and systems with external reporting processes.

3. **Software Incorporating XBRL:** Today's information systems are insufficient to enable companies to easily comply with the extensive and continuous reporting required by corporate governance regulation. To assist companies in addressing their XBRL needs, software developers like Rivet are embedding XBRL as a base component of their software (Hannon, 2005). The willingness of software developers to incorporate XBRL into their software will be key to increasing the use of XBRL. Unfortunately, it is a "Catch 22" situation. The software companies are waiting for the market to develop sufficiently, but their lack of development is hindering the development of that market.

Barriers to the Diffusion of XBRL

The pace of XBRL adoption may be slowed by several issues. Market participants have concerns about the integrity of XBRL financial statements. Management of companies using XBRL are concerned about the costs associated with XBRL implementation, the training of employees to use XBRL, and the updating of taxonomies in the face of changing regulation.

1. **Data Integrity:** Concerns over data integrity are shared by users and preparers of financial information and the concerns center on the nature, extent and timing of assurance services on information, the correctness of the information, and the security of the information provided via the Web (Boritz and No, 2004). Like other electronic languages, financial information in XBRL can

be easily created and manipulated and can be used without the organization's consent or knowledge thereby reducing information integrity (Boritz and No, 2004). Additionally, experiences with errors in the use of XBRL taxonomies in the United States underscore further concerns over data integrity. Users of financial information that is produced and distributed electronically require assurance that both errors in information and the manipulation of data are not material. To address these concerns, XBRL has the capability to include electronic tags which can clearly identify what data has been audited (BDO, 2010). In addition, XARL, Extensible Assurance Reporting Language, as an XML-based extension of XBRL enables assurance providers to report on the integrity of XBRL-tagged information which is disseminated over the internet (see Boritz and No (2004) for an overview of XARL).

2. **Cost:** Companies operating in the capital markets already report to regulators electronically but have complained that additional costs will be required to convert electronic reporting into XBRL. In a survey of XBRL filers most companies made no attempt to embed XBRL into their financial reporting system but instead manually converted their final reports into an XBRL format or hired a consultant to do so (Cohen, 2009). Proponents of XBRL claim that companies need to look beyond financial reporting to experience the additional benefits from having greater XBRL data accessibility and availability (Hannon, 2006). Instead of preparing reporting information for many formats as required by different regulatory bodies, XBRL data can be reused and redelivered in any format that companies need for investor relation purposes, websites, regulatory filings and internal reporting (Graziano, 2002; Trites, 2008; Hannon, 2006).

3. **Employee Knowledge of XBRL:** The introduction of a new technology like XBRL will require fluency in the XBRL "language". Adopters of XBRL will need to make an investment in XBRL training to learn the well-developed taxonomies and/or software that has embedded XBRL into its system. From an education and training perspective, XBRL will have a significant impact through the reconfiguring of work assignments and the realigning of skills with assignments. With increased automation (e.g. the use of XBRL taxonomies to prepare the multitude of reporting requirements) and the reduction of mechanical tasks (e.g. reduced need for spreadsheets to prepare reporting requirements), the tasks assigned to employees will differ (Cohen et al., 2005). In addition to preparers, users of XBRL data such as analysts, auditors, and regulators will need to familiarize themselves with XBRL and the techniques used to analyze financial data. It is likely that these companies will also have to invest in XBRL training programs (BDO, 2010).

4. **Infrastructure:** The infrastructure of XBRL centers on the taxonomies that are developed for reporting and other purposes. Standard taxonomies are not developed to meet the specific requirements of a single company but are a composite of reporting requirements and practices (Cohen, 2004). In addition, different taxonomies are required for different business reporting purposes, for different jurisdictions with jurisdiction-specific accounting and other reporting regulations, and for specific business reporting needs. Various versions of XBRL taxonomies exist and a typical XBRL document will contain reference to one or more XBRL taxonomies (Cohen et al., 2005).

The ability to customize XBRL also raises concerns. The extensible capability of XBRL allows users the flexibility to customize standard taxonomies to better reflect their company's situation. This inherent flexibility allows XBRL to be used for a broad scope of reporting options, however, it also introduces reduced comparability. Piechocki et al. (2009) analysed the use of multiple taxonomies across different European countries. By analysing four XBRL situations, the authors demonstrated how the flexibility in multiple taxonomy designs across different jurisdictions created difficulties comparing institutions across national borders (Piechocki et al., 2009). To reduce the proliferation of various taxonomies and to maintain comparability, the SEC has encouraged companies to relabel the standard tags rather than create extension tags in situations where the company uses a different description for the standard XBRL data element (Brashear, 2009). Given the importance of this issue, researchers such as Piechocki et al. (2009) have called for research on the tools that can assist in appropriate taxonomy design that will maximize comparability and interconnectivity.

An additional challenge is the updating and maintenance of XBRL taxonomies. XBRL standardized taxonomies will need to be updated to comply with changes to accounting standards and other reporting requirements (Boritz and No, 2004). For companies with customized taxonomies any change to a standardized taxonomy may conflict with customizations that have been implemented (Cohen, 2004).

CONCLUSION

XBRL is a powerful electronic language which has the potential to change business reporting and affect the delivery of corporate governance (XBRL International, 2010a). Challenges must be overcome before XBRL will be accepted globally. These challenges include concerns over data integrity, the limited knowledge of employees about XBRL, the perceived cost of XBRL adoption relative to its benefits, and the challenges of flexible taxonomies. As adoptions of XBRL occur globally in countries like China, India, Australia, the Netherlands and the United States and as regulators make XBRL mandatory, XBRL will become the standard for reporting and will also offer other possibilities.

There are numerous research opportunities on XBRL implementation and use. One area of research is the harmonization of national taxonomies. Different countries are in the process of developing and using their own taxonomies. China and the United States have XBRL International approved taxonomies which are specific to their countries' accounting systems. Research needs to be conducted to understand the interconnectivity of various taxonomies like those of the United States and China.

Related to interconnectivity is the impact of IFRS. XBRL was developed in coordination with the development of IFRS. IFRS, which represents the accounting profession's attempt to harmonize accounting standards, may enable increased comparability between companies reporting from different countries. IFRS, however, is a principles-based regime which allows for a level of flexibility in the selection and use of accounting policies. XBRL's power of comparability, in contrast, revolves around standardization and harmonization similar to a rules-based regime. Investigation of the impact of a rules-based XBRL language embedded in a principles-based accounting system needs to be explored. Other areas of investigation include measuring the effectiveness of users' abilities to generate XBRL reports, understanding the profile of companies who extend the use of XBRL beyond the financial statements, and assessing the impact of XBRL data availability on decision-making.

REFERENCES

Alles, M. (2009). Special issue: XBRL and the future of disclosure. *International Journal of Disclosure and Governance*, 6(3), 184–185. doi:10.1057/jdg.2009.10

Anonymous,. (2010). Internet information providers: Edgar Online is the first company to furnish corporate action information Using XBRL. *Computers, Networks. Communications*, 29, 48.

Australian Government. (2010). *Timeline, an Australian government initiative: Standard business reporting*. Retrieved on September 23, 2010, from http://www.sbr.gov.au/About_SBR/Timeline.aspx

Bartley, J., Chen, Y. S. A., & Taylor, E. (2010). Avoiding common errors of XBRL reporting. *Journal of Accountancy*, 209(2), 46–51.

BDO. (2010). *Extensible business reporting language (XBRL): The future of financial reporting*. Risk Advisory Services, BDO. Retrieved on August 13, 2010, from www.bdo.ca/ras

Boritz, J. E., & No, W. G. (2004). Assurance reporting for XML-Based Information Services: XARL. *Canadian Accounting Perspectives*, 2(3), 207–233. doi:10.1506/V8D9-QTUN-HDU1-93RB

Brashear, J. (2009). SEC mandates interactive data financial reporting. *The Corporate Governance Advisor*, 17(3), 27–30.

Callaghan, J., & Nehmer, R. (2009). Financial and governance characteristics of voluntary XBRL adopters in the United States. *International Journal of Disclosure and Governance*, 6(4), 321–336. doi:10.1057/jdg.2009.15

CICA. (2010). *Using the Internet in corporate reporting*. Canadian Institute of Chartered Accountants. Retrieved on September 23, 2010, from http://www.cica.ca/research-and-guidance/research-activities/activities-in-progress/accounting/item33149.aspx

Cohen, E. E. (2004). Compromise or customize: XBRL's paradoxical power. *Canadian Accounting Perspectives*, 2(3), 187–206. doi:10.1506/YAHN-CAE8-5CWQ-H4TE

Cohen, E. E. (2009). XBRL's global ledger framework: Exploring the standardised missing link to ERP integration. *International Journal of Disclosure and Governance*, 6(8), 188–206. doi:10.1057/jdg.2009.5

Cohen, E. E., Schiavina, T., & Servais, O. (2005). XBRL: The standardised business language for the 21st century reporting and governance. *International Journal of Disclosure and Governance*, 2(4), 368–394. doi:10.1057/palgrave.jdg.2040006

Debreceny, R., Farewell, S., Piechocki, M., Felden, C., & Graning, A. (2010). Does it add up? Early evidence on the data quality of XBRL filings to the SEC. *Journal of Accounting and Public Policy*, 29(3), 296–306. doi:10.1016/j.jaccpubpol.2010.04.001

Efendi, J., Smith, L. M., & Wong, J. (2009). *Longitudinal analysis of voluntary adoption of XBRL on financial reporting*. SSRN working paper. Retrieved August 3, 2010, from http://papers.ssrn.com/sol3/papers.cfm?abstract_id=1440956

Gray, G. L., & Miller, D. W. (2009). XBRL: Solving real-world problems. *International Journal of Disclosure and Governance*, 6(3), 207–223. doi:10.1057/jdg.2009.8

Graziano, C. de M. (2002). XBRL streamlining financial reporting. *Financial Executive*, 18(8), 52–55.

Hannon, N. (2005). Post Sarbanes-Oxley: Does XBRL hold the key? *Strategic Finance*, 86(7), 57–61.

Hannon, N. (2006). Does XBRL Cost too Much? *Strategic Finance*, 87(10), 59–61.

Jiang, Y., Raghupathi, V., & Raghupathi, W. (2009). Web-based corporate governance disclosure: An empirical investigation. *Information Resources Management Journal, 22*(2), 50–69. doi:10.4018/irmj.2009092203

Piechocki, M., Felden, C., Graning, A., & Debreceny, R. (2009). Design and standardisation of XBRL solutions for governance and transparency. *International Journal of Disclosure and Governance, 6*(3), 224–241. doi:10.1057/jdg.2009.9

Premuroso, R. F., & Bhattacharya, S. (2008). Do early and voluntary filers of financial information in XBRL format signal superior corporate governance and operating performance? *International Journal of Accounting Information Systems, 9*, 1–20. doi:10.1016/j.accinf.2008.01.002

Trites, G. (2006). Implications of e-filing. *CA Magazine, 139*(8), 51–52.

Trites, G. (2008). Corporate reporting on the Web. *CA Magazine, 141*(7), 16–17.

XBRL Canada. (2010). *What is XBRL?* Retrieved on August 10, 2010, from http://www.xbrl.ca/index.php/what-is-xbrl

XBRL International. (2010a). *What is XBRL?* Retrieved on August 10, 2010, from http://www.xbrl.org/WhatIsXBRL

XBRL International. (2010b). *Global ledger taxonomy – An introduction.* Retrieved on September 23, 2010, from http://www.xbrl.org/GLTaxonomy/

KEY TERMS AND DEFINITIONS

Capital Markets: The financial markets where equity and debt instruments are traded.

Corporate Governance: The systems, regulations and processes in place to ensure that management in a company makes decisions that reflect the rights and interests of the stakeholders in the company.

E-Governance: It is governance through the provision of information via electronic means.

Market Participants: The broad scope of individuals, organizations, institutions, regulatory bodies and financial intermediaries who engage in transactions in the capital markets.

XBRL: A specialized XML language with allows for the tagging of business information.

XML: An electronic language that requires the tagging of data along a number of dimensions and which allows for the efficient exchange of tagged data electronically.

ENDNOTES

[1]   The discussion of e-governance in this chapter is focused on the provision of information through an electronic means such as the internet. E-governance is often conceptualized in broader terms and its conceptualization may include the execution of transactions electronically and electronic interactivity between stakeholders and corporations.

[2]   Subsequently, the SEC introduced regulation that mandates reporting for all of its registrants by 2011.

Chapter 8

E–Governance in the Financial Capital Markets:
The Canadian Capital Market Regulatory Environment

Shantanu Dutta
University of Ontario Institute of Technology, Canada

Ken MacAulay
St. Francis Xavier University, Canada

Mary M. Oxner
St. Francis Xavier University, Canada

ABSTRACT

Studies of corporate governance in the capital markets area have focused on the mechanisms and structures of governance and less on the medium through which it is accomplished. This chapter examines the use of information and communications technologies (ICTs) as a medium to enhance governance in the capital markets, focusing in particular on the Canadian capital market. Parallels are drawn between the e-governance issues faced by governments and the capital markets. The chapter concludes with a discussion of future directions for e-governance in the capital markets.

INTRODUCTION

Academics, professionals, investors and citizens have become increasingly interested in the governance of the organizations with which they interact on a daily basis. In addition, over the past twenty years, advances in information and communica-

tions technologies (ICTs) have improved the ability of these organizations to provide relevant information to interested parties. As a result of the increased interest in governance and the increased availability of information, discussions of good or poor governance can be found everywhere, from the local, national and international media to academic journals and conferences.

DOI: 10.4018/978-1-60960-848-4.ch008

Academics have focused most of their efforts on the study of governance in corporations and government. In particular, an extensive literature on the use of ICTs as a medium to enhance governance in local, regional and national governments, also known as electronic governance or e-governance, has developed. The ICTs utilized by governments were often adopted from the corporate environment and subsequently used by governments to improve transparency and responsiveness (Perez, Bolivar and Hernandez, 2008). Interestingly, the corporate governance literature in accounting and finance has focused on the mechanisms and structures of governance (Durisin and Puzone, 2009) and less on the medium through which it is accomplished. This chapter will examine the use of ICTs as a medium to enhance governance in the capital markets, focusing in particular on the Canadian capital market.

The remainder of the chapter is organized as follows. First, the Canadian capital markets are briefly described. Second, governance practices generally and e-governance practices in particular are reviewed for the Canadian capital markets. Third, information from relevant studies of governance applicable to the Canadian capital markets are summarized and issues associated with the use of electronic governance are identified. Fourth, parallels in e-governance in the financial capital markets and in governments are identified. Finally, future directions of e-governance in the Canadian capital markets are discussed.

THE CANADIAN CAPITAL MARKETS AND THE REGULATORY ENVIRONMENT

Canada is characterized by well-developed capital markets as evidenced by the fact that the market capitalization of exchange-listed issuers is high relative to Canada's GDP[1] (Nicholls, 2006). The capital markets consist of a number of individual markets, the most well known are the markets for equities and fixed-income. In Canada, most equities are traded on organized exchanges (i.e., auction markets), primarily the Toronto Stock Exchange (TSX) and the TSX Venture Exchange[2]. In contrast, most fixed-income products are traded in dealer or "over-the-counter" (OTC) markets. According to the World Federation of Exchanges, the TMX Group, with a domestic market capitalization of $1.7 trillion in 2009, was the eighth largest stock market in the world.

The regulatory system for the capital markets in Canada is ranked as one of the best in the world. In 2009, the Organization for Economic Co-operation and Development (OECD) ranked Canada fifth in the world in investor protection. In Canada, the capital markets, and the financial industry more generally, are characterized by extensive use of technology, in fact, much of their business is conducted electronically. Further, most of the information required by regulators (to be distributed to the public or provided to the regulators) is disclosed electronically. These factors make Canada a particularly good example to use to examine the use of electronic governance.

The Canadian capital markets have two other distinct features. First, companies who are traded on the stock market must either comply with a set of recommended best practices for corporate governance or, alternatively, explain how they will achieve the same governance objective in a different manner (i.e., "comply or explain"). This principles-based approach to governance recognizes that the costs and benefits of the governance requirements are likely to be different for small firms as compared to large firms. This feature means that there should be more variability in governance practices than under a rules-based approach to corporate governance. A second feature of the Canadian capital markets is that it does not have a national regulator[3]. In Canada, the regulation of the securities business has been assumed by the provinces. In contrast to the United States (which has the Securities and Exchange Commission or SEC), no federal regulatory body for the securities industry exists in Canada. Each province (and the three territories) is responsible for creating the legislation and regulation under which the industry operates. This feature is important because it means that the rules and regulations to govern firms in Canada are the result of a process of consideration, cooperation and coordination. These governance rules reflect not only the diversity of firms but also the diversity of political regions.

There are three major parties in the Canadian capital markets: investors (providers of capital), issuers (users of capital), and markets/market intermediaries. The interactions among and within these parties are regulated by a number of groups: provincial securities regulators, stock exchanges, and other self-regulated organizations (SRO's)[4]. This chapter focuses on governance in the equity markets.

Provincial securities commissions regulate the capital markets in their respective provinces. To harmonize regulations and achieve high industry standards, the provincial regulators formed the Canadian Securities Administrators (CSA). The CSA does not engage in regulation directly. It develops policies and instruments that are implemented by the provincial securities commissions, enabling the harmonization of regulations in the Canadian capital markets (Carnaghan and Gunz, 2007). The mission of the CSA is to institutionalize a Canadian securities regulatory system that "protects investors from unfair, improper or fraudulent practices and fosters fair, efficient and vibrant capital markets" (CSA, 2010a).

Self Regulatory Organizations (SROs) are private industry organizations that regulate their own members. SROs are usually delegated the regulatory function by the provincial securities commissions. They are responsible for ensuring that their members act in a manner consistent with securities legislation and they often have the power to prescribe the rules of conduct for their members.

Stock exchanges can be viewed as SROs. The provincial securities acts or commissions delegate considerable power to the stock exchanges to set rules and regulations for the trading of securities. In addition, firms listed on the stock exchange must also comply with the exchange's reporting requirements. Other SROs are the Investment Industry Regulatory Organization of Canada (IIROC) and the Mutual Fund Dealers Association (MFDA). IIROC oversees all investment dealers and the trading of debt and equity securities. IIROC carries out its regulatory responsibilities in two ways. First, they set and enforce rules related to the proficiency and conduct of member firms and their employees. Second, IIROC sets and enforces universal market integrity rules (UMIRs) regarding the trading of securities in Canada. IIROC also monitors trading activity in the stock market (IIROC, 2010). The MFDA is the SRO for the mutual fund industry. It regulates the distribution of mutual funds to investors by mutual fund salespeople. The MDFA also sets standards to ensure that its members are competent. It has the authority to set and enforce rules and regulations for its members (MFDA, 2010).

GOVERNANCE IN THE CANADIAN CAPITAL MARKETS

Information disclosure is the key to governance in the Canadian capital markets. At present almost all information in the Canadian capital markets is either gathered electronically or disseminated electronically. In addition, the principle of "full, true and plain disclosure" is the basis of many of the regulations in Canada. Sarra (2007) argues that disclosure has three roles in capital markets. In addition to serving as a transaction cost control device and a regulatory tool, disclosure also serves as a governance signalling device. Disclosure works as a signalling device to the extent that it provides information to investors on corporate governance performance, the results of operations, management ability and board oversight. In addition, disclosure also provides a governance role to the extent that it informs the board of changes in the risks facing the corporation and to the extent that it allows oversight of management (Sarra, 2007).

The governance system in the Canadian capital markets consists of the laws and regulations implemented by securities commissions and the relevant SRO's. In addition, business corporation statutes at the provincial and federal levels also provide remedies and require disclosures that form part of the system of governance (Gray and Kitching, 2005). Governance in the capital markets exists at two levels. At one level, rules and regulations exist to ensure that there is appropriate disclosure by issuers to investors. The regulators of Canadian capital markets, consistent with the principles of accountability and transparency, require corporations to provide information to the public to allow for the assessment of overall corporate performance and an assessment of management stewardship and decision-making. At another level, rules and regulations exist to make sure that the market functions properly. These rules require that the trading of securities is conducted in a manner that is fair and transparent. In addition, these rules ensure that market intermediaries which assist in the trading of securities are competent and act appropriately.

At the first level, regulators require public companies to provide information related to the fundamental aspects of their businesses. The amount of filings required for Canadian public companies is extensive but the following is a summary of the major requirements:

- **Prospectus / offering memorandum:** The information that must be provided when selling securities to the public
- **Periodic filings:** Required ongoing disclosures of key information on the company and its performance. Examples include annual and interim financial statements, management discussion and analysis, annual information forms, management information circulars, proxy solicitations
- **Non-periodic disclosures:** Required disclosure of material information and material changes. Examples would include earnings announcements and take-over bids.

The information contained in the periodic and non-periodic filings is required under "continuous disclosure" obligations. Key governance disclosures can be found in the periodic filings. For example firms' reports on compliance with recommended corporate governance practices, executive compensation, and audit committee details can be found in the management information circular (MIC), the annual information form (AIF), or sometimes the management discussion and analysis (MDA). In addition, because information must be disclosed in a manner that is fair and transparent, corporations are prohibited from the practice of selective disclosure (Carnaghan and Gunz, 2007).

At the second level, regulators require disclosures with respect to the trading of equities and require the provision of information on people who act as market intermediaries. Insiders of public companies are required to report on their trading in companies securities (i.e., insider trading). They are required to report their trades for two reasons. First, it provides transparency and information to the market about their trading activity and second, it deters insiders from trading on confidential information (CSA, 2010[b]). Dealers and advisors (eg., stock brokers) are required to register annually with the appropriate provincial securities commission(s). This process is designed to ensure that only competent and reputable people and firms are licensed.

Recent Governance Developments in the Canadian Capital Markets

It is important to also briefly review recent developments in disclosure the Canadian capital markets. This review will not be exhaustive but will highlight several examples that will reveal two trends in disclosure: enhanced reporting and more rapid reporting (Trites, 2004). The focus will be to describe recent changes in the corporate governance rules. Changes in several other mandated disclosures will also be discussed.

An example of enhanced disclosure can be found in the recent changes to corporate governance rules. In Canada, the Dey report (1994) started the reform of corporate governance and resulted in the adoption of a "comply or explain" approach to governance by the Toronto Stock Exchange in 1995. In the early 2000's, regulators were again looking at improvements to corporate governance practices. The result was new corporate governance guidelines (National Policy 58-201 [Corporate Governance Guidelines] and

National Instrument 58-101 [Disclosure of Corporate Governance Practices]) issued by the CSA in 2005 and subsequently adopted by the TSX.

MacAulay et al. (2009) investigated the impact of the introduction of NP 58-201 and NI 58-101 and found that the enhanced disclosure requirements in NI 58-101 had the desired effect. Although compliance was voluntary, Canadian corporate governance practices improved. In the 5 year period surrounding the 2005 introduction, the average corporate governance score increased from 10.4 in 2003 to 14.5 in 2007 (measured on a 20 point scale). Further, the percentage of firms that scored 10 or less dropped from 46% in 2003 to 14% in 2007. The frequency of compliance with each of the 20 items in the MacAulay et al (2009) scale for 2003 and 2007 can be found in Table 1. A review of these items reveals that the

Table 1. Frequency of Compliance with Corporate Governance Disclosure 2003 & 2007[5]

Type of Corporate Governance Disclosure		2003	2007
#1	Majority of directors are independent	79%	87%
#2	Chair is a member of management	46%	41%
#3	If chair is a member of management, lead director is assigned	13%	23%
#4	Measures in place to allow for meetings of independent directors	67%	90%
#5	Integrity of CEO/other executive officers assessed	6%	46%
#6	Adopted a strategic planning process	94%	93%
#7	ID business risks and systems to manage these risks	93%	89%
#8	Position description developed for the CEO	71%	86%
#9	Education provided for new directors	18%	82%
#10	Continuing education provided for directors	23%	41%
#11	Code of business conduct and ethics exists	30%	36%
#12	Board monitors compliance with code	57%	70%
#13	Nominating committee composed of independent directors	67%	65%
#14	Nominating committee can engage/ use outside advisors	45%	67%
#15	When making a recommendation, nominating committee assesses skills of existing directors	79%	87%
#16	Compensation committee composed of independent directors	46%	41%
#17	Compensation committee can engage/ use outside advisors	13%	23%
#18	Compensation committee evaluates CEO performance per objectives	67%	90%
#19	Compensation committee recommends CEO compensation	6%	46%
#20	Effectiveness of each board member is assessed	94%	93%

greatest improvements were in the areas of board independence, assessment of integrity, education of the board, and compensation practices.

In addition to governance practices for corporations, regulators in Canada have also addressed a number of other governance issues around disclosure. These examples are also illustrative of the two trends of enhanced and more rapid reporting requirements in the capital markets.

- As part of its move to harmonize regulations in Canada, the CSA introduced a passport system in 2004 and completed its implementation in 2009. Because the system has been adopted by all provinces but Ontario, it allows participants, for the most part, to deal with only their home regulator (i.e., it is a mutual recognition system). Key parts of the system address the filing of prospectuses and the registration of dealers and advisors. For example, the registration of dealers and advisors is now done electronically. This has resulted in the more efficient gathering of information by regulators and enhanced access by investors through their ability to search the database online.
- In 2010, the CSA introduced new changes to its insider reporting requirements. The time required to file the report is being reduced from the current 10 calendar days to 5 calendar days. Note that prior to the current rules it had been 10 calendar days after the end of the month in which the trade occurred.
- The CSA introduced new requirements surrounding the disclosure of executive compensation, effective for 2009. Companies will have to prepare expanded disclosure in a compensation discussion and analysis (CDA) section. In addition, a total compensation number will have to be disclosed.
- The CSA have also started work on several other items. They are proposing a "notice

and access" model to shareholder communications. Under this model, companies will no longer be required to deliver certain materials but could post them on a website. The proposals should increase efficiency and equity in shareholder communications (Voore and Grewal, 2010). The CSA is also working on a plain language project (the "point of sale project") to simplify disclosures for mutual funds. Finally, the CSA is exploring developments on "say on pay" with the idea of determining whether shareholders would get to vote on executive pay packages (Council, 2010).

Like the industry it regulates, over the past decade the CSA has increasingly incorporated ICT in its regulatory changes. These e-governance practices are highlighted next.

E-Governance Practices in the Canadian Capital Markets

The recent advances in ICTs have transformed the relationship between market regulators and their stakeholders and allowed more efficient and more effective governance. Disclosure is required by regulators because it serves to inform investors and thereby increase confidence and improve transparency in the markets. The information required by regulators is increasingly made available electronically. Disclosure via an electronic medium, however, is in continuous evolution, making for more efficient, more interactive and more transparent e-governance.

E-governance practices that have been adopted in the Canada capital market are administered by the Canadian Securities Administrators (CSA). E-governance processes were introduced to improve the efficiency of the process, reduce costs and speed up dissemination of the information. E-governance in the Canada capital markets is accomplished through several distinct web applications.

1. **SEDAR.** The System for Electronic Document Analysis and Retrieval (SEDAR) is the system used for filing electronically almost all the information required by securities regulators. Since its development in 1997, SEDAR has enabled the cost-efficient electronic filing of prospectuses and continuous disclosure documents. The result is the creation of a database of information on Canada's public companies which can be searched by the public. In addition, SEDAR is also a forum for electronic communication between companies and regulators (CSA, 2010[b]). The SEDAR website can be accessed at www.sedar.com.

2. **SEDI.** The System for Electronic Disclosure by Insiders (SEDI) is a web-based service for insiders to file their insider reports and for the public to access and view these reports. SEDI replaced a paper-based reporting system which resulted in a more efficient process and more timely disclosure (CSA, 2010[b]). The SEDI website can be accessed at www.sedi.ca.

3. **NRD.** The National Registration Database (NRD) is a web-based service that enables dealers and advisers to register electronically. The NRD harmonizes and improves the registration process for capital market participants. Investors are able to search the NRD system (from a separate interface on the CSA website) to determine if a dealer or advisor is registered (CSA, 2010[c]). The NRD website is www.nrd.ca and it can be search by the public from the CSA website at www.securities-administrators.ca/nrs/nrsearch.aspx?id=850.

4. **Other.** As part of the enforcement mandate of securities regulators, the CSA maintains a searchable database on persons disciplined for violation of securities laws or inappropriate conduct in the markets. This database is searchable by the public and can be found on the CSA website at http://www.securi-ties-administrators.ca/disciplinedpersons.aspx?id=74.

PREVIOUS RESEARCH

Findings from research applicable to governance issues in the Canadian capital markets are briefly reviewed. The purpose of this review is to ascertain the issues and principles applicable to e-governance in the capital markets. First, the findings of corporate governance studies, with an emphasis on studies conducted in Canada, will be discussed. Second, findings from internet financial reporting (IFR) studies will be reviewed.

Corporate Governance

An extensive corporate governance literature exists in accounting and finance. Much of this research has been focused on examining the relationship between different measures of corporate governance and various measures of performance or firm characteristics (see Bhaget and Bolton, 2008; Black et al., 2006; Brown and Caylor, 2009; Gompers et al., 2003; Klapper and Love, 2004; Daines et al., 2008; Jog and Dutta, 2004; Klein et al., 2005). The results of studies on the relationship of corporate governance with performance have been mixed. In Canada, Jog and Dutta (2004) did not find any evidence of a relationship while Klein et al. (2005) and Adjaoud et al. (2007) find only weak evidence of a relationship. More recently, MacAulay et al. (2009) documented a significant positive relationship between corporate governance and performance in the period prior to the new governance regulations of 2005. Finally, research assessing the relative importance of the country characteristics on corporate governance has been conducted. Doidge et al. (2007) found that country characteristics explained the majority of the variance in firm corporate governance and further, that firm characteristics were useful in explaining the variance in corporate governance only in developed countries.

Another stream of research has examined whether companies with better governance make better disclosures. In Canada, Beekes, Brown and Chin (2006) found that firms with higher corporate governance scores released more documents to investors, attracted a larger analyst following and, as reflected in their share price, integrated value-relevant information more rapidly. In a related study, Foerster and Huen (2004) found that Canadian firms in highest quintile for corporate governance earned positive abnormal returns. They interpreted their results as evidence that in the longer-term corporate governance matters for investors. These findings are consistent with earlier surveys that found that corporate governance is important to investors, that is, investors have greater confidence in companies with higher corporate governance (see for example the McKinsey Global Investor Opinion Survey on Corporate Governance, 2002).

Corporate governance research has focused mainly on the analysis of the information that firms ought to disclose and the effects of disclosure generally, without considering the media involved (Bushman et al, 2004). A related literature on internet financial reporting (IFR) may provide some insights on the use of the internet as a medium of disclosure.

Internet Financial Reporting

With the development of ICTs, companies can report their traditional annual reports together with additional financial and non-financial information in multiple formats on the internet (Xiao et al., 2005). Empirical studies have shown the importance of the internet as a communications channel between firms and their investors. Evidence of web based practices in various countries can be found in a number of studies (see for example Trites, 1999; Debreceny et al., 2002; Almilia, 2009). In summary, these studies find the internet

is increasingly being used for the dissemination of corporate information such as annual reports (Mohamed et al, 2009). A smaller set of studies explores the usefulness of IFR. These studies tend to focus on how IFR can improve the timeliness or transparency of information. In Canada, Debreceny et al (2008) found that key non-financial information is associated with future earnings and contemporaneous stock returns and interpreted this as an indication that web-based disclosures are useful to investors. Debreceny et al. (2008) also classified web disclosures as either incremental disclosures or disaggregated disclosures. Interestingly, they found that the vast majority of voluntary web disclosures in Canada were incremental disclosures.

A number of benefits of web based applications and services are identified in the IFR literature on corporations. Those benefits should also be applicable to the e-governance practices used by capital market regulators who legislate and regulate the distribution of capital market information in Canada. The benefits include cost savings, the scope of distribution of information and the extent of the provision of information.

The main benefits of web based applications and services, and electronic disclosure more generally, are the cost savings associated with producing and distributing information. The internet allows companies and regulators to disclose more information, that is more timely, to a broader range of stakeholders at a lower cost (Sarra, 2007). Another benefit of electronic disclosure is that the information is more accessible. The electronic distribution of information makes it more accessible because information is more easily reached by stakeholders and further, it can be searched more easily by electronic search engines. Improved accessibility, in turn, means greater equity in the dissemination of the information (Mohamed et al., 2009). New technologies also enable the presentation of more information or the same information in different or complementary formats. Traditional information can be supplemented with richer multimedia disclosures to improve stakeholders' understanding of the information (Trites, 1999; Mohamed et al., 2009). These developments could potentially benefit users and market regulators. For example, more timely disclosures should improve market efficiency. Further, timely disclosure accompanied by more extensive disclosure and greater accessibility should also serve to reduce information asymmetry (Sarra, 2007).

There are also potential issues and challenges related to web-based reporting. Mohamed et al. (2009) summarizes several of the issues identified in the literature that are associated with the use of IFR. These issues range from accessibility to the reliability of the information being reported. First, access to web based information and services may be restricted to only those who possess the appropriate equipment and skills. Consequently inequities in financial information dissemination may arise. Second, there is the challenge of ensuring the security and integrity of published financial information. The reliability of the information may be affected by errors in entering or extracting the information; further, after information is published, it could intentionally or unintentionally be altered. Third, if websites are used for multiple purposes then it may become more difficult to locate relevant information. Sarra (2007) raises several additional issues. She notes that there is a concern for the integrity of information when hyperlinks are used, especially if they link to information on different websites. Thus there is a need for transparency to allow users to determine who is responsible for the information and to allow them to assess the quality of the information. In addition, increasing the quantity of information disclosed may reduce true access by making it difficult to assess the importance of the information. Finally, electronic filing may lead to additional information being added incrementally to the existing system without considering its implications for the quality of disclosure. The principle of plain disclosure would suggest that it should be integrated with existing information disclosures. In summary, the extent to which these issues are addressed affects the usefulness of the internet as a medium of financial information dissemination in the Canadian capital markets.

THE PARALLEL NATURE OF E-GOVERNANCE IN THE PUBLIC SECTOR AND THE CANADIAN CAPITAL MARKETS

Many of the e-governance issues in the Canadian capital markets parallel e-governance issues in the public sector. The parallels between government and capital markets exist along their conceptualization of the dimensions of e-governance, the expectations of stakeholders, the impact of new technologies and the incremental nature of the evolution of e-governance. The concept of e-governance in the public sector will be discussed briefly before addressing the parallels that are present.

Describing E-Governance in the Public Sector

E-governance is understood, in part, as the performance of governance through an electronic medium in order to facilitate an efficient, speedy and transparent process of the dissemination information to the public, and other agencies, to enhance the performance of administrative activities both internally and externally and to engage citizens in new ways (UNESCO, 2007). The purpose of implementing e-governance is to enhance good governance, which is generally characterized by participation, transparency and accountability (UNESCO, 2007). The recent advances in communication technology provide opportunities to transform the relationship between government and it stakeholders by involving a broader scope of stakeholders and by allowing more efficient and more effective governance.

A discussion of e-governance requires consideration of its conceptualization. Although many authors have used e-governance interchangeably with e-government, e-governance in the public sector is most often considered to be a wider concept than e-government (UNESCO, 2007). E-government may be understood as the performance of government via the Web to facilitate an efficient, speedy and transparent dissemination of information to the public and for conducting administrative activities (UNESCO 2007). Essentially e-government is the provision of both government information and routine transactions using electronic means, most notably those using the Web or other similar technologies (e.g. public kiosks). In contrast, e-governance is a broader conceptualization since it addresses not only the way in which most public services are executed, but it also addresses the potential to change the fundamental relationship between government and citizens by better engaging citizens.

Parallels between the Public Sector and the Canadian Capital Markets

Arguably, e-governance in the public sector is conceptualized differently than it is in the capital markets in large part because the nature of the relationship between governments and their citizens differs from the relationship between corporations and their stakeholders. Although those differences exist, there are parallels between the two in their respective conceptualizations of e-governance. The parallels between the public sector and the capital markets relate to the dimensions of e-governance, the expectations of citizens and/ or stakeholders, the impact of the introduction of new technologies (i.e. Web based practices) and the incremental nature of the evolution of e-governance.

Dimensions of E-Governance

Involved discussions of e-governance in the public sector inevitably require a discussion of the decomposition of e-governance into several categories or functions. Various authors have decomposed the conceptualization of e-governance into several different functions but not all decompositions use the same labels or are carved into similar functions. Regardless of labels and functions, the e-governance conceptualization generally collapses into four separate dimensions: 1) the enhanced delivery of, availability of and access to information by allowing citizens access to broader and deeper levels of that information, 2) the delivery of services by allowing citizens to conduct routine transactions (e.g. renew driver's license) using the Web, 3) the improved functioning of internal infrastructure and interfaces for conducting government business, and finally, 4) a changed relationship involving increased engagement between governments and their citizens.

E-governance in the capital markets exhibits similarities to the four identified dimensions of e-governance in the public sector. Firstly, the electronic dissemination of information by corporations and regulatory bodies has improved the availability, the quantity and the accessibility of information. Corporations now make available annual reports, quarterly reports, audio of financial analyst calls, etc. on their corporate websites. The information available on SEDAR, SEDI and NRD is also easily accessible by investors. The result is much greater transparency as information can be more easily located and more easily accessed. Secondly, the delivery of regulatory services has increased as the capability of conducting routine services between corporations and the regulators through the use of Web applications has improved. For example, the SEDAR website is used for communications/business between regulators and issuers. Further, the CSA requires reporting of regulated information to be done electronically, insider reports to be submitted electronically and dealer registration to be done on-line. The electronic disclosure requirements have been accompanied by harmonized disclosure requirements among provinces which represent significant changes to the processes of regulation. Thirdly, the use of Web-based technologies to deliver information has increased internal efficiencies for companies and further has allowed for significant cost savings. Finally, e-governance has the potential to enable greater engagement or interaction between corporations and their stakeholders (e.g. investors, regulators, stock exchanges, tax agencies, etc.). The "say on pay" issue is an example of the possibility of investors, if they receive the right to vote on executive pay packages, having the ability to have more direct engagement and input into a company's operations.

Expectations of Citizens and Stakeholders

The expectations of citizens concerning the availability of information and the provision of services via the Web have increased significantly. Technological advances and Web based processes in the private sector have helped to shape those citizens' expectations. Citizens are able to pay for services or products of a retailer using technology made available by financial institutions. Citizens are also able to access information through electronic search features and are able to interact using social media technologies. In this Web based age, citizens' expectations of governments' use of the Web for providing both information and services is growing.

The relationship that government has with its citizens parallels the relationship corporations and capital market regulators have with their stakeholders. Like the government's citizens, capital market stakeholders (e.g. investors, creditors, etc.) and other agencies (e.g. stock exchanges, securities commissions, etc.) require information about public companies to allow for the assessment of stewardship and to allow for resource allocation.

The information for making those decisions is increasingly made available electronically. Stakeholders, regulators and corporations themselves all operate in an industry that makes extensive use of technology and their expectations of the enhanced delivery of information and services on-line are evolving and need to be addressed.

Impact of New Technologies

Technology has made e-governance possible. The implementation of e-governance in the public sector has proliferated since the advent of the Web in the 1990s and is now used as an effective interface between the government and its citizens. Technology has allowed and has required governments to reconfigure their processes and structures for the purpose of enhancing good governance (UNESCO, 2007).

Like government, the advent of the Web allowed for the introduction of e-governance through an electronic platform in the Canadian capital markets. "The Web has emerged as the primary vehicle for communicating information to investors and other stakeholders" (Trites, 2008, p. 16). E-governance in the Canadian capital markets has allowed for (i) the provision of information by issuers through SEDAR, (ii) the ability to electronically register dealers through NRD, (iii) the ability of insiders to file insider reports through SEDI, (iv) the ability of security regulators to retrieve, review and accept required disclosures electronically, and (v) the ability of investors to access information electronically.

Incremental Nature of the Evolution of E-Governance

The Web like many other technologies was originally envisaged to be a major transformational force to engage citizens with their governments. The evolution of e-governance however has been incremental rather than transformational. That evolution can be characterized as incremental movements along a continuum anchored at one end with no electronic provision of information or services to full engagement with citizens on a technology based platform. The evolution of e-governance began with the provision of information for citizen use (e.g. information on income tax rules), to the provision of on-line services and transactions (e.g. renewal of permits) and finally to the provision of interactive capabilities for citizens (e.g. on-line plebiscites). E-governance was introduced initially to citizens by the public sector through the electronic provision of information. In fact, during that introduction the leading reason in the United States and Canada for government website visits was to obtain information regarding income tax (Boritz and No, 2004). Citizens seemed initially generally satisfied with that electronic provision of information. Eventually, transactional capabilities for routine services were implemented and provided to citizens. The evolution of e-governance to an interactive engagement with citizens (an activity that distinguishes e-governance from e-government) is the next frontier for governments and will be introduced both as technologies and infrastructures allow and as citizens demand.

The capital markets increasingly are requiring more effective governance of public companies (e.g. SOX, NP-201) and much of that governance is disclosed through an electronic medium. The implementation of e-governance in the Canadian capital markets has followed a similar incremental path as the implementation of e-governance in the public sector. The implementation of e-governance began with the provision of information (e.g. on-line access by stakeholders to an Annual Information Form) followed by the introduction of services (e.g. on-line registration of investment intermediaries) and the improvement in internal infrastructure (e.g. on-line review and acceptance of corporate filings by securities regulators). Like government, the next frontier in e-governance is toward more stakeholder engagement which may be possible through more sophisticated and evolved technological applications.

FUTURE DIRECTIONS

This chapter attempts to illustrate the nature and impact of e-governance in the Canadian capital markets. Much work remains to be done to understand when, where and how e-governance works best. Future research could involve comparative studies of electronic governance among different regulatory regimes, for example, principles-based versus rules-based regimes. This research could be further extended to understand the impact of country characteristics on e-governance in the capital markets. In addition, research could examine whether the characteristics of the disclosures impact governance. For example why are most voluntary web-based disclosures in Canada incremental disclosures as opposed to disaggregated disclosures? Finally, the history of e-governance in different countries or regions could be examined to understand the factors that cause incremental versus transformational changes in e-governance.

Several research ideas are provided but these are only several of many possibilities and further these are likely to change. The electronic medium is in continuous evolution which is allowing for more efficient, more interactive and more transparent e-governance. The evolutionary nature of e-governance in the Canadian capital markets has allowed for the provision of information through multiple platforms. The next evolution in e-governance may involve developing governance mechanisms to handle trends such as more interactive applications and the movement to more real-time reporting. Clearly more work is required to better understand the nature and impacts of e-governance in the Canadian capital markets.

REFERENCES

Adjaoud, F., Zeghal, D., & Andaleeb, S. (2007). The effect of board's quality on performance: A study of Canadian firms. *Corporate Governance: An International Review, 15*(4), 623–635. doi:10.1111/j.1467-8683.2007.00592.x

Almilia, L. S. (2009). Determining factors of Internet financial reporting in Indonesia. *Accounting and Taxation, 1*(1), 87–99.

Anand, A. I., & Klein, P. C. (2005). Inefficiency and path dependency in Canada's securities regulatory system: Towards a reform agenda. *Canadian Business Law Journal, 42*(1), 41–72.

Beekes, W., Brown, P., & Chin, G. (2006). *Do better governed firms make more informative disclosures? Canadian evidence.* Working Paper, Lancaster University Management School.

Bhagat, S., & Bolton, B. (2008). Corporate governance and firm performance. *Journal of Corporate Finance, 14*, 257–273. doi:10.1016/j.jcorpfin.2008.03.006

Black, B. S., Jang, H., & Kim, W. (2006). Does corporate governance predict firms' market values? Evidence from Korea. *Journal of Law Economics and Organization, 22*(2), 366–413. doi:10.1093/jleo/ewj018

Boritz, J. E., & No, W. G. (2004). Assurance reporting for XML-based Information Services: XARL (Extensible Assurance Reporting Language). *Canadian Accounting Perspectives, 3*(2), 207–233. doi:10.1506/V8D9-QTUN-HDU1-93RB

Brown, L. D., & Caylor, M. L. (2009). Corporate governance and firm operating performance. *Review of Quantitative Finance and Accounting, 32*, 129–144. doi:10.1007/s11156-007-0082-3

Bushman, R. M., Piotroski, J. D., & Smith, A. J. (2004). What determines corporate transparency? *Journal of Accounting Research, 42*(2), 207–252. doi:10.1111/j.1475-679X.2004.00136.x

Canadian Securities Administrators. (2010a). *About CSA.* Retrieved on August 2, 2010, from http://www.securities-administrators.ca/ aboutcsa.aspx? id=77& linkidentifier=id& itemid=77

Canadian Securities Administrators. (2010b). *Industry resources.* Retrieved on August 2, 2010, fromhttp://www.securities-administrators.ca/ industry_resources.aspx? id=48&linkidentifier=id& itemid=48

Canadian Securities Administrators. (2010c). *Registration.* Retrieved on August 2, 2010, from http://www.securities-administrators.ca/ registration. aspx?id=857& linkidentifier=id& itemid=857

Carnaghan, C., & Gunz, S. P. (2007). Recent changes in the regulation of financial markets and reporting in Canada. *Accounting Perspectives, 6*(1), 55–94. doi:10.1506/W733-67L7-0774-6336

Cohen, E. E. (2004). Compromise or customize: XBRL's paradoxical power. *Canadian Accounting Perspectives, 3*(2), 187–206. doi:10.1506/YAHN-CAE8-5CWQ-H4TE

Daines, R., Gow, I., & Larcker, R. (2008). *Rating the ratings: How good are commercial governance ratings?* Working Paper, Stanford University.

Debreceny, R., Gray, G. L., & Raham, A. (2002). The determinants of Internet financial reporting. *Journal of Accounting and Public Policy, 21*, 371–394. doi:10.1016/S0278-4254(02)00067-4

Debreceny, R., Lymer, A., & Trabelsi, S. (2008). An empirical examination of corporate websites as a voluntary disclosure medium. *Administrative Science Association of Canada Conference Proceedings, 29*(26), 1-22.

Doidge, C., Karolyi, G. A., & Stulz, R. M. (2007). Why do countries matter so much for corporate governance? *Journal of Financial Economics, 86*, 1–39. doi:10.1016/j.jfineco.2006.09.002

Durisin, B., & Puzone, F. (2009). Maturation of corporate governance research, 1993-2007: An assessment. *Corporate Governance: An International Review, 17*(3), 266–291. doi:10.1111/j.1467-8683.2009.00739.x

Foerster, S. R., & Huen, B. C. (2004). Does corporate governance matter to Canadian investors? *Canadian Investment Review*, (Fall): 19–25.

Gompers, P., Ishii, J., & Metrick, A. (2003). Corporate governance and equity prices. *The Quarterly Journal of Economics, 118*(1), 107–155. doi:10.1162/00335530360535162

Gray, T., & Kitching, A. (2005). *Reforming Canadian securities regulation*. Library of Parliament (PRB 05-28E). Retrieved on August 2, 2010, from http://www2.parl.gc.ca/ content/ lop/ researchpublications/ prb0528-e.htm

Investment Industry Regulatory Organization of Canada. (2010). *About IIROC*. Retrieved August 2, 2010, from http://www.iiroc.ca/ English/ About/ Pages/ default.aspx

Jog, V., & Dutta, S. (2004). Searching for the governance grail. *Canadian Investment Review*, (Spring): 33–43.

Klapper, L. F., & Love, I. (2004). Coporate governance, investor protection, and performance in emerging markets. *Journal of Corporate Finance, 10*, 703–728. doi:10.1016/S0929-1199(03)00046-4

Klein, P., Shapiro, D., & Young, J. (2005). Corporate governance, family ownership and firm value: The Canadian evidence. *Corporate Governance: An International Review, 13*(6), 769–784. doi:10.1111/j.1467-8683.2005.00469.x

MacAulay, K., Dutta, S., Oxner, M., & Hynes, T. (2009). The impact of a change in corporate governance regulations on firms in Canada. *Quarterly Journal of Finance & Accounting, 48*(4), 29–52.

McKinsey. (2002). *Global investor opinion survey on corporate governance*. Retrieved on August 2, 2010, from http://www.mckinsey.com/ clientservice/ organizationleadership/ service/ corpgovernance/ PDF/ GlobalInvestorOpinion Survey2002.pdf

Mohamed, E. K. A., Oyelere, P., & Al-Busaidi, M. (2009). A survey of Internet financial reporting in Oman. *International Journal of Emerging Markets, 4*(1), 56–71. doi:10.1108/17468800910931670

Mutual Funds Dealers Association of Canada. (2010). *About the MFDA*. Retrieved August 10, 2010, from http://www.mfda.ca/ about/ about MFDA.html

Nicholls, C. (2006). Research studies: The characteristics of Canada's capital markets and the illustrative case of Canada's legislative regulatory response to Sarbanes-Oxley. *Canada Steps Up, 4*, 127–204.

Perez, C. C., Bolivar, M. P. R., & Hernandez, A. M. L. (2008). E-government process and incentives for online public financial information. *Online Information Review, 32*(3), 379–400. doi:10.1108/14684520810889682

Provincial/Territorial Council of Ministers of Securities Regulation (Council). (2010). *Progress report, January 2009 to December 2009*. Retrieved on August 2, 2010, from http://www.securitiescanada.org/ 2010-0301-progress- report- english.pdf

Sarra, J. (2007). Disclosure as a public policy instrument in global capital markets. *Texas International Law Journal, 42*(3), 875–898.

Trites, G. (1999). Democratizing disclosure. *CA Magazine, 132*(8), 47–48.

Trites, G. (2004). Decline of the age of Pacioli: The impact of e-business on accounting and accounting education. *Canadian Accounting Perspectives, 3*(2), 171–177. doi:10.1506/G82C-H0W9-L4TM-YJ94

Trites, G. (2008). Corporate reporting on the Web. *CA Magazine*, 7(141), 16–17.

UNESCO. (2007). *United Nations Educational Scientific and Cultural Organization*. Retrieved on August 2, 2010, from http://portal.unesco.org/ ci/ en/ ev.php-URL_ID=4404& URL_DO=DO_TOPIC& URL_SECTION =201.html

Xiao, J. Z., Jones, M. J., & Lymer, A. (2005). A conceptual framework for investigating the impact of the Internet on corporate financial reporting. *International Journal of Digital Accounting Research*, 5(10), 131–170.

KEY TERMS AND DEFINITIONS

Capital Markets: The financial markets where equity and debt instruments are traded.

Corporate Governance: The systems, regulations and processes in place to ensure that management in a company makes decisions that reflect the rights and interests of the stakeholders in the company.

E-Governance: It is governance through the provision of information via electronic means.

Enhanced Reporting: A trend in corporate financial reporting to supplement traditional disclosure with additional disclosures or with alternative forms of disclosure.

Internet Financial Reporting: the use of the internet by companies to disclose financial and non-financial information to investors and other stakeholders.

Rapid Reporting: The trend by regulators to require more immediate disclosure of information to stakeholders.

Transparency: A quality of the disclosure environment of a company that is characterized by a high level of openness through enhanced disclosure, resulting in increased accountability.

ENDNOTES

[1] According to Nicholls (2006), it was approximately 110% of GDP in 2005.

[2] In Canada, equities can also be traded on several alternative trading systems (ATS).

[3] Anand and Klein (2005) note that Canada may be the only country represented in the 100+ countries of the International Organization of Securities Commissions that does not have a national securities regulator.

[4] Several areas of the financial markets are beyond the scope of this chapter. For example, other financial products such as insurance and pensions are subject to federal regulations. In addition, the various investor protection funds that exist are not examined.

[5] Adapted from MacAulay et al. (2009).

Chapter 9
Decimalization of Stock Exchanges

Bin Chang
University of Ontario Institute of Technology, Canada

ABSTRACT

Technological innovation is propelling the move in financial markets away from fractional trading and towards decimal trading, as in the example of The New York Stock Exchange (NYSE) tick size changed from $1/16 to $0.01 on January 29, 2001. This chapter examines the impact of that trend as it relates to market quality and trading behaviour, and draws on comparisons between NYSE and NASDAQ, as well as evidence from other markets and market-traded securities, in demonstrating how decimalization leads to a decrease in the bid-ask spread and depth and an improvement in the probability of information-based trading, while having seemingly no effect on the frequency of limit orders. Our examination also demonstrates how the 1996 decimalization of the Toronto Stock Exchange (TSX, formerly TSE) has had little impact on its giant competitor, NYSE.

INTRODUCTION

Technological innovations have long shaped the business world, and financial markets have certainly been no exception to that shaping. Over the last two decades, new financial reporting requirements and standards, new security regulations, and new trading rules and patterns have been accompanied by, and often arisen as a result of, new advances in technology. Even such traditional practices as equities trading and personal banking have been more or less replaced by online practices, and such advances show no signs of slowing as financial markets rely ever increasingly on electronic media and systems in carrying out relevant operations.

In this era of e-finance and e-governance, one of the most significant developments has been the

DOI: 10.4018/978-1-60960-848-4.ch009

introduction of 'decimal pricing' in stock markets. Up until the late 1990s, stock exchanges used 'fractional pricing' rules for trading stocks, trading in multiples of $1/8, for instance. With the development of reliable and efficient electronic based trading systems, however, stock market regulators began to demand a more specific pricing method.

Beginning in the year 2000, fuelled by technological innovation, the New York Stock Exchange (NYSE) selected a limited number of stocks for a pilot project on decimal pricing. Bolstered by the results of the project, it decided to implement the changes market-wide on January 29, 2001. Shortly thereafter, after completing its own pilot project on the matter, NASDAQ moved to decimal pricing as well, and in a matter of a few months, the smallest tick size on both NASDAQ and NYSE went from $1/16 to $0.01.

Harris (1994, 1997, and 1999) makes several predictions regarding the impact on execution quality of reducing tick size, all of which have implications with regards to liquidity and volatility. For example, Harris predicts that reducing tick size would result in a decrease in the bid-ask spreads and depth, an increase in trading volume, a better-informed market of traders, a move from limit-order to market-order, an adoption of fast-execution computer systems, and a speedier quote adjustment.

This chapter is divided into two parts: the first part examines those predictions made by Harris about decimalization, and the second part examines the empirical evidence gathered *after* decimalization as it relates to those predictions.

In particular, we examine the impact of decimalization on various aspects of market quality, such as spreads, depths, return volatility, trading volume, quote clustering, and quote adjustment, and demonstrate Whether Harris's predictions are confirmed to be accurate by several subsequent studies, including Bacidore, Battalio, & Jennings, 2003, Bessembinder, 2003c, Chakravarty, Wood, & Van Ness, 2004, Chung, Charoenwong, & Ding, 2004, Chung, Chuwonganant, & McCormick,

2004, Chung, Van Ness, & Van Ness, 2004, Gibson, Singh, & Yerramilli, 2003, and Goldstein & Kavajecz, 2000.

Furthermore, we perform an analysis of trading behaviour as evidenced by the frequency and order sizes of limit-orders versus market-orders, referencing the findings of Bacidor, Battalio, & Jennings (2003) on the subject, and utilize the work of Chakravarty, Van Ness, & Van Nexx (2005), Gibson, Singh, & Yerramilli (2003), and Zhao & Chung (2006) in analyzing Anshuman & Kalay's (1998) suggestion that a large tick size imposes large transaction costs on traders and thus reduces the value of private information.

In comparing the impact decimalization has had on NYSE and NASDAQ, respectively, we begin with the fact that NASDAQ spreads are greater than NYSE spreads prior to decimalization, and then examine bid-ask spreads and other market quality measures in NASDAQ in order to determine whether the pattern holds true following decimalization.

We also examine the effects of the switch to decimalization on the Toronto Stock Exchange (TSX), which occurred in 1996, well before NYSE made the move. In doing so, we determine whether or not an increase in order flow results, and reference Ahn, Cao, & Choe (1998) who find that order flows do not migrate from U.S. exchanges to TSX, thereby suggesting that the savings in transaction costs on TSX are not sufficient to offset the benefits of trading on NYSE.

This chapter is of interests from three perspectives. It is a costly move to decimalize an entire stock exchange, and thus the action is invariably undertaken with the expectation that great benefits will derive from doing so. Of course, whether or not those benefits outweigh the negatives of the move is an important question that should be asked, and this chapter seeks to answer that question. Harris (1994, 1997, and 1999) postulates that the move from fractional pricing to decimal pricing would result in lower bid-ask spreads, higher trading volume, greater liquidity, and more informed trading. However, Harris also predicts that decimalization would hurt large and limit order traders. We are able, therefore, to use the criteria provided by Harris as metrics to evaluate the effectiveness of a quoting system.

Moreover, through a comparison of the market quality of NYSE and NASDAQ, respectively, we are able to shed light on the problem of what exactly the optimal market structure might be. Granted, the NYSE is an auction market, while NASDAQ is a dealer's market, a difference which inherently stirs debate on which structure results in lower transaction costs. Our literature review, however, compares trading costs in the two exchanges in the pre- and post- decimalization period, and therefore provides an updated perspective on the issue.

Finally, there is, as noted, a body of international research that exists on the subject of decimalization, and the fact that our study also examines the increasingly competitive global environment amongst stock markets, by analyzing trading volumes on stocks cross-listed on both TSX and NYSE, adds a new arm to that research. That is, whether or not TSX's move, which pre-dated NYSE's move by five years, managed to draw traders away from NYSE is an obvious query that we resolve within the context of our evaluation of the effectiveness of decimalization.

PREDICTIONS MADE BEFORE DECIMALIZATION

Harris (1994, 1997, and 1999) makes several predictions regarding the impact of reducing tick size to a penny. Specifically, Harris (1994) empirically investigates the impact of tick size and predicts the quantitative change in bid-ask spreads, quoted sizes, and trading volume if tick size is changed from $1/8 to $1/16; Harris (1997) provides a comprehensive literature review on the arguments and evidence for and against decimalization; and Harris (1999) surveys the effects that trading in

pennies will have on investors, dealers, brokers, exchanges, and data vendors.

Bid-Ask Spread, Quote Size and Trading Volume

Harris (1994) provides a simple example to illustrate the significance of tick size: a $1/8 tick size on a $2 stock results in a bid-ask spread of 1/16 of the price. Comparing that to a $1/4 tick size on a $40 stock, which results in a bid-ask spread of 1/160 of the price— one tenth of the former example—makes it clear that the significant spread difference between bids on the $2 stock and bids on the $40 stock could inarguably influence trading costs, trading decisions, and even stock prices.

In addition, Harris (1994) makes predictions on the qualitative impact of reducing the tick size on bid-ask spreads, displayed quote size, and trading volume. Postulating that bid-ask spreads would decrease as a result of reducing tick size to a penny, he provides the rationale that since, as evidenced in the example above, the quoted spread could not be less than the tick size, traders would be forced to quote the tick size even if they would like to quote otherwise; however, if the tick size were reduced to a penny, traders would be able to quote the price that they would like to offer, thereby reducing the bid-ask spread.

Also, in predicting that the reduced bid-ask spreads would lead to smaller displayed quote sizes, Harris reasons that if the tick size were larger than the price that dealers would like to quote otherwise, then the spread would equal the tick size, and supplying liquidity could therefore be quite profitable, especially to small orders. Reducing tick size, Harris argues, would thus reduce the incentive to quote a large size.

Finally, Harris (1994) predicts that an increase in trading volume would result from decreasing tick size. He posits that reducing the minimum bid price would make it less expensive to trade, and that if tick size were greater than the increment that dealers would like to quote otherwise, then dealers might simply choose to not trade at all.

After forecasting the qualitative impact of the reduction of tick size, Harris (1994) then proceeds to estimate the quantitative impact of that change. It is important to note that, without the effect of tick size, the price level should not be related to the relative bid-ask spread (defined as bid-ask spread divided by the price, or bid-ask spread multiplied by the inverse of price). However, the example above suggests that the tick size may cause relative spreads for lower-priced stocks to be higher than they otherwise would be, indicating a positive relationship between relative spread and the inverse of price. Similar arguments can be applied to displayed quote sizes or trading volume. Thus, Harris (1994) uses a regression model with the relative spread, displayed quote size, or trading volume as dependent variables to estimate the coefficient of inverse price. This research applies an OLS model, a switching regression model, and a discrete model. Its sample includes firms listed in NYSE and the American Stock Exchange (AMEX) in 1989.

The estimated regression models are then used to project the quantitative impact of reducing tick size from $1/8 to $1/16. Within the models, Harris makes a critical assumption that the average price coefficient is statistically significant only because it is a proxy for the inverse of the relative tick size. That is, he assumes that halving the tick size would then imply a halving of the estimated inverse price coefficient. That said, Harris' models predict that for stocks priced under $10, spreads would decrease by 38 percent, quote sizes would decrease by 16 percent, and daily volume would increase by 24 percent.

Trading Behaviour and Liquidity

Harris (1997) focuses on three aspects of trading behaviour and liquidity: ease of use, market image, and competitiveness. As a result of the many advances in technology which have arisen in recent years, we can, for our purposes, dismiss ease of use as no longer being a concern. Similarly, the issue of market image is relatively insignificant as well, since stock exchanges in the United States are still the most liquid in the world despite the fact that several overseas exchanges have also moved to decimal trading. What remains critical to our study, therefore, is the effect of decimalization on competition, both cross-border and within the same market.

Based on Harris' prediction that decimalization would lead to lower bid-ask spreads and higher trading volumes, it follows that the decimalization of markets like TSX would put competitive pressure on US exchanges. Interestingly, even when it comes to competition within the same market, Harris (1997) predicts that decimalization would not affect everyone equally, as it would benefit some traders but hurt others. He provides the following example to illustrate: given that exchanges use price, time, and public order precedence rules to arrange trades, and given that professional traders are able to see the current price quotes on a given stock, they therefore have a clear advantage in a decimalized market where they need only bid one penny higher than the front running public bid. That is, suppose the highest limit buy price from a public trader is $30.00 when a market order to sell arrives. The professional trader, because he can see the order, can quite easily fill it himself by front-running the public trader with a bid of $30.01. What's even more inequitable about this system, from the standpoint of the public trader at least, is that if the price rises, then the professional trader profits to the extent of the price rise, and if it drops, his loss is limited to a mere $0.01, because he can still sell into public trader's existing $30.00 limit order. In other words, professional traders can, by virtue of the aforementioned strategy, have unlimited upside potential, but only $0.01 downside risk.

In order to defend against this professional strategy, public traders could seek to hide their trades through floor traders, break up their trades, and switch from limit-order strategy to market-order strategy (Harris, 1997, pp.4), but doing so would effectively result in smaller quote sizes, higher transaction costs, and less transparency. Harris therefore concludes that small market-order traders and professional traders would benefit from decimalization, but large traders and limit-order public traders would be hurt.

With regards to the ambiguous effect on liquidity of reducing tick size, Harris (1994) argues that if the tick size were greater than what the traders would be willing to offer, decimalization would reduce the profit of liquidity providers. Harris (1997) further argues that decimalization on one side would increase trading volume, but on the other side would reduce quote sizes.

Summary of Predictions

Harris (1999) summarizes previous research, arguments, and evidence, and makes twelve predictions on the effects of decimalization:

1. Spreads would narrow;
2. Quotation sizes would decrease significantly;
3. Large market orders would be broken up into smaller trades;
4. Smaller retail traders would move from limit orders to market orders;
5. Exchange specialists would trade more often and their trading would be more profitable, as they would be less bound by the public order precedence rule;
6. Prices for market orders would improve;
7. Electronic proprietary traders, because they are fast traders, would become more profitable;
8. A mix of electronic market and an upstairs floor would appear;
9. NASDAQ dealers would make less money trading active stocks because of narrower spreads;
10. Payments for order flow would decrease;
11. Some dealers would go out of business if they could not afford offer fast execution;
12. Large traders would adopt advanced electronic trading systems.

Clearly, advances in technology play a very large role in determining the response to decimalization. Without the development of fast-speed execution, for example, traders would be unable to break up big orders into smaller ones at the appropriate price level (prediction 3). Also without the innovation, it is impossible for professional traders to front-run a bid with a one cent increment and small traders wouldn't be as inclined to resort to market orders, as described in prediction 4. Similarly, predictions 7, 8, 11, and 12 are all directly dependant on the adoption of fast-speed computers and networks.

EMPIRICAL EVIDENCE ON MARKET QUALITY

Bid-Ask Spreads

Harris' (1994, 1997, and 1999) predictions are tested by later studies. For instance, in a sample that includes 300 common stocks from both NYSE and NASDAQ which are matched on the basis of market capitalization, Bessembinder (2003c) sought to assess the possible longer-term effects of decimalization, and indeed reports significant decreases in quoted spreads and depths on both exchanges after decimal pricing. Bessembinder's study compares the summary statistics on spreads as well as other market quality measures in the three weeks before NYSE switched to decimalization to 21 weeks after NASDAQ switched to decimalization, and reports that volume-weighted quoted spreads decreased from 10.98 cents to 5.54 cents for firms in all size groups, and that the relative quoted spread (i.e. the quoted spread divided by price) dropped greatly.

Charkravarty, Wood, & Van Ness (2004) find similar results using a sample that includes only NYSE firms, and which consists of six subsamples based on two cross-sectional divisions and three sub-periods. The two cross-sectional divisions are made up of the decimal-pilot securities as a control sample and the matched non-decimal securities, and the investigation period is comprised of a pre-decimal period, a decimal trial period, and an all-decimal period. The study reports a definitive reduction in spreads— 35 percent for decimal-pilot stocks in the trial period and 39 percent for control stocks in the all-decimal period. Of note, NYSE (2001a, b) declares similar results.

Although the studies cited above each confirms the decline of bid-ask spreads, it is still important to distinguish between institutional traders and retail traders when it comes to spread changes. Institutional traders, for instance, are typically larger than retail traders, and are more likely to use limit orders when trading. Reducing the tick size to one cent also generates an opportunity for fast-moving institutional traders to front run the retail trader by simply increasing their bids by a penny, and institutional traders may also be more inclined to break up their trades into smaller ones to avoid exposing their trading strategy. On that last point, Chakravarty, Panchapagesan, & Wood (2005) examine institutional execution costs in NYSE. Using proprietary data on orders and trades, they examine the trading costs of 34 large buy-side institutions trading NYSE stocks over a period of 41 days before and 44 days after decimalization, and find that even though overall trading costs may have declined in the period, trading costs in fact increased for orders that were executed within a single day.

By measuring the mutual fund trading costs in a four-month period before and after decimalization, Bollen & Busse (2006) examine the same issue using different data and technology. While defining trading cost as the difference between a mutual fund's daily return and a synthetic portfolio with the same holdings at zero costs, they find that trading costs of actively-managed mutual funds increase significantly post-decimalization. It is important to note, however, that there is a limitation to their research methodology, as they do not analyze the components of trading cost or the change in each component.

Quoted Size and Market Depth

If the market for a stock is "deep", there will be sufficient volume of pending orders on both the bid side and ask side, thereby preventing a large order from significantly moving the price. This factor comes into play with regards to Harris' prediction about the reduction of quote size— a prediction which is proved accurate by later empirical tests. Bessembinder (2003c), for one, reports that the full sample mean quote size for NYSE stocks decreased following decimalization by 65.2 percent, from 4,369 shares to 1,529 shares. Bessembinder reports the reductions in quote size as 74 percent for large capitalization stocks and 46 percent for small capitalization stocks. Results are similar in the report of Charkravarty, Wood, & Van Ness (2004).

However, though the literature cited above clearly illustrates the decline in both bid-ask spreads and market depth, it offers limited insight into the actual mechanisms by which decimalization affects such declines. Indeed, what the respective studies have not investigated empirically are the questions of what stocks were affected the most and why, and it is at this point that Chung, Charoenwong & Ding (2004) extend the research by summarizing four possible explanations for the noted declines, namely: binding constraint; front-running; price competition; and other stock attributes. The four explanations can be summed up as follows:

Firstly, with reference to binding constraint, we note that Harris (1994, 1997, and 1999) argues that if the tick size were larger than the price that dealers would like to quote otherwise (which is the definition of the term "binding"), then the spread would equal the tick size. The implication of this for Chung *et al.* is that if the tick size was binding, then spread and market depth would decline after decimalization. Secondly, a smaller tick size would result in a higher probability that front-running would occur, since for a single penny increase in their bids traders could reap the benefits of a conceivably unlimited upside. Thirdly, a smaller tick size would allow more intense competition, since it would entail a lower incremental cost. Moreover, even if the tick size were not binding, a smaller tick size would reduce the rounding-off of price quotes, and this would lead to better prices from both the bid and ask sides, as well as a reduction in bid-ask spreads. Lastly, decimalization could affect other attributes of stocks such as trading volume and volatility, thereby indirectly affecting spreads and depth.

Chung, Charoenwong & Ding (2004) analyze those arguments empirically by measuring binding constraint as being the proportion of spread quotes that are equal to the tick size of $1/16 before decimalization, front-running probability as being the portion of odd $1/16 trades before decimalization, and price competition as being the intensity of trading before decimalization. With regards to the final of their four possible explanations for the declines, they measure five stock attributes: change in price, the number of trades, trade size, return volatility, and market capitalization, to assess the extent to which, if at all, decimalization has an effect. Furthermore, in addition to the pre- versus post- comparisons that are used in most research, they use regressions to quantify the impact of the four sources.

Evidently, Chung, Charoenwong & Ding (2004) find evidence to support all four arguments. Stocks with higher proportions of one-tick spreads and odd-sixteenth quotes, and stocks that had more frequent trading before decimalization, do indeed experience a greater reduction in spreads and market depth. In addition, decimalization did in fact lead to an increased frequency of trades,

smaller trade sizes, and less volatility and those factors did affect spreads and depth.

Volatility, Frequency of Trade, and Trade Volume

There are two reasons why volatility may be affected by decimalization. One, it is related to liquidity, and we see Harris (1994, 1997, 1999), predicts that decimalization would lead to a decrease in liquidity supply. Bessembinder (2003c), too, argues that decreased liquidity supply could also be manifest in the form of more volatile prices. And the other reason is that volatility is related to risk. On that point, Charkravarty, Wood, & Van Ness (2004) argue that if the risk of trading in decimal stocks increases significantly following decimalization, we would expect to see higher volatility.

Bessembinder (2003c) investigates volatility after decimalization, and predicts more volatile prices would result from a decrease in the liquidity of supply. Contrary to that prediction, however, Bessembinder's empirical work, which calculates returns from quotation midpoints and then intraday return volatility, shows that the volatility actually declined following decimalization, and that the decline is statistically significant.

Bessembinder (2003c) goes on to test whether or not the reduction in volatility is permanent. He argues that if the reduction is permanent, the return will follow random work in the post-decimalization period, indicating a variance ratio of 1. If, on the other hand, the reduction is temporary, when the price is pushed above the long-term equilibrium it should reverse, resulting in a variance ratio that is less than 1. The results of Bessembinder's inquiry clearly show that statistically, the variance ratio is insignificantly different from 1, indicating that there is no systematic reversal of quote changes in the wake of decimalization.

Notably, Charkravarty, Wood, & Van Ness (2004), too, test volatility directly. They form a minute-by-minute return series for stocks in each category of trading volume, and find that volatility declined significantly in each category—a result that is consistent with Bessembinder (2003c).

Charkravarty, Wood, & Van Ness (2004), also examine trading frequency and volume. In their examination, they divide trades into five categories based on size, in order to see if the effects of decimalization differ from trade size to trade size. Their results reveal a decline in both the frequency of trades and in the trading volume of all trade sizes, decimal stocks and control stocks alike. In order to isolate the impact of decimalization, they report the net difference in trading volume and frequency in decimal stocks; that is, the difference between each decimal stock and its paired control stock for each trade size category. Their results show that the net difference in trading volume and frequency declines in each category, but the reduction is only significant for medium size trades. This result is further confirmed by Charkravarty, Van Ness, & Van Ness (2005).

Quote Custering and Quote Adjustment

Earlier studies, such as Ball, Torous, & Tschoegl, 1985; Barclay, 1997; Bessembinder, 1999; Christie &Schultz, 1994; Chung, Van Ness, & Van Ness, 2001, 2002; Godek 1996; Grossman et al., 1997; Harris, 1991; Huang & Stoll, 1996, illustrate the point that stocks with higher clustering exhibit higher spreads. Chung, Van Ness, & Van Ness (2004) is one of the first studies to investigate quote clustering after decimalization. Their work finds that, though intuitively, decimalization allows trading in all decimals equally frequently, after decimalization both NYSE and NASDAQ exhibit a high frequency of quote clustering (40 percent of quotes on nickels, 20 percent on dimes, and 12 percent on quarters). They further find that spreads are positively correlated with quote clustering using a structural regression model.

An important issue, too, is the speed at which quotes are adjusted in a decimalized market. Despite extensive documentation about the magnitude of bid-ask spreads, there is very little information available about the speed at which information is incorporated into a stock price. Hasbrouck (1991), for one, proposes that if the tick size is binding, and if it is greater than the spread that traders would like to quote otherwise, then traders may not seek to change the quote even after receiving updated information. If that holds true, then decimalization would accelerate a quote adjustment— an argument that in fact Chung, Chuwonganant, & Jiang (2008) provide support for by finding that the reduction in quote speed from the pre- to post-decimalization periods is indeed statistically significant.

Liquidity

A complete measurement of liquidity must encompass two dimensions: bid-ask spreads, which measure the incremental price that traders are looking to pay or receive for a stock, and market depth, which measures the quantity of stock offered at a particular price.

Yet in terms of research, bid-ask spreads are doubtless the dominant measure of liquidity. It is thus based only on that measure and evidence of reduced bid-ask spreads, that some of the researchers in our literature conclude that decimalization results in increased liquidity. Nevertheless, that conclusion does contribute to the research on liquidity. Fang, Noe, & Tice (2009), for instance, examine the relationship between stock liquidity and firm performance. As they note, a difficulty with research in the field is the endogeneity of the two variables, making it challenging to identify the causality between them. To account for this difficulty, they choose decimalization, an exogenous liquidity shock to solve this problem, and find that the increase in liquidity around decimalization improves firm performance. The reason given for this is that liquidity increases the informational content of market prices and of performance-sensitive managerial compensation.

Chordia, Roll, & Subrahmanyam (2008) study the relation between liquidity and market efficiency. Similar to Bessembinder (2003c), they also apply variance ratio tests, and find that prices were closer to random-walk benchmarks after decimalization, and further, that return variance ratios increased while return autocorrelations decreased. Their results suggest that private information is more incorporated into prices during more liquid regimes.

EMPIRICAL EVIDENCE ON TRADING BEHAVIOUR

Limit Order

Harris (1997) argues that decimalization would allow fast-moving professional traders to front run public limit-book orders by only $0.01, causing them to switch their trades to market order, or break up their trades into smaller ones. The following studies substantiate those predictions.

Bacidore, Battalio, & Jennings (2003) examine changes in trader behaviour, displayed quote size, and execution quality around decimalization. They use a decimal sample and a control sample to isolate the impact of decimalization from the possible impact of other contemporary market events. Regarding trade behaviour, they find: (1) the frequency of limit orders was unchanged relative to market order; (2) limit order size decreased; (3) limit orders were more likely to be cancelled.

On one hand, the evidence does suggest a decline in liquidity supply for the given liquidity demand after decimalization; however, with the finer tick size, traders can supply liquidity closer to the quoted spread's midpoint, and at more price points. Thus, the implication on liquidity supply is mixed.

Bacidore, Battalio, & Jennings (2003) next examine the change in displayed liquidity supply that results from decimalization. They document changes in the quoted size and, using a methodol-ogy similar to Goldstein & Kavajecz (2000), re-create the limit-order book to examine liquidity supply at prices away from the inside quote. Their study determines that lower quote size results from decimalization.

Finally, Bacidore, Battalio, & Jennings (2003) use effective spread to measure execution quality. As proved by Roll (1984), the effective spread represents the imputed cost of a round-trip trade relative to the spread midpoint. The Bacidore, Battalio, & Jennings (2003) study find that effective spreads decrease in both decimal stocks and control stocks after decimalization, with effective spreads of the former being less than those of the latter in smaller order-size categories. The finding leads them to conclude generally that "execution quality improves after decimalization for the smaller order sizes and does not deteriorate for the largest orders."

Informed Trading

A major consensus amongst our literature is that smaller tick size facilitates more informed trading. Ainshuman & Kalay (1998), for example, suggest that a large tick size imposes large transaction costs on traders and thus reduces the value of private information. Harris (1997) predicts that traders will hide their trades by breaking down large trades. Barclay & Warner (1993) argue that informed traders favour medium sized trades (labelled as "stealth trading") because large trades may give them away and small trades involve higher trade costs. Thus Chakravarty, Van Ness & Van Ness (2005) combine those arguments and project that if traders more frequently fragment trades after decimalization, adverse selection costs will increase on medium trades and decrease on large trades; and, on the contrary, if informed traders stay away from the market totally, adverse selection costs will decrease on even large trades. For their study, they gather a sample from January and February 2001 in NYSE and a matched sample in NASDAQ to examine the adverse selection

173

costs. Subsequently, they estimate the adverse selection component (percentage of the spread) through a regression model and then calculate dollar adverse selection costs (adverse selection percentage multiplied by the spread).

Chakravarty, Van Ness, & Van Ness (2005) go on to document an increase in the adverse selection component of spread. This increase, combined with an even greater reduction in bid-ask spread dollar amounts, is shown to lead to a reduction in dollar adverse selection costs after decimalization, with the strongest evidence coming from medium size trades, followed by small and large size trades. The researchers provide two possible explanations for this: stealth trading and institutional trading decreased, and institutional traders broke up their trades more frequently.

Gibson, Singh, & Yerramilli (2003) further investigate the impact on informed trading, and argue that the impact is unclear, ex-ante. On one hand, it may promote informed trading, since a larger bid-ask spread under fractional trading gives rise to higher trading costs and reduces the incentive to gather information. On the other hand, it may discourage informed trading, since decimalization can promote the practice of front-running, thereby hurting the profit of limit-order traders. It thus remains an empirical question as to whether or not decimalization results in more informed trading.

Using a sample of NYSE listed S&P 500 firms, Gibson, Singh, & Yerramilli (2003) hypothesize that a net increase in the incentives of traders to become privately informed post-decimalization will increase the dollar value of the adverse-selection costs. Following the methodology proposed by Huang and Stoll (1997), they deconstruct the traded spread into an inventory-plus-adverse-selection component and an order-processing component, and discover that the dollar amount of the inventory-plus-adverse-selection component remained unchanged, while that of the

order-processing component reduced substantially post-decimalization. As a result, the former became the major component after decimalization. Notably, the researchers interpret their results as no net change in informed trading, which is interesting when compared to Chakravarty, Van Ness, & Van Ness (2005) whose study indeed discerns an increase. One possible reason for the different findings is the sample selection: market wide stocks in one but only S&P 500 stocks in the other. That is, given that the S&P 500 consists of the biggest 500 firms in terms of market capitalization, and that those stocks are also the most frequently traded and most liquid in the entire market, it is easy to understand why they might differ from the broad market when it comes to the aforementioned studies.

Zhou & Chung (2006) continue the investigation on the impact of decimalization, showing support in their study for Chakravarty, Van Ness, & Van Ness (2005). Following Bessembinder (2003a) in making no allowance for trade reporting lags, and Lee and Ready (1991) in classifying trade directions, they proceed to estimate the probability of information-based trading (PIN) by employing the model used in earlier studies (Easley, Hvidkjaer, & O'Hara, 2002; Easley, Kiefer, O'Hara, 1996, 1997a, 1997 b; Easley, Kiefer, O'Hara, and Paperman, 1996; Easley & O'Hara, 1992; Glosten & Milgrom, 1985). Consistent with Chakravarty, Van Ness, & Van Ness (2005), they include all stocks in NYSE in their sample, although they do apply a different methodology. That is, instead of estimating the adverse selection cost component, they estimate the probability of informed trading, and their results display a significant increase in this probability after decimalization, suggesting that decimal pricing increased the value of private information and raised the informational efficiency of asset price. Their study also shows that their results are not driven by concurrent changes in stock attributes.

COMPARISON BETWEEN NYSE AND NASDAQ

NASDAQ started decimalization shortly after NYSE, using a pilot process of its own that involved decimalizing 14 securities on March 12, 2001 and 197 securities on March 25, 2001, before converting the remainder of its securities on April 9, 2001. It is insightful to examine the ways, similar and different, that decimalization has affected the two markets.

Our literature has already pointed out some of the differences between NYSE (well known to be an auction market) and NASDAQ (well known to be a dealer's market). Prior studies (e.g. Barclay, 1997; Bessembinder, 1999; Christie & Schultz, 1994; Chung, Van Ness, & Van Ness, 200; Huang & Stoll, 1996) have also shown that the spreads in the NASDAQ have historically been wider than the spreads on comparable stocks in NYSE, and illustrated how spreads have decreased when a stock has moved from NASDAQ to NYSE. In addition, previous research has shown that NAS-DAQ stocks exhibit less frequent $1/8 spreads than stocks on the NYSE, and that NASDAQ trading costs remained higher than NYSE trading costs even after NASDAQ undertook market reform in 1997.

With regards to the effects of decimalization, however, our literature explains that the effects on both NASDAQ and the NYSE were decidedly similar. Bessembinder (2003c), for example, shows that (1) quoted bid-ask spreads decline; (2) quote sizes decline; (3) intraday volatility declines; and (4) variance ratio becomes statistically insignificantly different from one. Chakravarty, Wood, & Van Ness (2004) also confirm that spreads and depth decrease in both exchanges, and Chung, Van Ness & Van Ness (2005), in examining quote clustering, find that stocks in both markets exhibit high degrees of quote clustering on nickels and dimes, and that quote clustering has a significant effect on spreads in both markets.

Nevertheless, the impact on each market is not quantitatively identical. Chung, Van Ness, & Van Ness (2005) compare trading costs and quote clustering in May 2001, the first month that both markets are fully decimalized. In order to differentiate between the impact decimalization may have had and the impact of other stock attributes, they match NYSE and NASDAQ stocks based on five criteria: price, the number of trades, trade size, return volatility and firm size.

Their study finds that the results differ by weighting scheme and firm size. That is, using equal weighting, the mean spread of NASDAQ stocks is greater than the mean spread of NYSE stocks, and the difference is greater for smaller stocks. On the contrary, using volume weighting, the mean NASDAQ spread is narrower than the mean NYSE spread, and the difference is statistically significant for large stocks. The results indicate that the respective markets are more suitable for certain firms than they are for others. For instance, the NASDAQ, because of the lower spread it offers small-size and lower volume stocks is better suited for those firms, while NYSE, because of the lower spread it offers large-size and higher volume stocks is better suited for those kinds of firms. This is a finding that is wholly consistent with the conventional street wisdom that says small firms should list on NASDAQ and then graduate to NYSE once they mature.

In terms of quote adjustment speed, another important point for comparison, Garfinkel & Nimalendran (2003) maintain that quote adjustment is faster in NYSE than in NASDAQ. Their reasoning is that NASDAQ dealers may not have strong incentives to make quick quote adjustments in response to information shock, since a significant portion of order flow is either internalized or preferred. Chung, Chuwonganant, & Jiang (2008) subsequently confirm the point using U.S. data: quote adjustment is faster in NYSE than it is in NASDAQ, following decimalization.

DECIMALIZATION OF TSX

TSX switched from a mix of fractional and decimal trading to full decimal trading on April 15, 1996, well ahead of the decimalization of NYSE and NASDAQ. Because it was so early in its conversion, its impact on multiple dimensions of market quality has been extensively studied (Ahn, Cao, & Choe, 1998; Bacidore, 1997; Chung, Kryzanowski, & Zhang, 1997; Huson, Kim, & Mehrotra, 1997; Weaver, 1997). The studies show that decimalization resulted in a $0.02 to $0.05 decrease in bid-ask spreads for stocks priced above $5, and had no prevailing effect on stocks priced below $5. The aforementioned studies also show that post-decimalization, quote size dropped between 26 and 52 percent for stocks priced above $5, and only slightly dropped for others, while trading volume and market share in general remained relatively the same.

United States regulators paid close attention to the decimalization of the Toronto market, for the simple reason of competition: The number of Canadian firms cross-listing shares on a U.S. exchange was substantial, suggesting that the early decimalization of TSX might have attracted order flow from U.S. markets. Ahn, Cao & Choe (1998) examine this issue and do not find any supporting evidence. Actually, their research indicates that the advantages US exchanges enjoy in terms of such things as image, liquidity and recognition far outpace any competitive strength TSX might have gathered as a result of decimalization.

SUMMARY AND CONCLUSION

Technological innovation has had a significant influence on stock markets around the world, facilitating, for instance, the transition from fractional pricing to decimal trading. NYSE converted to decimal trading on January 29, 2001, changing its smallest tick size from $1/16 to $0.01 in the process. Subsequent to that change, research-

ers, investors, and regulators alike have sought a greater understanding of the overall impact of decimalization on market quality and informational efficiency.

In this chapter, we have reviewed that impact and discovered, as widely predicted, that quoted bid-ask spreads declined substantially following decimalization, resulting in much lower transaction costs. We have also seen that quote size, which measures market depth, or the quantity that traders would like to trade at each price point, declined as well. Furthermore, volatility was shown to have declined, the number of trades and trading volume were shown to have increased, and quote adjustment was shown to have become much faster following decimalization. On the other hand, the impacts of decimalization were not always evident, as quote clusters, for instance, were shown to form around nickels and dimes whether decimalized or not, and there is mixed evidence on the impact of liquidity.

Furthermore, this chapter has summarized the evidence as it pertained to the effect of decimalization on trading behaviour. We showed, for instance, that the frequency of limit orders did not change relative to market orders, although limit order size did decrease, and in contrast, that limit orders were more likely to be cancelled in the post-decimalization period, and that the adverse selection component of bid-ask spreads increased.

This chapter also summarizes the similarities and differences of decimalization on NYSE and NASDAQ. They enjoy the common benefit of decreased bid-ask spreads. However, the impact is heterogeneous for stocks with different market capitalizations as the literature finds that the trading costs is smaller on NYSE for large-capitalization stocks, and smaller on NASDAQ for small-capitalizations stocks.

Finally, this chapter discusses the impact of the decimalization of TSX which occurred earlier than that on NYSE. Although it caused the reduction of bid-ask spreads, it had not attracted trading flows from NYSE to TSX as predicted, suggesting that the other advantages of trading on NYSE outpaced the benefit of decimalization of TSX.

REFERENCES

Ahn, H., Cao, C. Q., & Choe, H. (1998). Decimalization and competition among stock markets: Evidence from the Toronto Stock Exchange cross-listed securities. *Journal of Financial Markets*, *1*, 51–87. doi:10.1016/S1386-4181(97)00002-5

Anshuman, V., & Kalay, A. (1998). Market making with discrete prices. *Review of Financial Studies*, *11*, 81–109. doi:10.1093/rfs/11.1.81

Bacidore, J., Battalio, R., & Jennings, R. (2003). Order submission strategies, liquidity supply, and trading in pennies on the New York Stock Exchange. *Journal of Financial Markets*, *6*, 337–362. doi:10.1016/S1386-4181(03)00003-X

Bacidore, J., Battalio, R., Jennings, R., & Farkas, S. (2001). *Changes in order characteristics, displayed liquidity, and execution quality on the New York Stock Exchange around the switch to decimal pricing.* Working Paper, NYSE.

Bacidore, J. M. (1997). The impact of decimalization on market quality: An empirical investigation of the Toronto Stock Exchange. *Journal of Financial Intermediation*, *6*(2), 92–120. doi:10.1006/jfin.1997.0213

Ball, C., Torous, W., & Tschoegl, A. (1985). The degree of price resolution: The case of the gold market. *Journal of Futures Markets*, *5*, 29–43. doi:10.1002/fut.3990050105

Barclay, M. (1997). Bid-ask spreads and the avoidance of odd-eighth quotes on NASDAQ: An examination of exchange listings. *Journal of Financial Economics*, *45*, 35–60. doi:10.1016/S0304-405X(97)00010-X

Barclay, M., & Warner, J. (1993). Stealth and volatility: Which trades move prices? *Journal of Financial Economics*, *34*, 281–306. doi:10.1016/0304-405X(93)90029-B

Bessembinder, H. (1999). Trade execution costs on NASDAQ and NYSE: A post-reform comparison. *Journal of Financial and Quantitative Analysis*, *34*, 387–408. doi:10.2307/2676265

Bessembinder, H. (2003a). Issues in assessing trade execution costs. *Journal of Financial Markets*, *6*, 233–257. doi:10.1016/S1386-4181(02)00064-2

Bessembinder, H. (2003b). Quote-based competition and trade execution costs in NYSE-listed stocks. *Journal of Financial Economics*, *70*, 385–422. doi:10.1016/S0304-405X(03)00168-5

Bessembinder, H. (2003c). Trade execution costs and market quality after decimalization. *Journal of Financial and Quantitative Analysis*, *38*, 747–777. doi:10.2307/4126742

Bollen, N. R. B., & Busse, J. A. (1996). Tick size and institutional trading costs: Evidence from mutual funds. *Journal of Financial and Quantitative Analysis*, *41*(4), 915–937. doi:10.1017/S0022109000002696

Chakravarty, S., Panchapagesan, V., & Wood, R. A. (2005). Did decimalization hurt institutional investors? *Journal of Financial Markets*, *8*(4), 400–420. doi:10.1016/j.finmar.2005.05.002

Chakravarty, S., Van Ness, B., & Van Ness, R. (2005). The effect of decimalization on trade size and adverse selection costs. *Journal of Business Finance & Accounting*, *32*, 1063–1081. doi:10.1111/j.0306-686X.2005.00622.x

Chakravarty, S., Wood, R., & Van Ness, R. (2004). Decimals and liquidity: A study of the NYSE. *Journal of Financial Research*, *27*, 75–94. doi:10.1111/j.1475-6803.2004.00078.x

Chordia, T., Roll, R., & Subrahmanyam, A. (2008). Liquidity and market efficiency. *Journal of Financial Economics*, *87*(2), 249–268. doi:10.1016/j.jfineco.2007.03.005

Christie, W., & Schultz, P. (1994). Why do NASDAQ market makers avoid odd-eighth quotes? *The Journal of Finance*, *49*, 1813–1840. doi:10.2307/2329272

Chung, K. H., Charoenwong, C., & Ding, D. (2004). Penny pricing and the components of spread and depth changes. *Journal of Banking & Finance*, *28*, 2981–3007. doi:10.1016/j.jbankfin.2003.11.001

Chung, K. H., Charoenwong, C., & Jiang, J. (2008). The dynamics of quote adjustments. *Journal of Banking & Finance*, *32*(11), 2390–2400. doi:10.1016/j.jbankfin.2008.02.001

Chung, K. H., Charoenwong, C., & McCormick, D. (2004). Order preferencing and market quality on NASDAQ before and after decimalization. *Journal of Financial Economics*, *71*, 581–612. doi:10.1016/S0304-405X(03)00174-0

Chung, K. H., & Kim, V. (2009). Volatility, market structure, and the bid-ask spread. *Asia-Pacific Journal of Financial Studies*, *38*(1), 67–107. doi:10.1111/j.2041-6156.2009.tb00008.x

Chung, K. H., Van Ness, B., & Van Ness, R. (2001). Can the treatment of limit orders reconcile the differences in trading costs between NYSE and NASDAQ issues? *Journal of Financial and Quantitative Analysis*, *36*(2), 267–286. doi:10.2307/2676274

Chung, K. H., Van Ness, B., & Van Ness, R. (2002). Spreads, depths, and quote clustering on NYSE and NASDAQ: Evidence after the 1997 Securities and Exchange Commission rule changes. *Financial Review*, *37*, 481–505. doi:10.1111/1540-6288.00025

Chung, K. H., Van Ness, B., & Van Ness, R. (2004). Trading costs and quote clustering on NYSE and NASDAQ after decimalization. *Journal of Financial Research*, *27*, 309–328. doi:10.1111/j.1475-6803.2004.00096.x

Chung, R., Lawrence, K., & Zhang, H. (1997). Decimalization's winners and losers. *Canadian Investment Review*, (Winter): 35–39.

Easley, D., Hvidkjaer, S., & O'Har, M. (2002). Is information risk a determinant of asset returns? *The Journal of Finance*, *57*, 2185–2221. doi:10.1111/1540-6261.00493

Easley, D., Kiefer, N., & O'Hara, M. (1996). Cream-skimming or profit-sharing? The curious case of purchased order flow. *The Journal of Finance*, *51*, 811–834. doi:10.2307/2329223

Easley, D., Kiefer, N., & O'Hara, M. (1997a). One day in the life of a very common stock. *Review of Financial Studies*, *10*, 805–835. doi:10.1093/rfs/10.3.805

Easley, D., Kiefer, N., & O'Hara, M. (1997b). *Pooling or separating equilibriums in financial markets? Evidence from oil stocks*. Working Paper, Cornell University.

Easley, D., Kiefer, N., O'Hara, M., & Paperman, J. (1996). Liquidity, information, and infrequently traded stocks. *The Journal of Finance*, *51*, 1405–1436. doi:10.2307/2329399

Easley, D., & O'Hara, M. (1992). Time and the process of security price adjustment. *The Journal of Finance*, *47*, 577–605. doi:10.2307/2329116

Fang, V. W., Noe, T. H., & Tice, S. (2009). Stock market liquidity and firm value. *Journal of Financial Economics*, *94*(1), 150–169. doi:10.1016/j.jfineco.2008.08.007

Garfinkel, J., & Nimalendran, M. (2003). Market structure and trader anonymity: An analysis of insider trading. *Journal of Financial and Quantitative Analysis*, *38*, 591–610. doi:10.2307/4126733

Gibson, S., Singh, R., & Yerramilli, V. (2003). The effect of decimalization on the components of the bid-ask spread. *Journal of Financial Intermediation, 12,* 121–148. doi:10.1016/S1042-9573(03)00017-2

Glosten, L., & Milgrom, P. (1985). Bid, ask and transaction prices in a specialist market with heterogeneously informed traders. *Journal of Financial Economics, 14,* 71–100. doi:10.1016/0304-405X(85)90044-3

Godek, P. (1996). Why NASDAQ market makers avoid odd-eighth quotes? *Journal of Financial Economics, 41,* 465–474. doi:10.1016/0304-405X(95)00863-A

Goldstein, M., & Kavajecz, K. (2000). Eighths, sixteenths and market depth: Changes in tick size and liquidity provision on NYSE. *Journal of Financial Economics, 56,* 125–149. doi:10.1016/S0304-405X(99)00061-6

Goldstein, M., Shkilko, A., & Van Ness, B. &Van Ness, R. (2005). *Inter-market competition for NYSE-listed securities.* Working paper, University of Mississippi.

Grossman, S., Miller, M., Fischel, D., Cone, K., & Ross, D. (1997). Clustering and competition in dealer markets. *The Journal of Law & Economics, 40,* 23–60. doi:10.1086/467365

Harris, L. (1991). Stock price clustering and discreteness. *Review of Financial Studies, 4,* 389–416. doi:10.1093/rfs/4.3.389

Harris, L. (1994). Tick sizes, discrete bid-ask spreads, and quotation sizes. *Review of Financial Studies, 7,* 149–178. doi:10.1093/rfs/7.1.149

Harris, L. (1997). *Decimalization: A review of the arguments and evidence.* Working paper, University of Southern California.

Harris, L. (1999). *Trading in pennies: A survey of the issues.* Working paper, University of Southern California.

Hasbrouck, J. (1991). Measuring the information content of stock trades. *The Journal of Finance, 46,* 179–207. doi:10.2307/2328693

Huang, R., & Stoll, H. (1996). Dealer versus auction markets: A paired comparison of execution costs on NYSE and NYSE. *Journal of Financial Economics, 41,* 313–357. doi:10.1016/0304-405X(95)00867-E

Huson, M., Youngsoo, K., & Vikas, M. (1997). *Decimal quotes, market quality, and competition for order flow: Evidence from the Toronto stock exchange.* Working paper, University of Alberta

Lee, C., & Ready, M. (1991). Inferring trade direction from intraday data. *The Journal of Finance, 46,* 733–746. doi:10.2307/2328845

New York Stock Exchange. (2001a). *Comparing bid-ask spreads on the New York Stock Exchange and NASDAQ immediately following NASDAQ decimalization.* NYSE Research, July 26, 2001.

New York Stock Exchange. (2001b). *Decimalization of trading on the New York Stock Exchange: A report to the Securities and Exchange Commission.* NYSE Research, September 7, 2001.

Weaver, D. G. (1997). *Decimalization and market quality.* Working paper, Marquette University.

Zhao, X., & Chung, K. H. (2006). Decimal pricing and information-based trading: Tick size and informational efficiency of asset price. *Journal of Business Finance & Accounting, 33*(5-6), 753–766. doi:10.1111/j.1468-5957.2006.00622.x

KEY TERMS AND DEFINITIONS

Decimalization: The process of changing the prices that securities trade at from fractions to decimals.

Bid-Ask Spread: The amount by which the ask price exceeds the bid. This is essentially the difference in price between the highest price that a buyer is willing to pay for an asset and the lowest price for which a seller is willing to sell it.

Market Depth: The market's ability to sustain relatively large market orders without impacting the price of the security.

Liquidity: The degree to which an asset or security can be bought or sold in the market without affecting the asset's price.

Limit Order: An order placed with a brokerage to buy or sell a set number of shares at a specified price or better.

Market Order: An order to buy or sell securities or commodities at the best price with immediate effect.

Volatility: A statistical measure of the dispersion of returns for a given security or market index. Volatility can either be measured by using the standard deviation or variance between returns from that same security or market index.

Chapter 10
Internet Banking and Online Trading

Bin Chang
University of Ontario Institute of Technology, Canada

Shantanu Dutta
University of Ontario Institute of Technology, Canada

ABSTRACT

In the recent past, online or Internet based banking has become quite common. Banks have also realized the potential of Internet banking and have recognized that it is necessary to integrate the customers' new lifestyle and Web based activity preferences with their business models. Most of the empirical studies have reported positive impact of Internet banking on bank performance. Adoption of Internet banking leads to cost reduction and hence likely to increase banks' profitability. Introduction on internet banking has brought unprecedented speed in banking system and has been playing a major role in the globalization of banking system. As Internet banking makes inroads to banking business, market participants have also started to use Internet for security trading activities. Online trading has led to an upward trend in trading frequency, trading volume, and turnover ratio.

INTERNET BANKING AND ONLINE TRADING

Most of the households in the North America and in the developed economies have access to internet. Over the years, users have become more comfortable with and accustomed to internet use and started to rely on web based activities for daily and business needs. Banks have also realized the potential of internet banking and have recognized that it is necessary to integrate the customers' new lifestyle and web based activity preferences with their business models. Hence, internet banking has been introduced and started to impact customers' banking activities and personal portfolio management styles. Corrocher (2006) defines the term internet banking as follows:

DOI: 10.4018/978-1-60960-848-4.ch010

"The term Internet banking refers to the use of the Internet as a remote delivery channel for banking services, which include both traditional ones, such as opening an account or transferring funds, and new ones, such as electronic online payments" (p. 536).

Introduction on internet banking has brought unprecedented speed in banking system and has been playing a major role in the globalization of banking system. As Internet banking makes inroad to banking business, market participant have also started to use Internet for security trading activities. Online trading has led to an upward trend in trading frequency, trading volume, and turnover ratio. In this chapter, we will systematically discuss the issues relevant to Internet banking and online trading (i.e. Internet based trading). Although, there are similarities in the concepts of Internet banking and online trading as both are facilitated by web based transactions, for clarity and ease of understanding the practical and empirical issues in these two topics we present them separately.

INTERNET BANKING

In the first part of this chapter, we discuss the brief history of internet banking, its advantages, disadvantages and challenges faced by both banks and customers as a result of internet banking. We also look into the empirical research to find the impact of Internet banking on bank performance and the reasons for adopting Internet banking.

Brief History of Internet Banking

Modern internet banking system has evolved from the distance banking services over electronic media that were introduced in early 1980s.[1] As the case with any new technology, there were a number of trial and errors before the modern practices were adopted. In early 1980s, four major U.S. banks (Citibank, Chase Manhattan, Chemical and Manufacturers Hanover) started to use some form of home banking services that allowed customers to do distance banking. They introduced 'videotex system' to achieve the objective of home banking service – but the project did not success commercially.

In 1983, first online banking service was introduced in the U.K. by Bank of Scotland. They developed the service for the customers of Nottingham Building Society (NBS) that enabled online and distance services such as on-line viewing of statements, bank transfers and bill payments. The system was derived from the 'Prestel (press telephone) system' which was originally developed by the postal service department of U.K. and used a computer or keyboard connected to the telephone system and television set. In U.S., Stanford Federal Credit Union was the first financial institution to offer online internet banking services to all of its members in Oct, 1994.[2] Stanford Credit Union gradually developed its capabilities with a series of user friendly steps. It became one of the first to offer checking accounts and credit cards in the late 1970s. "In the early 1980s, it introduced ATMs and banking by telephone. In November 1993, Stanford Federal Credit Union conducted its first four internet transactions; and in 1994, it became the first financial institution to offer online banking when it launched its website; it offered online BillPay to its members in 1997, added account aggregation and mobile banking in 2002, and became one of the first institutions to implement the Passmark authentication system in 2005."[3]

In Canada, The bank of Montreal and the TD Canada Trust were among the first Canadian Banks to introduce internet banking to its customers. Over the time, there have been evolutions of other financial institutions that entirely operate on the internet. For such online banks or financial institutions, access to all accounts and transactions is available 24 hours a day, 7 days a week. Citizens Bank of Canada is the first online bank to offer its service entirely through online to its customer. Other exclusive Canadian online banks include ING Direct and President's Choice Financial (Kapoor et al. 2006).

Scope, Advantages and Disadvantages of Internet Banking

Scope

Through the internet banking service customers can get access to a list of services. In order to use internet banking service one needs access to the website of the bank. Generally there are distinct user name and password for each customer to access their accounts. Generally, following services are available to the customers through internet banking:

- Checking account balances
- Checking credit card balances
- Making payments for online purchases
- Bill payments
- Transferring funds
- Making mortgage payments
- Getting loans from banks

Banks are constantly including more and more services in internet banking. Therefore, we expect to see an expansion of the above list of online service offerings in the future.

Like any other new technological developments, internet banking system has its own advantages and disadvantages. Below, we discuss these advantages and disadvantages from both customer's and bank's perspectives.

Advantages and Disadvantages of Internet Banking: Customer Perspectives

There are a number of significant advantages of internet banking that attract millions of bank customers to online banking services over the world.

Convenience

Major advantage of internet banking for the customers is the convenience of banking from virtually anywhere from the world as long as there is an availability o internet service. As the internet coverage is increasing day-by-day, internet banking provides an enormous opportunity to the customers to access their banking services virtually any time of the day. Quite importantly, customers can access their accounts, withdraw money and make bill payments while they are outside of their own country.

Saving Costs

Customers can make bill payments instantly, check their accounts, arrange for loans, and set up mortgage payments with ease. Ad they can monitor their accounts very easily, customers can track their payment schedules and make sure that bills are paid on time – that saves them from paying penalties or extra interest charges.

Detecting Fraudulent Activities

Online banking has become also quite handy to detect fraudulent activities and charges. It is quite common these days for the customers to make payments for day to day purchases through debit card and credit card. Such payments could be risky and the accounts information can be stolen during online transaction. Financial institutions advise customers to report such incidents without any delay in order to take appropriate actions. Through online account access, customers could track any wrongdoing quite fast. This would help them to recover their money fast by reporting the events to the financial institutions - in most of the instances. Finally, internet banking also saves time and cost for the customers.

Though the advantages of internet banking are appealing, there are some distinct advantages with internet banking that make some people cautious and uncomfortable in using online services.

Safety in Internet Banking

Major concern with internet banking is the safety issue. There are security threats with wireless network and online network that may deter customers from using online banking. There are many big cyber scams reported in the recent past, and customers bank account related information has been stolen. Some of these events and consequences will be discussed in the later sections.

Lack of Support

While using internet banking, customers are generally left alone. There is no access to the traditional face to face customer support. It is not always easy for the customers to understand the intricate details of financial matters and they may need additional advices and suggestions before they carry out the transactions. In internet based banking such services are not available. Although, customers can call the bank's customers service department for further explanations and suggestions – often there are disappointments.

Knowledge of Computer and Internet

Customers using internet banking need to have access to computer hardware and internet. However, mere availability of these instruments is not enough; the customers need to understand how to use these tools. May people (specially the older people and people of developing countries) might not have access to these tools or are not comfortable in using these tools. This will keep a section of bank users away from using internet banking service.

Advantages and Disadvantages of Internet Banking: Bank Perspectives

Most of the traditional banks now provide internet banking services. There are some major advantages for adopting internet banking for these banks.

Going with the Trend

With the advent of internet system, people around the world want to take advantage of it whatever way possible. Banking system is not an exception. Most of the Banks introduced this service in order to satisfy the needs of modern bank customers. Good internet banking service is likely to attract customers who are comfortable with online services. More likely, young generation will be attracted to such services and this will ensure future customer base for the financial institutions.

Cost Saving

Internet banking, if properly planned and implemented, could save some cost for the financial institutions. Banks can provide services to more customers concurrently through internet banking service and free up the physical space requirements in the bank premises. Customers can also avoid long queues and delays. This is likely to increase customer satisfaction level. However, as the internet banking service is becoming pervasive and offered by any known banks, the service providers of internet banking need to be mindful of the quality of their service. Mere offering of internet banking services would not lead to customer satisfaction.

Attracting more Businesses

In earlier days, it was quite difficult for remotely located small businesses to have an access to quality banking services. In the era of internet banking that problem has been reduced significantly. This is advantageous for both parties. Small businesses get financial services more easily; at the same time financial institutions have access to border range and sizes of business.

Introduction of internet banking service also pose significant challenges for financial institutions. Some of these challenges are discussed by Cristina et al.[4]; the salient issues are summarized below:

Retention of Loyal Customers

Internet banking makes it easier for the customer to switch to other banks or get services from multiple banks. It is much easier for a new entrant to attract customers from other financial institutions by providing more competitive services. In the era of internet, it is quite easier for customers to know about the services of other banks and shop for the best options.

Threats from Competitors

As a bank or financial institutions rely more on internet banking – they have to make more online disclosure. This allows other competitors to set their own strategy and try to the rates and services of the said banks. Furthermore, internet banking helps in the flourishing of online brokers. These brokers can shop easily for the best deals for their customers. All of these factors create competitive pressure on a financial institution, which in turn erode profitability of the financial institutions.

Lending Risks

With internet banking, qualified customers have an option to get approval for bank loans electronically. However, such services could create significant challenges and risks for the lending organizations (Cristina et al. – please see the footnote 4) that include:

- Verification of customer identity for online credit application
- Ongoing assessment of customer credential

- Valuing collateral, monitoring loans and collecting loan payments over a wider geographic area.

Security and Reputational Risks

According to Cristina et al. (please see the footnote 4) security breaches can fall into three categories, "breaches with serious criminal intent (fraud, theft of commercially sensitive or financial information), breaches by 'casual hackers' (defacement of websites or 'denial of service' – causing websites to crash), and flaws in system design and/or set up leading to security breaches (genuine users seeing/ being able to transact on other users' accounts). If any of these security breaches occur, it could cost the financial institutions. There are legal implications for such breaches. Also security breaches would cause harm to the reputation of financial institutions. In financial industry, 'trust' is a critical element; if customers lose their trust in a financial institution, they are likely to look for other alternatives.

Empirical Research on Internet Banking

A number of research studies have examined the issues related to early adoptions of internet banking and relevant financial performance of the financial institutions. Main results from some of the relevant studies are presented below:

Adoption of Internet Banking

Furst et al. (2002) carry out a detail study to understand which banks are the early adaptors of internet banking. Their study covers the internet banking offerings of every national bank in the U.S. and the relevant information is gathered through a detail survey conducted by the Office of the Comptroller of the Currency (OCC) examiners completed between mid-August and Mid-September 1999 for 2535 national banks. Timing of this study is quite important, as Couch and Parker (2000) report that the number of banks and thrifts with Web sites more than doubled (from 1500 to 3500) between 1997 and 1999.[5] More importantly, approximately 1,100 websites were transactional by the end of 1999. Furst et al. (2002) identify the following characteristics of the banks and thrifts that explain the early adoption of internet banking in the U.S.:

- Membership in a bank holding
- Banks and thrifts those are located in the urban area
- Relatively higher premises and fixed cost to net revenue, and
- Higher level of non-interest income

Also, not surprisingly, the study report that among banks that offer internet banking, larger banks and banks with a longer history offer more services on the internet. Furst et al. (2002) further report that more profitable banks were relatively slow in adopting internet banking, possibly because these banks were not eager to destabilize their existing business model before evaluating the promise of the new technologies.

By using data made public by the U.S. National Credit Union Association (NCUA) for the 200-2003 period, Dow (2007) examines the decision to adopt web and personal computer banking by credit unions. Credit unions are non-profit financial institutions, thus are different from traditional banks. In the recent years credit unions have grown in size and have more resources for making technological offerings. Two reasons are cited for Credit union's size growth: relaxation of the so called "common bond requirement" for credit union establishments is and the reduction in the number of credit unions (Dow, 2007). As the credit unions are non-profit organizations, their goal is to benefit both their borrowers and depositions. In other words, they would like to maintain a lower interest spread. However, such goal may deter a credit union from officering internet banking services. Developing websites for

internet banking would cost credit unions, which would force them to increase the interest spread. On the other hand, internet banking service may itself benefit the credit unions by reducing operating cost. Dow (2007) addresses these issues in his research study and report the following:

- Credit unions that provide internet banking services tend to maintain higher interest spread
- Generally larger credit unions are likely to adopt internet banking earlier and are likely to offer more advanced version of the technology

Corrocher (2006) examines the determinants of adoption of Internet banking among Italian banks by using a dataset that lists all the adopters of Internet banking per month in Italy between September 1995 and December 2000. In addition to focussing on the more common variables such as bank size, this study also examines the impact of existing bank networks, internet diffusion levels in the markets and customer background. Main findings of this study are as follows:

- There is a negative relationship between (i) the intensity of bank branching and the probability of Internet adoption, and (ii) the size of the existing (local) demand and the probability of Internet adoption. These findings suggest that banks with an extensive branch networks and banks that are operating in a market with strong local demand are less likely to adopt internet banking. It implies that banks are interested in adopting internet banking mainly to capture new customers rather than to offer new value-added services to existing customers.
- Banks that offer and facilitate trading activities are more likely to adopt Internet banking compared the ones that are involved in traditional interest-based activi-

ties. This implies that banks need to cater to the requirements of the different groups of users.

- Banks are more likely to adopt internet banking while operating in a market with higher levels of internet diffusion and when customers have relatively higher income and education levels.

- Finally, the study also finds that bank size positively affects Internet banking adoption to a certain point and then the relationship is reverse. This implies that medium size banks are the first movers in adoption of Internet banking.

Impact of Internet Banking on Bank Performance

England et al. (1998) is one of the pioneering studies that has looked into the Internet banking in U.S. banks and reported the performance of such banks. England et al. show that by mid-1998, most of the transactional internet banks in the U.S. offered services like web based balance enquiries and fund transfer between accounts. However, they report no significance difference in operating performance of the banks that offer internet banking service and the ones that do not. Furst et al. (2002) examine the federally chartered U.S. banks in 1998 and finds that Internet banking outperforms non-Internet banks in terms of operating performance. However, they also report that start-up ('de novo') Internet banks were less profitable and less efficient than non-internet start-ups. It implies that Internet banks need more time to stabilize their business and implement new technology based banking services.

DeYoung (2005) examines the financial performance of a dozen U.S. based Internet-only banks and thrifts that started up between 1997 and 2001. The results of this study are quite important and interesting as, unlike most of other studies in this area, this study provides a clean test of the inter-only business model. DeYoung (2005) compares

operating performance of these Internet only banks with a sample of 644 branching banks and thrifts that also started up between 1997 and 2001. The results show that Internet-only start ups are significantly less profitable than branching bank start ups. However, DeYoung (2005) also finds that Internet only banks "successfully executes some elements of the business model (e.g. rapid growth, better prices on loans and deposits) but not others (e.g. lower overhead expenses)" (p. 895). Further, performance gaps between the 'better-run' Internet-only banks and branching banks and thrifts reduces over the years. DeYoung (2005) observes that Internet-only banks have access to "deeper scale economies" than the branching banks. Therefore, it is quite likely that as they grow larger, better-run Internet-only banks will be financially competitive with the branching banks.

DeYoung et al. (2007) examine the performance of U.S. community banks that offer internet banking. Data period for this study (from year-end 1999 through year-end 2001) is quite fitting as Internet banking was still a relatively new phenomenon at that time. DeYoung et al. (2007) mainly focus on small banks[6] (or so called community banks), as the larger banks already adopted Internet banking by that time. They contrast the change in performance of 424 community banks for the 1999-2001 period with that of 5175 branching-only community banks and find that Internet adoption improved community bank profitability, mainly by increasing revenues from deposit service charges. The study also report that "Internet adoption was also associated with movements of deposits from checking accounts to money market deposit accounts, increased use of brokered deposits, and higher average wage rates for bank employees" (p. 1033).

A few studies have also examined the impact of Internet adoption by European banks. Ciciretti et al. (2009) examine the impact of internet adoption by Italian banks with a sample of 105 banks over 1993-2002 period. They find that Internet adoption impacts bank performance positively and play a role in reducing bank risk. Hernando and Neito (2007) examine a sample of 72 commercial banks operating in Spain over the period 1994-2004 and find that adoption of Internet banking reduces overheard expenses (particularly, staff, marketing and IT) gradually. This cost reduction leads to an improvement in financial performance for the relevant banks. Sathye (2005) examines the effect of transactional web service introduction by major credit unions in Australia on their financial performance and risk profile. The study reports no significant effect on performance or risk profile of the Australian credit unions that adopted Internet banking.

In summary, we find that most of the empirical studies have reported positive impact of Internet banking on bank performance. Adoption of Internet banking leads to cost reduction and hence likely to increase banks' profitability.

ONLINE TRADING

Technological innovation enables individuals to trade financial securities through a computer and internet. A survey (Sachoff, 2008) reveals that in 2008, 82 percent U.S. households have internet access. To meet the surging demand of trading online, almost all brokerage houses provide this service. Litan & Rivlin (2001) argue that internet has changed the information acquisition, investment method, and trading behavior of investors. In order to get a deeper insight into online trading, in this part we focus on following issues: (i) who participate in online trading? (ii) how does internet affect trading behavior? (iii) how do individual online traders perform? (iv) what online information affects trading? (v) has it caused any structural change in financial market?

Participants of Online Trading

Choi, Laibson, & Metrick (2002) use two large corporate 401 (k) managed by Hewitt Associ-

ates to study the characteristics of online traders. 401 (k) is a defined contribution pension plan in which both employers and employees contribute certain percentage of salary. It has nice tax-deferral feature in that contributions are tax deductible, grow free of tax inside the plan, and only taxable upon withdrawal usually after retirement. It has become a major source of retirement planning. All employees in a corporation participate in it mandatorily. Although some choose online trading and others do not, mandatory participation eliminates the possibility of self-selection bias in securities trading. Their data consist of more than 60,000 participants from early 1997 to early 2000. They chose participants who completed at least one trade since August 1998 when web channel was opened.

Using a Logit estimation for two plans separately, they identify some common feature. First, participates who are male, younger, have higher salary or more wealth inside the plan are more likely to initiate an online trading. Second, people who are terminated from job or retired are less likely to start online trading. A possible reason is that they are less informed about the new channel. Third, people with previous experience with phone trading are less likely to start online trading. It is possible that they are already familiar with phone trading and are reluctant to change it for a while.

Barber & Odean (2002) also examine who goes online using a different sample. The original data is taken from a big brokerage account with data on all trades and monthly positions from 1991 and 1996. They include an online sample with 1,607 investors who switched from phone trading to online trading and a size (market value of common stock)-matched control sample who did not switch. Using summary statistics and logistic regression, they report that online traders are more likely to be younger men with higher income and net wealth, consistent with the finding of Choi, Laibson, & Metrick (2002). They also find that online traders have higher monthly turnover, less value-firm preference, and more investment experience.

Joo, Grable, & Choe (2007) use a different sample set to examine who use online retirement investment advices. The sample is generated through the Retirement Confidence Survey conducted by Employee Benefit Research Institute in 2004. They find that online advice users are those who are younger, participate in a defined contribution retirement plan, or make joint personal finance decisions with other family members.

Excessive Trading

Choi, Laibson, & Metrick (2002) find trading frequency and turnover increased after the introduction of online trading and 18 month later, it became the majority of trades. In addition to the introduction of online trading, the macroeconomic environment, like the volatility of the market, could have caused the increase of trading frequency. To isolate the impact of online trading, they use a regression model to control for non-web index which is the non-web traded subsample of Hewitt Associates 40-largest stock index. Other control variables include S&P return, S&P lag return, S&P squared return, S&P volatility, their own company's stock return and volatility and trend, and calendar-day effect. Prior research (Barber & Odean, 2000; Bergstrasser & Poterba, 2002; Chevalier & Ellison, 1997; Edelen, 1999; Grinblatt & Keloharju, 2000, 2001; Odean, 1998b, 1999) has found these variables to affect trading.

They construct an interaction of "web *time" where web is a dummy with 1 for online trading and 0 for phone trading, and time is the number of days since online trading is introduced. This interaction is positive and statistically significant. They further estimate the economic significance and find that "Web nearly doubles trading at an 18-month horizon." They conclude that the Web's effect on trading frequency was growing over time. They further attribute this observation to smaller size per trade of online trading.

Anderson (2007) extends the study with an international dataset. His sample includes 324,736 transactions by 16,837 investors at a Swedish internet discount brokerage firm from May 1999 to March 2002. Note this data consists of online trading only, thus it does not offer "online trading versus traditional method" comparison. It confirms some similarities between Swedish traders and U.S. traders since online traders are predominantly male with 82 percent population, 37 years old on average. They have strong preference for risk in that the average market beta is 1.4. However, Anderson also reports some differences. For example, a median trader only holds 2 stocks, which is even less than U.S. peers. Also Swedish traders' portfolio size is only USD 2000, which is also far less than U.S. traders.

Anderson's research explores trading behavior with respect to three dimensions: diversification, turnover, and portfolio size. First, diversification is positively related to risk preference and performance. More diversified portfolios consist of less technology stocks and perform better. Second, average individuals turn over portfolios twice a year with 20 percent of them turning over seven times a year. Intensive turnover leads to poor performance which is directly caused by transaction costs. Average underperformance is 8.4 percent annually. Third, the impact of transaction costs on performance is most severe on small portfolios since flat dollar amount of transaction costs means higher percentage costs on smaller transactions.

Performance of Online Traders

The evidence is mixed. Choi, Laibson, & Metrick (2002) find that web traders and phone traders do not differ significantly in performance. Again they use the two corporate 401 (k) plan sample. They adopt the methodology of Graham and Harvey's (1996) study and use transaction data following Goetzmann & Massa (2002). They use a regression model where the dependent variable is S&P 500 return in next month and independent variable is current web order flow, non-web order flow, and control variables. They find that the coefficients of the first two are not statistically different.

Note that the sample of Choi, Laibson, & Metrick (2002) is quite different from others. They use two corporate 401 (k) plans which are free of tax or transaction costs. The participation is mandatory, which exclude the probability of self-selection. The asset class is not restricted to stocks, which instead include many mutual funds. In such an environment, they conclude that excessive trade does not determinate performance.

Barber & Odean (2002) find that traders who participated in online trading later already showed a stronger performance even before online trading was available. Besides raw return and market return, this research measures performance by "alpha", i.e., the excess return of expected return calculated from CAPM and Fama-French model. Prior to the launch of online trading, they already beat the market by 0.354 percent a month, and beat the control sample by 0.172 percent a month. They also beat the market and the control sample after netting transaction costs or using CAPM and Fama-French models as benchmark. Beating the market would have fostered the overconfidence of online traders. Prior research has studied the overconfidence issue in general, not particularly of online traders (Barber & Odean, 2000, 2001; Grinblatt & Keloharju, 2001; Lewellen, Lease, & Schlarbaum, 1977; Odean, 1998a, 1999; Shapria & Venezia, 2001).

However, they soon discover that the performance dramatically dropped after switching to online trading. Online traders underperformed the market by 9 basis points a month before transaction costs and 30 basis points a month after transaction cost, which represents 3.6 percent annual loss.

They attribute the underperformance to excessive trading. Online traders suddenly doubled their average turnover ratio when switched to the new mode and then dropped and maintained it at the 50 percent higher level than the pre-online trading scenario. However, traders who did not switch to online trading did not change their turnover ratio. They find that speculative trading accounts for 60 percent of the increase in turnover for average online investor.

The poor performance of online trading is also found in other countries. For example, Oh, Parwada & Walter (2008) investigate the trading behavior and performance of online equity investors in comparison to non-online equity investors in Korea. They find that on aggregate, online investors perform poorly in comparison to non-online investors during 2001-2005.

Excessive trading causes huge loss to individual traders. Barber, Lee, Liu, & Odean (2009) explicitly estimate how much investors lose by trading. Using Taiwan's data, they find it costs individuals 3.8 percent annually. Their losses are equivalent to 2.2% of Taiwan's gross domestic product or 2.8% of the total personal income.

Besides excessive trading caused by overconfidence, there are other theories to explain the poor performance of active traders. Barberis & Thaler (2003) provide an excellent survey of the literature (Barber & Odean, 2008; Barber, Odean, & Zhu, 2009; Grinblatt & Keloharju, 2001; Huberman, 2001; Kahneman & Tversky, 1974; Massa & Simonov, 2005; Odean, 1999; Shefrin & Statman, 1985). They discuss the disposition effect which is to sell winners quickly and hold onto losers, the representative heuristic which is to buy attention grabbing stocks, familiarity bias that is to pick the same stocks again and again, the affection from peers to buy what others buy, and the lack of short position.

The above mentioned research focuses on individual traders, who may be considered naive or unprofessional. On the other hand, Mizrach & Sweets (2009) analyze a group of active traders who voluntarily post their trades in real time into a public Internet chat room called Activetrader. These are semi-professionals that are largely ignored by literature. It is conservative to assume that they are the online traders. This sample includes four snapshots of October 2000, April 2001, April

2002, and mid-June to mid-July 2003. A typical picture of the trader is a middle-aged male with $198,000 exposed in the market and five years of investment experience.

These semi-professionals behave differently from other active investors in the studies mentioned above. First, they have strong performance. Using Carhart (1997)'s model with Fama-French three factors enhanced with momentum factor, they estimate the alpha to be 0.444 in 2000, 0.221 in year 2001, 0.225 in year 2002, 0.003 (statistically insignificant) in year 2003, and 0.017 in the full sample. Second, traders in the most active quintile make 83 percent of all profits. This is in contrast to the finding of Barber & Odean (2000) that top quintile of most active traders make the worst performance. Third, they both long and short stocks. They double the return when short.

These semi-professionals also show similar behavior as other active investors. First, there is evidence of disposition effect. The average holding period for a losing trade is 47.87 minutes, but winners are held for 60.23 minutes. Second, they trade usually stocks with large market capitalization, high trading volumes and high betas. Third, they follow peers who already post a trade. Mizrach, & Sweets (2009) also find that semi-professionals learn from experience. More experienced traders make more profit. Also traders who reduce their selection of stocks make more profit.

Quality of Online Information

Another important issue is whether online information contains quality information. Individuals can find information by searching websites, joining chat rooms, subscribing to mailing lists, downloading newsgroups, or even receiving email spams. The findings in this set of studies are mixed mainly due to the selection of different samples.

One interesting research area involving quality of online information is earnings forecast. Bagnoli, Beneish, & Watts (1999) compare analyst forecasts with whispers – that is, unofficial

forecasts made on internet, Wall Street Journal website and Financial newswires. They find that analysts are on average optimistic while whispers are pessimistic. This finding is later verified by Zaima & Hrjoto (2005). Bagnoli, Beneish, & Watts (1999) compare First Call consensus of analysts forecast earnings and unofficial online whispers and find that the latter is more accurate. Different from the opinion above, Dewally (2008) finds that whispers do not contain unique information and so are no more accurate than analysts' consensus. These two studies come to different conclusions because of different sample.

Other research focuses on online stock recommendations such as buy or sell. Tumarkin & Whitelaw (2001) and Tumarkin (2002) contribute to what determinants online messenger board. Dewally (2003) analyzes the quality of online postings. This research analyzes two newsgroup sites, namely, misc.invest.stocks and alt.invest. penny-stocks in April 1999 and February 2001. Different from Yahoo messenger board where there is a unique chat room for a particular stock, newsgroups post all stock recommendations in one room, which allows researchers to identify hot stocks. The recommendations are overwhelmingly positive with buy-sell ratio to be 7:1. They find statistically insignificant abnormal return in a two-day window around stock recommendation, and the long term return is not significantly different from market returns.

Antweiler & Frank (2004) choose Yahoo Finance and Raging Bull, the most popular online messenger board. Their sample includes 1.5 million online postings on 45 stocks, the components of Dow Jones Industrial Average and Dow Jones Internet Index in the full year of 2000. First, they confirm the bullishness that is found in the sample of Dewally (2003). Second, they research the impact of stock return, and find it to be statistically significant but economically marginal. Third, the number of messages can predict stock return volatility and trading volume. Finally, disagreements of messages are related to soaring trading volume, which is consistent with Harris and Raviv (1993). Thus they conclude that online messages contain information.

Sabherwal, Sarkar, & Zhang (2009) continue this research with a much more recent data. They choose messages of 135 most actively discussed stocks from Thelion.com from July 18, 2005 to July 2006. Their sample is primarily consisted of thinly traded small-cap stocks. Their finding is different from Dewally (2003). Sabherwal, Sarkar, & Zhang find that "the number of messages posted about a stock on a given day is not only positively related with the stock's abnormal return on that day but it also positively predicts the next day's abnormal return" (pp. 424). The different results on whether online messages contain information are mainly caused by the sample selection.

There is a rising trend of spam emails. Hanke & Hause (2008) are among a very limited literature on this issue. Their sample includes 1,241 spam emails on 235 stocks in 2005. They first find that the inclusion of a spam email dummy increase the R-square of a regression model of excess return, turnover, and intra-day price change, suggesting that spam emails contains valuable information for investors. They further find that the positive news contained in spam emails have no lasting positive effect on stock prices. Also repeated spamming on successive days sustains excess demand for target stocks.

Impact on Financial Market

Online trading has greatly changed the financial market. Barber & Odean (2002) summarize the benefits to be lower commission, easier access, and speeder trade execution. For example, they document that bid-ask spreads and commissions drops for both online traders and phone traders, suggesting that there is a market-wide reduction in transaction costs. However, online trading also generates excessive trade. In turn, the trading costs on excessive trade have caused poor performance.

Bogan (2008) analyzes its impact. This research indentifies a structural change in the stock market between the periods 1980–1993 and 1994–2001 based on the following evidence. First, Survey of Consumer Finances documented that the percentage of U.S. households owning stocks took off in the second period. Research finds that a bull market alone does not explain it. In the same period, households with computer and internet access grew dramatically. Data from Charles Schwab, a large brokerage house shows that the portion of online trading increased from 20 percent to 85 percent, in contrast to the huge drop of trades made through phone, branches, service center and others. Third, U.S. stock market's volume, trades, and turnover increased sharply. Finally, transaction cost is much smaller for online trading versus broker-assisted trading. For example the former is $8, but the latter is $18 in Amertriade in 2000.

Bogan then develops the research question: Does internet trading affect stock market participation? Bogan's sample is the year 1992 and 2002 survey of the Health and Retirement Survey (HRS), which is a nationally representative longitudinal data set. This survey has been used in prior studies like Hong, Kubik, & Stein (2004). This survey includes one-cohort, i.e., people who were born in between 1941 and 1947. The one-cohort feature reduces the impact of age, which is found to affect trading behavior in other studies. This sample is not transaction data and so online trading cannot be directly identified. This study uses whether a home has computer or not to proxy for online trading, which obviously introduces measurement errors.

Bogan's research concludes that the use of internet has increased the likelihood to participate in trading, causing a reduction in a previous market friction of low stock market participant rates. It applies Probit models with the dependent variable to be an owning-stock dummy. Bogan makes a smart choice to include a dummy that is 1 if the participant already owns a stock in 1992. In this way, this work controls the omitted variables that represent the financial sophistication of a household and might have affected stock owning decisions. It finds that computer usage increases the probability to own stocks by 0.07. This is equivalent to $27,000 more mean household income or two more years of education.

CONCLUDING REMARKS ON ONLINE TRADING

The literature has done extensive research on online trading. With 82 percent U.S. households having internet access, online trading is becoming prevalent. The literature studies it from five dimensions including participants, trading behavior, performance, the use of online information, and the impact on the financial markets. First, the participants are more likely to be young male with investment experience, good salary, and large portfolio. Second, online traders are involved in excessive trading, causing an upward trend in trading frequency, trading volume, and turnover ratio. Third, individuals' performance dropped after switching from traditional brokerage-assisted trading to online trading. One major reason is the transaction cost related to excessive trading. Fourth, online information is abundant and easily accessed, but their impact on stock return is mixed and depends on sample selection. Finally, it caused a structural change in the financial market between the periods 1980–1993 and 1994–2001. The latter period witnessed increasing trade, volume, turnover, and participants.

REFERENCES

Anderson, A. (2007). All guts, no glory: Trading and diversification among online investors. *European Financial Management*, *13*(3), 448–471. doi:10.1111/j.1468-036X.2007.00368.x

Antweiler, W., & Frank, M. Z. (2004). Is all that talk just noise? The information content of Internet stock message boards. *The Journal of Finance*, *59*, 1259–1295. doi:10.1111/j.1540-6261.2004.00662.x

Bagnoli, M., Beneish, M. D., & Watts, S. G. (1999). Whisper forecasts of quarterly earnings per share. *Journal of Accounting and Economics*, *28*(1), 27–50. doi:10.1016/S0165-4101(99)00018-X

Barber, B., & Odean, T. (2000). Trading is hazardous to your wealth: The common stock investment performance of individual investors. *The Journal of Finance*, *55*, 773–806. doi:10.1111/0022-1082.00226

Barber, B., & Odean, T. (2001). The internet and the investor. *The Journal of Economic Perspectives*, *15*(Winter), 41–54. doi:10.1257/jep.15.1.41

Barber, B., & Odean, T. (2008). All that glitters: The effect of attention and news on the buying behavior of individual and institutional investors. *Review of Financial Studies*, *21*, 785–818. doi:10.1093/rfs/hhm079

Barber, B., Odean, T., & Zhu, N. (2009). Systematic noise. *Journal of Financial Markets*, *12*(4), 547–569. doi:10.1016/j.finmar.2009.03.003

Barber, B. M., Lee, Y. T., Liu, Y. J., & Odean, T. (2009). Just how much do individual investors lose by trading? *Review of Financial Studies*, *22*, 609–632. doi:10.1093/rfs/hhn046

Barberis, N., & Thaler, R. (2003). A survey of behavioral finance. In Constantinides, G., & Stulz, R. (Eds.), *Handbook of the economics of finance* (pp. 1053–1128). Amsterdam, The Netherlands: North-Holland Publishers.

Bergstrasser, D., & Poterba, J. (2002). Do after-tax returns affect mutual fund inflows? *Journal of Financial Economics*, *63*, 381–414. doi:10.1016/S0304-405X(02)00066-1

Bogan, V. (2008). Stock market participation and the Internet. *Journal of Financial and Quantitative Analysis*, *43*(1), 191–211. doi:10.1017/S0022109000002799

Carhart, M. M. (1997). On persistence in mutual fund performance. *The Journal of Finance*, *52*, 57–82. doi:10.2307/2329556

Chevalier, J., & Ellison, G. (1997). Risk taking by mutual funds as a response to incentives. *The Journal of Political Economy*, *105*, 1167–1200. doi:10.1086/516389

Choi, J. J., Laibson, D., & Metrick, A. (2002). How does the internet affect trading? Evidence from investor behavior in 401 (k) plans. *Journal of Financial Economics*, *64*, 397–421. doi:10.1016/S0304-405X(02)00130-7

Cicirretti, R., Hasan, I., & Zazzara, C. (2009). Do Internet activities add value? Evidence from the traditional banks. *Journal of Financial Services Research*, *35*(1), 81–98. doi:10.1007/s10693-008-0039-2

Corrocher, N. (2006). Internet adoption in Italian banks: An empirical investigation. *Research Policy*, *35*(4), 533–544. doi:10.1016/j.respol.2006.02.004

Couch, K., & Parker, D. L. (2000). Net interest grows as banks rush online. *Southwest Economy. Federal Reserve Bank of Dallas*, *2*, 1–5.

Dewally, M. (2003). Investing with a rock of sale. *Financial Analysts Journal*, *59*(4), 1–14. doi:10.2469/faj.v59.n4.2546

Dewally, M. (2008). The informational value of earnings whispers. *American Journal of Business*, *23*(1). Retrieved from http://www.bsu.edu/ mcobwin/ majb/ ?p=546. doi:10.1108/19355181200800003

DeYoung, R. (2005). The performance of Internet-based business models: Evidence from the banking industry. *The Journal of Business*, *78*(3), 893–947. doi:10.1086/429648

DeYoung, R., Lang, W. W., & Nolle, D. L. (2007). How the Internet affects output and performance at community banks. *Journal of Banking & Finance*, *31*(4), 1033–1060. doi:10.1016/j.jbankfin.2006.10.003

Dow, J. P. (2007). The adoption of web banking at credit unions. *The Quarterly Review of Economics and Finance*, *47*(3), 435–448. doi:10.1016/j.qref.2006.08.014

Edelen, R. M. (1999). Investor flows and the assessed performance of open-end mutual funds. *Journal of Financial Economics*, *53*, 439–466. doi:10.1016/S0304-405X(99)00028-8

England, K. L., Furst, K., Nolle, D. E., & Robertson, D. (1998). Banking over the Internet. *Quarterly Journal. Office of the Comptroller of the Currency*, *17*(4), 25–30.

Furst, K., Lang, W. W., & Nolle, D. E. (2002). Internet banking. *Journal of Financial Services Research*, *22*(1/2), 95–117. doi:10.1023/A:1016012703620

Goetzmann, W. N., & Massa, M. (2000). Daily momentum and contrarian behaviour of index fund investors. *Journal of Financial and Quantitative Analysis*, *37*, 375–389. doi:10.2307/3594985

Graham, J., & Harvey, C. (1996). Market-timing ability and volatility implied in investment newsletters' asset allocation recommendations. *Journal of Financial Economics*, *42*, 397–421. doi:10.1016/0304-405X(96)00878-1

Grinblatt, M., & Keloharju, M. (2000). The investor behavior and performance of various types: A study of Finland's unique data set. *Journal of Financial Economics*, *55*, 43–68. doi:10.1016/S0304-405X(99)00044-6

Grinblatt, M., & Keloharju, M. (2001). What makes investors trade? *The Journal of Finance, 56*, 589–616. doi:10.1111/0022-1082.00338

Hanke, M., & Hauser, F. (2008). On the effects of stock spam e-mails. *Journal of Financial Markets, 11*(1), 57–83. doi:10.1016/j.finmar.2007.10.001

Harris, M., & Raviv, A. (1993). Differences of opinion make a horse race. *Review of Financial Studies, 6*, 473–506. doi:10.1093/rfs/6.3.473

Hernando, I., & Nieto, M. (2007). Is the Internet delivery channel changing banks' performance? The case of Spanish banks. *Journal of Banking & Finance, 31*(4), 1083–1099. doi:10.1016/j.jbankfin.2006.10.011

Hong, H., Kubik, J., & Stein, J. (2004). Social interaction and stock market participation. *The Journal of Finance, 59*, 137–163. doi:10.1111/j.1540-6261.2004.00629.x

Huberman, G. (2001). Familiarity breeds investment. *Review of Financial Studies, 14*, 659–680. doi:10.1093/rfs/14.3.659

Joo, S. H., Grable, J. E., & Choe, H. (2007). Who is and who is not willing to use online employer-provided retirement investment advice. *Journal of Employment Counseling, 44*(2), 73–85.

Kahneman, D., & Tversky, A. (1974). Judgment under uncertainty: Heuristics and biases. *Science, 185*, 1124–1131. doi:10.1126/science.185.4157.1124

Kapoor, J. R., Dlabay, L. R., Hughes, R. J., & Ahmad, A. (2006). *Personal finance* (3rd Canadian edition). Toronto, Canada: McGraw-Hill Ryerson.

Lewellen, W. G., Lease, R. C., & Schlarbaum, G. G. (1977). Patterns of investment strategy and behavior among individual investors. *The Journal of Business, 50*, 296–333. doi:10.1086/295947

Litan, R. E., & Rivlin, A. M. (2001). Projecting the economic impact of the internet. *The American Economic Review, 91*(2), 313–317. doi:10.1257/aer.91.2.313

Massa, M., & Simonov, A. (2005). Behavioral biases and investment. *Review of Finance, 9*, 483–507. doi:10.1007/s10679-005-4998-y

Odean, T. (1998a). Are investors reluctant to realize their losses? *The Journal of Finance, 53*, 1775–1798. doi:10.1111/0022-1082.00072

Odean, T. (1998b). Volume, volatility, price, and profit when all traders are above average. *The Journal of Finance, 53*, 1887–1934. doi:10.1111/0022-1082.00078

Odean, T. (1999). Do investors trade too much? *The American Economic Review, 89*(5), 1279–1298. doi:10.1257/aer.89.5.1279

Oh, N. Y., Parwada, J. T., & Walter, T. S. (2008). Investors' trading behavior and performance: Online versus non-online equity trading in Korea. *Pacific-Basin Finance Journal, 1-2*, 26–43. doi:10.1016/j.pacfin.2007.04.009

Sabherwal, S., Sarkar, S. K., & Zhang, Y. (2008). Online talk: Does it matter? *Managerial Finance, 34*(6), 423–436. doi:10.1108/03074350810872813

Sachoff, M. (2008). *18% of U.S. households have no Internet access*. Retrieved on May 14, 2008, from http://www.webpronews.coanke m/topnews/2008/05/14/18-of-us-households-have-no-internet-access

Sathye, M. (2005). The impact of internet banking on performance and risk profile: Evidence from Australian credit unions. *Journal of Banking Regulation, 6*(2), 163–174. doi:10.1057/palgrave.jbr.2340189

Shapira, Z., & Venezia, I. (2001). Patterns of behavior of professionally managed and independent investors. *Journal of Banking & Finance, 25*, 1573–1587. doi:10.1016/S0378-4266(00)00139-4

Shefrin, H., & Statman, M. (1985). The disposition to sell winners too early and ride losers too long: Theory and evidence. *The Journal of Finance, 40*, 777–790. doi:10.2307/2327802

Tumarkin, R. (2002). Internet message board activity and market efficiency: A case study of the internet service sector using RagingBull.com. *Financial Markets Institutions and Instruments, 11*(4), 313–335. doi:10.1111/1468-0416.11403

Tumarkin, R., & Whitelaw, R. F. (2001). News or noise? Internet message board activity and stock prices. *Financial Analysts Journal, 57*(3), 41–51. doi:10.2469/faj.v57.n3.2449

Zaima, J. K., & Harjoto, M. A. (2005). Conflict in whispers and analyst forecasts: Which one should be your guide? *Financial Decisions, 17*(3), 1–16.

KEY TERMS AND DEFINITIONS

Internet Banking: Performing banking operations (such as fund transfer, opening an account, checking balance online) by using the website of financial institutions.

Internet Only Banks: Such banks operate only through internet. All services are provided online and there are no physical branch locations for such internet only banks.

Adoption of Internet Banking: Using internet as a medium of transactions for a significant part of banking transactions. A number of factors (such as size, location, demography) may influence a bank to adopt internet banking.

Internet Banking Performance: Financial returns of the banks that use internet as a medium of providing banking services.

Online Trading: Using internet for security transactions.

Online Trading Participants: Investors who use internet for security trading. It is generally found that the online trading participants are more likely to be young male with investment experience, good salary, and large portfolio. Online traders tend to do excessive trading.

Online Trading Performance: Returns generated to the investors who use online trading. It is reported that generally individuals' performance dropped after switching from traditional brokerage-assisted trading to online trading. One major reason is the transaction cost related to excessive trading.

ENDNOTES

1. http://en.wikipedia.org/wiki/Internet_banking
2. https://www.sfcu.org/about
3. http://en.wikipedia.org/wiki/Stanford_Federal_Credit_Union
4. Cristina, T., Beatrice, C., and Florentina, P., "E-Banking – Impact, Risk, Security". Accessed online on June 5, 2010.
5. By year end 1999, there were approximately 10,000 U.S. banks and thrifts (Furst et al., 2002).
6. Banks with less than $1 billion in assets.

Section 4
E–Government Adoption Perspectives

Chapter 11

Review of Open Source Software (OSS):
Advantages and Issues Related with its Adoption in E–Government

Bhasker Mukerji
St. Francis Xavier University, Canada

Ramaraj Palanisamy
St. Francis Xavier University, Canada

ABSTRACT

The popularity of Open Source Software (OSS) in developing countries is quiet evident from its widespread adoption across government departments and public sector organizations. The use of OSS saves economic resources of cash starved countries, provides an opportunity to promote e-government, and to utilize their resources in other sectors. Many developing countries have a large pool of skilled developers who can modify the source code of the OSS at a very low cost. Many governments in developing and developed countries have switched to OSS which probably encourages others to follow the trend. It was not possible to follow the adoption trend in all the developing countries but the usage of OSS in countries like India, Brazil, and Venezuela provides us an insight. The successful adoption of OSS requires thorough analysis of its advantages as well as the issues associated with it. This chapter will provide an overview of OSS, characteristics of OSS developers, and their motivation to volunteer by contributing in OSS projects, followed by the advantages and issues associated with OSS.

DOI: 10.4018/978-1-60960-848-4.ch011

OVERVIEW OF OSS

The term open source software (OSS) was coined in early 1998 and since then it has become a topic of great interest among practitioners and academics because of its potential to revolutionize the traditional software development process. It is very closely associated with the free software movement (FSM) which started in early eighties. When "free software" was becoming popular there was a lot of confusion about the word "free" and it was not getting any serious attention from the business community. Therefore, some supporters of FSM, who advocated the involvement of business community in the movement decided to look for another terminology which could replace it without losing its essence. Thus, open source initiative (OSI), a non - profit organization was formed which took the responsibility of promoting this unique software development methodology. The purpose was to sort out the confusion created by the word "free" and replace it with something that would be acceptable to the companies. Open Source Initiative, a non-profit organization was formed which provided the "Open Source Definition" to clearly define the concept of OSS and remove the misconceptions. The open source definition suggests that other than providing the access code of the software, the distribution terms should also meet the following criteria (www. opensource.org):

1. **Free Redistribution:** The license shall not restrict any party from selling or giving away the software as a component of an aggregate software distribution containing programs from several different sources. The license shall not require a royalty or other fee for such sale.
2. **Source Code:** The program must include source code, and must allow distribution of both source code as well as compiled form. When some form of a product is not distributed with source code, there must be a well-publicized means of obtaining the source code for no more than a reasonable reproduction cost preferably, downloading via the Internet without charge. The source code must be the preferred form in which a programmer would modify the program. Deliberately obfuscated source code is not allowed. Intermediate forms such as the output of a preprocessor or translator are not allowed.
3. **Derived Works:** The license must allow modifications and derived works, and must allow them to be distributed under the same terms as the license of the original software.
4. **Integrity of the Author's Source Code:** The license may restrict source-code from being distributed in modified form only if the license allows the distribution of "patch files" with the source code for the purpose of modifying the program at build time. The license must explicitly permit distribution of software built from modified source code. The license may require derived works to carry a different name or version number from the original software.
5. **No Discriminationagainst Persons or Groups:** The license must not discriminate against any person or group of persons for downloading and using the software.
6. **No Discrimination against Fields of Endeavor:** The license must not restrict anyone from making use of the program in a specific field of endeavor. For example, it may not restrict the program from being used in a business, or from being used for generic research.
7. **Distribution of License:** The rights attached to the program must apply to all to whom the program is redistributed without the need for execution of an additional license by those parties.
8. **License Must Not Be Specific to a Product:** The rights attached to the program must not depend on a specific particular software dis-

tribution agenda. If the program is extracted from that distribution and used or distributed within the terms of the program's license, all parties to whom the program is redistributed should have the same rights as those that are granted in conjunction with the original software distribution.

9. **License Must Not Restrict Other Software:** The license must not place restrictions on other software that is distributed along with the licensed software. For example, the license must not insist that all other programs distributed on the same medium must be open-source software.

10. **License Must Be Technology-Neutral:** No provision of the license may be predicated on any individual technology or style of interface.

Licenses

All software, either proprietary or open source are distributed with license. The proprietary software license does not allow users to copy or distribute the software without the consent of the software manufacturer whereas the OSS licenses do not restrict the users from copying, modifying and redistributing the software.

The license associated with Open source or free software enforces the guidelines set up by the community that developed the software. The objectives of attaching a license with the open source or free software are:

1. To save the developers from any legal liability and to protect the freedom of the source code. The developers of software write the source code to the best of their ability and knowledge therefore they should not be held legally responsible if the software doesn't work nor has many bugs. As mentioned in the open source definition, if any modification is made in the code of the OSS, the new

version will still remain OSS and the user has to redistribute it with the same terms.

2. Protect the contribution of the developers by denying appropriation efforts (Bonaccorsi and Rossi, 2003).

The free software licenses have two main characteristics:

A. The derived product based upon the modifications made in the original source code should also remain free software.

B. The license associated with the original source code should remain the same with the derived product. It restricts the usage of free software for commercial gains.

Open source initiative takes a more business friendly approach towards the companies who are willing to use open source software and invites their participation in the development process (AlMarzouq et al., 2005). According to OSI, there are 61 different licenses approved by the various companies. The most common components differentiating these licenses from one another are (Krishnamurthy, 2003):

A. whether modification of the source code is allowed without returning it back to the community.

B. whether the user is allowed to combine OSS with proprietary software

C. whether it has conditions to give privileges to the community that developed the software.

The "classic" open source licenses which are most commonly used are – GPL, LGPL, BSD, MIT and MPL. It is advised by the OSI to use one of the existing licenses but still the developers have come up with their own licenses creating legal complexities. The companies using OSS have to be very cautious and need the advice of legal experts to understand the legal interpretations of the license associated with the software (OSI, 2006).

OSS Community

The rise in the usage of Internet proved to be a boon for the OSS users because Internet linked the "virtual developers" scattered all across the globe. Business community which was not comfortable with the ideology of "free software" perceived benefits from joining the OSS movement because of the business friendly approach of the OSI. The benefits and business opportunities which motivate the companies to join the OSS movement are discussed in detail in this chapter. The increase in support from the business community along with the rise in the number of voluntary developers provided the much required boost to the movement. Open source movement is just over a decade old and is not yet completely explored by the academic researchers. Most of the contribution has come from the practitioners' world though the interest of the academic researchers is on the rise. In the development of OSS, virtual communities are formed because the members are located all across the globe. Efforts are made to understand how these communities are formed and managed so far, whereas the researchers have mainly focused upon exploring the motivation of the members to participate in the development of OSS and to learn more about the characteristics of the developers. A person interested in getting involved with any OSS project generally goes to its webpage and downloads the current version of the software. He/She uses the software and then based upon his/her programming skills modifications in the source code are made to fix the existing bugs and posts it back to the community explaining the modifications, which if approved gets integrated in the next version of the software. Once, (s)he mails his/her own modifications to the community, other members of the community review the modifications and gives their opinion to it. The community of any OSS development project comprises of developers of the software as well as those people who test the software and inform the developers about the bugs in the software. Earlier, people were apprehensive about the abilities of these unknown and unseen people. They were considered to be young amateurs but later on it was found that most of these developers are trained professionals.

The OSS developer survey carried out by the International Institute of Infonomics at the University of Maastricht in Netherland was one of the most comprehensive studies of the demographics of OSS developers. The survey was conducted online between February 2002 and April 2002 and was distributed freely among software developers globally (Ghosh et al., 2002). The questionnaire consisted of multiple choice questions designed to reveal the following:

- Personal profile of the developer (age, gender, occupation, income, education etc.)
- Activity and experience in the OSS community.
- Comparisons of experiences in the OSS community and in the proprietary software field.
- Involvement and activity in the development of proprietary software
- Motivation for involvement in the OSS community (whether monetary gain is a factor)
- Compensation for contributions to the OSS community (direct or indirect compensation)

The analysis of the survey was based on responses gathered from 2784 participants, 71 percent of whom lived in Europe or Russia, and 13 percent lived in the United States. Some of the important findings of the survey are - OSS developers are mostly young men in their twenties (99 percent are male and only 1 percent are female). The surveys also showed that majority of the respondents were aged between 19 and 33. Only 25 percent were older than 30 years of age, and only 10 percent were older than 35. One of the more interesting findings relating developers' characteristics is the fact that, out of the 98.9 percent male respondents, only 41.4 percent were single. 18.6 percent had partners but live separately, while 18.8 percent had live-in partners and another 21.1 percent were married. Only 17 percent of the respondents had children, with one half of those having only one child. With almost 60 percent of the surveyed sample in some kind of relationship, the study's authors noted that, this finding dispels the "often-mentioned assumption that OSS (open source/free software) developers are singles that are bored and have no partnership obligations and responsibilities". The survey shows that the bulk of OS developers are professional programmers with high level of education. A good number of developers possess university degrees which make up 70 percent of all degrees among the respondents. The study shows that universities and the IT sector play a critical role in the development of OS community. 83% of all developers surveyed are employed in the IT sector or involved in similar tasks at universities. Software engineers form the largest group with a share of 16%, followed by students, programmers, and IT consultants. Another significant finding of this report is that a large portion of developers are employed although the majority of them contribute to open source projects without pay. The authors also note among the employed, which comprise two thirds of the sample, a "relatively high" share of 14 percent is self-employed. They conclude that the employment status of a developer does not seem to play a significant role within the OS community. The survey also found that OS developers are not among the top earners, which may be explained by the large share of students that form the OS community. Seven percent of the respondents earned nothing, while another 45 percent earned $2000 US dollars or less per month. The study finds that while the majority of OS contributors are professional software developers, most of the developers in the sample develop OS software as part of a hobby rather than a profes-

sion. According to the study, almost 70 percent of the respondents spend 10 hours a week or less on open source projects, with 23 percent spending only 2 hours a week. Nine percent spend between 20 and 40 hours per week on open source, with 7 percent spending more than 40 hours a week. Out of those who spend more than 40 hours per week on open source projects, 38 percent also spend more than 40 hours per week developing proprietary software. The survey also found that the majority of the respondents (95 percent) do not only use OS/FS at home but also at work, or at school. Most of the developers surveyed were involved in networking and Web services projects. Almost 48% preferred the Debian operating system, followed by Red Hat with 13.8 percent, Mandrake with 9.8 percent, and SuSE with 9.2 percent. For favoured desktop environments, Gnome and KDE came on top among respondents with Gnome at 32.4 percent and KDE at 30.2 percent. Overall, 71.9 percent of the respondents said that their past experience consisted of 1-5 projects. Eighteen percent have worked on 6-10 projects and 68.4 percent claimed to have prior experience of leading projects.

MOTIVATIONS BEHIND INVOLVEMENT IN OSS DEVELOPMENT

The development of software requires programming skills and more importantly an in-depth understanding of the problem that the software intends to solve or simplify the process of doing any task. It requires a lot of time and effort which is well compensated by the software companies to their personnel engaged in developing proprietary software. Initially, one of the most baffling issues for the researchers was to understand the motivational factors of the participants in an OSS projects. Most of the participants who are developing OSS do not get any monetary benefit out of it then why do they utilize their precious time in developing something which is not even protected by intellectual property rights (Ljunberg, 2000; Raymond, 2001; Lerner & Tirole, 2002).This is the major focus of research in the field of OSS development. Research conducted to determine the motivational forces have found the presence of various factors behind the involvement of developers in OSS projects.

The "Altruism factor" was suggested to be one of probable reasons explaining the participation of the individuals in OSS projects. The participants believed in doing something for their community and making a software that would be available for free to everyone was their way of supporting their community (Kogut and Meitu, 2001;Lakhani and Von Hippel, 2003). This theory explained the participation of those members who contributed in their leisure time but failed to explain the contribution of the participants who have devoted significant time in all the activities of the project (Bonaccorsi and Rossi, 2003). It was also assumed that participants in the OSS projects have desire for non-monetary rewards like status and reputation (Bezroukov, 1999; McDonald *et al*., 2003). Some researchers tried to explain the participation by claiming that contributors believe that the proprietary software development companies have no right to keep the source code of the software secret and making money by charging license fees (Kogut and Meitu, 2001). They perceived the involvement as an act of participating in a social movement and the zeal to develop OSS comes from the perceived competition with the proprietary software developing companies and the desire to excel in it. Hertel *et at*., (2003) argued that although open source movement is not a social movement but it has some similar characteristics of the social movement. Klanderman's (1997) model that explains participation in social movement is also useful in understanding the motivation to join OSS projects. He proposed three classes of motives:

1. **Collective Motives:** if the person perceives the goals of the movement to be valuable and attainable then he will actively participate.
2. **Social Motives:** if positive response is expected from colleagues, friends and family then it motivates people to join social movements.
3. **Reward motives:** the expected rewards from joining the movement motivates people.

Another model that explains the motivation of individuals to participate in OSS projects is the VIST model. The four components of VIST model that facilitates active participation in OSS projects are:

1. **Valence:** The subjective evaluation of the team goals determines whether to participate in the group activity.
2. **Instrumentality:** The perceived importance of one's contribution in achieving the goal determines the motivation of the individual.
3. **Self-efficacy:** The perceived level of accomplishment determines the level of motivation. If the individual fails to complete his task, then it reduces the level of motivation.
4. **Trust:** The amount of trust in the group, group members determines the level of motivation.

Intrinsic and Extrinsic Motivation Theory

The other theory that throws light upon the volunteered participation of the individuals in OSS projects is the intrinsic and extrinsic motivation theory. Ryan and Desi (2000) have defined intrinsic motivation as "doing an activity for inherent satisfaction" which is inherently interesting and enjoyable. An intrinsically motivated person does a task because of the fun or challenge associated with it but not for any reward. The reward is integrated in the activity itself. Csikszentmihalyi (1975) was the first psychologist to study the enjoyment dimension of intrinsic motivation. Having fun or enjoyment is the only reward that is associated with some activities and those who pursue them, do them solely to get this reward. He proposed a state of "flow" in which enjoyment is maximum, characterized by intense and focused concentration, confidence in one's ability and the enjoyment of doing the activity itself regardless of the result (Nakamura and Csikszentmihalyi 2003). This state of flow occurs when the skill of the person matches with the challenges associated with the task. In OSS projects some people are motivated to join the community because of the challenge associated with it (Bezroukov, 1999).

On the other hand, a task that is too difficult for the person to finish successfully would induce anxiety whereas a task that is too easy to do induces boredom. Enjoyable activities generate a feeling of achievement when the hurdle is overcome and the problem is resolved. In OSS projects, developers choose projects and their role that matches with their interest and skills, which is not possible in their regular jobs. The sense of creativity while accomplishing a task is another concept closely related to enjoyment based intrinsic motivation. Amabile (1996) considered intrinsic motivation to be the key determining factor in creativity which has defined creativity as an accomplishment of a task that is heuristic and the solution is novel and appropriate.

Another determinant of intrinsic motivation can be explained by the need for affiliation theory proposed by McClelland (1975). The community goal gets the highest priority when the members of the community do not try to achieve personal advantage at the cost of jeopardizing the benefits for the whole community and take pride at becoming a member of a group or community. They are intrinsically motivated to behave in an appropriate manner consistent with the norms of the community. Researchers have found a strong desire of belongingness among the members involved in the development of OSS projects (Lakhani and Wolf 2005). Participants in OSS projects exhibit pride in collective identities. The word "hacker" is considered an honor in the world of OSS community because their task is to solve coding problems and share it with other members. It does not include those people who steal or break through the source codes for their own benefit and create problems for others thus earning bad name for the community. Intrinsic motivation is also an act of being motivated to do something without being forced by commands and without being paid to do it (Lindenberg 2001). The cognitive evaluation theory (CET) proposed by Deci and Ryan (1985) seems to explain the factors that enhance the motivation of the developers of OSS. The expectation of reward, positive feedback gives rise to a feeling of competence which satisfies the psychological need for competence. This theory also suggests that the feeling of competence in itself cannot enhance intrinsic motivation if the person does not have the freedom to determine his behaviour. If this theory is applied in the OSS development context, the members of an OSS project have the autonomy to choose their task and the type of contribution they want to make which increases the level of intrinsic motivation.

Extrinsic motivation is based upon the economic model of human behavior which suggests that people behave in a particular way because of the external awards associated with the accomplishment of the task (Frey 1997). Extrinsically motivated person does any task in order to get some separable outcome which can be rewards, ego gratification, and identification (conscious valuing of activity-self endorsement of goals). Lerner and Tirole (2002) suggested that programmers continue to participate in OSS projects as long as the benefit exceeds the costs. They proposed that the benefits can be classified under two categories - immediate payoffs and delayed pay offs. The immediate payoffs from participating in an OSS project include:

A. The user is getting paid to participate in the OSS projects - Firms using the OSS based software for IT solutions hire skilled programmers to participate in OSS projects (Hars and Ou 2002; Hertel et. al 2003; Lakhani and Wolf 2005).

B. The user might need the particular software for his use. Research has shown that users have strong incentives to create solutions to meet their particular needs and their needs are the major source of innovation in various other fields - scientific instruments (Riggs and Von Hippel 1994), Sports Equipments (Franke and Shah 2003) and Industrial products. Therefore, the need of the user for particular software may motivate him to participate in the related OSS projects.

The delayed benefits for being associated with OSS projects are:

C. Job market signaling (Holstrom 1999) - participants in the OSS projects show their skills by solving problems and reviewing the codes or suggestions made by other participants. Therefore, employers looking for people with particular skills keep a close watch on the performance of the participants and give job offers to the eligible participants.

D. Improving the personal skills by solving the problems and learning from others' suggestions and reviews (Moody 2001). It also provides an opportunity to hone their existing skills and learn new skills. Therefore, learning is one of the major driving forces that motivate people to join OSS development projects (Ye and Kishida, 2003). When a participant writes a code, it is reviewed intensely before it becomes a part of the new version. Even after it becomes a part of the official code base, other members of the community keep on testing the code base and suggesting modifications. The problems in the codes or faulty logics are communicated back to the author which is a source of learning for the author. Therefore this whole

process improves the quality of the codes in a very short period of time and at the same time helps the participants to improve their skills. Lakhani and wolf (2005) conducted a survey to understand the motivation of the participants in OSS projects. They interviewed 637 participants involved in 287 different OSS projects and found that 58% of them participate due to their own need, 41.8% considered it a good opportunity to improve their skills. This is consistent with the studies in the area of innovation where some users had the need of some specific functionality which has led to innovation.

Some Interesting Empirical Studies

1. Hertel *et. Al.* (2003) have categorized the motivation to join an OSS project into:
    A. Intrinsic motivations
    B. Social comparison motivations.

They found after discussing with the members of the Linux kernel community that the motivation to develop an OSS comes from the desire to fulfill some underserved needs and to improve the existing software. These are considered to be the intrinsic motivational factors. Other than that, the desire to prove one's own worth by demonstrating the programming skills to others and building reputation among the software developer community are the social comparison motives to get involved with OSS projects. An empirical study was conducted to explore the motives to join OSS projects. The sample had 141 participants from 28 different countries. Most of them were from North America and Europe, 48% and 37% respectively. Almost 49% participants were involved in writing the codes whereas 51% were the frequent readers of the mailing list. The other details about their employment and the incentives are given in Table 1.

Table 1. Location, Employment and Incentives

Region	Percentage
North America	48%
Europe	37%
Australia	7%
Asia, South America and Africa	8%
Occupation	**Percentage**
Full-time employees	67%
Part-time employees	5%
Unemployed	5%
Students	23%
Incentives	**Percentage**
Received salary for participating	20%
Received money sometimes	23%
Unpaid volunteers	57%

The results of the study found the following factors that motivated the participants to get involved with the Linux development kernel:

A. General Identification factor as Linux user
B. Specific Identification factor as Linux developer
C. Improvement of the existing software
D. Career goals
E. Norm-oriented motives: appreciation from friends and colleagues
F. Social and political motives: working for the development of an OSS software
G. Hedonistic motives: loves programming and writing source codes.

2. Zhao and Deek (2004) surveyed the 133 participating in 73 open source projects and found that the major motivational factor for 64% of the users who participated in the open source development projects was personal development needs. Thirty two percent of the users participated in the projects because of the needs of their employers. The survey revealed that most of the participants contribute in the OSS projects by finding bugs, usability problems and suggesting new features in the software. Other tasks performed by limited number of participants are writing source codes, reviewing others source codes and documentation.

3. Another study by Boston consulting group also found that skill improvement and intellectual challenge are the most important reasons for participating in OSS development projects. The contributors are classified into four categories:
   A. Those who believe source codes should be open
   B. Those who consider it fun and challenging.
   C. Those who believe that participation enhances their skills
   D. Those who participate due to their work related needs

4. The FLOSS developer survey (Ghosh *et al.*, 2002) found that the most popular reason for joining an open source project was to learn new skills. One of the key findings is that OSS developers were likely to get involved with OSS development out of a desire to improve their programming skills, however, with time their interest in open source became material and political in nature. Nearly 80 percent of the respondents claimed that they started working on OSS to learn and develop new skills, and half of the sample said that their involvement with OSS gave them a chance to share knowledge and skills with other developers.

In addition to the above motives, other reasons for working on open source projects included: the desire to spread the growth OSS, desire to limit the power of large proprietary software companies, solving a specific problem (such as removing a bug), giving something back for the OSS they use, building reputation within the community and to job opportunities, feeling of responsibility to the software itself and to colleagues working on project, and the desire to get the job done.

ADVANTAGES OF ADOPTING OSS IN GOVERNMENT ORGANIZATIONS

The most important advantage of adopting OSS is that it helps to reduce government's IT expenditure and promotes e-Government. Generally, government spends substantial amount of money for proprietary software license fees. In a study done by vital wave consulting in South Africa, it was found that the government spends $350-$450 million dollars annually on software licenses and over $1.5 billion dollars for support and upgrades. Thus OSS is considered to be an alternative to proprietary software. It is expected that switching to OSS results in huge savings but surprisingly, it is difficult to get evidence to support this claim. According to Mr. Crawford Beveridge, Chairman Sun Microsystems for Europe, Middle East and Africa, "South Africa is ahead of Europe and North America when it comes to the adoption of open source technology but behind countries such as Brazil, where president Lula da Silva has led the charge to transform the technology the country's government uses".

It is important to mention here that companies developing proprietary software invest heavily in developing and marketing their software. Almost one-fourth of all proprietary software projects fail and more than half of all proprietary software projects face increase in budgeted development costs. This raises two important questions – Are companies developing proprietary software justified in charging high license fees and how much it would cost the government to customize and continuously upgrade the OSS. The low adoption cost of OSS is encouraging governments in various countries to consider it as a viable alternative at national, provincial and municipal levels. The successful adoption will depend upon the government's interest at the national level to pursue this option. Many South American and European countries already have the mandate of using OSS in their government computers which includes countries like Brazil, Argentina, Mexico, France, Germany, Italy, Spain and United Kingdom. In Asia countries like China, Japan, South Korea and India have started using OSS at different levels of the government. One of the most cited reasons for the popularity of OSS in these countries is that it reduces the dependence of the government on proprietary software. Since all of these countries have in-house skills, it is easier for them to customize the OSS to meet their requirements. In a country like India having 114 major languages, the use of proprietary software based on one language does not encourage its citizens to use e-government services at different levels. Use of OSS allows citizens to access e-government services in their native language and also promotes the use of computers in small towns and villages. Provincial governments and Municipalities have more restricted budget compared to the national government therefore, increase in the usage of OSS not only promotes e-government but also reduces the cost of providing various services to the citizens. Instead of using traditional methods, governments can save significant amount of time and money by communicating with its citizens through Internet and can also increase its efficiency. One of the provincial governments in India has made it mandatory to use Linux operating system in all the government high schools.

The advantages sought by the developed countries from adopting OSS are not much different from the developing countries. In a study conducted in UK it was found that long term savings, reliability, scalability and customizability are the most important reasons behind adopting OSS. Other developed countries like France and Canada also look for reducing government's IT expenditure and utilize the resources in improving the services to their citizens. Another benefit of adopting OSS is related to the geographical location of the members of the OSS development community. They are working at different time zones and at different parts of the globe which ensures quick response in case of any problem with the software. Researchers have found the quality of OSS to be of higher quality compared to its equivalent proprietary software and the development cost is much lower (Haruvy *et al.*, 2003; Wheeler, 2001). As mentioned earlier, OSS is considered to be very reliable because of its stringent peer review during its development stage (Andersson *et al.*, 2005; Murphy, 2001; Vowler, 2003). It is assumed that the source code of the OSS is tested by a large number of members thus reducing the chances of having any bug in the software. In spite of all the claims, reliability and security of OSS is an ongoing debate and is not yet established.

ISSUES ASSOCIATED WITH OSS ADOPTION

All the advantages of OSS mentioned above are the most common justifications given by various government organizations in developing as well as developed countries who have switched from proprietary software to OSS. It is also important to discuss the issues associated with OSS adoption which should be considered before taking the decision to adopt OSS in the IT infrastructure. The accomplishment of government's objectives from adoption of OSS is contingent upon whether it has pondered upon the issues and has developed strategies to overcome them.

As compared to proprietary software the technical support for the OSS may not be available to the user if any OSS vendor is not given the contract to provide services. The OSS developing community does not have any responsibility to provide any support related to installation or technical problems. The level of required technical support would vary depending upon the level of adoption of OSS. In government organizations, it is critical to have 24/7 availability of technical support because one of the key objectives of the e-government is to provide services to the citizens in an efficient and timely manner. In the time of crisis, although literally, the whole community is there to fix the problem, but no one is bound to provide the desired help promptly. Therefore the desired support may not be available when required (AlMarzouq *et al.*, 2005).

Companies like Red Hat, fill this gap by providing the much required services and technical support to their customers who have adopted OSS. Therefore, it appears that the adoption of OSS does not necessarily remove the organization's dependence on vendors. The organization may also face problems in finding vendors providing services to a particular OSS. Generally, companies who have formed their business model by providing services to their customers using OSS develop their expertise in limited number of open source products; especially the ones which are popular and widely adopted. But, for the relatively less popular OSS products, the support only comes from the community that developed the software which is extremely unreliable (Ven *et al.*, 2008). The government organizations have to either approach the vendors and take their services in choosing, installing, maintaining and upgrading the OSS or develop in-house expertise to be able to fix the problems if services are not available from the vendors.

One of the most commonly cited advantages of OSS is the availability of source code to its users. This may sound tempting but realistically, it requires technical skills to tweak the code to customize it (Krishnamurthy, 2003). In a study, Andersson *et al.* (2005) have found that organizations require higher level of technical knowledge while using OSS compared to any proprietary software because technical support was not always available from the OSS developer community. Hence most OSS products are used by technically skilled users but non-technical users are comfortable with proprietary software which is relatively more user friendly and does not require advanced technical skills. The lack of detailed documentation is another major hindrance in making OSS popular among the non-technical users. It is essential for the government organizations to estimate the level of complexity of the chosen OSS and the availability of in-house technical skills.

The cost advantage of OSS has been cited in the literature as one of the major reasons for increase in its usage by various government organizations but till date, we do not have enough evidence to support this claim. Studies by proprietary software companies have found that the "total cost" of implementing OSS products are higher than using proprietary software. By using OSS, the organization would avoid the license fee but have to spend on in-house training of the employees, services and support from the vendors. The long term advantages of adopting OSS might be higher but the short term adoption cost could be significantly higher (Vaughan-Nichols, 2004). Other than that, switching from proprietary software to OSS software may not only prove to be expensive but, at the same time could also affect efficiency and performance. The government organizations should conduct a study within their organization to estimate the total cost of adopting the chosen OSS and how it would affect their efficiency and performance before taking decision. In 2007, the Berlin city government had to decide whether or not to switch to OSS to save IT costs. They expected a possible reduction in IT cost by 50% (annual expenditure on IT was approximately 340 million USD). The government finally decided not to take the risk of switching completely to OSS but to use a mix of OSS and proprietary software for economic and performance reasons (Blau, 2007).

The OSS development process is not standardized in OSS communities because the level of participation, communication varies in each OSS development project. There are numerous OSS projects at Sourceforge.net having only few members. Therefore the software produced also varies in quality and it would be unrealistic to assume that all OSS are of superior quality (Al-Marzouq *et al.*, 2005). Earlier, we have discussed in detail the characteristics and the motivations of the OSS developers involved in various OSS projects. The objective of a typical OSS developer is not to develop software for non-technical users and they do not focus upon the "ease of use" or "user friendly" aspects of the interface because the ultimate users are mostly highly skilled people, not requiring detailed instructions. On the other hand, proprietary software companies consider the "ease of use" to be their utmost priority which distinguishes the objectives of two different approaches of software development. Therefore the government organizations should analyze the complexity of the OSS, its "ease of use" and reliability before switching to OSS. The OSS development model also has very high risk of patent infringement therefore government organizations should properly analyze the OSS products before adoption. There are numerous OSS licenses but so far, they are not rigorously tested in the court. The complexity and the number of the licenses makes it difficult to understand the legal implications if the government organization is using many OSS products (Vowler, 2003).

CONCLUSION

The OSS development model is gradually evolving and more and more companies are now participating in the developing process which has its own pros and cons. The characteristics and motivations of a typical OSS developer described in this chapter still holds true because the majority of OSS developers are volunteers dedicating their time not for any direct financial gains. The OSS literature discusses mostly the advantages associated with its adoption and the freedom it provides to its users in terms of access to source code and the cost advantages but the issues discussed in this chapter should be taken into consideration before switching from the existing proprietary software. The government organizations should not be influenced by the popularity of OSS and the claimed cost advantages. Decision should be made after careful evaluation of the issues associated with OSS.

Various government organizations in developing as well as developed countries are adopting OSS which is expected to play an important role in the implementation of an effective and efficient e-Government but we require empirical studies to confirm it. The usability of the chosen OSS should also be assessed because the typical users of OSS are technically skilled. Usability is different from utility and has five characteristics (Nielsen, 1993) – ease of learning, efficiency, memorability, error frequency and subjective satisfaction. The technical skills required to efficiently use OSS is strongly related with the usability of the OSS. The non-technical employees will adopt OSS only if it scores high on the above mentioned five characteristics of usability. The widespread adoption and sustainability of OSS is contingent upon whether the government organizations have carefully evaluated all the issues associated with the OSS.

As discussed in this chapter, the major challenges in adopting OSS in e-government applications are lack of technical support, absence of proper documentation, reliability and security aspects of the OSS, usability and others. Before adopting OSS, these issues are to be addressed by the government agencies in consultation with their in-house system development personnel. Justifications for adopting OSS in specific application areas of e-government could be identified by bench marking of some of the already implemented systems by other agencies. It is reasonable to emphasize the need for tailoring the OSS to specific application requirements. Thereby the success of adoption depends on customizing the OSS for the given e-government situation. This demands a strong in-house team for doing this task. Case studies on these issues and challenges are suggested for further research.

REFERENCES

Al Marzouq, M., Li, Z., Guang, R., & Varun, G. (2005). Open source: Concepts, benefits and challenges. *Communications of the AIS, 16.*

Amabile, T. M. (1996). *Creativity in content.* New York, NY: Westview Press.

Andersson, A., Hassler, K., & Nedstam, J. (2005). *Open source business models in practice: A survey of commercial open source introduction.* Lund University.

Bezroukov, N. (1999). A second look at the cathedral and the bazaar. *First Monday, 4*(12).

Blau, J. (2007). Berlin rejects call for open source. *Computer World*, May.

Bonaccorsi, A., & Rossi, C. (2003). Why open source software can succeed. *Research Policy, 32*, 1243–1258. doi:10.1016/S0048-7333(03)00051-9

Csikszentmihalyi, M. (1975). *Beyond boredom and anxiety: The experience of play in work and games.* San Francisco, CA: Jossey-Bass, Inc.

Deci, E. L., & Ryan, R. M. (1985). *Intrinsic motivation and self-determinaton in human behaviour.* New York, NY: Pienum.

Franke, N., & Shah, S. (2003). How communities support innovative activities: An exploration of assistance and sharing among end users. *Research Policy, 32*(1), 157–178. doi:10.1016/S0048-7333(02)00006-9

Frey, B. (1997). *Not just for money: An economic theory of personal motivation.* Brookfield, WI: Edward Elger Publishing Company.

Hars, A., & Ou, S. (2002). Working for free? Motivations for participating in open-source projects. *International Journal of Electronic Commerce, 6*(3), 25–39.

Haruvy, E., Prasad, A., & Sethi, S. P. (2003). Harvesting altruism in open source software development. *Journal of Optimization Theory and Applications, 118*(2), 381–416. doi:10.1023/A:1025455523489

Hertel, G., Niedner, S., & Herrmann, S. (2003). Motivation of software developers in open source projects: An Internet-based survey of contributors to the Linux kernel. *Research Policy, 32,* 1159–1177. doi:10.1016/S0048-7333(03)00047-7

Holmstrom, B. (1999). Managerial incentive problems: A dynamic perspective. *The Review of Economic Studies, 66,* 169–182. doi:10.1111/1467-937X.00083

Klanderman, B. (1997). *The social psychology of protest.* Oxford, UK: Blackwell Publishers.

Kogut, B., & Metiu, A. (2001). Open-source software development and distributed innovation. *Oxford Review of Economic Policy, 17*(2), 248–264. doi:10.1093/oxrep/17.2.248

Krishnamurthy, S. (2003). A managerial overview of open source software. *Business Horizons,* 47–56. doi:10.1016/S0007-6813(03)00071-5

Lakhani, K., & von Hippel, E. (2003). How open source software works: "Free" user-to-user assistance. *Research Policy, 32,* 923–943. doi:10.1016/S0048-7333(02)00095-1

Lakhani, K. R., & Wolf, R. B. (2005). Why hackers do what they do: Understanding motivation and effort in free/open source software projects. In Feller, J., Fitzgerald, B., Hissam, S., & Lakhani, K. R. (Eds.), *Perspectives on free and open source software.* MIT Press.

Lerner, J., & Tirole, J. (2002). Some simple economics of open source. *The Journal of Industrial Economics, 50*(2), 197–234. doi:10.1111/1467-6451.00174

Lindenberg, S. (2001). Intrinsic motivation in a new light. *Kyklos, 54*(2/3), 317–342.

Ljungberg, J. (2000). Open source movements as a model for organizing. *European Journal of Information Systems, 9*(4). doi:10.1057/palgrave/ejis/3000373

McClelland, D. C. (1975). *Power: The inner experience.* New York, NY: Halstead.

McDonald, C. J., Schadow, G., Barnes, M., Dexter, P., Overhage, J. M., & Mamlin, B. (2003). Open source software in medical informatics. *International Journal of Medical Informatics, 69*(2/3), 175–184. doi:10.1016/S1386-5056(02)00104-1

Moody, G. (2001). *Inside Linux and the open source revolution.* New York, NY: Perseus Press.

Murphy, T. (2001). *Evaluate open source risks.* Retrieved from http://ftponline.com/wss/2002_10/online/tmurphy

Nakamura, J., & Csikszentmihalyi, M. (2003). The construction of meaning through vital engagement. In Keyes, C. L., & Haidt, J. (Eds.), *Flourishing: Positive psychology and the life well-lived.* Washington, DC: American Psychological Association. doi:10.1037/10594-004

Nielsen, J. (1993). *Usability engineering.* Boston, MA: Academic Press.

Raymond, E. S. (2001). *The cathedral & the bazaar* (2nd ed.). Sebastapol, CA: O'Reilly.

Riggs, W., & von Hippel, E. (1994). Incentives to innovate and the sources of innovation: The case of scientific instruments. *Research Policy, 23*(4), 459–469. doi:10.1016/0048-7333(94)90008-6

Ryan, R. M., & Desi, E. L. (2000). Intrinsic and extrinsic motivations: Classic definitions and new directions. *Contemporary Educational Psychology, 25,* 54–67. doi:10.1006/ceps.1999.1020

Vaughan-Nichols, S. J. (Jan 2004). Novell embraces open source. *eWeek.* Ziff Davis Media Inc.

Vowler, J. (April 2003). Finding out the hidden cost of open source. *Computer Weekly.*

Wheeler, D. A. (2001). More than a gigabuck: Estimating Linux's size. Retrieved on December 20, 2005, from http://www.dwheeler.com/sloc/redhat71-v1/redhat71sloc.html

Ye, Y., & Kishida, K. (2003). Toward an understanding of the motivation of open source software developers. In *Proceedings of the International Conference on Software Engineering*. Portland.

Zhao, L., & Deek, F. P. (2004). User collaboration in open source software development. *Electronic Markets, 14*(2), 89–103. doi:10.1080/10196780 410001675040

KEY TERMS AND DEFINITIONS

Open Source Software: The free distribution of software over the Internet containing programs from several different sources. The license shall not require a royalty or other fee for such sale.

Free Software Movement: The free distribution of software over the Internet and the license for such distribution shall not restrict any party from selling or giving away the software as a component of an aggregate software distribution containing programs from several different sources.

Open Source Initiative (OSI): A non - profit organization was formed which took the responsibility of promoting the free software development methodology.

E-Government: The use of new technologies such as Internet by the Government agencies to communicate, provide information and services in an interactive way to the citizens.

OSS Community: The developers of open source software scattered across the globe formed a virtual community known as OSS community.

OSS License: Licenses set up by the OSI for protecting the developers from any legal liability and to protect the freedom of the source code.

Chapter 12
Survey of Citizens' Perceptions in the Adoption of National Governmental Portals

Teta Stamati
National and Kapodistrian University of Athens, Greece

Athanasios Karantjias
University of Pireaus, Greece

Drakoulis Martakos
National and Kapodistrian University of Athens, Greece

ABSTRACT

The transformational role of e-government can be achieved through engagement of the citizens in the e-government rollout and subsequent adoption. The present study integrates constructs from the Technology Acceptance Model, Diffusions of Innovation Theory and Trust Models in order to propose a research model to guide future e-government initiatives. The critical acceptance factors, namely: trust, security, and regulation are analyzed for the citizens' adoption process. The citizen's perceptions of electronic services adoption are analyzed based on the case study of the National Governmental Portal.

INTRODUCTION

Electronic services have become a critical force in service oriented economies. The trend towards transformational government (t-Gov) has emerged mainly by the aspirations of citizens regarding Governments' performance and efficiency, regulation, trust and security (Gil-Garcial et al. 2007). The impact of technological innovations on

Governments has been profound, with increased collaboration between agencies to deliver seamless services, increased participation of citizens in policy and decision making, delivery of location aware public services, and new paradigms like connected governance, ubiquitous and ambient public services, knowledge-based administration and participatory budgeting.

Within this context, a significant number of Governments have constructed their presence on the web through the National Portals. In Greece,

DOI: 10.4018/978-1-60960-848-4.ch012

the public agencies are currently attempting to enhance their web presence providing electronic services to citizens through the National Governmental Portal, namely 'ERMIS' (www.ermis.gov.gr). Through the portal of 'ERMIS', the agencies have started offering various categories of online services, as introduced by Moon (2002), regarding information, interaction and transaction. E-government projects are becoming increasingly important for Greek Government and the public administration bases its decision to move forward with modern e-platforms expecting benefits such as better services, operational savings and increased program effectiveness (Stamati & Martakos, 2010).

'ERMIS' portal is attempting the modernization of the public administration providing added value services to citizens. The portal operates as a one-stop-shop service provider regarding the transactions with the Greek Government. From an operational point of view, 'ERMIS' is moved in three fundamental axes that concern: (i) the management of the information of the public administration and its disposal to the Internet in order to provide reliable briefing to citizens and enterprises regarding their transactions with the governmental mechanism; (ii) the growth of essential infrastructures providing interoperability between the information systems and the applications of the public administration for electronic transactions; (iii) the authentication of citizens and enterprises in the frame of benefit of secure services.

The chapter discusses the societal factors affecting the adoption of National Governmental Portals in the developing countries. The objective of the study is to present a model for e-government services adoption. The model identifies the fundamental concepts that impact intention to adopt e-government services. The proposed model, namely *t-Gov adoption Model*, identifies that the items of perceived trust, perceived security and supporting legislation and regulatory framework are determinant for e-government adoption. The

model is constructed based on the theory of reasoned action (TRA) (Ajzen & Fishbein, 1972). It extends and streamlines the Technology Acceptance Model proposed by Davis (1986) and the Diffusions of Innovation Theory proposed by Rogers (1995).

Based on the theoretical and empirical support from the services sciences, the study tested a number of research hypotheses which are formulated in the assessment phase. Based on qualitative research, the fundamental model constructs are evaluated using the interpretive techniques of focus groups and in depth interviews. The measurement of the model is conducted by creating the latent model. The statistic assessment is conducted in two phases, namely exploratory and confirmatory and it is based on methods and statistic indicators utilizing the statistic packages of SPSS and LISREL. The empirical assessment of the model is based on the positivistic approach. An assessment instrument has been developed for the data collection. The concepts of the model are operationalized to measurable variables and the measurement scales are created. The reliability and the validity of the measurement instrument are assessed. The data for the theory evaluation comes from the case study of the implementation of 'ERMIS'.

CONCEPTUAL MODEL

This study integrates constructs from well established adoption models based on the Technology Acceptance Model (Gefen & Straub, 2000; Moon & Kim, 2001; Pavlou, 2003), Diffusions of Innovation (Van Slyke et al., 2004), Security Theory (Karantjias, et al., 2009; Karantjias et al., 2010) and Trust Models (Bélanger et al., 2002; 2010; McKnight et al., 2002; Gefen et al., 2003; Stamati & Martakos, 2011) into a parsimonious model of e-government adoption.

Technology Acceptance Model

Examining the reasons that affect people's acceptance or rejection of new technologies has been one challenging issues in the study of services sciences (Stamati & Martakos, 2011). Among the various efforts to understand the process of user acceptance of an innovation, the Technology Acceptance Model (TAM), introduced by Davis (1986), is one of the most well established theoretical frameworks (Swanson, 1988). The model attempts both to explain the key factors of user acceptance of information systems and to predict the importance of the factors in the diffusion of technological systems (Davis, et al., 1989). The model is trying to derive the determinants of computer acceptance that is general, capable of explaining user behaviour across a broad range of end-user computing and systems technologies, while is trying to be parsimonious and theoretically justified (Davis et al., 1989).

TAM explores the factors that affect behavioural intention to use information systems and suggests a linkage between the key variables, namely, perceived usefulness and perceived ease of use and users' attitude, behavioural intention, and actual system adoption and use (Davis, 1986). According to TAM, perceived usefulness (PU) and perceived ease of use (PEOU) influence one's attitude towards system usage, which influences one's behavioural intention to use a system, which in turn, determines actual system usage (Davis et al., 1989).

TAM is a path model that begins with the impact of external factors. These can be system design characteristics, user characteristics, nature of the development or implementation process, political influences, organizational structure, and so on (Ajzen & Fishbein, 1980; Irani et al., 2005). It suggests that information system usage is determined by behavioural intention, which is viewed as being jointly determined by the user's attitude toward using the system and the PU of the system (Davis et al., 1989).

Since Davis' (1986) introduction of TAM, many studies have been conducted using it in a number of systems usages, testing its appropriateness and modifying it in different contexts. Past research on the model has largely focused on personal computer usage or relatively simple software applications (Chau, 1996; Davis, 1993; Davis et al., 1989; Mathieson, 1991). Recently, in line with the development of web-based technologies, applications of the TAM have been made in the areas of organizational contexts (Hu et al., 1999; Venkatsh, 1999), e-commerce (Jiang et al, 2000), digital library systems (Davies, 1997) and e-government (Carter & Bélanger, 2004; Stamati & Martakos, 2011).

Although TAM is a well established and documented model for explaining technology acceptance by users, the model has been unable to account comprehensively for the factors that affect users' acceptance of technology systems, due to the original model's intended generality and simplicity (Carter & Bélanger, 2004; Stamati & Martakos, 2011). The main TAM's drawback is its lack of explicit inclusion of predecessor variables that influence PEOU and PU (Dishaw & Strong, 1999; Irani et al., 2005). Davis (1989) also claimed that further research should explore other variables that could affect PEOU, PU and actual use. Thus, it is necessary to further investigate the users' acceptance of technology systems with additional constructs considering the specific technology adoption contexts.

Diffusion of Innovation

The Diffusion of Innovation (DOI) theory, introduced by Rogers (1995), explains user adoption and diffusion of new technologies. According to Rogers (1995), the term of 'diffusion' refers to the process by which an innovation is communicated through channels over time among the members of a social society. The rate of diffusion is affected by an innovation's relative advantage, complexity, compatibility, trialability and observability.

The construct of 'trialability' refers to the degree by which an idea can be experimented with on a limited basis (Rogers, 1995), while the construct of 'observability' refers to the degree by which the results of an innovation are visible (Rogers, 1995). Tornatzky & Klein (1982), according to their survey, concluded that relative advantage, compatibility and complexity are the most relevant constructs to adoption research, while they excluded the constructs of 'trialability' and 'observability'.

Trust and Security

Trust and security are key enablers of the Information Society since end-users should use and feel comfortable with electronic services and have confidence that their online transactions are trustworthy and secure. Similarly, consumers, small and medium enterprises as well as big organizations should use electronic services with confidence in the security and trust of their enterprise integrations and provided services. As access to the Internet diversifies, from personal computers to advanced mobile and wireless devices, people feel increasingly concerned about the protection of their assets and privacy in this networked world. These aspects will become more and more important as the service oriented economies moves towards the smart digital environments based on many interacting objects, devices and systems.

The introduction of cloud and social computing, which have grown from being a promising business concept to one of the fastest growing segments of the IT industry, trust and security are very important requirements of every new enterprise implementation. Recession-hit companies are increasingly realizing that simply by tapping into the cloud they can gain fast access to best-of-breed business applications or drastically boost their infrastructure resources, all at negligible cost. But as more and more information on individuals and companies is placed in the cloud and can be accessed from multiple communities, concerns are beginning to grow about just how safe an environment it is.

Current practices indicate e-Government services, despite their technological integration approach, succeed in their business goals when entities involved trust them. Surveys performed on this prove that the success of governmental portals is primarily attributed to the fact that they have built the trust of citizens (Karantjias et al., 2009; Karantjias et al., 2010). At the same time, the lack of citizens' trust, identified as one of the greatest barriers inhibiting online government transactions, continues to be high (Bélanger et al., 2002; 2010; McKnight et al., 2002; Gefen et al., 2003).

Security and privacy concerns are still holding up pilot projects/adoption plans, since social tools make many things that were normally private much more public, including policies, procedures, critical methods, corporate data, and intellectual property. Therefore many organizations choose to wait for best practices in dealing with this important issue to solidify before climbing very far up the social computing adoption curve.

Despite the technological advancements and the adoption of trust building mechanisms by online citizens, such as trust seals and security and privacy policies, the portion of Internet users who do not trust online sites has increased. This suggests that although Internet users become increasingly familiar with electronic services, they are also increasingly concerned and reluctant in engaging in online transactions. This paradox is possibly attributed to new threats and risks that emerge in a non-stop fashion, such as product-based deception, or old ones that have never ceased to exist, such as privacy and information misuse (Karantjias et al., 2010). Therefore, building citizens' trust is still a major challenge for Governments and how it can be accomplished within an e-government environment remains an open issue.

An e-government service should make use of security services and mechanisms supported by the environment or architecture where it is deployed.

There are five critical security requirements that need to be satisfied (Karantjias et al., 2010):

- **authentication:** the method with which an entity is uniquely identified and its identity verified;
- **integrity:** the method that ensures that every system, resource, file and information in general can be modified only by authorized entities;
- **privacy and confidentiality:** the method by which access to the content of information is available only to authorized recipients;
- **non-repudiation:** the method that produces cryptographic data that ensure that an entity cannot repudiate its actions; and
- **availability:** the method that ensures that a system can fulfil its purpose with a given degree of success.

Security mechanisms are stand alone instances of components that are directly embedded within an e-government enterprise service and that addresses a security requirement based on a policy. Security services on the other hand, are independent services within an e-government architecture that are available to any enterprise service wishing to perform a security goal as part of a policy. Security services integrate security mechanisms, and may interact with other security services as part of their operation. Security mechanisms may also interact with security services to send and receive information.

The latest incarnation of a distributed computing framework is the Services Oriented Architectures (SOAs). However, these objectives are often completely lost when advanced security integration is added. Until now, most SOA developments have relied on application or system level authentication and authorization for

establishing simple trusted user identity features, causing the following obstacles such as (Karantjias et al., 2010):

i. the service providers (SPs) have to implement multiple, different and separate authentication and authorization mechanisms for their applications and systems. This is rather expensive and difficult for an SP to manage and administer, while is inefficient for the end-users who have to manage multiple identities;

ii. every attempt to interconnect separate applications in order to add value and build more advanced e/m-services, often means linking separate user e/m-access security processes. This is rather complex and difficult to achieve from the technical point of view. The usual solution is to lower the level of security and privacy to these systems and applications, while the end-users are not able to easily handle their identifiers and credentials; and

iii. very few of these solutions adopt the user perspective, who needs to simplify his entrance in a large scale enterprise framework and receive high quality of advanced e-Government services.

The increasing regulatory compliance and audit requirements are additional burdens for the SPs forcing them to consider a higher assurance level for user identity in e/m-provision of services, which impose the implementation of proprietary security mechanisms with questionable levels of usability, manageability, and scalability (Karantjias et al., 2010).

Worldwide accepted and mature standards, specifications, and protocols lay on the foundation for solutions and new security models that allow trusted user identity to be digitally and effectively managed across multiple and different security domains and enterprise systems. However, current implementations and architectures based on these do not actually gain the benefits of a truly parametrizable e/m-environment in which existing modules can be easily merged.

The uplift of the above mentioned obstacles requires more than advanced communications protocols. What is needed is an efficient and practical way to use these standards and integrate a synchronous architecture, which will be able to introduce automation and system support of the identity management equally at the user and the SP sides. Based on it, enterprises should be able to easily build end-to-end identity infrastructures, supporting interoperable applications.

Regulatory Framework

E-government is conceptualized as the intensive or generalized usage of information technologies for the provision of added-value e-services, and the improvement of its managerial effectiveness, promoting high democratic values and mechanisms. Therefore, the integration of ICTs for the public sector should also produce changes and reengineering of current administrative units workflows which are affected from the established legal and regulatory framework in every country (Stamati & Karantjias, 2011).

However, public administrations are governed by specific regulations that are different from those which govern the relationships between individuals. Current legal frameworks are characterized by the assignment of significant powers to public bodies and the recognition of relevant formal guarantees for citizens, based typically on a correct observance by public administrations of a legally predetermined bureaucratic-based sequence of steps. Consequently, many rules become obstacles to the effective implementation of e-Government, while they erode its confidence among citizens, since they are made too rigid to accommodate the changes made possible by the solutions conveyed by ICT professionals.

Taking this into account, initiatives promoted by European Member States to develop the use of ICT in the public sector, aimed at trying to over- come potential problems arising from the need to adapt the legal framework of their public administrations to the new challenges and problems. However, essential reforms are still necessary in order to overcome some of the barriers imposed by specific parts of the Administrative Law regulation, such as the Directives on data protection, the use of digital signatures, and the Personal Identification Information (PII) management.

Focusing on the security and privacy, previously described, legislation and laws should provide the basis for ensuring an adequate level of compliance to international regulations and laws as well as giving internal direction. Recent regulatory developments in the liability of enterprises and management, such as the USA Sarbanes-Oxley Act, the Australian equivalent, the Corporate Law Economic Reform Program and the requirements stated in Basel II have made senior executives more accountable for ensuring the quality of organizational information, which is achieved through effective information assurance management. The increased demand from society for the protection of privacy and personal data has led several countries to develop their own privacy laws, for example the Australian Privacy Act and the European data protection directive.

Many developed countries have yet to consider adopting adequate legislation related to information security management, laws that criminalize cyber attacks and enable police to adequate investigate and prosecute such activities.

Research Hypotheses

The proposed adoption model is based on the Theory of Reasoned Action (TRA), according to which beliefs influence intentions, and intentions influence one's actions (Ajzen & Fishbein, 1972). TRA, introduced by Martin Fishbein and Icek Ajzen (1975, 1980), is derived from previous research that started out as the theory of attitude, which led to the study of attitude and behaviour. TRA stresses that individual behaviour is driven

Figure 1. Conceptual framework 1 – t-Gov adoption model

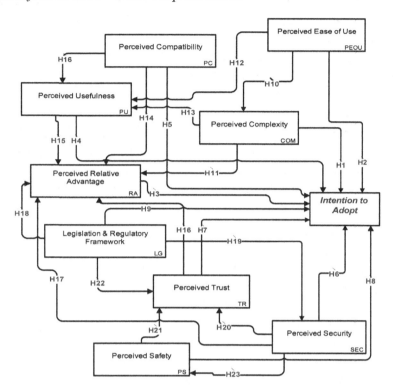

by behavioural intentions, where behavioural intentions are a function of an individual's attitude toward the behaviour and subjective norms (Ajzen & Fishbein, 1972). Attitude toward the behaviour is defined as the individual's feelings about performing the behaviour (Ajzen and Fishbein, 1972). It is designated through an evaluation of one's beliefs regarding the consequences arising from a behaviour and an evaluation of the desirability of these consequences (Ajzen & Fishbein, 1972). Thus, overall attitude can be assessed as the sum of the individual consequence multiplied by the desirability assessments, for all expected consequences of the behaviour. Subjective norm is defined as an individual's perception of whether people important to the individual think the behaviour should be performed (Ajzen & Fishbein, 1972). The contribution of the opinion of any given referent is weighted by the motivation that an individual has to comply with the wishes of that

referent. Hence, overall subjective norm can be expressed as the sum of the individual perception multiplied by the motivation assessments, for all relevant referents.

Considering the aforementioned adoption theories, the initial conceptual framework of for e-government adoption extends the existing theoretical frameworks, as presented in figure 1.

The Conceptual Framework 1 of the t-Gov Adoption Model consists of nine research constructs, namely:

- **perceived ease of use (PEOU):** the degree to which a person believes that using a particular system would enhance his or her job performance (Davis, 1986);
- **perceived usefulness (PU):** the degree to which one person believes that using a particular system would be free of effort (Davis, 1986);

- **perceived complexity (COM):** the degree to which a person believes that an innovation is being relatively difficult to use and understand (Rogers, 1995). Complexity is comparable to the construct 'Perceived Ease of Use';
- **perceived compatibility (PC):** the degree to which a person believes that an innovation is seen to be compatible with existing values, beliefs, experiences and needs of adopters (Rogers, 1995). This means that the person believes that using a particular system would be according to the way that the person is used to interact with other people;
- **perceived relative advantage (RA):** the degree to which a person believes that an innovation is seen as being superior to its predecessor (Rogers, 1995);
- **perceived security (SEC):** the degree to which a person believes that using a particular system would be secure;

Table 1. Initial research hypotheses

Hypothesis 1 (H1)	Higher levels of perceived complexity will reduce intention to adopt 'ERMIS'
Hypothesis 2 (H2)	Higher levels of perceived ease of use will increase intention to adopt 'ERMIS'
Hypothesis 3 (H3)	Higher levels of perceived relative advantage will increase intention to adopt 'ERMIS'
Hypothesis 4 (H4)	Higher levels of perceived usefulness will increase intention to adopt 'ERMIS'
Hypothesis 5 (H5)	Higher levels of perceived compatibility will increase intention to adopt 'ERMIS'
Hypothesis 6 (H6)	Higher levels of perceived security will increase intention to adopt 'ERMIS'
Hypothesis 7 (H7)	Higher levels of perceived trust will increase intention to adopt 'ERMIS'
Hypothesis 8 (H8)	Higher levels of perceived safety will increase intention to adopt 'ERMIS'
Hypothesis 9 (H9)	Higher levels of perceived supporting legislation and regulatory framework will increase intention to adopt 'ERMIS'
Hypothesis 10 (H10)	Higher levels of perceived ease of use will reduce perceived complexity of 'ERMIS'
Hypothesis 11 (H11)	Higher levels of perceived complexity will reduce perceived relative advantage of 'ERMIS'
Hypothesis 12 (H12)	Higher levels of perceived ease of use will be positively related to higher levels of perceived usefulness of 'ERMIS'
Hypothesis 13 (H13)	Higher levels of perceived complexity will reduce perceived usefulness of 'ERMIS'
Hypothesis 14 (H14)	Higher levels of perceived compatibility will be positively related to higher levels of perceived relative advantage of 'ERMIS'
Hypothesis 15 (H15)	Higher levels of perceived usefulness will be positively related to higher levels of perceived relative advantage of 'ERMIS'
Hypothesis 16 (H16)	Higher levels of perceived trust will be positively related to higher levels of perceived relative advantage of 'ERMIS'
Hypothesis 17 (H17)	Higher levels of perceived security will be positively related to higher levels of perceived relative advantage of 'ERMIS'
Hypothesis 18 (H18)	Higher levels of perceived supporting legislation and regulatory framework will be positively related to higher levels of perceived relative advantage of 'ERMIS'
Hypothesis 19 (H19)	Higher levels of perceived supporting legislation and regulatory framework will be positively related to higher levels of perceived security of 'ERMIS'
Hypothesis 20 (H20)	Higher levels of perceived security will be positively related to higher levels of perceived trust of 'ERMIS'
Hypothesis 21 (H21)	Higher levels of perceived safety will be positively related to higher levels of perceived security of 'ERMIS'
Hypothesis 22 (H22)	Higher levels of perceived supporting legislation and regulatory framework will be positively related to higher levels of perceived trust of 'ERMIS'
Hypothesis 23 (H23)	Higher levels of perceived security will be positively related to higher levels of perceived safety of 'ERMIS'

- **perceived trust (TR):** the degree to which a person believes that using a particular system would be trustfulness;
- **perceived safety (PS):** the degree to which a person believes that using a particular system would be safe;
- **perceived supporting legislation and regulatory framework (LG):** the degree to which a person believes that using a particular system would be according to the legislation.

The resulting research hypotheses of the theoretical framework are as follows in Table 1:

DATA COLLECTION

In order to explain and justify the choice of the methodology that the researchers employed in conducting the empirical study, we present a short description of the reasons for selecting the research approach and strategy together with a short description of the most appropriate methods of collecting data for the research. The following table summarizes the main characteristics of the three main types of philosophy namely the positivist school, the interpretivist school and the critical social school.

The study is conducted according both to the interpretivist school and the positivist school as figure 2 presents.

Interpretive Research

The study deals with the adoption of e-government services, and it is therefore necessary to understand in depth the adoption process from the point of view of its meaning for the citizens as a social contract. Therefore, the research approach that was initially followed is described as being broadly

Table 2. Types of philosophy for IS research

School of Philosophy	Characteristics	References
Positivist	- assumes reality is objectively given and can be described by measurable properties; - independent of researchers and their instruments; - tends to produce quantitative data; - concerns hypothesis testing; - seeks to test theory; - knowledge consists of facts that are independent; - data are highly specific and precise.	Walsham (1995); Yin (2003); Remenyi (1998); Denzin & Lincoln (1998); Hussey & Hussey (1997); Lee & Baskerville (2003); Myers (1997); Orlikowski & Baroudi (1991); Oates (2006).
Interpretivist	- seeks to describe, understand and translate phenomena through meanings that people assign to them; - aims to understand the context of IS and how it is influenced by context; - aims to understand the deeper structure of phenomena within cultural and contextual situations; - data rich and subjective; - tends to produce qualitative data; - often concerned with generating theories.	Yin (2003a); Remenyi (1998); Denzin & Lincoln (1998); Hussey & Hussey (1997); Lee & Baskerville (2003); Myers (1997).
Critical	- reality is historically constituted; - the epistemological position is that the researcher and the investigated object are interactively linked; - knowledge of the social world is value loaded; - it exposes and critiques unjust and inequitable conditions in society from which people require liberation; it does not only seek to understand social phenomenon.	Guba & Lincoln (1994); Lee (1991); Orlikowski and Baroudi (1991); Oates (2006).

Figure 2. Research method

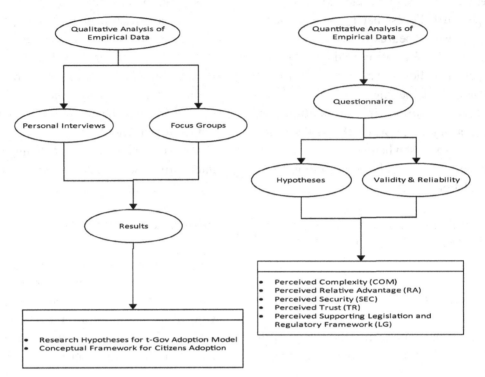

interpretive. The main reasons behind this choice are the following:

- interpretive studies usually attempt to understand phenomena through the meanings that people assign to them. In our case, the interpretivist approach allowed the researchers to study empirically the factors that encourage or hinder the adoption of 'ERMIS' in a natural setting. These factors are influenced by many research issues and disciplines; such as organizational, managerial, technical and social; and
- the unit of analysis in this research is the Greek Government which is a complex social structure and is managed and controlled by different people's sense-making: that is the e-government adoption process influences and is influenced by them. Therefore, the interpretivist approach is

the most useful approach to adopt in understanding this process.

The following paragraphs explain the data collection methods that have been used under the umbrella of the case study.

Focus Groups

Focus groups refer to the form of group interview that capitalizes on communication between research participants in order to generate data. Although group interviews are often used simply as a quick and convenient way to collect data from several people simultaneously, focus groups explicitly use group interaction as part of the method.

The research conducted four focus group sessions designed to elicit perceptions from various stakeholder groups involved with 'ERMIS'. These focus groups occurred throughout the first eight months of the study. A total of 57 citizens were

Table 3. Focus groups

Focus Group (FG)	Duration	Participants No	Role of Participants
FG1	4 h	30	employees of public sector, staff from private IT companies, citizens
FG2	3 h	14	employees from the Ministry of Interior, employees from the private IT company that was implementing the 'ERMIS' portal
FG3	2,5 h	5	the team that was responsible for the implementation of 'ER-MIS' portal
FG4	3,5h	8	potential adopters of 'ERMIS' portal

participated in these sessions. Table 3 summarizes the types of participants at each focus group.

Focus groups brought together 'ERMIS' stakeholders who shared interests in common themes (e.g. public interest, technological and managerial issues, etc). The focus group sessions provided opportunities to explore shared beliefs and goals concerning 'ERMIS' portal. The researchers included selected individuals at each focus group session to ensure content rich qualitative data from perspectives that would encompass the range of users and stakeholders beliefs and concerns.

In Depth Interviews

In depth interviews, the researchers made use of unstructured or semi-structured set of issues and topics to guide the discussions. The objective of the exercises was to explore and uncover deep seated emotions, motivations and attitudes. The researchers attempted to deal with sensitive matters considering that the respondents were likely to give evasive or even misleading answers when directly questioned. The interviewers adhered to the following six fundamental rules according to Dillon et al. (1994):

• avoid appearing superior or condescending and make use of only familiar words;
• put question indirectly and informatively;
• remain detached and objective;

• avoid questions that encourage 'yes' or 'no' answers;
• probe until all relevant details, emotions and attitudes are revealed; and
• provide an atmosphere that encourages the respondent to speak freely, yet keeping the conservation focused on the issues being researched.

Summarizing, the purpose of the depth interviews was twofold: (i) to determine what interviewees expected the potential effects of the 'ERMIS'; and (ii) to inquire about possible measures and focus of the study. Table 4 presents the details of the interviews within the specific case study.

Hermeneutic Analysis and Findings

Participants interviewed during the sessions completed a profile sheet which included quantitative and qualitative questions related to 'ERMIS'. The profile sheet asked respondents to assess, in a quantitative manner, adoption of 'ERMIS' provided services. The participants used a Likert type scale (Likert, 1932) (from '1' to '5' in which '1' indicated 'strong adoption' and '5' indicated 'not adoption') to assess adoption of 'ERMIS' provided e-services.

The researchers developed separate profile sheets for each of the session in order to match the information needs of the research project with the various stakeholder groups. The profile

Table 4. In depth interviews

Interview	Duration	Interviewer
PI1	1 h	Political Staff of Public Administration with place of responsibility in the Greek Strategy of Electronic Governance
PI2	2 h	Professor with expertise and rich published material in e-government
PI3	1 h & 15 min	CEO in the biggest Greek IT company. He has been responsible for more than 100 big public projects. He holds Phd and MBA.
PI4	1h & 45 min	CFO in big Greek IT company. He holds MSc in Finance and Business Administration.
PI5	2 h	Technical Director in private IT company which is running e-government projects. He holds MS in Computer Science and Phd in Information Systems.
PI6	1 h & 45 min	Execute staff in private IT company. He was the Project Manager for 'ERMIS' project. He holds MSc in Computing.
PI7	1 h & 10 min	Business Unit Manager in big IT company. He has been working in UK and Germany in consortiums. He has extensive experience in e-government projects abroad. He holds an MBA.
PI8	1 h	Employee in the Ministry of Interior. He was the president of the committee of 'ERMIS' project.
PI9	1 h	Employee in the Ministry of Finance. He holds BSc in Legal Studies.
PI10	1 h	Employee in the Technical Department of the Ministry of Interior. He has the role of administrator in 'ERMIS' portal.

provided the researchers with assessments about participant knowledge of 'ERMIS' characteristics and attitudes, as well as qualitative information concerning expected user benefits, lessons learned and perceived barriers or threats to the adoption of 'ERMIS'.

Included on the profile sheet was a question which asked respondents to identity a favorite alternative Governmental website to 'ERMIS' when trying to locate government information and the reasons explaining the particular alternative as a favorite. These questions enabled the researchers to identify online sources of government information which were used in addition to 'ERMIS' and would reflect a user based choice for accessing federal government information.

Prior to each of the session, the researchers developed the interview questions which were pre-tested by researchers and selected participants. These questions guided the interview process, though the researchers varied from the session protocols when interviewee responses opened new avenues for data collection. The recorders at each session wrote a detailed description of

comments made by participants and an analysis of the issued discussed.

The researchers created a database from these summaries and used database management software to organize the data collected. The researchers defined a set of coding categories based on the actual data; the evaluation framework sensitized the researchers to the broader categories. The coding factors represented content found within the narrative summaries. Specific coding categories included categories for 'ERMIS' issues and information policy issue. The researchers used coding as a means of analyzing the data obtained from this data collection technique. Once analyzed, the coding scheme provided a data reduction technique for project researchers. As a result of this analysis, researchers were able to query the database for specific incidents of particular factors without losing the ability to focus on the data content from a holistic perspective.

The aforementioned interpretive techniques regarding the produced conceptual framework of the adoption model, revealed the following significant results:

In the *t-Gov adoption Model*, the concepts of RA, PC and PU are loaded together. The constructs RA and PC have loaded together in other DOI research (Moore & Benbasat, 1991; Carter & Bélanger, 2003). Moore and Benbasat conducted a thorough study using several judges and sorting rounds to develop reliable measures of diffusion of innovation constructs (Rogers, 1995). Although the items for RA, PC and PU were identified separately by the judges and sorters, they all loaded together.

Regarding RA and PC, Moore and Benbasat concluded, 'this may mean that, while conceptually different, they are being viewed identically by respondents, or that there is a causal relationship between the two (Moore & Benbasat, 1991)'. For instance, Moore & Benbasat (1991) refer that 'it is unlikely that respondents would perceive the various advantages of using e-government services, if its use were in fact not compatible with the respondents' experience or life style'.

PU also loaded with RA and PC. A similar argument to the one used to justify RA and PC loading together can be used to explain PU and RA loading together. PU refers to the belief that a new technology will help one accomplish a task, while RA refers to the belief that an innovation will allow one to complete a task more easily than he or she can currently. Conceptually, these two constructs are very similar. They both refer to the use of an innovation to facilitate and ease the attainment of some goal. As RA and PU capture essentially the same concept, we decided to drop PU from further analysis.

Similarly, the concepts of PEOU and COM are loaded together. The constructs of PEOU and COM are loaded together in the Carter and Bélanger's study (2005). Although the items for PEOU and COM were identified separately by the judges and sorters, they all loaded together. This may mean that it is unlikely that respondents would perceive the provided services as ease of use if the governmental portal's use is complex.

Finally, the concepts of TR and PS are loaded together. Again, although the items for TR and PS were identified separately, it is unlikely that respondents would perceive the provided services as trustworthy if the governmental portal does not provide mechanisms for safe transactions.

Considering the aforementioned issues, the model and the hypotheses tests were conducted with five independent variables – COM, RA, TR, LG and SEC as presented in the following diagram. The produced research hypotheses are: H1, H3, H6, H7, H9, H11, H16, H17, H18, H19, H20 and H22. Figure 3 presents the produced conceptual framework.

Positivist Research

An empirical study has been performed to test the model and the depicted relationships. The study was a laboratory experiment where 'ERMIS' was the National Portal used for the data analysis. The data collection procedure and the development of measures used are described in the following paragraphs.

Sample

Data were collected by administering an online questionnaire to a sample of 250 citizens. There was no information given about the actual purpose of the study. The subjects were first asked to answer to questionnaire items regarding the character of 'ERMIS' portal. Then they were requested to visit the Governmental Portal assuming that they are interested in a specific service provision. They were asked to look for the provision of e-services, find information about it and go through the procedure of completing in an electronic manner the transaction they were looking for. Actual running of the service was not required. After that, they were asked to indicate their responses to questionnaire items about using the provided electronic service.

Figure 3. Conceptual framework 2: t-Gov adoption model

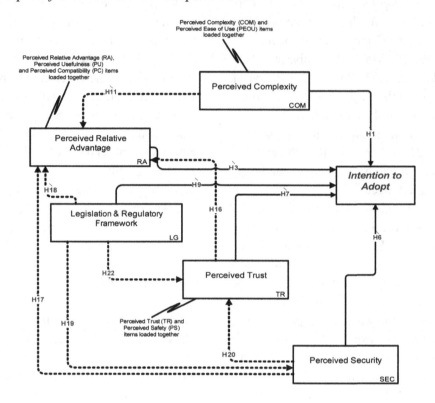

A total of 227 responses were collected yielding an effective response rate of 90.8%. Questionnaires that were incomplete were discarded resulting in 207 usable responses.

Participants were mostly male (56.5%), between 26 and 45 years old (58.5%), mainly graduated from a University (46.9%), resident of Athens (77.3%). Their income is mainly between 700-1,500 Euros per month (53.1%).

Measures

Each of the five model constructs was operationalised using multiple items scales, based on Churchill's (1979) paradigm. New scales were developed for some constructs. Items were generated based on the definition of the constructs and a review of the relevant literature so as to capture their conceptual meaning. For the rest of the constructs, items were borrowed from existing validated measures, as suggested by Straub (1989),

adapted with slight modifications where necessary to apply for electronic government context. All items were measured using a 5-point Likert-type scale, ranging from '1' - strongly disagree to '5' - strongly agree.

The measurement instrument was pretested with the sample of 10 people from personal interviews. The participants were presented with the list of items and a list of constructs, and were asked to assign each item to the construct that captured it best and to comment on the item's applicability to other constructs. Based on this test, the initial discriminant and convergent validity of the items was assessed to produce a refined set of measures which was used for data collection. The final version of the scales can be found in Table 5.

Data Analysis

Data were analyzed with structural equation modeling techniques using SPSS and LISREL. Data

Table 5. List of items measures

COM	Object	Source
COM1	If something is complicated I do not deal with	Rogers (1995)
COM2	If something it is not easy to use I do not deal	Davis (1986)
COM3	The ease of use of new technological software plays important role in order to I utilize it	Davis (1986)
COM4	If I think that the an electronic service is simpler I will try to avoid the realisation of transaction with natural presence in the public authority	Carter & Bélanger (2004)
COM5	I easily can acquire the essential expertise in order to use the electronic provided services from the 'ERMIS'	New Object
COM6	I consider that the electronic transactions through 'ERMIS' is easy and evident process	New Object
RA	**Object**	**Source**
RA1	In general if something is useful in everyday routine or in work I will adopt it	Davis (1986)
RA2	If something is according to my the experiences my way of living I will adopt it	Rogers (1995)
RA3	I will do something if I believe that it offers me relative advantage	Rogers (1995)
RA4	I consider that 'ERMIS' will be useful regarding my transactions with the Public Administration	New Object
RA5	I will use 'ERMIS' if the way of running and completing a transaction is conformed with the way that I have learned to deal with the Public Authorities	New Object
SEC	**Object**	**Source**
SEC1	In general I have need to feel safety	Gefen (2000)
SEC2	I consider that the Government have the necessary mechanisms for citizens to feel safety	Gefen (2000)
SEC3	The security issue is significant for me	Cheung & Lee (2000)
SEC4	I feel secure to use the Internet for electronic transactions	Cheung & Lee (2000)
SEC5	I am sure that 'ERMIS' will provide secure transactions	New Object
TR	**Object**	**Source**
TR1	In general I trust people	Gefen (2000)
TR2	I think that in general people are reliable	Gefen (2000)
TR3	I trust Public Administration	Cheung & Lee (2000)
TR4	I trust the new technologies and the Internet	Cheung & Lee (2000)
TR5	'ERMIS' offers trust mechanisms and thus I can entrust it for my electronic transactions with the Public Sector	New Object
TR6	I would execute an online transaction through 'ERMIS' that requires money exchange	New Object
LG	**Object**	**Source**
LG1	I consider important the existence of a transparent and unambiguous legislation and regulatory framework to support my transactions with the others	Carter & Bélanger (2005)
LG2	I feel confident that the legal framework will protect me in the internet	Carter & Bélanger (2005)
LG3	If the electronic transactions with the Government are imposed by the legislation framework, I will realize them through 'ERMIS'	New Object
LG4	I have been informed regarding the legislative framework that covers the electronic transactions in the internet	New Object
LG5	I believe that 'ERMIS' covers advanced legal issues in order to complete an electronic transaction with Public Administration	New Object

Table 6. Variables fit indices

Variable	KMO	Bartlett's Test of Sphericity	Eigenvalue	Correlation Matrix min value	Limits
COM	0.944	χ^2: 1635.128 P<0,01	7.712	0.832	KMO>0,8 Eigenvalue>1 Correlation Matrix min value>0,3
RA	0.857	χ^2: 739.336 P<0,01	3.445	0.304	
SEC	0.891	χ^2: 818.808 P<0,01	3.840	0.538	
TR	0.883	χ^2: 988.593 P<0,01	4.114	0.243	
LG	0.915	χ^2: 1149.068 P<0,01	4.310	0.792	

analysis was based on the covariance matrix of the observed variables and was performed using maximum likelihood estimation method. The analysis was done in a two-stage procedure (Anderson & Gerbing, 1988; Gerbing & Anderson, 1988; Kline, 1998) with which the measurement model is first developed and estimated separately from the full structural equation model which models simultaneously measurement and structural relationships (Gerbing & Anderson, 1988).

Measurement Model

The measurement model, which is described by a set of structural equations representing the rela-

tionships between observed and latent variables, was assessed first. The model fit was adequate, with fit indices being within acceptable levels as presented in table 6 (Segars & Grover, 1993; Gefen et al., 2000; Straub et al., 2004; Lewis et al., 2005).

The goodness-of-fit indices suggest evidence of convergent and discriminant validity as well as unidimensionality of the model constructs (Hair et al., 1998; Gefen et al., 2000; Straub et al., 2004).

The measurement model was further assessed for construct reliability and validity through a Confirmatory Factor Analysis (CFA). All constructs demonstrated adequate reliability, with Cronbach's alpha value being .785 (Nunally, 1978;

Table 7. Factor loadings

COM			TR			
	COM1	0.955			TR1	0.834
	COM2	0.938			TR2	0.793
	COM3	0.937			TR3	0.787
	COM4	0.930			TR4	0.755
	COM5	0.940			TR5	0.166
	COM6	0.927			TR6	0.779
RA	RA1	0.867	LG		LG1	0.847
	RA2	0.477			LG2	0.891
	RA3	0.914			LG3	0.861
	RA4	0.905			LG4	0.848
	RA5	0.901			LG5	0.864
SEC	SEC1	0.744				
	SEC2	0.897				
	SEC3	0.913				
	SEC4	0.892				
	SEC5	0.923				

Straub et al., 2004). Reliability was assessed by computing the composite reliability of the constructs (Gefen et al., 2000). Composite reliability scores were .70 or higher, providing evidence of internal consistency (Hair et al., 1998). Thus, all constructs are deemed reliable.

Convergent validity was assessed by examining the ratio of factor loadings to their respective standard errors (Segars, 1997). This ratio, represented by the t statistic value, should be greater than |2.00|, to indicate that each factor loading is greater than twice its associated standard error and should be significant for each factor loading. The model constructs satisfy both criteria for convergent validity. Each factor loading was more than double its standard error.

Discriminant validity was assessed with a chi-square difference test (Segars, 1997). This involves setting the correlation between a pair of constructs to unity and comparing the chi-square of this model to the chi-square of the original unconstrained model. Discriminant validity between the two constructs in question is evidenced if the chi-square difference between the constrained and the unconstrained model is significant, smaller for the unconstrained model (Anderson & Gerbing, 1988). The chi-square difference was estimated for all construct pairs, providing evidence for the discriminant validity of the model constructs.

Structural Model

Having tested the measurement model, the full structural model was estimated, to test the hypothesized relationships between the model constructs. The main model fit indices are as follows in Table 8:

The aforementioned indices were within acceptable levels (Segars & Grover, 1993; Gefen et al., 2000; Straub et al., 2004; Lewis et al., 2005). The explanatory power of the proposed model was assessed by observing the R2 of the endogenous constructs in the structural model estimation. The squared multiple correlations, equivalent to

R2, for the endogenous model constructs are shown in the following figure. R2 must be at least 0.10 in order for the latent construct to be judged adequate (Falk & Miller, 1992). All model R2 values satisfy this recommendation. The model with path coefficients and t-values for each endogenous construct are presented in figure 4 and table 9.

Hypotheses 16, 17 and 18 were not supported as they were to be significant. Specifically, there was not significant impact between the concepts of perceived trust and relative advantage, perceived security and relative advantage, and finally between legislation and regulatory framework and relative advantage.

DISCUSSIONS

This study presents an integrated model for e-government adoption that incorporates constructs from TAM, DOI and Trust Models. Previous studies regarding e-government adoption have revealed that the constructs of perceived ease of use, compatibility and trustworthiness are significant indicators of citizens' intention to use state e-government services (Carter & Bélanger, 2005). The present research extends previous adoption research by collecting and analyzing data from a diverse pool of citizens. The large ranges in age, occupation and region are presented in the study. Such a diverse sample provides insight into citizen perceptions of the Governmental Portals' role in providing e-government services. Additionally, the proposed model introduces the construct of supporting legislation and regulatory framework.

Table 8. Model fit indices

x2/d.f.	1.40	NFI	0.94
RMSEA	0.05	NNFI	0.95
CFI	0.98	RMSR	0.078

Figure 4. Conceptual framework 3: Proposed t-Gov adoption model – structural model estimation

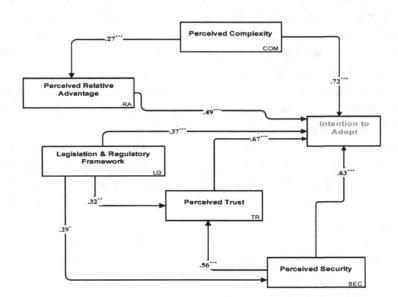

*	significant at the .05 level	***	significant at the .001 level
**	significant at the .01 level	n.s.	not significant at the .05 level

Table 9. Hypotheses testing results

Hypothesis	Path	Path Coefficient	t-value	Description
H1	COM->ADOPT	.72	7.11	examined the effect of perceived complexity to intention to adopt
H3	RA -> ADOPT	.49	3.23	examined the effect of perceived relative advantage to intention to adopt
H6	SEC -> ADOPT	.63	5.87	examined the effect of perceived security to intention to adopt
H7	TR -> ADOPT	.67	6.31	examined the effect of perceived trust to intention to adopt
H9	LG -> ADOPT	.37	3.21	examined the effect of the supporting legislation and regulatory framework to intention to adopt
H11	COM -> RA	.27	2.66	examined the effect of perceived complexity to relative advantage
H19	LG -> SEC	.29	2.87	examined the effect of perceived supporting legislation and regulatory framework to security
H20	SEC -> TR	.56	3.43	examined the effect of perceived security to trust
H22	LG -> TR	.32	3.12	examined the effect of perceived legislation and regulatory framework to trust

Perceived complexity, relative advantage, trust and security and supporting legislation were all significant indicators of citizens' intention to use state e-government services.

There are many ways in which government agencies can reduce perceived complexity. This can be achieved by providing online tutorials that offer tips and illustrations of how to transact with the sites. Governmental Portals should enhance their search and help features to enable citizens quickly to find relevant information and complete required transactions.

Perceived relative advantage was found to have a significant relationship with use intentions in the context of e-government. The research proved that 'ERMIS' portal should operate in a manner that is consistent with individuals' values, beliefs and experiences and provide information and work support as being superior to its predecessors. For instance, non-paper forms should be similar to paper forms that citizens are familiar with and facilitate citizens to complete their transactions with the public agencies. Authors believe that the agencies' involvement in e-government initiatives will enforce standardization filling citizens' requirements for relative advantage.

Trust and security proved to be significantly in adoption of e-government services. Perceptions of trust and security affect intention to adopt e-government services (Lee & Turban, 2001). Although ICTs permit Governments to create interoperable services and applications, their original definition did not include a strong, built-in security model. Today, security is one of the primary challenges when implementing e-strategies for the public sector. Modern ICTs (e.g. second generation PKIs) support a large scale deployment of a number of security services, such as origin authentication, content integrity, confidentiality, and non-repudiation, establishing trust chains at local, national and international level. Electronic signatures and related services that allow data authentication can, therefore, play an important role in this aspect by ensuring security and trust in every e-transactions.

From a legal perspective, in service oriented economies, public administrations should be governed by specific regulations that are different from those which govern the relationships between individuals. In general, current regulatory frameworks are characterized by the assignment of significant powers to public bodies and the recognition of relevant formal guarantees for citizens, based typically on a correct observance by public administrations of a legally predetermined bureaucratic-based sequence of steps. Consequently, many rules become obstacles to the effective implementation of e-Government, while they erode its confidence among citizens, since they are made too rigid to accommodate the changes made possible by the solutions conveyed by ICT professionals.

REFERENCES

Ajzen, I., & Fishbein, M. (1972). Attitudes and normative beliefs as factors influencing intentions. *Journal of Personality and Social Psychology, 21*, 1–9. doi:10.1037/h0031930

Ajzen, I., & Fishbein, M. (1980). *Understanding attitudes and predicting social behavior*. Englewood Cliffs, NJ: Prentice-Hall.

Anderson, J. C., & Gerbing, D. W. (1988). Structural equation modeling in practice: A review and recommended two-step approach. *Psychological Bulletin, 103*, 411–423. doi:10.1037/0033-2909.103.3.411

Bélanger, F., & Carter, L. (2008). Trust and risk in e-government adoption. *Strategic Information Systems, 17*, 165–176. doi:10.1016/j.jsis.2007.12.002

Bélanger, F., & Hiller, J. (2006). A framework for e-government: Privacy implications. *Business Process Management Journal, 12*(1), 48–60. doi:10.1108/14637150610643751

Bélanger, F., Hiller, J., & Smith, W. (2002). Trustworthiness in electronic commerce: The role of privacy, security, and site attributes. *The Journal of Strategic Information Systems, 11*, 245–270. doi:10.1016/S0963-8687(02)00018-5

Carter, L., & Bélanger, F. (2003). Diffusion of innovation and citizen adoption of e-government services. *Proceedings of the 1st International E-Services Workshop*, (pp. 57–63).

Carter, L., & Bélanger, F. (2004). Citizen adoption of e-government initiatives. *Proceedings of the 37th Hawaiian International Conference on Systems Sciences*, (pp. 5–8).

Chau, P. Y. K. (1996). An empirical assessment of a modified technology acceptance model. *Journal of Management Information Systems*, *13*(2), 185–204.

Churchill, G. J. (1979). A paradigm for developing better measures of marketing constructs. *JMR, Journal of Marketing Research, 16*, 64–73. doi:10.2307/3150876

Davies, C. (1997). Organizational influences on the university electronic library. *Information Processing & Management, 33*(3), 377–392. doi:10.1016/S0306-4573(96)00070-2

Davis, F. (1989). Perceived usefulness, perceived ease of use and user acceptance of Information Technology. *Management Information Systems Quarterly, 13*, 319–340. doi:10.2307/249008

Davis, F. D. (1986). *A technology acceptance model for empirically testing new end-user Information Systems: Theory and results*. Unpublished doctoral dissertation, Massachusetts Institute of Technology.

Davis, F. D. (1993). User acceptance of Information Technology: System characteristics, user perceptions, and behavior impacts. *International Journal of Man-Machine Studies, 39*, 475–487. doi:10.1006/imms.1993.1022

Davis, F. D., Bagozzi, R. P., & Warshaw, P. R. (1989). User acceptance of computer technology: A comparison of two theoretical models. *Management Science, 35*(8), 982–1003. doi:10.1287/mnsc.35.8.982

Denzin, N. K., & Lincoln, Y. S. (1998). *Collecting and interpreting qualitative materials*. Thousand Oaks, CA: Sage Publications.

Dillon, W. R. Madden, T. J., & Firtle, N. H. (1994). *Marketing research in a marketing environment*, 3rd edition, (pp. 124-125). Irwin.

Dishaw, M. T., & Strong, D. M. (1999). Extending the technology acceptance model with task-technology fit constructs. *Information & Management, 36*(1), 9–21. doi:10.1016/S0378-7206(98)00101-3

Falk, R. F., & Miller, N. B. (1992). *A primer soft modeling*. Akron, OH: University of Akron Press.

Gefen, D., Karahanna, E., & Straub, D. (2003). Trust and TAM in online shopping: An integrated model. *Management Information Systems Quarterly, 27*, 51–90.

Gefen, D., & Straub, D. (2000). The relative importance of perceived ease of use in IS adoption: A study of e-commerce adoption. *Journal of the Association for Information Systems, 1*, 1–28.

Gerbing, D. W., & Anderson, J. C. (1988). An updated paradigm for scale development incorporating unidimensionality and its assessment. *JMR, Journal of Marketing Research, 25*, 186–192. doi:10.2307/3172650

Gil-Garcia, J. R., Chengalur-Smith, I., & Duchessi, P. (2007). Collaborative e-government: Impediments and benefits of information-sharing projects in the public sector. *European Journal of Information Systems, 16*, 121–133. doi:10.1057/palgrave.ejis.3000673

Guba, E. G., & Lincoln, Y. S. (1994). Competing paradigms in qualitative research. In Denzin, N. K., & Lincoln, Y. S. (Eds.), *Handbook of qualitative research* (2nd ed.). London, UK: Sage Publications.

Heeks, R. (1999). *Reinventing government in the information age: International practice in IT-enabled public sector reform.* New York, NY: Routledge. doi:10.4324/9780203204962

Hu, P. J., Chau, P. Y. K., Sheng, O. R. L., & Tam, K. Y. (1999). Examining the technology acceptance model using physician acceptance of telemedicine technology. *Journal of Management Information Systems, 16,* 91–112.

Hussey, J., & Hussey, R. (1997). *Business research: A practical guide for undergraduate and postgraduate students.* Basingstoke, UK: Macmillan Business.

Irani, Z., Elliman, T., & Jackson, P. (2007). Electronic transformation of government in the UK: A research agenda. *European Journal of Information Systems, 16,* 327–335. doi:10.1057/palgrave.ejis.3000698

Irani, Z., & Love, P. E. D. (2001). The propagation of technology management taxonomies for evaluating investments in manufacturing resource planning (MRPII). *Journal of Management Information Systems, 17*(3), 161–177.

Irani, Z., Love, P. E. D., Elliman, T., Jones, S., & Themistocleous, M. (2005). Evaluating e-government: Learning from the experiences of two UK local authorities. *Information Systems Journal, 15,* 61–82. doi:10.1111/j.1365-2575.2005.00186.x

Jiang, J. J., Hsu, M., & Klein, G. (2000). E-commerce user behavior model: An empirical study. *Human Systems Management, 19,* 265–276.

Karantjias, A., Polemi, N., Stamati, T., & Martakos, D. (2010). A user-centric & federated single-sign-on IAM system for SOA e/m-frameworks. *International Journal of Electronic Government, 7*(3), 216–232. doi:10.1504/EG.2010.033589

Karantjias, A., Stamati, T., & Martakos, A. (2010). Advanced e-government enterprise strategies & solutions. *International Journal of Electronic Governance, 3*(2). doi:10.1504/IJEG.2010.034094

Karantjias, A., Stamati, T., Polemi, N., & Martakos, D. (2009). A synchronous, open, user-centric, federated identity and access management system (OpenIdAM). *Electronic Journal on E-Commerce Tools and Applications (eJETA), 3*(1).

Kline, R. B. (1998). *Principles and practice of structural equation modeling.* New York, NY: The Guilford Press.

Lee, A., & Baskerville, R. (2003). Generalizing in information systems research. *Information Systems Research, 14*(3), 221–243. doi:10.1287/isre.14.3.221.16560

Lee, A. S. (1991). Integrating positivist and interpretative approaches to organizational research. *Organization Science, 2*(4), 342–365. doi:10.1287/orsc.2.4.342

Lee, M. K. O., & Turban, E. (2001). Trust in business-to-consumer electronic commerce: A proposed research model and its empirical testing. *International Journal of Electronic Commerce, 6*(1), 75–91.

Likert, R. (1932). A technique for the measurement of attitudes. *Archives de Psychologie, 140.*

Mathieson, K. (1991). Predicting user intentions: Comparing the technology acceptance model with the theory of planned behavior. *Information Systems Research, 2,* 173–191. doi:10.1287/isre.2.3.173

McKnight, H., Choudhury, V., & Kacmar, C. (2002). Developing and validating trust measures for e-commerce: An integrative typology. *Information Systems Research, 13,* 334–359. doi:10.1287/isre.13.3.334.81

Moon, J., & Kim, Y. (2001). Extending the TAM for a World Wide Web context. *Information & Management, 28,* 217–230. doi:10.1016/S0378-7206(00)00061-6

Moon, M. J. (2002). The evolution of e-government among municipalities: Rhetoric or reality? *Public Administration Review, 62*(4), 424–433. doi:10.1111/0033-3352.00196

Moore, G., & Benbasat, I. (1991). Development of an instrument to measure the perceptions of adopting an information technology innovation. *Information Systems Research, 2,* 173–191. doi:10.1287/isre.2.3.192

Myers, M. D. (1997). Qualitative research in information systems. *Management Information Systems Quarterly, 21*(2), 241–242. doi:10.2307/249422

Oates, B. J. (2006). *Researching information systems and computing.* London, UK & Thousand Oaks, CA: Sage Publications.

Orlikowksi, W. J., & Baroudi, J. (1991). Studying information technology in organizations: Research approaches and assumptions. *Information Systems Research, 2*(1), 1–28. doi:10.1287/isre.2.1.1

Pavlou, P. (2003). Consumer acceptance of electronic commerce: Integrating trust and risk with the technology acceptance model. *International Journal of Electronic Commerce, 7,* 69–103.

Remenyi, D. (1998). *Doing research in business and management: An introduction to process and method.* London, UK & Thousand Oaks, CA: Sage Publications.

Rogers, E. M. (1995). *Diffusion of innovations* (4th ed.). New York, NY: Free Press.

Segars, A. H. (1997). Assessing the unidimensionality of measurement: A paradigm and illustration within the context of Information Systems research. *Omega, 25*(1), 107–121. doi:10.1016/S0305-0483(96)00051-5

Simon, J. L. (1969). *Basic research methods in social science: The art of empirical investigation.* New York, NY: Random House.

Stamati, T., & Martakos, D. (2011). Electronic transformation of local government: An exploratory study. [IJEGR]. *International Journal of Electronic Government Research, 7*(1), 20–37. doi:10.4018/jegr.2011010102

Straub, D., Boudreau, M. C., & Gefen, D. (2004). Validation guidelines for IS positivist research. *Communications of the Association for Information Systems, 13,* 380–427.

Straub, D. W. (1989). Validating instruments in MIS research. *Management Information Systems Quarterly, 13*(2), 147–169. doi:10.2307/248922

Swanson, E. B. (1988). *Information System implementation: Bridging the gap between design and utilization.* Homewood, IL: Irwin.

T. Stamati, A. Karantjias. Inter-sector practices reform for e-Government integration efficacy, *Journal of Cases on Information Technology (ICIT),* IGI Global, in press.

Tornatzky, L., & Klein, K. (1982). Innovation characteristics and innovation adoption implementation: A meta-analysis of findings. *IEEE Transactions on Engineering Management, 29,* 28–45.

Van Slyke, C., Bélanger, F., & Comunale, C. (2004). Adopting business-to-consumer electronic commerce. The effects of trust and perceived innovation characteristics. *The Data Base for Advances in Information Systems, 35,* 32–49.

Venkatesh, V. (1999). Creation of favourable user perceptions: Exploring the role of intrinsic motivation. *Management Information Systems Quarterly, 23*(2), 239–260. doi:10.2307/249753

Walsham, G. (1995). The emergence of interpretivism in IS research. *Information Systems Research, 6*(4), 376–394. doi:10.1287/isre.6.4.376

Welch, J. L. (1985). Research marketing problems and opportunities with focus groups. *Industrial Marketing Management*, *14*, 247. doi:10.1016/0019-8501(85)90017-3

Yin, R. K. (2003). *Case study research: Design and methods* (3rd ed.). Thousand Oaks, CA: Sage Publications.

KEY TERMS AND DEFINITIONS

Transformational Government (t-Gov): An update of the concept of e-government and refers to the initiative of the UK government which sets out the vision for the delivery of public services using new technologies in order to change Government's works.

Service Oriented Economy: An economy mainly dominated by services rather than products.

Services Sciences: A new discipline which is about the adoption of scientific methods and tools in service sectors in order to serve the services.

Trust: In traditional settings, trust has been conceptualized in terms of beliefs related to the attributes of the other party in an exchange. The term has been mainly defined around the trustor's beliefs in the benevolence, competence and integrity of the trustee.

Information Security: Protecting information by providing Strong Authentication, with which an entity is uniquely identified and its identity is verified; Message Integrity that ensures that every system, resource, file and information in general can be modified only by authorized entities; Confidentiality, by which access to the content of information is available only to authorized recipients; Non-repudiation that produces cryptographic data that ensure that an entity cannot repudiate its actions; and Availability that ensures that a system can fulfill its purpose with a given degree of success.

Privacy: The ability of an individual to seclude information about him and thereby reveal himself selectively. In Information Technology privacy is related to anonymity, pseudonimity, linkability and unlinkability.

Regulation: Controlling human or societal behavior by rules or restrictions.

Complexity of an Information System: The degree to which a person believes that the system is being relatively difficult to use and understand.

Compatibility: The degree to which a person believes that an innovation is seen to be compatible with existing values, beliefs, experiences and needs of adopters. This means that the person believes that using a particular system would be according to the way that the person is used to interact with other people.

Information Systems: The hardware, software, policies, procedures and people that capture, transmit, store, retrieve, manipulate, and display information.

Chapter 13
Security and Privacy Issues in E-Government

Ramaraj Palanisamy
St. Francis Xavier University, Canada

Bhasker Mukerji
St. Francis Xavier University, Canada

ABSTRACT

Government is a unique actor as a provider of online public services to its citizens and enterprises. The e-citizens expect that the e-government services are safe and secure, that the privacy of the e-citizen is protected. As security and privacy are primary concerns in e-government, this chapter describes the security and privacy issues faced by the government, the sources and applications of these threats, the ways of protecting security and citizens' personal information, and the challenges in managing the security threats. The purpose of this chapter is to provide guidelines for the administrators of state-level & federal-level e-government services and IT professionals that they need for continuous improvement of e-government security and privacy.

INTRODUCTION

As web technologies have developed from the pure information-sharing phase to interactive, transactional, and intelligent phases, many states and countries started making use of these technologies for web-based government (e-government) services for improving government efficiency, transparency, and competitiveness in the global

DOI: 10.4018/978-1-60960-848-4.ch013

economy. Over 90% of United Nations member countries now operate their government Websites (Swartz, 2004) and engage their e-citizens in e-government systems and services. The businesses and citizens easily find the information or services they need by using the e-government websites and thereby strengthening their competitiveness and growth (Brush, 2007). The easy access to the e-government websites for availing the government services has made the government more transparent and efficient (Digital Task Force, 2004). The e-government benefits are numerous: U.S. federal e-government saved more than U.S. $133 million in software costs (Evans, 2008); about four million citizens filed income taxes online for free in 2007 by using IRS Free File; Forrester Research predicts that more than $600 billion of government fees and taxes will be processed Worldwide through the web; in Europe citizens saved seven million hours a year on the time they spent for filing income taxes; European Union firms save about € 10 per transaction when doing it online (European Commission, 2005) to name a few. Chevallerau (2005) identified several tangible benefits of e-government: improved quality of information supply, reduced work-process time, fewer administrative burdens, reduced operational cost, improved service level, increased work efficiency, and increased customer satisfaction.

Despite the increasing popularity and substantial growth in the development of e-government services on the internet, the e-government stumbles upon security and privacy threats (Thibodeau, 2000). In general, the internet users have growing concerns of cyberspace identity thefts and privacy violations. Citizens may be skeptical and mistrust e-government services, perceiving them as invasions of citizens' security and privacy (James, 2000). Security and privacy issues are big concerns in using commercial Websites; there is even more of a concern for citizens engaging with e-government services (McDowell, 2002), led to a lack of trust which was identified to be a significant barrier to the adoption of e-government (Cremonini and Valeri, 2003). The e-government sites become potential targets for cyber attackers and terrorists. Cyber intrusions into e-government network systems could harm e-government services any time if the e-government sites were not properly secured (Halcnin, 2004). Moen et al., (2007) reported that 82% of the e-government sites around the world were vulnerable to common web application attacks such as cross site scripting and structured query language (SQL) injection.

In particular, 90% of the European e-government sites and 76% of the North American (United States and Canada) e-government sites were vulnerable to common web application attacks. The U.S. was targeted by most denial of services (DoS) attacks during the first half of 2007, accounting for 61% of the worldwide total (Symantec, 2007). The types of cyber intrusions and attacks were DoS attacks, unauthorized access to networks, theft of employee or customer information, online financial fraud, website defacement, web-application attacks, and system penetration (e.g., Halcnin, 2004; Moen et al., 2007; Richardson, 2008; Symantec, 2007). These attacks mainly aimed networks' TCP/IP (Layer 4), SSL (Layer 5), HTTP and FTP (Layer 7) according to the Open Systems Interconnection Reference Model (McNurlin & Sprague, 2006). Besides, some states and local e-government sites posted citizens' names, social security numbers, property tax records, or other private information on their site without any password protection (Myers, 2007). This private information lured the cyber attackers for causing nuisance, destructive attacks, and misusing this for financial gains (Symantec, 2007).

Government is a unique actor as a supplier of online public services to its citizens and enterprises, arguably, it is of primary importance that the usage of e-government services is safe and secure, that the privacy of the e-citizens is protected. As security concerns are an important reason for people not to access the Internet, this chapter describes the security and privacy issues faced by the e-government, the sources and applications of these threats, the ways of protecting security as well as citizens' personal information, and the challenges in managing the security threats. The purpose of this chapter is to provide guidelines for the administrators of state-level & federal-level e-government services and IT professionals that they need for continuous improvement of e-government security and privacy.

SECURITY ISSUES

Security Threats in E-Government

With the more intensive use of the Internet for e-government services, security problems are increasing. In spite of the frequent warnings about the online security to be found in the media, many online users of e-government services unthinkably embrace the e-government because it is quick and simple. On the other hand, the consumers of online government services seem somewhat accepting the internet's insecurity and the government agencies are increasingly worried about possible security breaches. The frauds with credit or debit cards are causing serious barrier to engaging in e-government. This raises the challenge for government agencies to convince the citizens that e-government can be conducted in a safe online environment. In the e-government context, security refers to the perceptions about security regarding the means of payment and the mechanism for storing and transmission of information (Kolsaker and Payne, 2002) and it refers to the technical aspects that ensure the integrity, confidentiality, authentication and non-recognition of relationships (Flavia´n and Guinalı´u, 2006). In summary, security refers to the technical guarantees that ensure that the legal requirements and good practices with regard to privacy will be met effectively (Casalo´ et al., 2006).

Impact of Security Threats

A survey on computer security was conducted by Computer Security Institute in 2008 and reported in Richardson (2008). Computer security practitioners in U.S. corporations, government agencies, financial institutions, medical institutions, and universities participated in the survey. The survey results reported the following threats experienced by a number of the participating organizations: virus attacks occurred to 50% of the participating organizations; insider abuse, 44%;

laptop computer theft, 42%; unauthorized access, 29%; denial of service, 21%; instant messaging abuse, 21%; malware, 20%; theft or loss of customer data, 17%; abuse of wireless network, 14%; system penetration, 13%; financial fraud, 12%; misuse of web application, 11%; password sniffing, 9%; theft or loss of proprietary information, 9%; DNS server attacks, 8%; website defacement, 6%; telecommunication fraud, 5%; and sabotage, 2%. It becomes imperative that the e-government administration should identify the internet security vulnerabilities in a proactive manner and prevent the network systems from being attacked.

The survey results indicated that the government websites have several spots vulnerable to cyber intrusions and hacker attacks because after knowing the IP address of a website, cyber intruders know how to access the server of the site. Besides, the open portal systems of government websites would enable cyber intruders and hackers to identify the ports' detailed information such as server names and versions, service status, and operating systems. By knowing these sensitive information, cyber intruders and hackers would be able to explore ways to intrude into and hack those open, vulnerable ports. As a result, web services could be hampered by DoS attacks (Symantec, 2007) and important information could be changed, stolen, or deleted by cross site scripting and by injecting structured query language (SQL) commands.

Managing the Security Threats

In order to prevent the damages caused by the cyber intruders and hackers, many e-government sites came out with security and policy statements and made them available in their sites. Besides the posting of privacy and security policies, anti-hacking notices are also made available in the sites. Prevention systems such as data transmission encryption systems, intrusion detection systems, investigation-systems for improper web activities, login authentication systems, and web-traffic monitoring systems could be established by the e-government web administration. Intrusion Detection System (IDS) is considered to be a standard requirement in building network security infrastructure. A mobile agent could be used for a distributed IDS that detects intrusion not only from outside the network but also from inside. Information security auditing could be used to determine the e-government's compliance of the legislation such as the Privacy Act, and the Sarbanes-Oxley Act which specify how organizations must handle information and protect policy. Besides, for network security the computer network security mapping is a major method of using software tools for assessing the vulnerability of an entire computer network system without intrusion and identifying areas of potential security threats (e.g., Garcia, 2004). For example, to examine the vulnerability of the e-government network systems, a popular free network mapping tool, Nmap provided by the insecure.org could be used. Nmap is a software for port scanning and network mapping. The software uses raw internet protocol (IP) packets to determine what hosts are available on the network, what ports are open, filtered, or closed. Also, the software assesses what services (application name and version) those hosts are offering; what operating systems (OS) and OS versions they are running; what type of packet filters and firewalls are in use and many other such characteristics. It becomes necessary for the administrators of the e-government sites to consider the following security measures: posting guidelines for proper use of e-government services in the e-government sites, authentication for account access (using login to protect account privacy and security), encryption (using Secure Socket Layer (SSL) encryption to protect data transmissions), monitoring (using software programs to monitor traffic), auditing (identifying unauthorized attempts to cause damage), investigation (investigating improper activities), using intrusion detection software for identifying intrusions and hackings, using server management

software for monitoring internet traffic, investigating improper activities to identify individual persons and a proper-use or anti-hacking note in security policy.

Network address translation (NAT) and port address translation (PAT) technologies are available for hiding sites' IP addresses and port information. The e-government administrators should make use of such technologies for hiding e-government sites' IP addresses and port information. NAT is a technique used to assess network traffic through a router that involves rewriting the source or destination IP addresses and the port numbers of IP packets as they pass through the NAT-enabled router or firewall. PAT is a device that translates or replaces IP addresses and ports of its internal hosts and this device hides the true IP address and ports of the internal hosts. On the other hand, the external hosts are only aware of the IP address of the PAT device and the port used to communicate on behalf of the internal host and not that of the internal host's (e-government's site) IP address. As an alternative, for ensuring security, high anonymity proxy servers could be used for hiding website's original IP address. These proxy servers, though expensive, avoid identifying themselves as proxy servers, thereby making their sites anonymous on the internet. By this way, the e-government websites' original IP addresses could be hidden and thereby cyber intruders have difficulties of getting the portal's network information. Besides, the e-government administrators should consider firewalling the ports and allowing proxy servers or NAT/ PAT enabled routers for the internet access. By doing so, the e-government ports' server names and versions, service status, and operating systems would not be available to intrusion and hacking. In case if the IT budget does not allow installing proxy servers and firewalls, site administrators have to use server management software to watch the ports' traffic and detect hacker's fingerprints used in exploitation of web servers and applications.

Security breaches proved that most of the authentication methods are not secure. For instance, there are many methods such as secured information interchange using cryptography and by authenticating users with the help of passwords or online signatures before the access is granted. The drawback of such technique is causing inconvenience for the users by remembering multiple passwords. Besides passwords can be easily guessed and online signatures can be forged. To overcome these problems, biometrics-based verification like face, voice, fingerprints, iris, DNA, and vein are being used for authenticating users (Tanveer, 2006). In face recognition, the captured images of the individuals are matched to the already stored image in a database. In this way, the authorization is made within less than 5 seconds. As human eyes are very unique and hard to fake, iris and retina based recognition is used for authentication. In voice recognition, the user's low and high sound frequencies are validated. Since face or hand vein thickness and their locations are considered to be unique, the scanned images through vascular scanning process are given for comparing and matching with the database records. The fingerprinting method is also used to identify an individual.

Challenges in Managing Security Threats

The e-government service delivery programs are facing tough challenges. On one hand the e-government services are to be rendered with more improvements in the dimensions of speed, quality, reliability, convenience, and cost. On other hand the e-governments are facing regulatory compliances and cost cutting. Managing both becomes a big challenge for e-government agencies. In this regard, Information Technology plays a crucial role for delivering 24 hours and one-stop government services. Obviously, governments are laying foundations for multi-channel, inter-connected government and starting to adopt many of the

customer relationship management capabilities mostly seen in the private world-class organizations. The service delivery paradigm is also fast changing from department centric approach to citizen centric approach and from process orientation to service orientation. Integrated service delivery thru' web portal is another evolving service mechanism in e-government.

PRIVACY ISSUES

Privacy in E-Government

In general, privacy refers to the protection of an individual's personal information. Specifically, privacy is defined as the individual's right to be alone and privacy has different dimensions including individual's behaviour, communications and personal data (Clarke, 1999). In the context of Internet privacy affects aspects such as obtaining, distributing and non-authorized use of personal information (Wang et al., 1998) and privacy issues refer to a set of legal requirements and good practices with regard to the handling of personal data (Casalo´ et al., 2006). The growing technological capabilities for information processing have made privacy an increasingly important issue. The privacy issues are increasing online user's distrust as personal data is being collected and processed in online transactions. A survey of online consumers revealed that privacy was more important compare to the issues of cost, ease of use, and unsolicited marketing; also privacy was found to be the biggest barrier preventing the online consumers from using websites (Green et al., 1998). A Forrester research study shows that two-thirds of consumers worried about protecting personal information online (Branscum, 2000). Another interesting study was a 2000 National Consumers League survey in which respondents ranked personal privacy above healthcare, education, crime and taxes as concerns (Paul, 2001). In some cases, online individuals have not purchased internet fearing the misuse of their personal information. Fears of privacy violations and misuse of private information are the big concerns for online e-citizens in using the e-government sites. As a result, privacy becomes a major obstacle to the spread of e-government.

Sources of Privacy Issues

Online sites collect data about individuals for several reasons including signing on, customization, for better service, convenience, and others. The online collection of data about individuals has always triggered the issues of privacy. The availability of sophisticated online technology increases privacy concerns as it allows for faster, easier storage of more data, aggregation of the data possibly without the online e-citizen's knowledge. The government agencies make use of the same technologies for collecting, aggregating, and cross-referencing individuals' data. The data collection allows personalization and customization of the e-citizen's interaction with the government agencies. As a result, e-citizens often agree to give personal information on the web for a better service, convenience, or benefits on the particular e-government site. Despite this, government collection of personal data is often seen as an invasion of privacy. As a result, in the e-government world, the serious privacy concerns are often outweighed by several advantages for e-government. Although online businesses collect and aggregate individuals' personal data, often without consent, a survey of 1000 adults revealed that online consumers were more likely to trust business to secure their private information, and expressed concerns about the misuse of information in governments' hands (ITAA, 2000).

Another source for collecting the individuals' information is through the various data forms available in websites. The current technology allows easy and fast loading of data forms on websites and fast transfer of data directly into databases. For online companies this is a great

advantage since the data are loaded in a faster and accurate way without any possibilities for errors or without encountering any problems related with unreadable writing. Internet tools such as cookies make these tasks easier. Cookies collect private information such as an IP address without the consent or knowledge of the online user. Though business organizations practice the habit of collecting individual information using cookies, government agencies must report their data collection policies, procedures, and practices by notifying the individuals that data are collected and explaining how the collected data would be used.

One of the biggest public disagreements has happened when two companies DoubleClick and Abacus Direct Corp decided to merge their databases. DoubleClick used cookies for collecting information on anonymous online purchasing data and browsing habits. The second company had a database of 88 million buyer profiles collected by direct markets and online retailers. The decision for merging the two databases was announced after the announcement of the two companies. The public raised their concerns for cross referencing real offline consumer data with their online purchasing habits (collected with or without the concern). After the public disagreement, the two companies stopped their plans to merge their two databases. Accordingly, a potential cross-referencing online data with other online data between two government agencies is also a concern of privacy advocates. In e-government, there are several possibilities for cross-referencing the online data among the different government agencies. The government agencies share the data for various reasons, such as debt collection (for instance, the Department of Education matches data with Postal service to find postal employees offending on student loans), eligibility verification (for example, the Department of Education matches data with the Social Security Administration to verify social security numbers and citizenship of student aid applicants), fraud and/or ineligibility detection (for instance, the Department of Education matches data with the Internal Revenue Service to locate tax payers who have failed to pay on student loans), and data reconciliations (e.g. two government agencies share data to update their records). These cross-referencing of data contained in databases of government agencies may raise privacy issues and there is a need for the respective agencies announcing their information sharing programs from time to time.

In addition to the issue of cross-referencing data between the government agencies, collection of data without the knowledge of citizens is the biggest issue privacy advocates are raising with e-government websites. This hidden data collection may occur when the users customize their web browsers with their personal information. When they do so, they do not always realize that their personal information can be accessed by websites they are visiting and then stored in the web site's databases. Since these tasks are accomplished by the cookies, the US government agencies were directed not to use cookies without prior consent from the users and a clear notice about the usage of cookies are to be given in their websites.

Applications of Privacy Information

There are many examples of "identity theft" using personal information (such as birthdates, driving licence numbers, credit card numbers, etc.) provided online by individuals. This personal information was used by cyber intruders and hackers for scams aimed at leashing funds from online banking accounts of people. This is a common example of misusing the personal information for scams. This is not only an issue for financial institutions and e-commerce but also for e-government services. The other applications of privacy information in e-government are phishers trying to reel in tax payers, net thieves shift their focus from nuisance to financial gain and control, and others. As a result, the FBI warns frequently about email scams, advices the online users for securing their network, and instructs the online users for keeping their money safe on the internet.

Prevention Measures for the Damages Caused by Privacy

The policy of a consumer-centric e-government should focus on the opinion of its citizen. Considering the major concerns of citizens with online privacy issues, the e-government initiatives must analyze critically e-government decisions with regards to privacy information. For instance, when initially e-government sites were launched information was provided on hours of operation, phone numbers, and a listing of events highlighted the pages but now many public records such as real estate records, property valuations, and court documents are being posted online. The important question is: should public records be posted online? Though the technical ability increased the government's capability to put this information on the web, these information are readily available to anyone around the world, including the hackers/ cyber intruders who would use social security numbers, addresses and maiden names to perpetrate identity theft. The reason is what has been publicly available becomes automatically publicly accessible once posted on the web. Consequently, the governments should limit such postings of individually identifiable information on the web. Thereby, the disclosure of individual information could be controlled. Specifically, the e-government administrators should ensure the use of a "Privacy policy" on their sites as the link name to the privacy policy statement in order to control the cyber intrusions.

SECURITY AND PRIVACY ISSUES IN E-GOVERNMENT

A stage model for e-government growth was proposed comprising initiation, infusion, customization (Watson and Mundy, 2001). Symonds (2000) describes a four stage model to e-government: one-way communications, two-way communications, exchanges, and portals. These models focus on the evolution of e-government in different stages. In one-way communication, governmental information is disseminated by posting the information on websites for constituents. The challenge with these sites is to make sure that the information provided is accurate and timely. Thousands of such e-government web sites are available. In two-way communications model, there are information exchanges (say thru' email) by making simple requests and changes. The governmental agencies may allow online requests but the information is returned via online/ mail/ email. An example would be citizens applying for medicare cards online and the mailing the cards by mail. In exchanges (transactions) stage, the government sites are available for actual transactions online. The examples include renewing licences, paying fines, and applying for financial aid. In the portal stage (integration), all government services are integrated with a single portal. The biggest challenge is the integration of all online and back-office systems. Examples of portals include the US' FirstGov (http://firstgov.gov/), Australia's State of Victoria's MAXI system (www.maxi.com.au/), and Singapore's eCitizen Centre (www.ecitizen. gov.sg/index_low.html).

However, these models do not include the types and governmental relationships with various constituents. The various types and categorization are government-to-citizen (G2C), government-to-employee (G2E), government-to-government (G2G), and government-to-business (G2B). In G2C model, the government establishes or maintains a direct relationship with individual citizens to deliver service or benefit. For instance the US Social Security Administration provides its delivery of services and benefits through web. This could be two way communications in which the citizen requesting information about the various services and benefits and the government may require the citizen's information for processing the

benefits. Other examples include voting online, and citizen participation in commenting on various governmental issues, policies, and procedures. In G2G environment, the various government agencies collaborate and exchange services with one another. An example of this category would be the US National Science Foundation's online funding request system called FastLane (www.nsf.gov).

As the perceived lack of web site security and privacy is one of the main reasons for e-citizens' distrust in e-government, the analysis of the complex issue of security and privacy begins with the first stage: the one-way communications (posting of information). No matter what stage the e-government is, the security and privacy considerations are to be given by identifying the unique constituency interests within the constraints. However, in case of businesses the scenario could be different in this context. The reason is the businesses may not restrict the presence of their information online at government websites. In fact, they likely support the posting of their private information in an electronic form that their customers can use to contact them.

Managing the Security and Privacy Issues in E-Government

In the context of e-government, security and privacy issues are not for merely e-citizens and businesses but really should involve all stakeholders in the online industry. Of course, the responsibility for personal internet security ultimately rests with the concerned individual. At the same time, many organizations that have a stake in the internet could do more to promote personal internet security. For instance, the manufacturers of hardware and software, retailers, Internet Service Providers (ISPs), businesses that operate online, police and the criminal justice system have to work together to protect the security and privacy.

The internet security vulnerabilities and attacks keep changing from time to time. For example the annual research reports by SANS Institute (2007,

2008) says that the kind of vulnerabilities being exploited in 2007 were somewhat different from that of in 2006. The top vulnerabilities in 2006 were (i) operating systems (OS) vulnerabilities in internet Explorer, Windows libraries, Microsoft Office, Windows services, Windows configuration, Mac OS X, and UNIX configuration; (ii) cross platform vulnerabilities in web applications, database software, peer-to-peer file sharing applications, instant messaging, media players, DNS (domain name system) servers, backup software, and security/ enterprise/directory management servers; (iii) network device vulnerabilities in network and other devices configurations, and VoIP(voice-over-internet protocol) servers and phones; (iv) policy and personnel vulnerabilities in excessive user rights and unauthorized devices, phishing and spear phishing; and (v) zero-day attacks, which occur when attackers discover and exploit previously unknown flaws (SANS, 2007). On the contrary, the top vulnerabilities in 2007 were (i) client-side vulnerabilities in web browsers, office software, email clients, and media players; (ii) server-side vulnerabilities in web applications, Windows services, Unix and Mac OS services, backup software, antivirus software, management server, and database software; (iii) policy and personnel vulnerabilities in excessive user rights and unauthorized devices, phishing and spear phishing, and unencrypted laptops and removable media; (iv) application abuse in instant messaging and peer-to-peer programs; (v) network device vulnerabilities in VoIP servers and phones; and (vi) zero-day attacks (SANS, 2008). Accordingly, to cope with the changes over the time, internet security professionals ought to develop and adopt newer security measures in a more continuous manner.

Another big challenge is assessing the costs of cyber-crimes. The major types of cyber crimes were found to be the following: viruses, worms or Trojans, financial fraud, denial of service, equipment theft, telecoms fraud, usage of systems for criminal or illegitimate purposes, unauthorized

access to business systems, theft of information/ data, sabotage of data or networks, and website defacement (Hi-tech crime survey, Serious organized crime agency). An OECD report (2006) on information security in Norway depicts the challenges posed in assessing the costs of cyber crime. In evaluating the costs of information security failures there are a number of methodological challenges. Some of them are: how to quantify the loss of a sensitive information asset that was stolen, who holds that information, what time, and what use will be made of it; and how to measure cascading effects such as the consequences of a system's disruption on other linked systems. Besides, how to account for indirect costs such as security expenses (for example the overhead costs of an incident response team). In reality, there is no availability of standard and widely accepted method for dealing with these questions. Due to lack of information and consistent cost assessment method, the cost estimates of e-crimes and the security failures are commonly based on surveys among organizations. Despite the survey, such survey results can not be interpreted as accurate measures of the cost of cyber crimes simply because of the lack of consistent method for quantifying costs. The information security industry provides the most general cost assessments based on extrapolation from surveys although the precise methodology of these assessments are not made public and can not be assessed objectively (OECD, 2006).

In response to the security attacks and privacy threats on the government websites/ networks, a cyber initiative to overhaul the cyber defences is required. For example, the U.S. federal government launched such a cyber initiative to overhaul U.S. cyber defences. One of the goals in the initiative was to reduce the number of communication ports, through which their networks linked to Internet (Grow et al., 2008). The e-government administrators should enhance the levels of their website security and privacy as perceived by the e-citizen. In order to achieve this, it becomes necessary to properly manage the legislative, technical and business measures that determine the levels of security and privacy. In managing these aspects, priorities are to be given to the two-way communications as this will help to increase e-citizen's trust. Besides, the technologies used for enhancing the security and privacy could be highlighted to ensure security in email communications. These technologies such as digital certificates, digital signatures, firewalls, and antivirus programs can prevent anonymous surfing by the unauthorized users. Furthermore, the e-citizens/ users are to be trained to increase their levels of perceived online privacy and security. For this purpose, the governments may collaborate with the private sector for providing training to online users. Furthermore, designing complex websites with full of multimedia effects should be avoided as far as possible. The e-government sites should have simple structure instead of a highly sophisticated one and easy for the online user to understand. So, usability / ease-of-use must be getting top priority in web site development. The usability of the e-government website improves the understanding the contents and the services provided over the site. Also, usability gives a more comfortable atmosphere for the user which creates a feeling of security in using the site and thereby increases the level of trust for online users.

As a starting point, the government authorities can accept or use digital signatures (in case of business organizations signatures of both the employee and the organization would be required) in the documents, signed emails, sign/verify blank forms in two-way communications. Other forms of secure connections such as logging in via a pin code or an access code or using a digital signature would be required in the government websites. Installation of firewalls, virus protection software, off-site data backup, backup power unit, spam filtration of received emails, installation of intrusion detection software and other related technologies are other ways of enhancing the levels of security and privacy in e-government websites.

For ensuring privacy, the usage of cookies on the e-government websites should be avoided as far as possible. For instance, in June 2000, US federal agencies were directed to control the use of cookies on their sites. The usage of cookies has to be avoided because of the cyber laws and traditions about government access to citizens' personal information. Only when there is a valid and compelling reason for using the cookies, the agency head can approve for the same. However, the websites need to notify to its citizens about this practice of using cookies for collecting the citizens' personal information.

Besides, the Privacy Act (1974) controls the government agencies from collecting personal information of online users. Any agency who would like to record, use, share, distribute, and allow access to individual information such as individual name, identifiable number or other identifier must obtain prior permission from the individual to do so. There could be exceptions in cases of routine uses of individuals' information, intra-agency use, use on a need to know basis, and other exceptional reasons. A senior agency member could be appointed to be responsible for privacy. The member may continuously review and monitor the records in light of the internet. The guidelines are to be developed emphasizing the necessity for review of agency records and security & privacy features in e-government environment. Law enforcement is required for specifically address posting of information on government websites.

CONCLUSION

Security and privacy are the two related variables and the close relationships between the two must be emphasized especially to the e-citizens. Managing both the concepts jointly as running side by side would avoid any kind of confusion. The government policy makers have to set security and privacy as an important goal in providing e-government services. This will increase the confidence level of e-citizens and will avail the e-government services in a reliable, safe and secure way. There is no doubt that e-government is advancing democracy and civic participation but at the same time it may also involve threats to democratic values such as security and privacy. For the years to come, the important trend will be providing secure e-government web services by applying the internet technology. Future research should focus on secured web services for delivering dependable services to the end-users. The reason being the citizens expect the same level and type of services from government that they receive from the private sector. Besides, the government also anticipates increased efficiency, improved productivity, and cost savings similar to those experienced by the private sector (Clark, 2003).

In general, there is a growing awareness among the citizens about security and privacy. For instance, in most countries, individuals have already taken single or multiple security measures to protect against virus attacks and other malware. The security problems are to be prioritized and the appropriate action needs to be taken. For instance, spam is the number one security problem and many types of malware are distributed through spam, it would be a good idea to collect data on spam. In case of business users, most organizations have already built security features in place. For instance, firewalls are rapidly being implemented by several organizations across different countries. As a result, the number of security problems encountered has decreased. However, protecting security and privacy in e-government sites is an ongoing process.

REFERENCES

Branscum, D. (2000). Guarding online privacy. *Newsweek, 135*(23), 77-8.

Brush, M. (2007). MoEIS increases accuracy and efficiency of e-government solutions. *Tier News*. Retrieved January 10, 2007, from http://www.tier.com/ news/ pf.cfm?id= 166

Casalo, L. V., Flavian, C., & Guinalı'u, M. (2006). Trust: Key concept in the development of virtual communities. In Putnik, G. D., & Cunha, M. M. (Eds.), *Encyclopedia of networked and virtual organizations*. Hershey, PA: Idea Group Reference.

Clark, E. (2003). Managing the transformation to e-government: An Australian perspective. *Thunderbird International Business Review, 45*(4), 377–397. doi:10.1002/tie.10087

Clarke, R. (1999). Internet privacy concerns confirm the case for intervention. *Communications of the ACM, 42*(1), 61–70.

Cremonini, L., & Valeri, L. (2003). *Benchmarking security and trust in Europe and the US*. (Rand Monograph Report MR-1763), Europe. Retrieved from http://www.rand.org/ pubs/ monograph_reports/ MR1736/

Digital Task Force. (2004). *The Danish e-government strategy 2004-2006*. Retrieved from http://e.gov.dk/ uploads/ media/ strategy_pixi.pdf

European Commission. (2005, January 14). *E-government services yield real benefits for EU citizens and businesses*. Retrieved from http://europa.eu.int/ rapid/ pressReleasesAction.do? reference=IP/ 05/ 41&format= HTML&aged=0& language=EN&guiLanguage=en

Evans, K. S. (2008). *Expanding e-government: Achieving results for the American people*. Retrieved from http://www.whitehouse.gov/ omb/ egov/ documents/ 2008_Expanding_E-Gov_Report.pdf

Flavia'n, C., & Guinalı'u, M. (2006). Consumer trust, perceived security, and privacy policy: Three basic elements of loyalty to a web site. *Industrial Management & Data Systems, 106*(5/6), 601–620. doi:10.1108/02635570610666403

Garcia, R. C. (2004). Network security: Mapping intrusion and anomaly detection to very-high-degree polynomials. *Signals, Systems, and Computers, 2*(7), 1449–1452.

Green, H., Yang, C., & Judge, P. C. (1998). A little privacy, please. *Business Week, 3569*(1), 98-9.

Grow, B., Epstein, K., & Tschang, C. (2008, April 21). The new espionage threat. *Business Week*, 32–45.

Halcnin, L. E. (2004). Electronic government: Government capability and terrorist resources. *Government Information Quarterly, 21*(4), 406–419. doi:10.1016/j.giq.2004.08.002

ITAA. (2000). *Keeping the faith: Government information security in the internet age*. Retrieved from www.itaa.org/ infosec/ faith.pdf

James, G. (2000). Empowering bureaucrats. *MC Technology Marketing Intelligence, 20*(12), 62–68.

Kolsaker, A., & Payne, C. (2002). Engendering trust in e-commerce: A study of gender-based concerns. *Marketing Intelligence & Planning, 20*(4), 206–214. doi:10.1108/02634500210431595

McDowall, R. (2002). *What is the probability of e-government?* (IE4C). Retrieved from http://www.it-director.com/ content.php? id=2767

McNurlin, B. C., & Sprague, R. H. Jr. (2006). *Information systems management in practice* (7th ed.). Upper Saddle River, NJ: Pearson Prentice Hall.

Moen, V., Klingsheim, A. N., Simonsen, K. F., & Hole, K. J. (2007). Vulnerabilities in e-governments. *International Journal of Electronic Security and Digital Forensics, 1*(1), 89–100. doi:10.1504/IJESDF.2007.013595

Myers, L. (2007, February 5). Online public records facilitate ID theft: Is your local government unwittingly aiding identity thieves? *MSNBC: Nightly News*. Retrieved from http://www.msnbc.msn.com/ id/ 16813496/

OECD. (2006). *Norway: Information Security. OECD Reviews of Risk Management Policies*. Paris, France: OECD.

Paul, P. (2001). Mixed signals. *American Demographics, 23*, 44–49.

Richardson, R. (2008). *The 2008 computer crime and security survey*. Computer Security Institute. Retrieved from http://www.gocsi.com/ forms/ csi_survey.jhtml;jsessionid= 1GW0KB43ZOYT-KQSND LPSKH0CJ UNN2JVN

SANS Institute. (2007). *SANS top-20 internet security attack targets: The 2006 annual update*. Retrieved from http://www.sans.org/ top20/ 2006/

SANS Institute. (2008). *SANS top-20 2007 security risks: The 2007 annual update*. Retrieved from http://www.sans.org/ top20/

Swartz, N. (2004). E-government around the world. *Information Management Journal, 38*(1), 12.

Symantec. (2007, September). Symantec internet security threat report. *Symantec Enterprise Security, 12*, 1-30. Retrieved from http://www.symantec.com

Symonds, M. (2000). Government and the internet: No gain without pain. *The Economist, 355*(1), S9-S14.

Tanveer, S. (2006). Voice biometric based user verification: An exemplary tool for secure identification. In J. Bhattacharya (Ed.), *Technology in government*. New Delhi, India: GIFT publishing.

Thibodeau, P. (2000). E-government spending to soar through 2005. *Computerworld, 34*(17), 12.

Wang, H., Lee, M., & Wang, C. (1998). Consumer privacy concerns about internet marketing. *Communications of the ACM, 41*(1), 63–70. doi:10.1145/272287.272299

Watson, R. T., & Mundy, B. (2001). A strategic perspective of electronic democracy. *Communications of the ACM, 44*(1), 27–30. doi:10.1145/357489.357499

KEY TERMS AND DEFINITIONS

E-Government Challenges: The challenges faced by the government agencies to promote e-government among the citizens.

E-Government Services: The different types of government services (e.g., registration, renewal driver's licence, e-passport etc.) provided electronically by the government agencies to the citizens.

E-Government: The use of new technologies such as Internet by the Government agencies to communicate, provide information and services in an interactive way to the citizens. of storing and transmission of information.

Privacy: Privacy refers to the protection of citizens' personal information from non-authorized usage.

Security: Security refers to maintaining integrity, confidentiality, and authentication.

Technology Management: The effective and efficient management of new technologies to improve e-government services to the citizens.

Web-Technologies: New Internet based technologies used to communicate process and provide services to the citizens.

Compilation of References

Accenture (2009). From e-government to e-governance: Using new technologies to strengthen relationships with citizens.

Accenture Report. (2005). *Leadership in customer service: New expectations, new experiences.* E-Government Report.

Accenture. (2003). *E-government leadership – Realizing the vision.* The Government Executive Series.

Accenture. (2004). *E-government leadership: High performance, maximum value.* The Government Executive Series.

Adjaoud, F., Zeghal, D., & Andaleeb, S. (2007). The effect of board's quality on performance: A study of Canadian firms. *Corporate Governance: An International Review,* *15*(4), 623–635. doi:10.1111/j.1467-8683.2007.00592.x

AGIMO (Australian Government Information Management Office). (2006). *Responsive government- A new service agenda.* Department of Finance and Administration, Australian Government.

Ahn, H., Cao, C. Q., & Choe, H. (1998). Decimalization and competition among stock markets: Evidence from the Toronto Stock Exchange cross-listed securities. *Journal of Financial Markets,* *1,* 51–87. doi:10.1016/S1386-4181(97)00002-5

Ahuja, A. (2008). Open and secure solutions for empowering governments. Retrieved September 21, 2009, from www.egovonline.net/.../4194-indian-society-is-it-ready-for-online-government-services.html

Ajzen, I., & Fishbein, M. (1972). Attitudes and normative beliefs as factors influencing intentions. *Journal of Personality and Social Psychology, 21,* 1–9. doi:10.1037/h0031930

Ajzen, I., & Fishbein, M. (1980). *Understanding attitudes and predicting social behavior.* Englewood Cliffs, NJ: Prentice-Hall.

Al Marzouq, M., Li, Z., Guang, R., & Varun, G. (2005). Open source: Concepts, benefits and challenges. *Communications of the AIS, 16.*

Al-adawi, Z., Yousafzai, S., & Pallister, J. (2005). *Conceptual model of citizen adoption of e-government.* The Second International Conference on Innovations in Information Technology (IIT'05), (2005).

Alhabshi, S. M. (2008). E-government in Malaysia: Barriers and progress. (International Federation for Information Processing (IFIP) Working Group 9.4). *Information Technology in Developing Countries, 18*(3), 6–15.

All About Market Research. (2008). *Internet world stats.* Retrieved from http://www.allaboutmarketresearch.com/internet.htm

Alles, M. (2009). Special issue: XBRL and the future of disclosure. *International Journal of Disclosure and Governance, 6*(3), 184–185. doi:10.1057/jdg.2009.10

Allison, P. D. (1999). *Logistic regression using the SAS system.* Cary, NC: SAS Institute.

Al-Mashari, M. (2007). A benchmarking study of experiences with electronic-government. *Benchmarking: An International Journal, 14*(2), 172–185. doi:10.1108/14635770710740378

Almilia, L. S. (2009). Determining factors of Internet financial reporting in Indonesia. *Accounting and Taxation, 1*(1), 87–99.

Amabile, T. M. (1996). *Creativity in content.* New York, NY: Westview Press.

Anand, A. I., & Klein, P. C. (2005). Inefficiency and path dependency in Canada's securities regulatory system: Towards a reform agenda. *Canadian Business Law Journal, 42*(1), 41–72.

Andersen, K. V., & Henriksen, H. Z. (2006). E-government maturity models: Extension of the Layne and Lee model. *Government Information Quarterly, 23,* 236–248. doi:10.1016/j.giq.2005.11.008

Anderson, J. C., & Narus, J. A. (1998). Business marketing: Understand what customers value. *Harvard Business Review, 76*(6), 53–65.

Anderson, A. (2007). All guts, no glory: Trading and diversification among online investors. *European Financial Management, 13*(3), 448–471. doi:10.1111/j.1468-036X.2007.00368.x

Anderson, J. C., & Gerbing, D. W. (1988). Structural equation modeling in practice: A review and recommended two-step approach. *Psychological Bulletin, 103,* 411–423. doi:10.1037/0033-2909.103.3.411

Anderson, K. (1999). Reengineering public sector organizations using Information Technology. In Heeks, R. (Ed.), *Reinventing government in the information age* (pp. 312–330). New York, NY: Routledge.

Andersson, A., Hassler, K., & Nedstam, J. (2005). *Open source business models in practice: A survey of commercial open source introduction*. Lund University.

Anshuman, V., & Kalay, A. (1998). Market making with discrete prices. *Review of Financial Studies, 11,* 81–109. doi:10.1093/rfs/11.1.81

Anthopoulos, L. G., Siozos, P., & Tsoukalas, L. A. (2007). Applying participatory design and collaboration in digital public services for discovering and re-designing e-government services. *Government Information Quarterly, 24,* 353–376. doi:10.1016/j.giq.2006.07.018

Anttiroiko, A.-V. (2005). Towards ubiquitous government: The case of Finland. *E-Service Journal, 4*(1), 65–99. doi:10.2979/ESJ.2005.4.1.65

Antweiler, W., & Frank, M. Z. (2004). Is all that talk just noise? The information content of Internet stock message boards. *The Journal of Finance, 59,* 1259–1295. doi:10.1111/j.1540-6261.2004.00662.x

Archer, N. (2007). Mobile e-health: Making the case. In Kushchu, I. (Ed.), *Mobile government: An emerging direction in e-government* (pp. 155–170). Hershey, PA: IGI Global. doi:10.4018/978-1-59140-884-0.ch008

Australian Government 2.0 Taskforce Final Report. (2009). *Engage getting on with government 2.0.*

Australian Government. (2010). *Timeline, an Australian government initiative: Standard business reporting.* Retrieved on September 23, 2010, from http://www.sbr.gov.au/About_SBR/Timeline.aspx

Bacidore, J., Battalio, R., & Jennings, R. (2003). Order submission strategies, liquidity supply, and trading in pennies on the New York Stock Exchange. *Journal of Financial Markets, 6,* 337–362. doi:10.1016/S1386-4181(03)00003-X

Bacidore, J. M. (1997). The impact of decimalization on market quality: An empirical investigation of the Toronto Stock Exchange. *Journal of Financial Intermediation, 6*(2), 92–120. doi:10.1006/jfin.1997.0213

Bacidore, J., Battalio, R., Jennings, R., & Farkas, S. (2001). *Changes in order characteristics, displayed liquidity, and execution quality on the New York Stock Exchange around the switch to decimal pricing.* Working Paper, NYSE.

Bagnoli, M., Beneish, M. D., & Watts, S. G. (1999). Whisper forecasts of quarterly earnings per share. *Journal of Accounting and Economics, 28*(1), 27–50. doi:10.1016/S0165-4101(99)00018-X

Ball, C., Torous, W., & Tschoegl, A. (1985). The degree of price resolution: The case of the gold market. *Journal of Futures Markets, 5,* 29–43. doi:10.1002/fut.3990050105

Banas, M. J., & Hillard, F. (SECOM). (2010). *Brazil embraces digital age with new interactive e-gov portal - Brasil.Gov.Br.* The Secretariat for Social Communication (SECOM) of the Presidency of Brazil.

Barber, B., & Odean, T. (2000). Trading is hazardous to your wealth: The common stock investment performance of individual investors. *The Journal of Finance, 55,* 773–806. doi:10.1111/0022-1082.00226

Barber, B., & Odean, T. (2001). The internet and the investor. *The Journal of Economic Perspectives, 15*(Winter), 41–54. doi:10.1257/jep.15.1.41

Barber, B., & Odean, T. (2008). All that glitters: The effect of attention and news on the buying behavior of individual and institutional investors. *Review of Financial Studies, 21*, 785–818. doi:10.1093/rfs/hhm079

Barber, B., Odean, T., & Zhu, N. (2009). Systematic noise. *Journal of Financial Markets, 12*(4), 547–569. doi:10.1016/j.finmar.2009.03.003

Barber, B. M., Lee, Y. T., Liu, Y. J., & Odean, T. (2009). Just how much do individual investors lose by trading? *Review of Financial Studies, 22*, 609–632. doi:10.1093/rfs/hhn046

Barberis, N., & Thaler, R. (2003). A survey of behavioral finance. In Constantinides, G., & Stulz, R. (Eds.), *Handbook of the economics of finance* (pp. 1053–1128). Amsterdam, The Netherlands: North-Holland Publishers.

Barclay, M. (1997). Bid-ask spreads and the avoidance of odd-eighth quotes on NASDAQ: An examination of exchange listings. *Journal of Financial Economics, 45*, 35–60. doi:10.1016/S0304-405X(97)00010-X

Barclay, M., & Warner, J. (1993). Stealth and volatility: Which trades move prices? *Journal of Financial Economics, 34*, 281–306. doi:10.1016/0304-405X(93)90029-B

Bartley, J., Chen, Y. S. A., & Taylor, E. (2010). Avoiding common errors of XBRL reporting. *Journal of Accountancy, 209*(2), 46–51.

BDO. (2010). *Extensible business reporting language (XBRL): The future of financial reporting*. Risk Advisory Services, BDO. Retrieved on August 13, 2010, from www.bdo.ca/ras

Beekes, W., Brown, P., & Chin, G. (2006). *Do better governed firms make more informative disclosures? Canadian evidence.* Working Paper, Lancaster University Management School.

Bélanger, F., & Carter, L. (2008). Trust and risk in e-government adoption. *Strategic Information Systems, 17*, 165–176. doi:10.1016/j.jsis.2007.12.002

Bélanger, F., & Hiller, J. (2006). A framework for e-government: Privacy implications. *Business Process Management Journal, 12*(1), 48–60. doi:10.1108/14637150610643751

Bélanger, F., Hiller, J., & Smith, W. (2002). Trustworthiness in electronic commerce: The role of privacy, security, and site attributes. *The Journal of Strategic Information Systems, 11*, 245–270. doi:10.1016/S0963-8687(02)00018-5

Bélanger, F., & Carter, L. (2005). Trust and risk in e-government adoption. *Proceedings of the 11th Americans Conference on Information Systems*, Omaha, NE, USA.

Bergstrasser, D., & Poterba, J. (2002). Do after-tax returns affect mutual fund inflows? *Journal of Financial Economics, 63*, 381–414. doi:10.1016/S0304-405X(02)00066-1

Bertot, J. C., & Jaeger, P. T. (2008). The e-government paradox: Better customer service doesn't necessarily cost less. *Government Information Quarterly, 25*(2), 149–154. doi:10.1016/j.giq.2007.10.002

Bessembinder, H. (1999). Trade execution costs on NASDAQ and NYSE: A post-reform comparison. *Journal of Financial and Quantitative Analysis, 34*, 387–408. doi:10.2307/2676265

Bezroukov, N. (1999). A second look at the cathedral and the bazaar. *First Monday, 4*(12).

Bhagat, S., & Bolton, B. (2008). Corporate governance and firm performance. *Journal of Corporate Finance, 14*, 257–273. doi:10.1016/j.jcorpfin.2008.03.006

Bhatnagar, S. (2006). *E-governance – An assessment framework. Department of Information Technology.* New Delhi: Government of India.

Bhatnagar, S. (2007). *E-government in Asia Pacific regions – An assessment of issues and challenges.* Ahmadabad: Indian Institute of Management.

Bhatnagar, S. (2002). E-government: Lessons from implementation in developing countries. *Regional Development Dialogue, 24*, 1–9.

Bhatnagar, S. (2003). Access to information report: E-government. In Hodess, R., Inowlocki, T., & Wolfe, T. (Eds.), *Global corruption report 2003* (pp. 24–32). London, UK: Profile Books Lt.

Black, B. S., Jang, H., & Kim, W. (2006). Does corporate governance predict frms' market values? Evidence from Korea. *Journal of Law Economics and Organization, 22*(2), 366–413. doi:10.1093/jleo/ewj018

Blackman, M. (2006). Municipalities move to mobile government. *Government Procurement*, 54-55. Retrieved from www.govpro.com

Blau, J. (2007). Berlin rejects call for open source. *Computer World*, May.

Bodkar, S., et al. (2008). Framework for expanding e-government: The e-governance project. Paper presented at 5th Scandinavian Workshop on E-Government, Copenhagen.

Bogan, V. (2008). Stock market participation and the Internet. *Journal of Financial and Quantitative Analysis*, *43*(1), 191–211. doi:10.1017/S0022109000002799

Bollen, N. R. B., & Busse, J. A. (1996). Tick size and institutional trading costs: Evidence from mutual funds. *Journal of Financial and Quantitative Analysis*, *41*(4), 915–937. doi:10.1017/S0022109000002696

Bonaccorsi, A., & Rossi, C. (2003). Why open source software can succeed. *Research Policy*, *32*, 1243–1258. doi:10.1016/S0048-7333(03)00051-9

Bonham, M., & Seifert, J. (2003). *The transformative potential of e-government in transitional democracies*. Congressional Research Service.

Boritz, J. E., & No, W. G. (2004). Assurance reporting for XML-Based Information Services: XARL. *Canadian Accounting Perspectives*, *2*(3), 207–233. doi:10.1506/V8D9-QTUN-HDU1-93RB

Boritz, J. E., & No, W. G. (2004). Assurance reporting for XML-based Information Services: XARL (Extensible Assurance Reporting Language). *Canadian Accounting Perspectives*, *3*(2), 207–233. doi:10.1506/V8D9-QTUN-HDU1-93RB

Branscum, D. (2000). Guarding online privacy. *Newsweek*, *135*(23), 77-8.

Brashear, J. (2009). SEC mandates interactive data financial reporting. *The Corporate Governance Advisor*, *17*(3), 27–30.

Brown, L. D., & Caylor, M. L. (2009). Corporate governance and firm operating performance. *Review of Quantitative Finance and Accounting*, *32*, 129–144. doi:10.1007/s11156-007-0082-3

Brown, D. (1999). Information Systems for improved performance management: Development approaches in US public agencies. In Heeks, R. (Ed.), *Reinventing government in the information age* (pp. 113–134). New York, NY: Routledge.

Browne, M. W., & Cudeck, R. (1993). Alternative ways of assessing model fit. In Bollen, K. A., & Long, J. S. (Eds.), *Testing structural equation models*. Newbury Park, CA: Sage.

Brush, M. (2007). MoEIS increases accuracy and efficiency of e-government solutions. *Tier News*. Retrieved January 10, 2007, from http://www.tier.com/ news/ pf.cfm?id= 166

Bushman, R. M., Piotroski, J. D., & Smith, A. J. (2004). What determines corporate transparency? *Journal of Accounting Research*, *42*(2), 207–252. doi:10.1111/j.1475-679X.2004.00136.x

Cabinet Office. (2005). *Transformational government enabled by technology*. Retrieved from www.cabinetoffice.gov.uk

Callaghan, J., & Nehmer, R. (2009). Financial and governance characteristics of voluntary XBRL adopters in the United States. *International Journal of Disclosure and Governance*, *6*(4), 321–336. doi:10.1057/jdg.2009.15

Canadian Securities Administrators. (2010a). *About CSA*. Retrieved on August 2, 2010, from http://www.securities-administrators.ca/aboutcsa.aspx?id=77&linkidentifier=id&itemid=77

Canadian Securities Administrators. (2010b). *Industry resources*. Retrieved on August 2, 2010, from http://www.securities-administrators.ca/industry_resources.aspx?id=48&linkidentifier=id&itemid=48

Canadian Securities Administrators. (2010c). *Registration*. Retrieved on August 2, 2010, from http://www.securities-administrators.ca/registration.aspx?id=857&linkidentifier=id&itemid=857

Carhart, M. M. (1997). On persistence in mutual fund performance. *The Journal of Finance*, *52*, 57–82. doi:10.2307/2329556

Carnaghan, C., & Gunz, S. P. (2007). Recent changes in the regulation of financial markets and reporting in Canada. *Accounting Perspectives*, *6*(1), 55–94. doi:10.1506/W733-67L7-0774-6336

Carroll, J. (2005). Risky business: Will citizens accept m-government in the long term? In I. Kushchu & M. Halid Kuscu (Eds.), *The Proceedings of the 1ˢᵗ European Mobile Government Conference* (Euro mGov 2005), Brighton, UK, (2005), 10-12 July, Mobile Government Consortium International Pub, UK.

Carter, L., & Bélanger, F. (2005). The utilization of e-government services: Citizen trust, innovation and acceptance factors. *Information Systems Journal*, *15*, 5–25. doi:10.1111/j.1365-2575.2005.00183.x

Carter, L., & Bélanger, F. (2003). Diffusion of innovation and citizen adoption of e-government services. *Proceedings of the 1st International E-Services Workshop*, (pp. 57–63).

Carter, L., & Bélanger, F. (2004). Citizen adoption of e-government initiatives. *Proceedings of the 37th Hawaiian International Conference on Systems Sciences*, (pp. 5–8).

Casalo, L. V., Flavian, C., & Guinalı'u, M. (2006). Trust: Key concept in the development of virtual communities. In Putnik, G. D., & Cunha, M. M. (Eds.), *Encyclopedia of networked and virtual organizations*. Hershey, PA: Idea Group Reference.

Castells, M. (2000). *End of millennium, the information age: Economy, society and culture* (*Vol. III*). Cambridge, MA/ Oxford, UK: Blackwell.

Chakravarty, S., Panchapagesan, V., & Wood, R. A. (2005). Did decimalization hurt institutional investors? *Journal of Financial Markets*, *8*(4), 400–420. doi:10.1016/j.finmar.2005.05.002

Chakravarty, S., Van Ness, B., & Van Ness, R. (2005). The effect of decimalization on trade size and adverse selection costs. *Journal of Business Finance & Accounting*, *32*, 1063–1081. doi:10.1111/j.0306-686X.2005.00622.x

Chakravarty, S., Wood, R., & Van Ness, R. (2004). Decimals and liquidity: A study of the NYSE. *Journal of Financial Research*, *27*, 75–94. doi:10.1111/j.1475-6803.2004.00078.x

Chandler, S., & Emanuels, S. (2002). Transformation not automation. *Proceedings of 2ⁿᵈ European Conference on E-government*, (pp. 91-102). St Catherine's College Oxford, UK.

Chandra, S., & Lyons, K. (2001). *Undertaking land administration projects: Sustainability, affordability, operational efficiency and good practice guidelines*. Australian Government Overseas Aid Program, Quality Assurance Series, AusAid.

Chatfield, A. T. (2009). Public service reform through e-government: A case study of "e-tax" in Japan. *Electronic. Journal of E-Government*, *7*(2), 135–146.

Chau, P. Y. K. (1997). Reexamining a model for evaluating information center success: Using a structural equation modeling approach. *Decision Sciences*, *28*(2), 309–334. doi:10.1111/j.1540-5915.1997.tb01313.x

Chau, P. Y. K. (1996). An empirical assessment of a modified technology acceptance model. *Journal of Management Information Systems*, *13*(2), 185–204.

Chawla, R. (2004). Online delivery of land titles to rural farmers in Karnataka, India. A paper presented at Scaling up Poverty Reduction: A Global Learning Process: E-Governance Conference, Shanghai.

Chawla, R. (2007). Freedom in the fields: Bhoomi online delivery of land records. Retrieved on September 29, 2009, from www.bhoomi.kar.nic.in

Chen, Z., Gangopadhyay, A., Holden, S. H., Karabatis, G., & McGuire, P. (2007). Semantic integration of government data for water quality management. *Government Information Quarterly*, *24*(4), 716–735. doi:10.1016/j.giq.2007.04.004

Chen, Y.-C., & Thurmaier, K. (2005). *Government-to-citizen electronic services: Understanding and driving adoption of online transactions*. The Association for Public Policy & Management (APPAM) Conference, Washington, D.C., November 3-6, (2005).

Chevalier, J., & Ellison, G. (1997). Risk taking by mutual funds as a response to incentives. *The Journal of Political Economy*, *105*, 1167–1200. doi:10.1086/516389

Choi, J. J., Laibson, D., & Metrick, A. (2002). How does the internet affect trading? Evidence from investor behavior in 401 (k) plans. *Journal of Financial Economics, 64*, 397–421. doi:10.1016/S0304-405X(02)00130-7

Chordia, T., Roll, R., & Subrahmanyam, A. (2008). Liquidity and market efficiency. *Journal of Financial Economics, 87*(2), 249–268. doi:10.1016/j.jfineco.2007.03.005

Choudrie, J., Weerakkody, V., & Jones, S. (2005). Realising e-government in the UK: Rural and urban challenges. *Journal of Enterprise Information Management, 18*(5), 568–585. doi:10.1108/17410390510624016

Christie, W., & Schultz, P. (1994). Why do NASDAQ market makers avoid odd-eighth quotes? *The Journal of Finance, 49*, 1813–1840. doi:10.2307/2329272

Chung, K. H., Charoenwong, C., & Ding, D. (2004). Penny pricing and the components of spread and depth changes. *Journal of Banking & Finance, 28*, 2981–3007. doi:10.1016/j.jbankfin.2003.11.001

Chung, K. H., Charoenwong, C., & Jiang, J. (2008). The dynamics of quote adjustments. *Journal of Banking & Finance, 32*(11), 2390–2400. doi:10.1016/j.jbankfin.2008.02.001

Chung, K. H., Charoenwong, C., & McCormick, D. (2004). Order preferencing and market quality on NASDAQ before and after decimalization. *Journal of Financial Economics, 71*, 581–612. doi:10.1016/S0304-405X(03)00174-0

Chung, K. H., & Kim, V. (2009). Volatility, market structure, and the bid-ask spread. *Asia-Pacific Journal of Financial Studies, 38*(1), 67–107. doi:10.1111/j.2041-6156.2009.tb00008.x

Chung, K. H., Van Ness, B., & Van Ness, R. (2001). Can the treatment of limit orders reconcile the differences in trading costs between NYSE and NASDAQ issues? *Journal of Financial and Quantitative Analysis, 36*(2), 267–286. doi:10.2307/2676274

Chung, K. H., Van Ness, B., & Van Ness, R. (2002). Spreads, depths, and quote clustering on NYSE and NASDAQ: Evidence after the 1997 Securities and Exchange Commission rule changes. *Financial Review, 37*, 481–505. doi:10.1111/1540-6288.00025

Chung, K. H., Van Ness, B., & Van Ness, R. (2004). Trading costs and quote clustering on NYSE and NASDAQ after decimalization. *Journal of Financial Research, 27*, 309–328. doi:10.1111/j.1475-6803.2004.00096.x

Chung, R., Lawrence, K., & Zhang, H. (1997). Decimalization's winners and losers. *Canadian Investment Review,* (Winter): 35–39.

Churchill, G. A. (1979). A paradigm for developing better measures of marketing constructs. *JMR, Journal of Marketing Research, 16*, 64–73. doi:10.2307/3150876

CICA. (2010). *Using the Internet in corporate reporting.* Canadian Institute of Chartered Accountants. Retrieved on September 23, 2010, from http://www.cica.ca/research-and-guidance/research-activities/activities-in-progress/accounting/item33149.aspx

Cicirretti, R., Hasan, I., & Zazzara, C. (2009). Do Internet activities add value? Evidence from the traditional banks. *Journal of Financial Services Research, 35*(1), 81–98. doi:10.1007/s10693-008-0039-2

CID. (2006). *Readiness for the networked world: A guide for developing countries.* Center for International Development at Harvard University.

Clark, E. (2003). Managing the transformation to e-government: An Australian perspective. *Thunderbird International Business Review, 45*(4), 377–397. doi:10.1002/tie.10087

Clarke, R. (1999). Internet privacy concerns confirm the case for intervention. *Communications of the ACM, 42*(1), 61–70.

Cohen, E. E. (2004). Compromise or customize: XBRL's paradoxical power. *Canadian Accounting Perspectives, 2*(3), 187–206. doi:10.1506/YAHN-CAE8-5CWQ-H4TE

Cohen, E. E. (2009). XBRL's global ledger framework: Exploring the standardised missing link to ERP integration. *International Journal of Disclosure and Governance, 6*(8), 188–206. doi:10.1057/jdg.2009.5

Cohen, E. E., Schiavina, T., & Servais, O. (2005). XBRL: The standardised business language for the 21st century reporting and governance. *International Journal of Disclosure and Governance, 2*(4), 368–394. doi:10.1057/palgrave.jdg.2040006

Cohen, E. E. (2004). Compromise or customize: XBRL's paradoxical power. *Canadian Accounting Perspectives, 3*(2), 187–206. doi:10.1506/YAHN-CAE8-5CWQ-H4TE

Corrocher, N. (2006). Internet adoption in Italian banks: An empirical investigation. *Research Policy, 35*(4), 533–544. doi:10.1016/j.respol.2006.02.004

Couch, K., & Parker, D. L. (2000). Net interest grows as banks rush online. *Southwest Economy. Federal Reserve Bank of Dallas, 2,* 1–5.

Cremonini, L., & Valeri, L. (2003). *Benchmarking security and trust in Europe and the US.* (Rand Monograph Report MR-1763), Europe. Retrieved from http://www.rand.org/pubs/ monograph_reports/ MR1736/

Critical Issues in E-Governance. (2007). Summary of discussion using issue process methodology panel discussion. Paper presented at the 5th International Conference on e-Governance (ICEG 2007). Available at http://www.csi-sigegov.org/critical_issues_on_e_governance.pdf accessed on 21.9.2009

Cronin, J. J., & Taylor, S. A. (1992). Measuring service quality: A reexamination and extension. *Journal of Marketing, 56,* 55–68. doi:10.2307/1252296

Csikszentmihalyi, M. (1975). *Beyond boredom and anxiety: The experience of play in work and games.* San Francisco, CA: Jossey-Bass, Inc.

Daines, R., Gow, I., & Larcker, R. (2008). *Rating the ratings: How good are commercial governance ratings?* Working Paper, Stanford University.

Dale, P. (1999, October). Is technology a blessing or a curse in land administration? Presented at the UN-FIG Conference on Land Tenure and Cadastral Infrastructure for Sustainable Development, Melbourne, Australia.

Dale, P. (2000). The importance of land administration in the development of land markets - A global perspective. Land Markets and Land Consolidation in Central Europe, TU Delft – Report of UDMS 2000.

Damodaran, L., Nicholls, J., & Henney, A. (2005). The contribution of sociotechnical systems thinking to the effective adoption of e-government and the enhancement of democracy. *The Electronic. Journal of E-Government, 3*(1), 1–12.

Davies, C. (1997). Organizational influences on the university electronic library. *Information Processing & Management, 33*(3), 377–392. doi:10.1016/S0306-4573(96)00070-2

Davis, F. D. (1989). Perceived usefulness, perceived ease of use and user acceptance of Information Technology. *Management Information Systems Quarterly, 13*(3), 319–340. doi:10.2307/249008

Davis, F. D., Bagozzi, R. P., & Warshaw, P. R. (1989). User acceptance of computer technology: A comparison of two theoretical models. *Management Science, 35*(8), 982–1003. doi:10.1287/mnsc.35.8.982

Davis, F. (1989). Perceived usefulness, perceived ease of use and user acceptance of Information Technology. *Management Information Systems Quarterly, 13,* 319–340. doi:10.2307/249008

Davis, F. D. (1993). User acceptance of Information Technology: System characteristics, user perceptions, and behavior impacts. *International Journal of Man-Machine Studies, 39,* 475–487. doi:10.1006/imms.1993.1022

Davis, F. D., Bagozzi, R. P., & Warshaw, P. R. (1989). User acceptance of computer technology: A comparison of two theoretical models. *Management Science, 35*(8), 982–1003. doi:10.1287/mnsc.35.8.982

Davis, F. D. (1986). *A technology acceptance model for empirically testing new end-user Information Systems: Theory and results.* Unpublished doctoral dissertation, Massachusetts Institute of Technology.

Dawes, S. S., Gregg, V., & Agouris, P. (2004). Digital government research: Investigations at the crossroads of social and Information Science. *Social Science Computer Review, 22*(1), 5–10. doi:10.1177/0894439303259863

De, R. (2006). The impact of e-government initiatives: Issues of poverty and vulnerability reduction. *Regional Development Dialogue, 27*(2), 88–100.

De, R. (2005). E-government systems in developing countries: Stakeholders and conflict. In Wimmer, M. A. (Eds.), *E-Gov - 2005, LNCS 3591* (pp. 26–37).

Debreceny, R., Farewell, S., Piechocki, M., Felden, C., & Graning, A. (2010). Does it add up? Early evidence on the data quality of XBRL filings to the SEC. *Journal of Accounting and Public Policy, 29*(3), 296–306. doi:10.1016/j.jaccpubpol.2010.04.001

Debreceny, R., Gray, G. L., & Raham, A. (2002). The determinants of Internet financial reporting. *Journal of Accounting and Public Policy, 21*, 371–394. doi:10.1016/S0278-4254(02)00067-4

Debreceny, R., Lymer, A., & Trabelsi, S. (2008). An empirical examination of corporate websites as a voluntary disclosure medium. *Administrative Science Association of Canada Conference Proceedings, 29*(26), 1-22.

Deci, E. L., & Ryan, R. M. (1985). *Intrinsic motivation and self-determinaton in human behaviour*. New York, NY: Pienum.

Deepak, B. (2004). *Measuring the impact of e-government. E-Government Applications Practice Lead, Global ICT Department*. World Bank.

Deininger, K. (2007). *Land policies for growth and poverty reduction. Organization for Economic Cooperation and Development*. India: World Bank.

Denzin, N. K., & Lincoln, Y. S. (1998). *Collecting and interpreting qualitative materials*. Thousand Oaks, CA: Sage Publications.

Department of Information Technology. (2007). *National e-governance report*. New Delhi.

Department of Public Service and Administration. (2007). *South African government information*. Retrieved from www.gov.za

Dewally, M. (2003). Investing with a rock of sale. *Financial Analysts Journal, 59*(4), 1–14. doi:10.2469/faj.v59.n4.2546

Dewally, M. (2008). The informational value of earnings whispers. *American Journal of Business, 23*(1). Retrieved from http://www.bsu.edu/mcobwin/majb/?p=546. doi:10.1108/19355181200800003

DeYoung, R. (2005). The performance of Internet-based business models: Evidence from the banking industry. *The Journal of Business, 78*(3), 893–947. doi:10.1086/429648

DeYoung, R., Lang, W. W., & Nolle, D. L. (2007). How the Internet affects output and performance at community banks. *Journal of Banking & Finance, 31*(4), 1033–1060. doi:10.1016/j.jbankfin.2006.10.003

Digital Task Force. (2004). *The Danish e-government strategy 2004-2006*. Retrieved from http://e.gov.dk/uploads/ media/ strategy_pixi.pdf

Dillon, W. R. Madden, T. J., & Firtle, N. H. (1994). *Marketing research in a marketing environment*, 3rd edition, (pp. 124-125). Irwin.

Dishaw, M. T., & Strong, D. M. (1999). Extending the technology acceptance model with task-technology fit constructs. *Information & Management, 36*(1), 9–21. doi:10.1016/S0378-7206(98)00101-3

District, C. (2008). *Revenue department report*. India.

Doidge, C., Karolyi, G. A., & Stulz, R. M. (2007). Why do countries matter so much for corporate governance? *Journal of Financial Economics, 86*, 1–39. doi:10.1016/j.jfineco.2006.09.002

Dow, J. P. (2007). The adoption of web banking at credit unions. *The Quarterly Review of Economics and Finance, 47*(3), 435–448. doi:10.1016/j.qref.2006.08.014

Durisin, B., & Puzone, F. (2009). Maturation of corporate governance research, 1993-2007: An assessment. *Corporate Governance: An International Review, 17*(3), 266–291. doi:10.1111/j.1467-8683.2009.00739.x

Dutta, S., & Mia, I. (Eds.). (2009). *The global Information Technology report 2008–2009*. Geneva, Switzerland: INSEAD and World Economic Forum.

Dwivedi, P., & Sahu, G. P. (2008). *Challenges of e-government implementation in India. Emerging technologies in e-government* (pp. 210–215). E-Governance Publication.

Easley, D., Hvidkjaer, S., & O'Har, M. (2002). Is information risk a determinant of asset returns? *The Journal of Finance, 57*, 2185–2221. doi:10.1111/1540-6261.00493

Easley, D., Kiefer, N., & O'Hara, M. (1996). Cream-skimming or profit-sharing? The curious case of purchased order flow. *The Journal of Finance, 51*, 811–834. doi:10.2307/2329223

Easley, D., Kiefer, N., O'Hara, M., & Paperman, J. (1996). Liquidity, information, and infrequently traded stocks. *The Journal of Finance, 51*, 1405–1436. doi:10.2307/2329399

Easley, D., & O'Hara, M. (1992). Time and the process of security price adjustment. *The Journal of Finance, 47*, 577–605. doi:10.2307/2329116

Economist Intelligence Unit. (2009). *E-readiness rankings 2009: The usage imperative*.

Edelen, R. M. (1999). Investor flows and the assessed performance of open-end mutual funds. *Journal of Financial Economics, 53*, 439–466. doi:10.1016/S0304-405X(99)00028-8

Edmiston, K. D. (2003). State and local e-government: Prospects and challenges. *American Review of Public Administration, 33*(1), 20–45. doi:10.1177/0275074002250255

Efendi, J., Smith, L. M., & Wong, J. (2009). *Longitudinal analysis of voluntary adoption of XBRL on financial reporting*. SSRN working paper. Retrieved August 3, 2010, from http://papers.ssrn.com/sol3/papers.cfm?abstract_id=1440956

EGAT/NRM/LRM/USAID. (2009). *Land tenure, poverty and economic growth in India*. Briefing Paper.

eGovWorld. (2007). *Global dialogue, mobile innovations for social and economic transformation*.

England, K. L., Furst, K., Nolle, D. E., & Robertson, D. (1998). Banking over the Internet. *Quarterly Journal. Office of the Comptroller of the Currency, 17*(4), 25–30.

Espinoza, M. M. (1999). Assessing the cross-cultural applicability of a service quality measure: A comparative study between Quebec and Peru. *International Journal of Service Industry Management, 10*(5), 449–468. doi:10.1108/09564239910288987

European Commission. (2005, January 14). *E-government services yield real benefits for EU citizens and businesses*. Retrieved from http://europa.eu.int/ rapid/ pressReleasesAction.do? reference=IP/ 05/ 41&format= HTML&aged=0& language=EN&guiLanguage=en

European Union. (2002). *Evolution of e-government in the European Union*. Report commissioned by the Spanish Presidency of the Council of the European Union. Retrieved from http://www.map.es/csi/pdf/ eGovEngl_definitivo.pdf

Evans, D., & Yen, D. C. (2006). E-government: Evolving relationship of citizens and government, domestic, and international development. *Government Information Quarterly, 23*(2), 207–235. doi:10.1016/j.giq.2005.11.004

Falk, R. F., & Miller, N. B. (1992). *A primer soft modeling*. Akron, OH: University of Akron Press.

Fang, Z. (2002). E-government in digital era: Concept, practice and development. *International Journal of the Computer. The Internet and Information, 20*, 193–213.

Fang, V. W., Noe, T. H., & Tice, S. (2009). Stock market liquidity and firm value. *Journal of Financial Economics, 94*(1), 150–169. doi:10.1016/j.jfineco.2008.08.007

Fishbein, M., & Ajzen, I. (1975). *Beliefs, attitude, intention, and behavior: An introduction to theory and research*. Reading, MA: Addison-Wesley.

Flavia'n, C., & Guinalı'u, M. (2006). Consumer trust, perceived security, and privacy policy: Three basic elements of loyalty to a web site. *Industrial Management & Data Systems, 106*(5/6), 601–620. doi:10.1108/02635570610666403

Foerster, S. R., & Huen, B. C. (2004). Does corporate governance matter to Canadian investors? *Canadian Investment Review*, (Fall): 19–25.

Fornell, C., & Larcker, D. F. (1981). Evaluating structural equation models with unobservable variables and measurement error. *JMR, Journal of Marketing Research, 18*(1), 39–50. doi:10.2307/3151312

Fountain, J. (2001). *Building the virtual state: Information Technology and institutional change*. Washington, DC: Brookings Institution Press.

Franke, N., & Shah, S. (2003). How communities support innovative activities: An exploration of assistance and sharing among end users. *Research Policy, 32*(1), 157–178. doi:10.1016/S0048-7333(02)00006-9

Frey, B. (1997). *Not just for money: An economic theory of personal motivation*. Brookfield, WI: Edward Elger Publishing Company.

Furst, K., Lang, W. W., & Nolle, D. E. (2002). Internet banking. *Journal of Financial Services Research, 22*(1/2), 95–117. doi:10.1023/A:1016012703620

Garcia, R. C. (2004). Network security: Mapping intrusion and anomaly detection to very-high-degree polynomials. *Signals, Systems, and Computers, 2*(7), 1449–1452.

Garfinkel, J., & Nimalendran, M. (2003). Market structure and trader anonymity: An analysis of insider trading. *Journal of Financial and Quantitative Analysis, 38*, 591–610. doi:10.2307/4126733

Gefen, D., Karahanna, E., & Straub, D. W. (2003). Trust and TAM in online shopping: An integrated model. *Management Information Systems Quarterly, 27*, 51–90.

Gefen, D., & Straub, D. (2000). The relative importance of perceived ease of use in IS adoption: A study of e-commerce adoption. *Journal of the Association for Information Systems, 1*, 1–28.

Gerbing, D. W., & Anderson, J. C. (1988). An updated paradigm for scale development incorporating unidimensionality and its assessment. *JMR, Journal of Marketing Research, 25*, 186–192. doi:10.2307/3172650

Gibson, S., Singh, R., & Yerramilli, V. (2003). The effect of decimalization on the components of the bid-ask spread. *Journal of Financial Intermediation, 12*, 121–148. doi:10.1016/S1042-9573(03)00017-2

Gil-Garcia, J. R., & Martinez-Moyano, I. J. (2007). Understanding the evolution of e-government: The influence of systems of rules on public sector dynamics. *Government Information Quarterly, 24*(2), 266–290. doi:10.1016/j.giq.2006.04.005

Gil-Garcia, J. R., Chengalur-Smith, I., & Duchessi, P. (2007). Collaborative e-government: Impediments and benefits of information-sharing projects in the public sector. *European Journal of Information Systems, 16*, 121–133. doi:10.1057/palgrave.ejis.3000673

Gilmore, A., & D'Souza, C. (2006). Service excellence in e-governance issues – An Indian case study. *Journal of Administration and Governance, 1*(1).

Glosten, L., & Milgrom, P. (1985). Bid, ask and transaction prices in a specialist market with heterogeneously informed traders. *Journal of Financial Economics, 14*, 71–100. doi:10.1016/0304-405X(85)90044-3

Godek, P. (1996). Why NASDAQ market makers avoid odd-eighth quotes? *Journal of Financial Economics, 41*, 465–474. doi:10.1016/0304-405X(95)00863-A

Goetzmann, W. N., & Massa, M. (2000). Daily momentum and contrarian behaviour of index fund investors. *Journal of Financial and Quantitative Analysis, 37*, 375–389. doi:10.2307/3594985

Goldstein, M., & Kavajecz, K. (2000). Eighths, sixteenths and market depth: Changes in tick size and liquidity provision on NYSE. *Journal of Financial Economics, 56*, 125–149. doi:10.1016/S0304-405X(99)00061-6

Goldstein, M., Shkilko, A., & Van Ness, B. & Van Ness, R. (2005). *Inter-market competition for NYSE-listed securities*. Working paper, University of Mississippi.

Gompers, P., Ishii, J., & Metrick, A. (2003). Corporate governance and equity prices. *The Quarterly Journal of Economics, 118*(1), 107–155. doi:10.1162/00335530360535162

Gore, A., Jr. (1993). *From red tape to results: Creating a government that works better and costs less*. Washington DC: Government Printing Office. Retrieved from http://govinfo.library.unt.edu/npr/library/nprrpt/annrpt/redtpe93/index.html

Gottschalk, P. (2009). Maturity levels for interoperability in digital government. *Government Information Quarterly, 26*(1), 75–81. doi:10.1016/j.giq.2008.03.003

Government of India. (2007). *Right to information India*. New Delhi.

Graham, J., & Harvey, C. (1996). Market-timing ability and volatility implied in investment newsletters' asset allocation recommendations. *Journal of Financial Economics, 42*, 397–421. doi:10.1016/0304-405X(96)00878-1

Grande, C. (1999, 10 December). E-envoy vows to raise Internet use by ministries. *Financial Times*.

Grandi, F., Mandreoli, F., Scalas, M. R., & Tiberio, P. (2004). Management of the citizen's digital identity and access to multi-version norm texts on the Semantic Web. In *Proceedings of the International Symposium on Challenges in the Internet and Interdisciplinary Research*.

Gray, G. L., & Miller, D. W. (2009). XBRL: Solving real-world problems. *International Journal of Disclosure and Governance, 6*(3), 207–223. doi:10.1057/jdg.2009.8

Gray, T., & Kitching, A. (2005). *Reforming Canadian securities regulation*. Library of Parliament (PRB 05-28E). Retrieved on August 2, 2010, from http://www2.parl.gc.ca/content/lop/researchpublications/prb0528-e.htm

Graziano, C. de M. (2002). XBRL streamlining financial reporting. *Financial Executive, 18*(8), 52–55.

Green, H., Yang, C., & Judge, P. C. (1998). A little privacy, please. *Business Week, 3569*(1), 98-9.

Grinblatt, M., & Keloharju, M. (2000). The investor behavior and performance of various types: A study of Finland's unique data set. *Journal of Financial Economics, 55*, 43–68. doi:10.1016/S0304-405X(99)00044-6

Grinblatt, M., & Keloharju, M. (2001). What makes investors trade? *The Journal of Finance, 56*, 589–616. doi:10.1111/0022-1082.00338

Grossman, S., Miller, M., Fischel, D., Cone, K., & Ross, D. (1997). Clustering and competition in dealer markets. *The Journal of Law & Economics, 40*, 23–60. doi:10.1086/467365

Grow, B., Epstein, K., & Tschang, C. (2008, April 21). The new espionage threat. *Business Week*, 32–45.

Guba, E. G., & Lincoln, Y. S. (1994). Competing paradigms in qualitative research. In Denzin, N. K., & Lincoln, Y. S. (Eds.), *Handbook of qualitative research* (2nd ed.). London, UK: Sage Publications.

Guijarro, L. (2007). Interoperability frameworks and enterprise architectures in e-government initiatives in Europe and the United States. *Government Information Quarterly, 24*, 89–101. doi:10.1016/j.giq.2006.05.003

Halcnin, L. E. (2004). Electronic government: Government capability and terrorist resources. *Government Information Quarterly, 21*(4), 406–419. doi:10.1016/j.giq.2004.08.002

Hanke, M., & Hauser, F. (2008). On the effects of stock spam e-mails. *Journal of Financial Markets, 11*(1), 57–83. doi:10.1016/j.finmar.2007.10.001

Hannon, N. (2005). Post Sarbanes-Oxley: Does XBRL hold the key? *Strategic Finance, 86*(7), 57–61.

Hannon, N. (2006). Does XBRL Cost too Much? *Strategic Finance, 87*(10), 59–61.

Hanstad, T., & Nielsen, R. (2009). Land tenure reform in India. In Prosterman, R. L., Mitchell, R., & Hanstad, T. (Eds.), *One billion rising: Law, land and alleviation of global poverty*. Leiden University Press.

Harris, L. (1991). Stock price clustering and discreteness. *Review of Financial Studies, 4*, 389–416. doi:10.1093/rfs/4.3.389

Harris, L. (1994). Tick sizes, discrete bid-ask spreads, and quotation sizes. *Review of Financial Studies, 7*, 149–178. doi:10.1093/rfs/7.1.149

Harris, M., & Raviv, A. (1993). Differences of opinion make a horse race. *Review of Financial Studies, 6*, 473–506. doi:10.1093/rfs/6.3.473

Harris, L. (1997). *Decimalization: A review of the arguments and evidence*. Working paper, University of Southern California.

Harris, L. (1999). *Trading in pennies: A survey of the issues*. Working paper, University of Southern California.

Hars, A., & Ou, S. (2002). Working for free? Motivations for participating in open-source projects. *International Journal of Electronic Commerce, 6*(3), 25–39.

Haruvy, E., Prasad, A., & Sethi, S. P. (2003). Harvesting altruism in open source software development. *Journal of Optimization Theory and Applications, 118*(2), 381–416. doi:10.1023/A:1025455523489

Hasbrouck, J. (1991). Measuring the information content of stock trades. *The Journal of Finance, 46*, 179–207. doi:10.2307/2328693

Heeks, R. B., & Bailur, S. (2007). Analyzing e-government research: Perspectives, philosophies, theories, methods, and practice. *Government Information Quarterly, 24*(2), 243–265. doi:10.1016/j.giq.2006.06.005

Heeks, R. (1999). *Reinventing government in the information age: International practice in IT-enabled public sector reform*. New York, NY: Routledge. doi:10.4324/9780203204962

Hernando, I., & Nieto, M. (2007). Is the Internet delivery channel changing banks' performance? The case of Spanish banks. *Journal of Banking & Finance, 31*(4), 1083–1099. doi:10.1016/j.jbankfin.2006.10.011

Hernon, P., Reylea, H. C., Dugan, R. E., & Cheverie, J. F. (2002). *United States government information: Policies and sources* (p. 388). Westport, CT: Libraries Unlimited.

Hernon, P., Reylea, H. C., Dugan, R. E., & Cheverie, J. F. (2002). *United States government information: Policies and sources* (p. 388). Westport, CT: Libraries Unlimited.

Hertel, G., Niedner, S., & Herrmann, S. (2003). Motivation of software developers in open source projects: An Internet-based survey of contributors to the Linux kernel. *Research Policy, 32,* 1159–1177. doi:10.1016/S0048-7333(03)00047-7

Hiller, J. S., & Bélanger, F. (2001). Privacy strategies for electronic government. In Abramson, M. A., & Means, G. E. (Eds.), *E-government 2001* (pp. 162–198). Lanham, MD: Rowman & Littlefield Publishers.

Holden, S. H., Norris, D. F., & Fletcher, P. D. (2003). Electronic government at the local level, progress to date and future issues. *Public Performance and Management Review, 26*(4), 325–344. doi:10.1177/1530957603026004002

Holmstrom, B. (1999). Managerial incentive problems: A dynamic perspective. *The Review of Economic Studies, 66,* 169–182. doi:10.1111/1467-937X.00083

Hong, H., Kubik, J., & Stein, J. (2004). Social interaction and stock market participation. *The Journal of Finance, 59,* 137–163. doi:10.1111/j.1540-6261.2004.00629.x

Howard, M. (2001). E-government across the globe: How will "E" change government? *Government Finance Review, 17*(4), 6–9.

Hu, L.-T., & Bentler, P. M. (1999). Cutoff criteria for fit indexes in covariance structure analysis: Conventional criteria versus new alternatives. *Structural Equation Modeling, 6*(1), 1–55. doi:10.1080/10705519909540118

Hu, P. J., Chau, P. Y. K., Sheng, O. R. L., & Tam, K. Y. (1999). Examining the technology acceptance model using physician acceptance of telemedicine technology. *Journal of Management Information Systems, 16,* 91–112.

Huang, R., & Stoll, H. (1996). Dealer versus auction markets: A paired comparison of execution costs on NYSE and NYSE. *Journal of Financial Economics, 41,* 313–357. doi:10.1016/0304-405X(95)00867-E

Huberman, G. (2001). Familiarity breeds investment. *Review of Financial Studies, 14,* 659–680. doi:10.1093/rfs/14.3.659

Huson, M., Youngsoo, K., & Vikas, M. (1997). *Decimal quotes, market quality, and competition for order flow: Evidence from the Toronto stock exchange.* Working paper, University of Alberta

Hussey, J., & Hussey, R. (1997). *Business research: A practical guide for undergraduate and postgraduate students.* Basingstoke, UK: Macmillan Business.

i4d. (2007). From e-government to m-government. *ICTD Project Newsletter,* 33-36.

IMF Report. (2007). *Global financial stability report, market developments and issues.*

IMF. (2008). *World economic outlook database*-October 2008, Washington, DC.

India Corruption Study. (2005). To improve governance. Centre for Media Studies, New Delhi.

India, U. N. D. P. (2009). Project E-Setu: Reaching the unreached. New Delhi, India: United Nations Development Program. Retrieved from http://www.undp.org.in/events/ict-goa/e-setu15-16dec03goa.PPT

Indian Brand Equity Foundation. (2004). *Ministry of Commerce.* Government of India.

Internet World Stats. (2009). Retrieved from http://www.allaboutmarketresearch.com/internet.htm

Investment Industry Regulatory Organization of Canada. (2010). *About IIROC.* Retrieved August 2, 2010, from http://www.iiroc.ca/English/About/Pages/default.aspx

Irani, Z., Elliman, T., & Jackson, P. (2007). Electronic transformation of government in the UK: A research agenda. *European Journal of Information Systems, 16,* 327–335. doi:10.1057/palgrave.ejis.3000698

Irani, Z., & Love, P. E. D. (2001). The propagation of technology management taxonomies for evaluating investments in manufacturing resource planning (MRPII). *Journal of Management Information Systems, 17*(3), 161–177.

Irani, Z., Love, P. E. D., Elliman, T., Jones, S., & Themistocleous, M. (2005). Evaluating e-government: Learning from the experiences of two UK local authorities. *Information Systems Journal, 15,* 61–82. doi:10.1111/j.1365-2575.2005.00186.x

Irani, Z., Al-Sebie, M., & Elliman, T. (2006). Transaction stage of e-government systems: Identification of its location & importance. *Proceedings of the 39th Hawaii International Conference on System Sciences.*

Irkhin, I. U. V. (2007). Electronic government and society: World realities and Russia (a comparative analysis). *Sociological Research, 46*(2), 77–92. doi:10.2753/SOR1061-0154460206

ITAA. (2000). *Keeping the faith: Government information security in the internet age.* Retrieved from www.itaa.org/ infosec/ faith.pdf

ITU. (2008). *World telecommunication/ICT indicators 2008.* International Telecommunication Union.

I-Ways. (2009). E-government for development information exchange. *Journal of E-Government Policy and Regulation, 32,* 20–22.

Jadhav, S. (2003). *Evaluation study on e-governance applications in ULBs.* Pune, India: YASHADA.

James, G. (2000). Empowering bureaucrats. *MC Technology Marketing Intelligence, 20*(12), 62–68.

Janssen, M., & Van Veenstra, A. F. (2005). Stages of growth in e-government: An architectural approach. *Electronic. Journal of E-Government, 3*(4), 193–200.

Jayaradha, N. (2003). *E-governance: Tackling the hurdles. Tamil Inaiyam 2003.* India: Tamilnadu.

Jeong, K., & Kim, H. (2003). After the introduction of the government portal services: Evolution into the m-government initiatives. *Proceedings of the ICA 37th Conference,* (2003).

Jha, R. (2005). Land fragmentation and its implications for productivity: Evidence from Southern India. (ASARC Working Paper 2005/01).

Jiang, Y., Raghupathi, V., & Raghupathi, W. (2009). Web-based corporate governance disclosure: An empirical investigation. *Information Resources Management Journal, 22*(2), 50–69. doi:10.4018/irmj.2009092203

Jiang, J. J., Hsu, M., & Klein, G. (2000). E-commerce user behavior model: An empirical study. *Human Systems Management, 19,* 265–276.

Jog, V., & Dutta, S. (2004). Searching for the governance grail. *Canadian Investment Review,* (Spring): 33–43.

Joo, S. H., Grable, J. E., & Choe, H. (2007). Who is and who is not willing to use online employer-provided retirement investment advice. *Journal of Employment Counseling, 44*(2), 73–85.

Kahneman, D., & Tversky, A. (1974). Judgment under uncertainty: Heuristics and biases. *Science, 185,* 1124–1131. doi:10.1126/science.185.4157.1124

Kapoor, J. R., Dlabay, L. R., Hughes, R. J., & Ahmad, A. (2006). *Personal finance* (3rd Canadian edition). Toronto, Canada: McGraw-Hill Ryerson.

Kapugama, N. (2009). *Colloquium: Identifying conditions for the delivery of m-government services to the BOP: India.* Retrieved from www.lirneasia.net

Karantjias, A., Polemi, N., Stamati, T., & Martakos, D. (2010). A user-centric & federated single-sign-on IAM system for SOA e/m-frameworks. *International Journal of Electronic Government, 7*(3), 216–232. doi:10.1504/EG.2010.033589

Karantjias, A., Stamati, T., & Martakos, A. (2010). Advanced e-government enterprise strategies & solutions. *International Journal of Electronic Governance, 3*(2). doi:10.1504/IJEG.2010.034094

Karantjias, A., Stamati, T., Polemi, N., & Martakos, D. (2009). A synchronous, open, user-centric, federated identity and access management system (OpenIdAM). *Electronic Journal on E-Commerce Tools and Applications (eJETA), 3*(1).

Klanderman, B. (1997). *The social psychology of protest.* Oxford, UK: Blackwell Publishers.

Klapper, L. F., & Love, I. (2004). Coporate governance, investor protection, and performance in emerging markets. *Journal of Corporate Finance, 10,* 703–728. doi:10.1016/S0929-1199(03)00046-4

Klein, P., Shapiro, D., & Young, J. (2005). Corporate governance, family ownership and firm value: The Canadian evidence. *Corporate Governance: An International Review, 13*(6), 769–784. doi:10.1111/j.1467-8683.2005.00469.x

Klievink, B., & Janssen, M. (2009). Realizing joined-up government — Dynamic capabilities and stage models for transformation. *Government Information Quarterly, 26*(2), 275–284. doi:10.1016/j.giq.2008.12.007

Kline, R. B. (2005). *Principles and practice of structural equation modeling.* New York, NY: The Guilford Press.

Kline, R. B. (1998). *Principles and practice of structural equation modeling.* New York, NY: The Guilford Press.

Knight, P. T. (2007, June). *Knowledge management and e-government in Brazil.* Paper Prepared For The Workshop On Managing Knowledge To Build Trust In Government, 7th Global Forum on Reinventing Government, 26-29 June 2007, Vienna, Austria. Retrieved from www.e-brasil.org.br

Kochhar, S., & Dhanjal, G. (2004). *From governance to e-governance: An initial assessment of some of India's best projects.* Skoch E-Governance Report Card.

Koga, T. (2006). *Policy issues regarding electronic government and Web accessibility in Japan.* World Library and Information Congress: 72nd Ifla General Conference and Council 20-24 August 2006, Seoul, Korea.

Kogut, B., & Metiu, A. (2001). Open-source software development and distributed innovation. *Oxford Review of Economic Policy, 17*(2), 248–264. doi:10.1093/oxrep/17.2.248

Kolsaker, A., & Payne, C. (2002). Engendering trust in e-commerce: A study of gender-based concerns. *Marketing Intelligence & Planning, 20*(4), 206–214. doi:10.1108/02634500210431595

Kraemer, K. L., & King, J. L. (2003). *Information Technology and administrative reform: Will the time after e-government be different?* CRITO, Center For Research On Information Technology And Organizations. Retrieved from http://www.crito.uci.edu

Krishna, S., & Walsham, G. (2005). Implementing public Information Systems in developing countries: Learning from a success story. *Information Technology for Development, 11*(2), 123–140. doi:10.1002/itdj.20007

Krishnamurthy, S. (2003). A managerial overview of open source software. *Business Horizons,* 47–56. doi:10.1016/S0007-6813(03)00071-5

Kumar, R. (2006). Impact and sustainability of e-government services in developing countries: Lessons learned from Tamilnadu, India. *The Information Society, 22,* 1–12. doi:10.1080/01972240500388149

Kumar, M., & Sinha, O. P. (2007). *M-government – Mobile technology for e-government* (pp. 294–301). Computer Society of India.

Kumar, V., Kumar, U., & Shareef, M. A. (2006). Implementation of quality management practice in EC. *Proceedings of the Administrative Sciences Association of Canada Conference,* Banff, Calgary, Canada, 27, 146-163.

Kushchu, I., & Kuscu, H. (2003). *From e-government to m-government: Facing the inevitable.* 3rd European Conference on E-Government (ECEG03), July 1–2 at Trinity College, Dublin, (2003).

Kyama, G. W. (2005). E-government: A view from South Africa. Retrieved from http://www.uneca.org/aisi/ NICI/ Documents/eGovernment %20A%20view%20from% 20Southern%20Africa%20- %20Godfrey%20Kyama.ppt

Lakhani, K., & von Hippel, E. (2003). How open source software works: "Free" user-to-user assistance. *Research Policy, 32,* 923–943. doi:10.1016/S0048-7333(02)00095-1

Lakhani, K. R., & Wolf, R. B. (2005). Why hackers do what they do: Understanding motivation and effort in free/open source software projects. In Feller, J., Fitzgerald, B., Hissam, S., & Lakhani, K. R. (Eds.), *Perspectives on free and open source software.* MIT Press.

Lallana, E. (2008). *E-government for development information exchange.* University of Manchester's Institute for Development Policy and Management. Retrieved from http://www.egov4dev.org/mgovernment/ applications/

Layne, K., & Lee, J. (2001). Developing fully functional e-government: A four stage model. *Government Information Quarterly, 18,* 122–136. doi:10.1016/S0740-624X(01)00066-1

Lee, C., & Ready, M. (1991). Inferring trade direction from intraday data. *The Journal of Finance, 46,* 733–746. doi:10.2307/2328845

Lee, A., & Baskerville, R. (2003). Generalizing in information systems research. *Information Systems Research, 14*(3), 221–243. doi:10.1287/isre.14.3.221.16560

Lee, A. S. (1991). Integrating positivist and interpretative approaches to organizational research. *Organization Science*, *2*(4), 342–365. doi:10.1287/orsc.2.4.342

Lee, M. K. O., & Turban, E. (2001). Trust in business-to-consumer electronic commerce: A proposed research model and its empirical testing. *International Journal of Electronic Commerce*, *6*(1), 75–91.

Lee, J. K., Kim, D. J., & Rao, H. R. (2005). An examination of trust effects and preexisting relational risks in e-government services. *Proceedings of the 11th Americas Conference on Information Systems*, Omaha, NE, USA.

Lerner, J., & Tirole, J. (2002). Some simple economics of open source. *The Journal of Industrial Economics*, *50*(2), 197–234. doi:10.1111/1467-6451.00174

Lewellen, W. G., Lease, R. C., & Schlarbaum, G. G. (1977). Patterns of investment strategy and behavior among individual investors. *The Journal of Business*, *50*, 296–333. doi:10.1086/295947

Likert, R. (1932). A technique for the measurement of attitudes. *Archives de Psychologie*, 140.

Lindenberg, S. (2001). Intrinsic motivation in a new light. *Kyklos*, *54*(2/3), 317–342.

Litan, R. E., & Rivlin, A. M. (2001). Projecting the economic impact of the internet. *The American Economic Review*, *91*(2), 313–317. doi:10.1257/aer.91.2.313

Ljungberg, J. (2000). Open source movements as a model for organizing. *European Journal of Information Systems*, *9*(4). doi:10.1057/palgrave/ejis/3000373

Local Government Association. (2002). *egov@local: Towards a national strategy for local e-government.* London, UK: Local Government Association.

Löfgren, K. (2007). The governance of e-government. *Public Policy and Administration*, *22*(3), 335–352.

Loiacono, E. T., Watson, R. T., & Goodhue, D. L. (2002). WEBQUAL: A measure of website quality. In Evans, K., & Scheer, L. (Eds.), *Marketing educators' conference: Marketing theory and applications, 13* (pp. 432–437).

MacAulay, K., Dutta, S., Oxner, M., & Hynes, T. (2009). The impact of a change in corporate governance regulations on firms in Canada. *Quarterly Journal of Finance & Accounting*, *48*(4), 29–52.

Madon, S., Sahay, S., & Sudan, R. (2007). E-government policy and health information systems implementation in Andhra Pradesh, India: Need for articulation of linkages between the macro and the micro. *The Information Society*, *23*(5), 327–344. doi:10.1080/01972240701572764

Madu, C. N. (1989). Transferring technology to developing countries – Critical factors for success. *Long Range Planning*, *22*(4), 115–124. doi:10.1016/0024-6301(89)90089-7

Maenpaa, O. (2004). E-governance: Effects on civil society, transparency and democracy. Paper presented at Challenges and Opportunities for Democracy, Administration and Law IIAS-ISA, Workshop, Helsinki.

Massa, M., & Simonov, A. (2005). Behavioral biases and investment. *Review of Finance*, *9*, 483–507. doi:10.1007/s10679-005-4998-y

Mathieson, K. (1991). Predicting user intentions: Comparing the technology acceptance model with the theory of planned behavior. *Information Systems Research*, *2*, 173–191. doi:10.1287/isre.2.3.173

McClelland, D. C. (1975). *Power: The inner experience.* New York, NY: Halstead.

McDonald, C. J., Schadow, G., Barnes, M., Dexter, P., Overhage, J. M., & Mamlin, B. (2003). Open source software in medical informatics. *International Journal of Medical Informatics*, *69*(2/3), 175–184. doi:10.1016/S1386-5056(02)00104-1

McDowall, R. (2002). *What is the probability of e-government?* (IE4C). Retrieved from http://www.it-director. com/ content.php? id=2767

McKinsey. (2002). *Global investor opinion survey on corporate governance.* Retrieved on August 2, 2010, from http://www.mckinsey.com/clientservice/organizationleadership/service/corpgovernance/PDF/GlobalInvestorOpinionSurvey2002.pdf

McKnight, H., Choudhury, V., & Kacmar, C. (2002). Developing and validating trust measures for e-commerce: An integrative typology. *Information Systems Research*, *13*, 334–359. doi:10.1287/isre.13.3.334.81

McNurlin, B. C., & Sprague, R. H. Jr. (2006). *Information systems management in practice* (7th ed.). Upper Saddle River, NJ: Pearson Prentice Hall.

Ministry of Information and Communication. (2005). E-readiness report of New Delhi.

Ministry of Rural Development. (2004). Land reforms. Retrieved on September 29, 2009, from http://rural.nic.in/book01-02/ch-24.pdf

Misuraca, G. C. (2009). E-government 2015: Exploring m-government scenarios, between ICT-driven experiments and citizen-centric implications. *Technology Analysis and Strategic Management, 21*(3), 407–424. doi:10.1080/09537320902750871

Moen, V., Klingsheim, A. N., Simonsen, K. F., & Hole, K. J. (2007). Vulnerabilities in e-governments. *International Journal of Electronic Security and Digital Forensics, 1*(1), 89–100. doi:10.1504/IJESDF.2007.013595

Mohamed, E. K. A., Oyelere, P., & Al-Busaidi, M. (2009). A survey of Internet financial reporting in Oman. *International Journal of Emerging Markets, 4*(1), 56–71. doi:10.1108/17468800910931670

Moody, G. (2001). *Inside Linux and the open source revolution*. New York, NY: Perseus Press.

Moon, M. J., & Bretschneider, S. (2002). Does perception of red tape constrain IT innovativeness in organizations: Unexpected results from simultaneous equation model and implications. *Journal of Public Administration: Research and Theory, 12*(2), 273–291.

Moon, M. J., & Norris, D. F. (2005). Does managerial orientation matter? The adoption of reinventing government and e-government at the municipal level. *Information Systems Journal, 15*, 43–60. doi:10.1111/j.1365-2575.2005.00185.x

Moon, M. J. (2002). The evolution of e-government among municipalities: Rhetoric or reality? *Public Administration Review, 62*(4), 424–433. doi:10.1111/0033-3352.00196

Moon, J. (2004). *From e-government to m-government? Emerging practices in the use of m-technology by state governments*. IBM Center for the Business of Government.

Moon, J., & Kim, Y. (2001). Extending the TAM for a World Wide Web context. *Information & Management, 28*, 217–230. doi:10.1016/S0378-7206(00)00061-6

Moore, G., & Benbasat, I. (1991). Development of an instrument to measure the perceptions of adopting an information technology innovation. *Information Systems Research, 2*, 173–191. doi:10.1287/isre.2.3.192

Mosse, B., & Whitley, E. A. (2009). Critically classifying: UK e-government website benchmarking and the recasting of the citizen as customer. *Information Systems Journal, 19*(2), 149–173. doi:10.1111/j.1365-2575.2008.00299.x

Murphy, T. (2001). *Evaluate open source risks*. Retrieved from http://ftponline.com/wss/2002_10/online/tmurphy

Muta, M. (2005). *Japanese e-government and e-commerce since Dec. 2001*. Retrieved from http://www.manaboo.com/ english/egov_japan.htm

Mutual Funds Dealers Association of Canada. (2010). *About the MFDA*. Retrieved August 10, 2010, from http://www.mfda.ca/about/aboutMFDA.html

Myers, M. D. (1997). Qualitative research in information systems. *Management Information Systems Quarterly, 21*(2), 241–242. doi:10.2307/249422

Myers, L. (2007, February 5). Online public records facilitate ID theft: Is your local government unwittingly aiding identity thieves? *MSNBC: Nightly News*. Retrieved from http://www.msnbc.msn.com/ id/ 16813496/

Nakamura, J., & Csikszentmihalyi, M. (2003). The construction of meaning through vital engagement. In Keyes, C. L., & Haidt, J. (Eds.), *Flourishing: Positive psychology and the life well-lived*. Washington, DC: American Psychological Association. doi:10.1037/10594-004

Naqvi, S. J., & Al-Shihi, H. (2009). M-government services initiatives in Oman. *Informing Science and Information Technology, 6*, 817–824.

National Informatics Centre. (2009). *Computerization of land records*. New Delhi: Land Records Division, Ministry of Information Technology.

Ndou, V. (2004). E–government for developing countries: Opportunities and challenges. *Electronic Journal on Information Systems in Developing Countries, 18*(1), 1–24.

Ndou, V. D. (2004). E-government for developing countries: Opportunities and challenges. *Electronic Journal of Information Systems in Developing Countries, 18*(1), 1–24.

Netter, J., Kutner, M. H., Nachtsheim, C. J., & Wasserman, W. (1996). *Applied linear regression models* (3rd ed.). Chicago, IL: Irwin.

Nicholls, C. (2006). Research studies: The characteristics of Canada's capital markets and the illustrative case of Canada's legislative regulatory response to Sarbanes-Oxley. *Canada Steps Up, 4*, 127–204.

Nielsen, J. (1993). *Usability engineering*. Boston, MA: Academic Press.

Nolan, R. L. (1979). Managing the crises in data processing. *Harvard Business Review, 57*(March/April), 115–126.

Norris, P. (2001). *Digital divide: Civic engagement, information poverty, and Internet worldwide*. New York, NY: Cambridge University Press.

Northxsouth. (2010). *Brazil launches new version of their electronic government portal.* Retrieved from http://news.northxsouth.com/2010/03/07/brazil-launches-new-version-of-their-electronic-government-portal/

NPR Reports. (1994). *Vice President Albert Gore's national performance review.*

Nunnally, J. C., & Bernstein, I. H. (1994). *Psychometric theory*. New York, NY: McGraw-Hill.

Nye, J. S. Jr. (1999). Information Technology and democratic governance. In Democracy.com? In Ciulla, E., Joseph, K., & Nye, S. Jr., (Eds.), *Governance in networked world* (pp. 1–18). Hollis, NH: Hollis Publishing Company.

Oates, B. J. (2006). *Researching information systems and computing*. London, UK & Thousand Oaks, CA: Sage Publications.

Odean, T. (1999). Do investors trade too much? *The American Economic Review, 89*(5), 1279–1298. doi:10.1257/aer.89.5.1279

OECD. (2006). *Norway: Information Security. OECD Reviews of Risk Management Policies*. Paris, France: OECD.

OECD. (2009). *Rethinking e-government services: User-centered approaches*. Paris, France: OECD.

OECD E-Government Studies. (2010). *Denmark, efficient e-government for smarter public service delivery.*

OECD Report. (2005). *OECD peer review of e-government in Denmark.* Pre-Publication Draft: Version 2 – 29, September 2005.

Oh, N. Y., Parwada, J. T., & Walter, T. S. (2008). Investors' trading behavior and performance: Online versus non-online equity trading in Korea. *Pacific-Basin Finance Journal, 1-2*, 26–43. doi:10.1016/j.pacfin.2007.04.009

Olsen, D. (2005). Local e-government in Norway - Current status and emerging issues. *Scandinavian Journal of Information Systems, 17*(2), 41–84.

Oracle Report. (2004). Urban local bodies in Tamilnadu deliver improved citizen services. Oracle – E-Governance News, 6, pp 1- 14.

Orlikowksi, W. J., & Baroudi, J. (1991). Studying information technology in organizations: Research approaches and assumptions. *Information Systems Research, 2*(1), 1–28. doi:10.1287/isre.2.1.1

Pacific Council on International Policy. (2002). *Roadmap for e-government in the developing world*. Report of the Working Group on E-Government in the Developing World.

Parasuraman, A., Zeithaml, V. A., & Berry, L. L. (1988). SERVQUAL: A multiple-item scale for measuring customer perceptions of service quality. *Journal of Retailing, 64*(1), 12–40.

Parent, M., Vandebeek, C. A., & Gemino, A. C. (2005). Building citizen trust through e-government. *Government Information Quarterly, 22*, 720–736. doi:10.1016/j.giq.2005.10.001

Paul, P. (2001). Mixed signals. *American Demographics, 23*, 44–49.

Pavlou, P. (2003). Consumer acceptance of electronic commerce: Integrating trust and risk with the technology acceptance model. *International Journal of Electronic Commerce, 7*, 69–103.

Perez, C. C., Bolivar, M. P. R., & Hernandez, A. M. L. (2008). E-government process and incentives for online public financial information. *Online Information Review, 32*(3), 379–400. doi:10.1108/14684520810889682

Piechocki, M., Felden, C., Graning, A., & Debreceny, R. (2009). Design and standardisation of XBRL solutions for governance and transparency. *International Journal of Disclosure and Governance, 6*(3), 224–241. doi:10.1057/jdg.2009.9

Premuroso, R. F., & Bhattacharya, S. (2008). Do early and voluntary filers of financial information in XBRL format signal superior corporate governance and operating performance? *International Journal of Accounting Information Systems, 9*, 1–20. doi:10.1016/j.accinf.2008.01.002

PRISM. (2005). *Department of IT*. Government of Punjab.

Provincial/Territorial Council of Ministers of Securities Regulation (Council). (2010). *Progress report, January 2009 to December 2009.* Retrieved on August 2, 2010, from http://www.securitiescanada.org/2010-0301-progress-report-english.pdf

Quick, S. (2003). *International e-government, special report: Government*. EBSCO Publishing.

Rai, K., & Bhalla, D. K. (2005). Computerization of land records in India. Retrieved on September 9, 2009, from http://www.gisdevelopment.net/application/lis/overview/lisrp0015.htm

Ramachandran, V. (2005). *E-Dhara: Land records management system*. India: Revenue Department, Government of Gujarat.

Raymond, E. S. (2001). *The cathedral & the bazaar* (2nd ed.). Sebastapol, CA: O'Reilly.

Reddick, C. G. (2005). Citizen-initiated contacts with Ontario local e-government: Administrators' responses to contacts. *International Journal of Electronic Government Research, 1*(4), 45–62. doi:10.4018/jegr.2005100103

Reddick, C. G. (2009). Factors that explain the perceived effectiveness of e-government: A survey of United States city government information technology directors. *International Journal of Electronic Government Research, 5*(2), 1–15. doi:10.4018/jegr.2009040101

Reddick, C. G. (2006). Information resource managers and e-government effectiveness: A survey of Texas state agencies. *Government Information Quarterly, 23*(2), 249–266. doi:10.1016/j.giq.2005.11.006

Remenyi, D. (1998). *Doing research in business and management: An introduction to process and method.* London, UK & Thousand Oaks, CA: Sage Publications.

Report, A. (2003). *E-government leadership – Realizing the vision*. The Government Executive Series.

Reserve Bank of India. (2008). Foreign exchange department report.

Richardson, R. (2008). *The 2008 computer crime and security survey*. Computer Security Institute. Retrieved from http://www.gocsi.com/ forms/ csi_survey. jhtml;jsessionid= 1GW0KB4 3ZOYTKQSND LP-SKH0CJ UNN2JVN

Riggs, W., & von Hippel, E. (1994). Incentives to innovate and the sources of innovation: The case of scientific instruments. *Research Policy, 23*(4), 459–469. doi:10.1016/0048-7333(94)90008-6

Riley, T. B. (2002). *Government and the invisible current of change*. Retrieved from http://www.electronicgov.net

Ritu, A. (2008). E-learning in land record Information System sharing good practices: E-learning in surveying, geo-Information Sciences and land administration. FIG International Workshop, Enschede, The Netherlands.

Robin, G., Andrew, G., & Sasha, M. (2009). How responsive is e-government? Evidence from Australia and New Zealand. *Government Information Quarterly, 26*(1), 69–74. doi:10.1016/j.giq.2008.02.002

Rogers, E. M. (1995). *Diffusion of innovations* (4th ed.). New York, NY: Free Press.

Ryan, R. M., & Desi, E. L. (2000). Intrinsic and extrinsic motivations: Classic definitions and new directions. *Contemporary Educational Psychology, 25*, 54–67. doi:10.1006/ceps.1999.1020

Sabherwal, S., Sarkar, S. K., & Zhang, Y. (2008). Online talk: Does it matter? *Managerial Finance, 34*(6), 423–436. doi:10.1108/03074350810872813

Sachoff, M. (2008). *18% of U.S. households have no Internet access*. Retrieved on May 14, 2008, from http://www.webpronews.coankem/topnews/2008/05/14/18-of-us-households-have-no-internet-access

SAFAD. (2000). *The 24/7 agency criteria for 24/7 agencies in the networked public administration.* The Swedish Agency For Administrative Development Publication Service. Retrieved from http://www.statskontoret.se/upload/ Publikationer/2000 /200041.pdf

Sakowicz, M. (2007). *How to evaluate e-government? Different methodologies and methods.* Retrieved from http://unpan1.un.org/intradoc /groups/public/documents/ NISPAcee/ UNPAN009486.pdf

Sandoval, R., & Gil-García, J. R. (2005). *Assessing e-government evolution in Mexico: A preliminary analysis of the state portals.* Paper presented at the 2005 Information Resources Management Association International Conference, San Diego.

SANS Institute. (2007). *SANS top-20 internet security attack targets: The 2006 annual update.* Retrieved from http://www.sans.org/ top20/ 2006/

SANS Institute. (2008). *SANS top-20 2007 security risks: The 2007 annual update.* Retrieved from http://www.sans.org/ top20/

Sarra, J. (2007). Disclosure as a public policy instrument in global capital markets. *Texas International Law Journal, 42*(3), 875–898.

Sathyamurthy, D. (2002, October). KAVERI - Karnataka valuation and e-registration. Paper presented at the sixth national conference on E-Governance, Chandigarh.

Sathye, M. (2005). The impact of internet banking on performance and risk profile: Evidence from Australian credit unions. *Journal of Banking Regulation, 6*(2), 163–174. doi:10.1057/palgrave.jbr.2340189

Saxena, K. B. S. (2005). Towards excellence in e-governance. International Journal of Public Sector Management, 18, 498–513. Retrieved on September 29, 2009, from http://www.emeraldinsight.com/10.1108/09513550510616733

Schedler, K., & Summermatter, L. (2007). Customer orientation in electronic government: Motives and effects. *Government Information Quarterly, 24*, 291–311. doi:10.1016/j.giq.2006.05.005

Schelin, S. H. (2003). E-government: An overview. In Garson, G. D. (Ed.), *Public Information Technology: Policy and management issues* (pp. 120–137). Hershey, PA: Idea Group Publishing.

Scholl, H. J. (2005). The mobility paradigm in government theory and practice: A strategic framework. In Ibrahim Kushchu & M. Halid Kuscu (Eds.), *Proceedings of the 1ˢᵗ European Mobile Government Conference* (Euro mGov 2005), Brighton, UK, (2005), 10-12 July, Mobile Government Consortium International Pub, UK.

Schware, R., & Deane, A. (2003). Deploying e-government program: The strategic importance of 'I' before 'E.'. *Info, 5*(4), 10–19. doi:10.1108/14636690310495193

Schware, R., & Deane, A. (2003). Deploying e-government program- The strategic importance of 'I' before 'E.'. *Info, 5*(4), 10–19. doi:10.1108/14636690310495193

Second Administrative Reforms Commission. (2008). Government of India report.

Segars, A., & Grover, V. (1993). Re-examining perceived ease of use and usefulness: A confirmatory factor analysis. *Management Information Systems Quarterly, 17*(4), 517–527. doi:10.2307/249590

Segars, A. H. (1997). Assessing the unidimensionality of measurement: A paradigm and illustration within the context of Information Systems research. *Omega, 25*(1), 107–121. doi:10.1016/S0305-0483(96)00051-5

Seifert, J. W. (2003). *A primer on e-government: Sectors, stages, opportunities and challenges of online governance.* Congressional Research Service, Library of Congress.

Shapira, Z., & Venezia, I. (2001). Patterns of behavior of professionally managed and independent investors. *Journal of Banking & Finance, 25*, 1573–1587. doi:10.1016/S0378-4266(00)00139-4

Shareef, M. A., Kumar, U., & Kumar, V. (2008). The e-government and e-governance: Conceptual alignment or subtle difference. *International Journal of Knowledge, Culture, and Change Management, 8*(1), 129–136.

Shareef, M. A., Kumar, U., & Kumar, V. (2007). Developing fundamental capabilities for successful e-government implementation. *Proceedings of ASAC Conference,* Ottawa.

Sharma, L. P. (2006). Technology fusion for e-land record. Paper presented at 4th International Conference on E-governance held at IIT, Delhi.

Shastri, P. (2001, May 1). Digitizing land records key to reform. Hindustan Times. Retrieved on September 29, 2009, from http://www.hindustantimes.com/News/business/Digitising-land-records-key-to-reform/Article1-219609.aspx

Shefrin, H., & Statman, M. (1985). The disposition to sell winners too early and ride losers too long: Theory and evidence. *The Journal of Finance, 40*, 777–790. doi:10.2307/2327802

Shirin, M. (2004). Evaluating the developmental impact of e-governance initiatives: An exploratory framework. *Electronic Journal of Information Systems in Developing Countries, 20*(5), 1–13.

Simon, J. L. (1969). *Basic research methods in social science: The art of empirical investigation*. New York, NY: Random House.

Sipiar, J., et al. (2005). Bridging the digital divide for e-government inclusion: A United States case study. The Electronic Journal of E-Government, 3(3), 137-146. Retrieved on September 9, 2009, at www.ejeg.com

SITA (Pty) Ltd. (2002). *Government experience in South Africa*. Retrieved from http://www.sita.co.zae

Stamati, T., & Martakos, D. (2011). Electronic transformation of local government: An exploratory study. [IJEGR]. *International Journal of Electronic Government Research, 7*(1), 20–37. doi:10.4018/jegr.2011010102

Steyaert, J. (2000). Local government online and the role of the resident. *Social Science Computer Review, 18*, 3–16. doi:10.1177/089443930001800101

Stokes, J., & Clegg, S. (2003). Once upon a time in the bureaucracy: Power and public sector management. *Organization, 9*(2), 225–247.

Straub, D., Boudreau, M. C., & Gefen, D. (2004). Validation guidelines for IS positivist research. *Communications of the Association for Information Systems, 13*, 380–427.

Straub, D. W. (1989). Validating instruments in MIS research. *Management Information Systems Quarterly, 13*(2), 147–169. doi:10.2307/248922

Sundar, D. K., & Garg, S. (2009). *M-governance: A framework for Indian urban local bodies*. Retrieved from http://www.mgovernment.org/resrces/euromgov2005/PDF/41_R359SK.pdf

Swanson, E. B. (1988). *Information System implementation: Bridging the gap between design and utilization*. Homewood, IL: Irwin.

Swartz, N. (2004). E-government around the world. *Information Management Journal, 38*(1), 12.

Symantec. (2007, September). Symantec internet security threat report. *Symantec Enterprise Security, 12*, 1-30. Retrieved from http://www.symantec.com

Symonds, M. (2000). Government and the internet: No gain without pain. *The Economist, 355*(1), S9-S14.

T. Stamati, A. Karantjias. Inter-sector practices reform for e-Government integration efficacy, *Journal of Cases on Information Technology (ICIT)*, IGI Global, in press.

Tanveer, S. (2006). Voice biometric based user verification: An exemplary tool for secure identification. In J. Bhattacharya (Ed.), *Technology in government*. New Delhi, India: GIFT publishing.

Tavares, M. (2001). *Brazilian policy for electronic government*. Federal Republic Of Brazil Ministry Of Planning, Budget And Management, Constituent Units and E-Government, organized by The Forum of Federations, Montreal.

Thakur, V. (2005). *Social impact of computerization of land records. Adopting e-governance*. New Delhi, India: Computer Society of India Publications.

Thibodeau, P. (2000). E-government spending to soar through 2005. *Computerworld, 34*(17), 12.

Titah, R., & Barki, H. (2005). *E-government adoption and acceptance: A literature review*. HEC Montréal.

Tornatzky, L., & Klein, K. (1982). Innovation characteristics and innovation adoption implementation: A meta-analysis of findings. *IEEE Transactions on Engineering Management, 29*, 28–45.

Trimi, S., & Sheng, H. (2008). Emerging trends in m-government. *Communications of the ACM, 51*(5), 53–58. doi:10.1145/1342327.1342338

Trinkle, S. (2001). *Moving citizens from in line to online: How the Internet is changing how government serves its citizens*. Retrieved from http://www.bcinow.com/demo /oel /Resources Articles.htm

Tripathi, R. (2006). *Selected aspects of interoperability in one-stop government portal of India. Towards next generation e-governance.* New Delhi, India: Computer Society of India Publications.

Trites, G. (2006). Implications of e-filing. *CA Magazine, 139*(8), 51–52.

Trites, G. (2008). Corporate reporting on the Web. *CA Magazine, 141*(7), 16–17.

Trites, G. (1999). Democratizing disclosure. *CA Magazine, 132*(8), 47–48.

Trites, G. (2004). Decline of the age of Pacioli: The impact of e-business on accounting and accounting education. *Canadian Accounting Perspectives, 3*(2), 171–177. doi:10.1506/G82C-H0W9-L4TM-YJ94

Trites, G. (2008). Corporate reporting on the Web. *CA Magazine, 7*(141), 16–17.

Trusler, J. (2003). South African e-government policy and practices: A framework to close the gap. In R. Traunmüller (Ed.), *EGOV 2003* (LNCS 2739, pp. 504-507).

Tumarkin, R. (2002). Internet message board activity and market efficiency: A case study of the internet service sector using RagingBull.com. *Financial Markets Institutions and Instruments, 11*(4), 313–335. doi:10.1111/1468-0416.11403

Tumarkin, R., & Whitelaw, R. F. (2001). News or noise? Internet message board activity and stock prices. *Financial Analysts Journal, 57*(3), 41–51. doi:10.2469/faj.v57.n3.2449

Tung, L. L., & Rieck, O. (2005). Adoption of electronic government services among business organizations in Singapore. *The Journal of Strategic Information Systems, 14*, 417–440. doi:10.1016/j.jsis.2005.06.001

Turner, M., & Desloges, C. (2002). *Strategies and framework for government online: A Canadian experience.* World Bank E-Government Learning Workshop, Washington D.C., June 18.

Umashankar, C. (2002). Transforming district administration using e-governance -Tiruvarur experience. Retrieved on September 29, 2009, from http://www.groups/yahoo.com/group/India-egov

Umashankar, C., & Bhaskara, R. (2000, January). Implementation of an integrated land records system - A case study at Kudavasal Taluk, Tiruvarur District, Tamilnadu. Paper presented at Technical proceedings, Geomatics 2000.

UN E-Government Service. (2008). *From e-government to connected governance.* Department of Economic and Social Affairs Division for Public Administration and Development Management.

UN/ASPA. (2002). *Benchmarking of e-government: A global perspective.* New York, NY: United Nations Division of Public Economics and Public Administration and the American Society for Public Administration.

UNESCO. (2007). *United Nations Educational Scientific and Cultural Organization.* Retrieved on August 2, 2010, from http://portal.unesco.org/ci/en/ev.php-URL_ID=4404&URL_DO=DO_TOPIC&URL_SECTION=201.html

United Nations. (2006). *Compendium of innovative e-government practices (Vol. II).* Department of Economic & Social Affairs.

United Nations. (2008). *From e-government to connected governance.* E-government survey 2008.

Update, N. (2004). *Municipal Initiatives in E-Governance, 2(1).* New Delhi: Institute of Social Sciences.

USA.gov. (2002). *Home page.* Retrieved from http://www.firstgov.gov/

Van Dijk, Jan A. G. M., Peters, O., & Ebbers, W. (2008). Explaining the acceptance and use of government Internet services: A multivariate analysis of 2006 survey data in the Netherlands. *Government Information Quarterly, 25*(3), 379–399. doi:10.1016/j.giq.2007.09.006

Van Slyke, C., Bélanger, F., & Comunale, C. (2004). Adopting business-to-consumer electronic commerce. The effects of trust and perceived innovation characteristics. *The Data Base for Advances in Information Systems, 35*, 32–49.

Vaughan-Nichols, S. J. (Jan 2004). Novell embraces open source. *eWeek.* Ziff Davis Media Inc.

Venkatesh, V. (1999). Creation of favourable user perceptions: Exploring the role of intrinsic motivation. *Management Information Systems Quarterly, 23*(2), 239–260. doi:10.2307/249753

Vincent, J., & Harris, L. (2008). Effective use of mobile communication in e-government: How do we reach the tipping point? *Information Communication and Society, 11*(3), 395–413. doi:10.1080/13691180802025632

Vowler, J. (April 2003). Finding out the hidden cost of open source. *Computer Weekly*.

Wagner, C., Cheung, K., Lee, F., & Ip, R. (2003). Enhancing e-government in developing countries: Managing knowledge through virtual communities. *The Electronic Journal on Information Systems in Developing Countries, 14*(4), 1–20.

Walsham, G. (1995). The emergence of interpretivism in IS research. *Information Systems Research, 6*(4), 376–394. doi:10.1287/isre.6.4.376

Wang, Y.-S. (2002). The adoption of electronic tax filing systems: An empirical study. *Government Information Quarterly, 20*, 333–352. doi:10.1016/j.giq.2003.08.005

Wang, H., Lee, M., & Wang, C. (1998). Consumer privacy concerns about internet marketing. *Communications of the ACM, 41*(1), 63–70. doi:10.1145/272287.272299

Wangpipatwong, S., Chutimaskul, W., & Papasratorn, B. (2005). Factors influencing the adoption of Thai e-government websites: Information quality and system quality approach. *Proceedings of the 4th International Conference on eBusiness*, November 19-20, (2005), Bangkok, Thailand.

Watson, R. T., & Mundy, B. (2001). A strategic perspective of electronic democracy. *Communications of the ACM, 44*(1), 27–30. doi:10.1145/357489.357499

Weaver, D. G. (1997). *Decimalization and market quality*. Working paper, Marquette University.

Welch, J. L. (1985). Research marketing problems and opportunities with focus groups. *Industrial Marketing Management, 14*, 247. doi:10.1016/0019-8501(85)90017-3

West, D. M. (2004). E-government and the transformation of service delivery and citizen attitudes. *Public Administration Review, 64*(1), 15–27. doi:10.1111/j.1540-6210.2004.00343.x

West, D. M. (2005). *Digital government: Technology and public sector performance*. Princeton, NJ: Princeton University Press.

Wheeler, D. A. (2001). More than a gigabuck: Estimating Linux's size. Retrieved on December 20, 2005, from http://www.dwheeler.com/sloc/redhat71-v1/redhat71sloc.html

Wolfinbarger, M., & Gilly, M. C. (2003). eTailQ: Dimensionalizing, measuring, and predicting retail quality. *Journal of Retailing, 79*(3), 183–198. doi:10.1016/S0022-4359(03)00034-4

Wong, W. (2000). *At the dawn of e-government*. New York, NY: Deloitte Research, Deloitte and Touche.

World Bank. (2003). *A definition of e-government*. Washington, DC.

World Bank. (2007). *India: Land policies for growth and poverty reduction* (pp. 74–79). New Delhi, India: Oxford University Press.

XBRL Canada. (2010). *What is XBRL?* Retrieved on August 10, 2010, from http://www.xbrl.ca/index.php/what-is-xbrl

Xiao, J. Z., Jones, M. J., & Lymer, A. (2005). A conceptual framework for investigating the impact of the Internet on corporate financial reporting. *International Journal of Digital Accounting Research, 5*(10), 131–170.

Ye, Y., & Kishida, K. (2003). Toward an understanding of the motivation of open source software developers. In *Proceedings of the International Conference on Software Engineering*. Portland.

Yin, R. K. (2003). *Case study research: Design and methods* (3rd ed.). Thousand Oaks, CA: Sage Publications.

Yoo, B., & Donthu, N. (2001). Developing a scale to measure the perceived quality of an Internet shopping site (Sitequal). *Quarterly Journal of Electronic Commerce, 2*(1), 31–46.

Zaima, J. K., & Harjoto, M. A. (2005). Conflict in whispers and analyst forecasts: Which one should be your guide? *Financial Decisions, 17*(3), 1–16.

Zambrano, R., & Dandjinou, P. (2003). *E-governance service delivery*. India and South Africa: United Nations Development Project.

Zhang, J. J., Yuan, Y., & Archer, N. (2002). Driving forces for m-commerce success. *Journal of Internet Commerce, 1*(3), 81–105. doi:10.1300/J179v01n03_08

Zhao, X., & Chung, K. H. (2006). Decimal pricing and information-based trading: Tick size and informational efficiency of asset price. *Journal of Business Finance & Accounting, 33*(5-6), 753–766. doi:10.1111/j.1468-5957.2006.00622.x

Zhao, L., & Deek, F. P. (2004). User collaboration in open source software development. *Electronic Markets, 14*(2), 89–103. doi:10.1080/10196780410001675040

About the Contributors

Mahmud A. Shareef is currently a post doctorate researcher in DeGroote School of Business, McMaster University, Hamilton, Canada. He is the recipient of Post Doctoral Fellow from Social Sciences and Humanities Research Council (SSHRC), Canada to conduct research on Electronic-government. Previously, he was a Research Associate in Ontario Research Network for Electronic Commerce (ORNEC), Ottawa, Canada. He has done his PhD in Business Administration from Sprott School of Business, Carleton University, Ottawa, Canada. He received his graduate degree from both the Institute of Business Administration, University of Dhaka, Bangladesh in Business Administration and Carleton University, Ottawa, Canada in Civil Engineering. His research interest is focused on development and performance of electronic-government and quality management of electronic-commerce. He is the principal author of the recently published book, Proliferation of the Internet Economy: E-Commerce for the Global Adoption, Resistance and Cultural Evolution, which has drawn enormous attention from scholarly researchers. He has published more than 30 papers addressing adoption and quality issues of e-commerce and e-government in different refereed conference proceedings and international journals. He is the author of 2 book chapters in Information Technology Handbook (IGI group) and has published 2 reputed books on quality management issues. He is an internationally recognized Information Technology (IT) consultant and has presented seminal papers in IT seminars. He was the recipient of more than 10 academic awards including 2 Best Research Paper Awards in the UK and Canada.

Norm Archer is Professor Emeritus in the Information Systems Area of the DeGroote School of Business, McMaster University, Canada. He is also Special Advisor to the McMaster eBusiness Research Centre (MeRC), which he founded in 1999 as its first director. From December 2000 to his retirement in July 2002 as a Full Professor, he held the Wayne C. Fox Chair in Business Innovation. He is currently involved in a variety of activities in research, consulting, teaching, and supervising graduate student research on e-government, e-business, and e-health topics. He is extensively involved in the development and operation of the MSc program in e-health, a unique collaborative program between the Faculties of Business, Health Sciences, and Engineering. Dr. Archer has published more than 100 papers in refereed journals and conferences, and has given many invited talks on e-government, e-business, and e-health at universities and conferences around the world. In his research he is active, along with his graduate students and colleagues, in the study of organizational problems relating to the implementation of e-business and e-government approaches, particularly pertaining to mobile applications in business, health, and government organizations, and the resulting impacts on processes, employees, customers, and suppliers. Current research projects involve various aspects of mobile e-health, mobile government, identity theft, and change management in organizations.

Shantanu Dutta is an Assistant Professor of Finance at University of Ontario Institute of Technology (UOIT). Previously, he taught at St. Francis Xavier University, Nova Scotia and Assumption University, Bangkok as a full-time faculty member. Before his career in academia, he served as a Finance Manager and Project Controller at Lafarge - a world leader in construction materials. Professor Dutta's research focuses on corporate governance, mergers and acquisitions, market efficiency, dividend policy, and technology management. He has published (or his articles have been accepted for publication) in Journal of Banking and Finance, Global Finance Journal, Canadian Investment Review, International Journal of Theoretical and Applied Finance, International Journal of Managerial Finance, International Journal of Technology Transfer, and International Journal of Global Energy Issues. He has also participated and presented papers in many scholarly conferences. Shantanu Dutta is a recipient of the Barclay Global Investor Canada Research Award.

* * *

Bin Chang is an Assistant Professor of Finance in the Faculty of Business & IT at the University of Ontario Institute of Technology. Prior to joining UOIT, Dr. Chang received her BA, LLB, and MA from Wuhan University in China, MA from Queen's University, and Ph.D. from the University of Toronto. Dr. Chang was also a credit derivatives risk t at CIBC and an instructor at the University of Toronto. Dr. Chang's research areas are in empirical asset pricing and empirical corporate finance. Her research on "Information asymmetry, dividend status and SEO announcement-day returns" has been accepted by Journal of Financial Research. Her other research on "Bias in equity recommendations on Canadian stocks" is accepted by Canadian Investment Review. She has presented her papers in Financial Management Association annual meetings, Northern Finance Association annual meetings, Eastern Finance Association annual meeting, and Midwest Finance Association annual meeting.

M. P. Gupta is Professor and Chair-Information Systems Group & Coordinator-Center for Excellence in E-gov at the Department of Management Studies, Indian Institute of Technology Delhi. His research interests lie in the areas of IS/ IT planning and e-government. Prof. Gupta has authored the acclaimed book "Government Online" and edited two others, entitled "Towards E-Government" and "Promise of E-Government," published by McGraw Hill, 2005. His research papers have appeared in national and international journals/conference proceedings. He was the recipient of the prestigious Humanities & Social Sciences (HSS) fellowship of Shastri Indo Canadian Institute, Calgary (Canada) and a Visiting Fellow at the University of Manitoba. He supervised the e-government portal "Gram Prabhat," which won the IBM Great Mind Challenge Award for the year 2003. He has steered several seminars and also founded the International Conference on E-governance (ICEG) in 2003, which is running into its sixth year. He is on the jury of Computer Society of India (CSI) E-gov Awards and also a member of Program Committee of several International Conferences. He is life member of Global Institute of Flexible Systems Management (GIFT), Systems Society of India (SSI) and Computer Society of India (CSI).

Athanasios Karantjias has obtained the Degree of Electrical and Computer Engineering from University of Patras in 2000 and a PhD in Computer Science from National Technical University of Athens in 2005. He is currently Assistant Professor at the Department of Computer Science of University of

Piraeus. His current research interests include identification, design, and evaluation of synchronous security and interoperability issues on enterprise architectures and advanced wireless Information Systems

Uma Kumar is a Full Professor of Management Science and Technology Management and Director of the Research Centre for Technology Management at Carleton University. She has published over 120 papers in journals and refereed proceedings. Ten papers have won best paper awards at prestigious conferences. She has won Carleton's prestigious Research Achievement Award and, twice, the Scholarly Achievement Award. Recently, she won the teaching excellence award at the Carleton University. She has been the Director of Sprott School's Graduate Programs. Uma has extensive consulting experience in both private and public sectors in India and Canada primarily working on technology incubation, technology transfer to developing countries, and innovation management. She has consulted DND, CIDA, the Federal partners of technology transfer, and the Canadian Association of Business Incubators. Uma has taught in executive MBA program in Hong Kong and in Sprott MBA in Ottawa, Iran, and China. Over last twenty years, she has supervised more than 70 MBA, MMS, and EMBA student's projects; most of these projects dealt with real practical problems of organizations. She has also given invited lectures to academics and professionals in Brazil, China, Cuba, and India.

Vinod Kumar is a Professor of Technology and Operations Management of the Sprott School of Business (Director of School, 1995–2005), Carleton University. He received his graduate education from the University of California, Berkeley and the University of Manitoba. Vinod is a well known expert sought in the field of technology and operations management. He has published over 150 papers in refereed journals and proceedings. He has won several Best Paper Awards in prestigious conferences, Scholarly Achievement Award of Carleton University for the academic years 1985–1986 and 1987–1988, and Research Achievement Award for the year 1993 and 2001. Vinod is a well known expert sought in the field of technology and operations management. He has consulted DND, CIDA, Canada Post, Industry Canada, CHEO, Federal partners of technology transfer, and Canadian Association of Business Incubators to name a few. Before joining academia in the early eighties, Vinod worked for five electronics and manufacturing firms for over 15 years in Canada, India, and the U.S. in various line and staff management positions. Vinod has given invited lectures to professional and academic organizations in Australia, Brazil, China, Iran, and India among others. He has taught in Executive MBA programs in Canada and Hong Kong and in Sprott MBA in Ottawa, Iran, and China, where he enjoys connecting his industry and research experience with management theories.

Kenneth MacAulay is an Associate Professor of accounting in the Gerald Schwartz School of Business and Information Systems at St. Francis Xavier University. He has co-authored three university-level accounting and financial planning texts in addition to a high school financial planning text. Ken is also actively involved in researching corporate governance issues in Canada. He holds degrees from St. Francis Xavier University (BBA) and Queen's University (PhD). He is active in his profession, having taught in the Atlantic School of Chartered Accountancy and having served as a member of the Nova Scotia Securities Commission from 2000 to 2009.

Drakoulis Martakos is an Associate Professor at the Department of Informatics and Telecommunications at the National and Kapodistrian University of Athens. He received his B.Sc. in Physics, MSc in

Electronics and Radio Communications, and Ph.D. in Real-Time Computing from the same university. Professor Martakos is a consultant to public and private organizations and a project leader in numerous national and international projects. He is author or co-author of more than 100 scientific publications and a number of technical reports and studies.

N. Mathiyalagan is an Associate Professor at the Post Graduate and Research Department of Communication, PSG College of Arts and Science, Coimbatore. He has an academic experience of over 25 years and his specific area of interest includes e-governance implementation, developmental communication, new media activities, and prime developmental projects undertaken by the government machinery. He has published a number of research articles in developmental communication. He has been guiding research programs leading to M.Phil and Ph.D in media studies.

Bhasker Mukerji is an Assistant Professor of Marketing at St. Francis Xavier University. He has received education in three continents – Asia, Europe, and North America and has worked for number of years in the private sector. He has also taught various Marketing courses at Eric Sprott School of Business (Carleton University) and Telfer School of Management (University of Ottawa). His research interests are in the areas of e-government, Internet marketing, technology commercialization, and open source software.

Morteza Niktash completed his Ph.D. degree program in Electrical Engineering from the Department of Systems and Computer Engineering, Carleton University in 1985. He has been working over thirty years for the private, academic, not-for profit, as well as public sectors at various technical, engineering, and management capacities for planning and development of business, services, applications, and systems. He has built and managed communities of practice & expertise (CoE); participated in various e-technology projects including e-government, knowledge management, and expert systems; published conference papers and held workshops in various areas including knowledge based systems, e-government, enterprise wide IM/IT architecture, as well as systems architecture for large business applications. He served as a Professor of Systems and Computer Engineering at Carleton University (1985-1990); planned, architected, designed, developed, and maintained distributed Information Systems for private sector (1977-1992); and joined the Department of Public Works and Government Services of Government of Canada in 1992. He is the former president of the Society for Collaborative Advancement of Professionals (SCOAP); a member of team of judges for selection of the best projects and leaders for the yearly Government Technology (GTEC) awards, as well as a member of the program committee of the Montreal international Conference in E-Technology.

Mary M. Oxner is an Associate Professor in the Gerald Schwartz School of Business and Information Systems at St. Francis Xavier University in Antigonish Nova Scotia. Mary primarily teaches in the accounting area, particularly managerial accounting and financial accounting theory. Mary's research interests include corporate governance, financial analysts, e-governance, ethical decision making, auditor expertise, educational strategies, and community board development.

Ramaraj Palanisamy is the Associate Professor of the Gerald Schwartz School of Business and Information Systems at St. Francis Xavier University. Prior to his current appointment, Dr. Palanisamy worked for 10 years with various academic institutions including Wayne State University (Detroit, USA), Universiti Telekom (Malaysia) and National Institute of Technology, (NITT), Deemed University, India. Dr. Palanisamy teaches courses in Enterprise Resources Planning implementation, Database Management Systems, Systems design, e-commerce architecture, and operations research.

Senthil Priya is a research scholar from the Department of Communication, PSG College of Arts and Science, Coimbatore, India. She has completed her M.S (Communication) from Manipal Institute of Communication, Manipal and M.Phil from PSG College for Arts and Science, Coimbatore. The chapter from this book is part of her M.Phil dissertation work titled, "A Qualitative study of E-Governance implementation in Coimbatore revenue administration – With particular reference to STAR and NILAM projects." Her major interests are e-governance, poverty alleviation through e-governance implementation, new media activities, and developmental communication. She is currently pursuing PhD research on implementation of e-agriculture in Coimbatore taluks.

Velamala Ranga Rao is currently working as a Computer Programmer Group 'A,' gazetted in the Remote Sensing Centre of Soil and Land Use Survey of India, Department of Agriculture and Cooperation, Ministry of Agriculture, Government of India. He obtained his Ph. D. in Statistics in 1993 from Andhra University. He has more than 18 years of experience in the field of Information Technology in the Government Sector. He has been Head of the Department of Computer Science of Engineering at Indira Gandhi Institute of Technology (IGIT), Delhi (2002-2003). His paper, "Key Issues of Personal Information Integration in E-Government," was published at 6th International Conference on E-governance 18– 20 December 2008, Department of Management Studies, IIT Delhi and "Public Safety: Secured Emergency Integrated Communications Network – Issues and Challenges for M-Government" published at 7th International Conference on E-Governance, 22 - 24 April, 2010, Indian Institute of Management, Bangalore.

Teta Stamati has obtained a Degree in Computer Science from National and Kapodistrian University of Athens (Greece) in 1998. She also holds an MPhil Degree in Enterprise Modelling Techniques from University of Manchester Institute of Science and Technology (UMIST) (UK), an MBA Degree from Lancaster University Business School (UK) and a PhD in Information Systems from Informatics and Telecommunication Department from National and Kapodistrian University of Athens (Greece). She has extensive experience in top management positions in leading IT companies of the Greek and European private sector. She is currently Research Fellow at the Department of Informatics and Telecommunications of National and Kapodistrian University of Athens. Her current research interests include Information Systems, services sciences, electronic and mobile government, green IT, social computing, trust, and security.

Rakhi Tripathi is a doctoral student at School of Information Technology, Indian Institute of Technology Delhi (IIT Delhi). Earlier, she obtained her MS in Computer Science from Bowie State University (University System of Maryland, USA) in 2003. Her present work relates to issues involved in achieving interoperability for one-stop government portal in India. Besides, she is also keenly interested in the area of Semantic Web. Her research has appeared in the edited volumes of International Conference on

E-Governance (ICEG) and is forthcoming in International Journal of Electronic Government Research (IJEGR). Besides, she has also worked as a Project Scientist with the project 'Establishment of Nation-wide QoS Test-bed' at the Department of Computer Science, IIT Delhi for two years.

Gerald D. Trites is a chartered accountant and was elected a Fellow in 1988. He also is a Certified Information Systems Auditor (1988). Currently, Jerry is Project Director of XBRL Canada under contract with the CICA and is serving on the XBRL International Assurance Committee. Previously, Jerry was a tenured Full Professor of St Francis Xavier University, Antigonish, Nova Scotia, and prior to that, was a partner with KPMG. He has published twelve books, including five research studies and a textbook on e-business entering into its fourth edition.

Index